RACE, ETHNICITY,
AND SEXUALITY

SOAS LIBRARY
WITHDRAWN

D0281840

833350

T

RACE, ETHNICITY, AND SEXUALITY

Intimate Intersections, Forbidden Frontiers

JOANE NAGEL
University of Kansas

New York   Oxford
OXFORD UNIVERSITY PRESS
2003

Oxford University Press

Oxford New York
Auckland Bangkok Buenos Aires Cape Town Chennai
Dar es Salaam Delhi Hong Kong Istanbul Karachi Kolkata
Kuala Lumpur Madrid Melbourne Mexico City Mumbai
Nairobi São Paulo Singapore Taipei Tokyo Toronto

Copyright © 2003 by Oxford University Press, Inc.

Published by Oxford University Press, Inc.
198 Madison Avenue, New York, New York, 10016
http://www.oup-usa.org

Oxford is a registered trademark of Oxford University Press

All rights reserved. No part of this publication may be reproduced,
stored in a retrieval system, or transmitted, in any form or by any means,
electronic, mechanical, photocopying, recording, or otherwise,
without the prior permission of Oxford University Press.

Library of Congress Cataloging-in-Publication Data

Nagel, Joane.
    Race, ethnicity, and sexuality : intimate intersections, forbidden frontiers / Joane Nagel.
      p. cm.
    Includes bibliographical references and index.
    ISBN 0-19-512746-3 (cloth : alk. paper)—ISBN 0-19-512747-1 (pbk. : alk. paper)
    1. Sex. 2. Race. 3. Ethnicity. 4. Nationalism. I. Title.
HQ21 .N195 2003
305.8—dc21   2002029269

Printing number: 9 8 7 6 5 4 3 2 1

Printed in the United States of America
on acid-free paper

SOAS LIBRARY

TO BESSIE BRITTON

CONTENTS

[Color Plate section appears between pages 148 and 149]

ILLUSTRATIONS

Figures

Plates (following page 148)

PREFACE

In May 1995 I spent a month in Italy. During that month I got interested in men. Later that summer, when I was back in Kansas, I got interested in sex. In Italy I was working at the Rockefeller Foundation's Bellagio Study and Conference Center, a wonderful interdisciplinary scholarly retreat that brought together researchers from around the world. My interest in men developed when I met a couple of fellow scholars from India: Zoya Hasan and her husband, Mushirul. Zoya was studying Muslim-Hindu politics and the dilemmas faced by Muslim intellectuals in the context of an increasingly conservative Islam. Central to her work was the analysis of the different places for women and men in nationalist movements. Zoya Hasan's "positionality"—the social space she occupied as a woman intellectual in Indian ethnonationalist politics—allowed her to see things in a way that, as a white woman living in the United States, I could not. Her work led me to question a number of assumptions and absences in my thinking about ethnopolitics—macro and micro.

Throughout my academic career as a comparative historical political sociologist, my work has centered on race, ethnicity, and nationalism in several national contexts. The sociological training I received at Stanford University in the mid-1970s, however, did not educate me in the sociology of gender or feminist theory, much less the sociology of sexuality, and certainly not in the study of sexualities. So, until my trip to Italy, I had tended to overlook—sometimes consciously, more often unconsciously—the role of gender and sexuality in any and all things racial, ethnic, or nationalist. Zoya Hasan's work changed that. In many ways, as a Muslim feminist, Zoya was damned if she did and damned if she didn't. If she was loyal to her feminist beliefs and criticized policies or practices contributing to the inequality of Muslim women in India, her comments could make her appear to be disloyal to her people and seen to be providing ammunition to Hindu critics of India's Muslims. Zoya Hasan's position and her analysis made it clear that nationalism was a profoundly gendered phenomenon.

As a scholar and intellectual, Zoya Hasan confronted issues that I did not. She did not have the luxury of choosing whether or not to acknowledge the structure and implications of gender in her work and life. When I attempted to look out from the standpoint that Zoya occupied, I could see for the first time how gender complicated racial, ethnic, and national identities, boundaries, movements, and conflicts. It was a short step from thinking about gender to considering the ways that sexuality/ies constituted race, ethnicity, and the nation—to recognizing the *ethnosexual* aspects of social life.

This book is the result of that ethnosexual journey I began in 1995. I have been fortunate to have met many fellow travelers along the way; without their hospitality and guidance I could never have arrived at this destination. Early in my work on ethnicity and sexuality I met sociologist and queer theorist Steven Seidman, who introduced me to sociological thinking about the social construction of sexuality. Steven confirmed what was becoming clear in my readings—that much of the most interesting work on sexuality was being done in the humanities, and much of it was being done in a language foreign to most social scientists—the discourse of cultural studies. It was clear that I needed a translator and a guide. I found two—Barry Shank and Tony Clark.

Barry was my smart, impertinent, and patient colleague in American Studies at Kansas. He answered and tolerated my endless queries about cultural studies' vocabularies of meaning: "discursive," "performative," "metonymic," "liminal" (this last he illustrated by leaping into a doorway to occupy liminal space—half in and half out). During the past several years Barry has taken hours and hours from his own work on the political and symbolic economy of popular culture to read my work and challenge my thinking. Even though he left Kansas in 2000 to join the Comparative Studies faculty at Ohio State University, he has continued to be a generous and constant, albeit virtual, intellectual companion. I honestly can say that without Barry Shank's help I could not have written this book.

My other guide, Tony Clark, is the embodiment of the commonly heard assertion about how much we can learn from our students. I met Tony when he was a first-year graduate student in American Studies and a student in one of my graduate seminars. He quickly began educating me by generously sharing with me his already deep knowledge of gender history, ethnic studies, and American ethnic history. Tony has helped me refine ideas, find literature, and finish the book research; we are already coauthors on articles and a book, and in 2002 Tony Clark became an official colleague when he joined the University of Kansas American Studies faculty.

Many other colleagues, students, and institutions have given me crucial ideas and support during the last several years. My friends and colleagues Norm Yetman and Donna Darden have been present in my intellectual and personal life throughout this research and writing. Norm has been a wonderful mentor since I first joined the Kansas faculty in 1977, and Donna has spent hundreds of hours during a decade of daily on-line exchanges offering witty commentary and consistent encouragement. Hsiu-hua Shen, my Ph.D. dissertation student and colleague, has helped me with the ideas and research for the book; her work on the sexual economy of Taiwanese-Chinese relations has broadened my understanding of the ethnosexual aspects of globalization. University of Kansas colleagues and graduate students have heard and commented on various ideas and sections of this book: in Sociology Department graduate seminars on ethnicity and sexuality, in faculty seminars sponsored by the Hall Center for the Humanities: the Gender Seminar, Performance Studies Seminar, Gender and Nationalism Seminar, Globalization Roundtable Series; the Hall Center also gave me an opportunity to present my work in its public lecture series. A University of Kansas sabbatical leave during 1999/2000 allowed me the time I needed to write the first complete draft of the book. Colleagues at a number of other universities invited me to present aspects of this work while it was in progress and provided essential feedback for refining my ideas and revising my thinking and writing—at Duke University, University of Illinois, Indiana University, College of William and Mary, Northwestern University, University of California at Santa Cruz and at San Diego, University of Wisconsin, University of Michigan, University of Virginia, University of Delaware, University of Pittsburgh. Finally I benefited from the technical assistance and ideas of many creative collaborators including Brendan Cope, Emily Eichler, Penny Fritts, Dori Gerdes, and John McCluskey.

Oxford University Press sought the opinions and advice of a number of outstanding reviewers at various points in the development of this book. Many of these readers identified themselves during the review process, allowing me to thank them directly; they include Adalberto Aguirre Jr., Rebecca Bach, Stephen Cornell, Yen Le Espiritu, Mary E. Kelly, Michael Kimmel, and Barry Shank; I am also grateful to the several anonymous reviewers for their excellent and constructive feedback and to Peter Labella and Sean Mahoney on Oxford's editorial staff for their handholding and facilitation during the last year of the book's writing.

My dear husband of twenty years, Mike Penner, has been in the unenviable, though sometimes interesting (he tells me) position of being closely connected to someone who, during the course of their marriage, became a sex researcher. His constant presence in my life has given me a safe base and conferred on me a respectability that allowed me to do this research. I am immensely grateful to him for his support.

This book is dedicated to my maternal grandmother, Bessie Britton. Bessie was part of the early-twentieth-century migration of poor whites out of the rural South. In the 1920s she moved from Huntington, West Virginia, to Cleveland, Ohio, where she worked as a seamstress and learned to read as an adult; her hard work and her whiteness allowed her to buy a house and accumulate what would become for me a small inheritance. The six thousand dollars Bessie Britton left me made it possible for me to go to college and to change the course of my life.

Finally, I am indebted to the courageous sexual studies and queer studies scholars whose creative thinking I depended on to theorize and illustrate this work. Much of their daring scholarship is new, undertaken in the past two decades, and many of them have no doubt felt the sting of suspicious criticism for their "prurient" interests or for "fetishizing" the subjects of their study. They have forged on despite such obstacles, and their pioneer spirit has blazed the trail that we will follow in the pages of this book.

Lawrence, Kansas   J.N.

INTRODUCTION

SEX MATTERS
Racing Sex and Sexing Race

What's sex got to do with it? With race? With ethnicity? With nationalism? And what about sex? What do race, ethnicity, and nationalism have to do with sex? These are the questions that lie at the center of this book. In the pages that follow we will explore the intimate intersections and forbidden frontiers where ethnicity and sexuality meet face to face. We will observe the power of sex to shape ideas and feelings about race, ethnicity, and the nation, and we will see how sexual images, fears, and desires shape racial, ethnic, and national stereotypes, differences, and conflicts. We will examine historical and contemporary moments in the United States and abroad when ethnicity and sexuality join hands to fashion new, hybrid communities and cultures, and we will witness the volatility and violence that can accompany *ethnosexual*[1] joint ventures and adventures. This book is about how sex matters in ethnic relations, and about how sexual matters insinuate themselves into all things racial, ethnic, and national.

Differences of color, culture, country, ancestry, language, and religion are the materials out of which ethnic, racial, and national identities and boundaries are built. Ethnic boundaries are also sexual boundaries. Ethnicity and sexuality join together to form a barrier to hold some people in and keep others out, to define who is pure and who is impure, to shape our view of ourselves and others, to fashion feelings of sexual desire and notions of sexual desirability, to provide us with seemingly "natural" sexual preferences for some partners and "intuitive" aversions to others, to leave us with a taste for some ethnic sexual encounters and a distaste for others. Ethnicity and sexuality blend together to form sexualized perimeters around ethnic, racial, and national spaces. Ethnic and sexual boundaries converge to mark the edges of ethnosexual frontiers.

1

Despite the visceral power of sexual matters in general, especially those involving race, ethnicity, or the nation, the connection between ethnicity and sexuality often is hidden from view. Sex is the whispered subtext in spoken racial discourse. Sex is the sometimes silent message contained in racial slurs, ethnic stereotypes, national imaginings, and international relations. Although the sexual meanings associated with ethnicity may be understated, they should never be underestimated. An obscured ethnosexual connection, once revealed, can illuminate many taken-for-granted features of social life. One example is urban racial segregation in the United States. Let me illustrate by telling a personal story to show what sex has to do with race, how sex matters, and how race and sex combine to contribute to patterns of "hypersegregation" in American cities.[2] Some of the language in this narrative may be offensive to some readers, but I believe that it is essential to the telling:

> I was born in Cleveland, Ohio. My family lived in the city when I was young, and in the 1950s I attended Cleveland Public Schools—an urban school system in which most of the schools were racially integrated to some extent. For instance, I had several African American classmates throughout my six years at Hazeldell Elementary School. We were in a special curriculum called "Major Work" where we had French lessons throughout elementary school as well as special music and art classes. Despite the advantages of my participation in this enhanced curriculum at Hazeldell, and despite my promised access to Major Work classes when I moved on to Patrick Henry Junior High, when I was in the sixth grade my parents began to talk about moving to the suburbs. They clearly stated why we had to move. Patrick Henry had a larger percentage of black students than Hazeldell, and my parents did not want me to go to school with "too many" blacks.
>
> Now, on the face of it, this story looks very much like a tale of typical U.S. urban ethnic politics and demographics: racism and white flight. Like many U.S. cities, Cleveland is a multiethnic, multiracial city with a long history of black-white and white ethnic (Polish, Irish, Italian, Jewish) segregation and tensions. I grew up constantly hearing comments about Dagos, Bohunks, Niggers, Micks, Polacks, Kikes, and hillbillies in all settings—family, school, neighborhood. Racism and ethnic denigration permeated virtually all social interactions in Cleveland, and much time was spent by everyone I knew identifying who was what ethnically ("what IS he?") and assigning meanings to these attributions ("oh, you know how THEY are!"). So, it is not surprising that my parents, who were products of this racist and racialized world (as am I), would plan to move to a white suburb at some point since African American migration into Cleveland was expanding in the 1950s as a continuing part of the post–World War II "Great Migration" of blacks out of the rural south.[3] What is interesting and revealing about this sequence of events was the timing of their decision: I was eleven years old as I moved from sixth to seventh grade, and I was developing sexually. I was wearing

a bra and had started menstruating. As these changes occurred, the urgency of my family's plan to move to the suburbs increased. In addition to my physical maturation, my impending entry into junior high seemed to represent a kind of sexual passage into a world that my parents wanted to be white like me.

What does this personal narrative tell us about race and sex and the connections between them? It tells us that ethnic and racial boundaries are also sexual boundaries. It tells us that the calculations that go into the decision to retreat into ethnic enclaves and neighborhoods and to erect and strengthen ethnic borders have an important sexual component that is part of the invisible foundation upon which ethnic boundaries rest. There are many reasons for racial segregation and white flight in U.S. cities—economic, political, historical, cultural—but readers should not expect to find the word *sex* in many, if any, of the indexes of books that offer explanations of patterns of U.S. urban racial segregation.[4] I would argue, however, that most people living in American cities make these kinds of sexual calculations consciously or unconsciously in their decisions to move their families, homes, jobs, and businesses. Ethnosexual considerations are intrinsic, though seldom explicitly expressed aspects of rationales for moving to the suburbs, rationales that are articulated as issues of "safety," "neighborhood," "schools," and "quality of life."

SEARCHING FOR SEX IN RACIAL, ETHNIC, AND NATIONAL SPACES

Urban racial segregation is only one of a number of areas of social life in the United States and elsewhere where the sexual underlies and even magnifies the racial. Exposing the connections between ethnicity and sexuality is the core project of this book. We will be looking for evidence of sexuality in:

- depictions of men and women of various races, ethnicities, and nationalities,
- fantasies and fears conjured up in racial stereotypes,
- rules governing contact between different ethnic groups,
- the regulation of men's and women's places in the nation,
- the ethnic face of desire and disgust,
- beliefs and myths about the practices, characteristics, and potency or impotency of ethnic and immigrant groups,
- appetites and aversions directed toward different racial groups,
- ethnic cleansing and genocide in nationalist conflicts and wars.

We will look for ethnosexual stereotypes in popular culture such as films, music, magazines, television, literature. We'll examine "sex-baiting" as a strategy of "race-baiting" in politics. We'll investigate the role of sex as a weapon in propaganda and warfare. We'll survey the uses of sex in the construction of racial, ethnic, and national identities—"ours" and "theirs." Our explorations of ethnicity and sexuality will span time and space. Sometimes the shifts we will make and the turns we will take might seem abrupt and even dizzying as we move from the past to the present, from country to country, region to region, place to place, from one racial, ethnic, or national group to another. The goal of this book is not to conduct an in-depth analysis of any single era or country or to focus on any one racial or ethnic group. The goal is to illustrate the power and ubiquity of sexuality as a feature of racial, ethnic, and national identities, boundaries, and tensions. When we have completed this ethnosexual journey, we will have seen numerous examples of the sexual aspects of race and racism, the sexual dimensions of ethnic identity and community, and the sexual agendas of nationalists and nationalism.

We will use many different lenses to inspect the sexual side of ethnicity. The chapters in this book will include census data, poetry, fieldwork, Internet postings, interviews, pictures, literature, ethnographies, historical texts, archival documents, biographies, and personal accounts. We will examine tables and charts; we will look at photographs and images; we will read excerpts from drama, fiction, fieldnotes, journals, newspapers, and legal texts. My voice and voices of others will intrude into the narrative at various points throughout the book to tell a story, provide an example, or draw a comparison. We will strive to interpret the meaning and implications of these various forms of data. We will try to contribute to social theory and to broaden the sociological method.

This book will incorporate methodologies and styles of evidence and interpretation from both the social sciences and the humanities—from sociology, anthropology, political science, history, gender studies, ethnic studies, literary studies, queer theory, and cultural studies. Readers accustomed to one tradition or another may find themselves puzzled at some times, skeptical at others, and even occasionally uncomfortable with the comparisons being made and the conclusions being drawn. We will adopt critical race theory's strategy of using "storytelling, counterstorytelling, and the analysis of narrative" to challenge "the myths, presuppositions, and received wisdoms that make up the common culture."[5] This book not only is intended to question assumptions about the irrelevance of sexuality for understanding race, ethnicity, and nationalism, it is intended to stretch the boundaries of sociological methods and evidence.

In order to draw out the connections between ethnicity and sexuality, we will cast a broad net across time and space, making comparisons among different eras in one nation's history and among different nations. I will ask the reader to be open to the comparative historical interpretative style used here, to try to relax into the variety of materials and techniques that you will encounter, and to look for common threads running through the many varying voices and examples I'll present. Some of these historical and contemporary voices will speak clearly for themselves about the ways in which they have been racialized and sexualized; others will require explanation and interpretation. Readers will not always be given a great deal of background on the examples presented; for those wishing to know more about a particular case, place, or event, I have included resources and suggestions for further reading in the chapter endnotes.

This will not be an objective survey or a search for negative evidence. I will pick and choose examples where ethnicity and sexuality collide and collude to construct social realities. We will not look for locations where race and sex do not mix. We will try, instead, to identify intersections where they are intimates, where they give power to one another. The approach here assumes that the ethnosexual connection is so hidden that our time is best spent exposing and mapping it. We will leave for others the work of conducting in-depth case studies, designing large-scale historical or international investigations, and specifying the limits of sexuality for understanding ethnic, racial, and national relations.

CONSTRUCTING ETHNICITY AND SEXUALITY

The conceptual framework of this book is social constructionism, an approach that questions the naturalness of the social order and looks for the underlying social motivations and mechanisms that shape human social relations and societies.[6] We will *not* examine the biological aspects of sexuality, race, ethnicity, or nationalism. We will *not* debate or detail physical differences between "blacks" and "whites" or "women" and "men" or "gays" and "straights."[7] We will *not* draw conclusions about the inherent nature of differences between people with dark skin or light skin, or between people with clitorises or penises, or between people who have opposite sex or same sex desires or partners.

We will examine, instead, *assertions* of physical or biological differences between people made in various eras by various groups and individuals in various settings. We will try to understand the social, economic, political, cultural, and/or religious agendas behind difference claims made in social constructions of ethnicity, gender, or sexuality. By using a social constructionist approach, we will try to question our own and others' assumptions about the *realness, naturalness,* and *timelessness* of black and white, women and men, gay and straight. We will look at how racial, gender, and sexual constructions are interconnected and depend on one another for their potency and familiarity. We will examine the racing of sex and the sexing of race; we will try to understand how race defines and constructs sexuality and how sexuality defines and constructs race, ethnicity, and nationality.

DEFINING ETHNICITY

The terms *race, ethnicity,* and *nationality* all were used in the last sentence to emphasize that they are related social categories. Chapter 2 will lay out in more detail a constructionist model of ethnicity, but in order to avoid confusion now, here are some definitions. By *ethnicity* I refer to differences between individuals and groups in skin color, language, religion, culture, national origin/nationality, or sometimes geographic region. Ethnicity subsumes both nationalism and race. Current notions of *race* are centered exclusively on visible (usually skin color) distinctions among populations, although its historical origins and usage were broader and included religious and linguistic groups (such as Jews or the Irish) who were considered to be "races." *Nationalism* commonly is viewed as a particular kind of ethnically based social identity or movement generally involving claims to statehood or political autonomy, and most often rooted in assertions of cultural distinctiveness, a unique history, and ethnic or racial purity.[8] Because of the power of race and nationalism to organize social life in the United States and around the world, I will discuss in detail a number of sexualized, gendered aspects of race and nationalism in several chapters of this book. For conceptual purposes, however, I consider ethnicity as the core concept; thus, race and nationalism are two major forms of ethnicity.

It is important to acknowledge the prominence, some would say preeminence, of race in historical and contemporary U.S. ethnic relations, in particular the volatility and controversy associated with the American black-white color line.[9] But race should not be considered as the *most* or *only* volatile or violent basis of ethnic division in the United States or elsewhere. A quick survey of some sites of twentieth-century ethnic conflict around the world—Canada, Northern Ireland, the Indian subcontinent, Germany, Rwanda, or the republics of the former Yugoslavia—reveals a great deal of antagonism and bloodshed along nonracial (i.e., non-color-based) ethnic divisions. The fact that many of these differences get vocalized and vilified in ways that have a familiar racial ring, speaks to the ideological interconnectedness of race, ethnicity, and nationalism.[10]

While Americans tend to grapple with race and immigration, in other countries ethnic controversies and conflicts center on sometimes different, sometimes similar issues. For instance, in Canada language politics dominate the national ethnic agenda as Francophone nationalists push for Quebec's independence from Canada; in New Zealand, indigenous Maori rights represent a central ethnic concern; in India ethnic tensions continue to haunt the Hindu-Muslim ethnic boundary, especially in the region of Kashmir where nuclear powers India and Pakistan confront one another; in Nigeria, ethnic political and economic violence has led to protest by and repression of the Ogoni minority; in Ethiopia, Eritreans have mobilized successfully for independence and Oromos seek expanded political rights; in Sudan, an ethnic divide separates Sudanese of Muslim Arab ancestry from darker-skinned non-Muslim "African" Sudanese; in Spain, Basque and Catalan nationalists seek autonomy or independence from the central state; in Tibet, Tibetans and Buddhist followers of the Dalai Lama seek to gain independence from Chinese political rule and policies designed to promote the Sinoization of Tibetan culture.[11]

Ethnicity, race, and nationalism are closely related, yet different facets of the same phenomenon. For that reason, they are sometimes given a single name, such as "cultural pluralism," "multiculturalism," "diversity," "identity politics," or "minorities."[12] In this book I will sometimes speak in terms of ethnicity as a general concept meant to include race and nationalism. At other times I'll speak specifically about race or nationalism. Unless I specify otherwise, my arguments about ethnicity are meant to apply to all three.

DEFINING SEXUALITY

Sexuality is less likely than ethnicity to be seen by scholars or, I expect, by most readers of this book, as a social construction. Sexuality seems to many people to be in large part a natural feature of physiology.[13] The prevailing biological model underlying everyday understandings of sexuality, however, is beginning to show some cracks in its foundational assumptions. Just as gender researchers in the 1970s and 1980s raised doubts about the purely biological origin of men's and women's different gender roles,[14] during the past decade there has emerged an interesting critique of the "essentialist" natural science model of sexuality—desire, orientation, action—as based simply in human physiology. By *essentialist* I refer to the notion that there is a fundamental, often physical or biological basis for human behavior, identity, and difference. We will explore the new anti-essentialist literature on sexuality in Chapter Two, but some basic definitions will be helpful here.

By *sexuality* I refer to "men" and "women" as socially, mainly geni-
tally defined individuals with culturally defined appropriate sexual tastes,
partners, and activities. There is no single universally shared conception of
natural or proper sexual desires, sexual partners, or sexual activities, rather,
there is as much variety in sexual practice as there are human cultures. Despite that diversity, in any historical period and society, there will be a dominant or *hegemonic*[15] sexuality that will define socially approved men's and
women's sexualized bodies (fat or thin, strong or weak, black or white), approved kinds of sexual desires for approved numbers and types of sexual partners (e.g., a monogamous relationship with an opposite sexed, same raced
partner), and approved sorts of sexual activities at appointed times and places
(e.g., vaginal-penile intercourse in the bedroom, out of public view). There
are many ways of having sex and being sexual, and sexual rules are frequently broken. Nevertheless, the assumption of heterosexuality as a normative ideal is common in many if not most contemporary societies. Two
examples, one from the United States, the other from Papua New Guinea,
illustrate the hegemony of heterosexuality even in the face of diverse, sometimes homoerotic sexual practices.

In 1961, Albert Reiss published a paper whose title illustrates the evo-
lution of the social meaning of the word *queer*, a word that has come full
circle from a term of derision to one of defiance: "The Social Integration of
Peers and Queers."[16] In this paper, Reiss described the self-imposed hypermasculine rules of behavior of a group of young male prostitutes ("peers")
who defined themselves as heterosexuals, but who engaged in homosexual
acts with mainly adult men ("queers") for profit. How can an individual rec-
oncile *being* a heterosexual while simultaneously *acting* like a homosexual,
Reiss asked? His answer: the heterosexual identities of these boys survived
the challenges posed by homosexual activities because of rigid, masculinist
rules for behavior the boys imposed on each other. In order to retain private
and public heterosexual identities peers engaged in the excessive, sometimes
gratuitous use of violence against queers, enforced a variety of rules about
when and where sex with queers could take place, and defined strictly circumscribed relationships with queers that allowed no emotional ties and permitted only a limited set of sexual acts. For instance, peers could only sexually penetrate and never be penetrated by queers.

A similar scenario combining heterosexual identities with queer behaviors is reported in a very different setting by anthropologist Gilbert Herdt.[17]
Herdt has documented the sexual practices of a small society in Papua New
Guinea whose members he refers to by the pseudonym, "Sambians." Before
adolescence Sambian boys undergo an initiation into male adulthood during
a roughly two-year period when they live in isolation from the women and

girls of their community. During this *rite de passage* boys are taught the skills associated with Sambian manhood, and they acquire the sperm needed to perform as heterosexual husbands in future marriages. The boys obtain sperm by sucking it from the penises of young adult Sambian men in a series of acts of fellatio during their period of gender isolation. Are Sambian young men "homosexuals" during the time they occupy either active or passive roles in oral sex? Or are Sambian boy fellators and their young adult male "sperm donors" simply behaving as would any average heterosexual Sambian male preparing for sexual adulthood? Herdt and his colleague, the late psychoanalyst Robert Stoller, embrace the latter view, arguing that Sambian homosexual practices are preparation for and indeed are defined as heterosexual since almost without exception Sambian boys grow up to marry women and cease to engage in even ritual fellatio.[18]

Are the peers in Reiss's study or the Sambian fellators described by Stoller and Herdt *really* heterosexual or *really* homosexual? Or are they something else—bisexual, situationally homosexual, serially homo/heterosexual? These questions make a strong presumption that individuals have a sexual *identity* (e.g., "gay" or "straight") that can be determined by observing their sexual *behavior*—you *are* what you *do* in bed. This assumed connection between sexual identity and behavior is not a cultural universal, nor is it timeless. In any society, however, there will be a prevailing standard for proper sexual behavior, and that sexual hegemony will be enforced against those defined as sexually deviant—often these are members of other classes, races, ethnic groups, or nationalities. Reiss's peers and queers were from different classes—working-class peers viewed themselves as models of appropriate masculine heterosexuality and expressed contempt for middle-class queers. Herdt reported that the Sambian men not only viewed themselves as exclusively heterosexual, but they also expressed masculinity through acts of violence—by criticizing and competing with other New Guinean ethnic groups, Sambians asserted and maintained their masculine superiority.

ETHNOSEXUAL INTERSECTIONS

The sexual ideologies of many groups define members of other classes or ethnicities as sexually different from, usually inferior to their own *normal* and proper ways of being sexual. These class or ethnic "Others" might be seen to be oversexed, undersexed, perverted, or dangerous.[19] For instance, Judith Halberstam argues that in contemporary United States society dominant notions of acceptable masculinity and male sexuality reflect the behaviors and desires of white middle-class men. These race- and class-based sexual standards tend to define African American and Latino men as exces-

sively masculine and oversexed or "hypersexual" and Asian men as insuffi-
ciently masculine and undersexed or "hyposexual."[20]

This pattern of contrasting valorized dominant group sexuality with devalued nondominant group sexualities can be found in descriptions of ethnic
relations around the world. Sexual stereotypes commonly depict "us" as sexually vigorous (usually our men) and pure (usually our women), and depict
"them" as sexually depraved (usually their men) and promiscuous (usually
their women). Much of this book will be devoted to detailing these ethnosexual constructions, showing how hegemonies and regimes of sexuality shape
ethnic relations, conflicts, and boundaries, and documenting the prevalence and
importance of sexuality in all things racial, ethnic, and national. In the chapters that follow we will see how definitions of ethnicity are imbued with sexual meanings and expectations, how the construction of ethnic boundaries depends on the establishment and enforcement of rules and regulations governing
sexual demeanor, partners, and reproduction, how the domestic and international politics of ethnicity revolve around the defense of ethnic homelands from
sexual invasion and attack, and how strategies of competition and domination
include the sexual control of ethnic Others' bodies and territories.

Chapter 1 will provide a more detailed answer to the questions posed at
the beginning of this introduction: what's sex got to do with race, ethnicity,
and the nation, and what does ethnicity have to do with sexuality? Chapter 2
will lay out the conceptual framework for the rest of the book by outlining a
social constructionist, boundary model of ethnicity and sexuality, describing
the role of sexuality in the construction of ethnicity, and discussing the ways
in which race, ethnicity, and nationalism shape sexual boundaries and meanings. The next six chapters will detail specific ethnosexual frontiers in the
United States and around the world. Chapters 3 and 4 focus on United States
history: Chapter 3 examines sex and the conquest of the U.S. West and the
role played by sexuality in defining the frontier, wilderness, and ultimately
America; Chapter 4 turns to sex and race, in particular the role of sexuality in
African American history and in the institution of slavery. Chapters 5 through
8 move offshore, examining the intersections of ethnicity and sexuality in nationalism, war, tourism, and globalization, respectively. The Conclusion briefly
summarizes the point of this book—that sex is raced and race is sexed.

NOTES

1. By *ethnosexual*, I refer to the intersection and interaction between ethnicity
and sexuality and the ways in which each defines and depends on the other for its
meaning and power.

2. For a definition of "hypersegregation" and a discussion of more structural policies contributing to patterns of U.S. urban racial segregation, see Kevin F. Gotham, *Race, Real Estate, and Uneven Development: The Kansas City Experience, 1900–2000* (Albany: State University of New York Press, 2002).

3. Joe William Trotter Jr., ed., *The Great Migration in Historical Perspective: New Dimensions of Race, Class, and Gender* (Bloomington: Indiana University Press, 1991).

4. See, for instance, Douglas S. Massey and Nancy A. Denton, *American Apartheid: Segregation and the Making of the Underclass* (Cambridge, MA: Harvard University Press, 1993).

5. Richard Delgado, *Critical Race Theory: The Cutting Edge* (Philadelphia: Temple University Press, 1995), xiv; see also Adrien Katherine Wing, *Global Critical Race Feminism: An International Reader* (New York: New York University Press, 2000); Richard Delgado and Jean Stefancic, *Critical Race Theory: An Introduction* (New York: New York University Press, 2001); Kimberle Crenshaw, Neil Gotanda, Gary Peller, Kendall Thomas, *Critical Race Theory: The Key Writings That Formed the Movement* (New York: New Press, 1995); my thanks to Adalberto Aguirre Jr. for bringing this literature to my attention.

6. See Peter L. Berger and Thomas Luckmann, *The Social Construction of Reality: A Treatise on the Sociology of Knowledge* (Garden City, NY: Anchor Books, 1967); Malcolm Spector and John I. Kitsuse, *Constructing Social Problems* (New York: Aldine de Gruyter, 1977); for a recent assessment of social constructionism, see James A. Holstein and Gale Miller, eds., *Reconsidering Social Constructionism: Debates in Social Problems Theory* (New York: Aldine de Gruyter, 1993).

7. For discussion of biological arguments about the nature of gender, sexuality, race, ethnicity, and nationalism, see J. Richard Udry, "Biological Limits of Gender Construction," *American Sociological Review* 65 (2000): 443–57; Michael Banton, *Racial Theories* (Cambridge: Cambridge University Press, 1998).

8. I want to distinguish here between "nationalism," which refers to political identification and mobilizations, and "nationality," which refers simply to the country of one's own or one's ancestors' origin. In the United States nationality is often a synonym for ethnicity, and in the United States and abroad it is often used only to denote citizenship. Nationalism is the more interesting and relevant concept for our purposes here since it goes beyond a social category or background characteristic; for discussions of historical and contemporary conceptual formulations of race, ethnicity, and nationalism, see Donald Horowitz, *Ethnic Groups in Conflict* (Berkeley: University of California Press, 1985); Walker Connor, "When Is a Nation?" *Ethnic and Racial Studies* 13 (1990): 92–103; Eric J. Hobsbawm, *Nations and Nationalism since 1970* (Cambridge: Cambridge University Press, 1985); Anthony D. Smith, "The Origins of Nations," *Ethnic and Racial Studies* 3 (1989): 340–67; Max Weber, *Economy and Society: An Outline of Interpretative Sociology*, volume 1, ed. Gunther Roth and Claus Wittich (Berkeley: University of California Press, 1978); Michael Omi and Howard Winant, *Racial Formation in the United States: From the 1960s to the 1980s* (New York: Routledge and Kegan Paul, 1986).

9. See Howard Winant, *Racial Conditions: Politics, Theory, and Comparisons* (Minneapolis: University of Minnesota Press, 1994).

10. For a discussion of the historical similarities in the development of racist and nationalist discourses, see Zillah Eisenstein, *Hatreds: Racialized and Sexualized Conflicts in the 21st Century* (New York: Routledge, 1996); Charles W. Mills *The Racial Contract* (Ithaca: Cornell University Press, 1997).

11. Abdul-Rasheed Na'Allah, ed., *Ogoni's Agonies: Ken Saro-Wiwa and the Crisis in Nigeria* (Trenton, NJ: Africa World Press, 1998); Ann Mosely Lesch, *The Sudan* (Bloomington: Indiana University Press, 1998); Joseba Zulaika, *Basque Violence: Metaphor and Sacrament* (Reno: University of Nevada Press, 1988); Albert Balcells, *Catalan Nationalism: Past and Present* (New York: St. Martin's Press, 1996); Melvyn C. Goldstein, *The Snow Lion and the Dragon: China, Tibet, and the Dalai Lama* (Berkeley: University of California Press, 1997); Asafa Jalata, *Fighting Against the Injustice of State and Globalization: Comparing the Black and Oromo Movements* (New York: Palgrave, 2001).

12. For a discussion of these concepts, see Crawford Young, *The Politics of Cultural Pluralism* (Madison: University of Wisconsin Press, 1976) and *The Rising Tide of Cultural Pluralism* (Madison: University of Wisconsin Press, 1993); T. Modood and P. Werbner, eds., *The Politics of Multiculturalism in the New Europe: Racism, Identity, and Community* (London: ZED, 1997); Zoya Hasan, ed., *Forging Identities: Gender, Communities, and State in India* (Boulder: Westview Press, 1994) and *Quest for Power: Oppositional Movements and Post-Congress Politics in Uttar Pradesh* (Delhi: Oxford University Press, 1998); Norman R. Yetman, *Majority and Minority: The Dynamics of Race and Ethnicity in American Life* (Boston: Allyn and Bacon, 1999).

13. See, for instance, Bobbi S. Low, *Why Sex Matters: A Darwinian Look at Human Behavior* (Princeton: Princeton University Press, 2000); my thanks to Donna Darden for bringing this latter work to my attention.

14. See Judith Gerson and Kathy Peiss, "Boundaries, Negotiation, Consciousness: Reconceptualizing Gender Relations," *Social Problems* 32 (1985); Judith Lorber, *Paradoxes of Gender* (New Haven: Yale University Press, 1994); Michael S. Kimmel, *The Gendered Society* (New York: Oxford University Press, 2000).

15. By *hegemonic* I refer to both coercive and ideological domination; coercive domination is easier to see; it refers to the actual use of power—in laws, courts, police, military—to enforce specific rules for behavior (who can marry whom, when, and where, who serves in military combat, who controls childbirth and child rearing); ideological domination can be more or less subtle; it refers both to explicit propaganda or "messages" contained in political discourse, commercial marketing, or popular culture, as well as to popular beliefs that are so ingrained, so assumed, so unconsciously held that they are taken for granted, "feel" right, seem "natural." Hegemonic ideologies are hard even to think about; the alternatives seem so inconceivable; truly revolutionary thought challenges hegemonies.

16. Albert J. Reiss Jr., "The Social Integration of Peers and Queers," *Social Problems* 9 (1961): 102–20; about the term *queer*, Reiss writes: "The word 'queer' is of the 'straight' and not the 'gay' world. In the "gay" world it has all the qualities of a negative stereotype but these are not intended in this paper. The paper arose out of the perspective of boys in the 'straight' world" (102); for a discussion of the history and uses of the term *queer*, see Donna Penn, "Queer: Theorizing Politics and History," *Radical History Review* 62 (1995): 24–42.

17. Gilbert Herdt, *Guardians of the Flutes* (New York: McGraw-Hill, 1981) and *Rituals of Manhood* (Berkeley: University of California Press, 1982).

18. They present as evidence the case of a man whom they considered to be a "real" homosexual. "Kalutwo" was a Sambian male who preferred to continue same sex fellatio after the "proper" period when young men stopped such sexual relations with Sambian boys and married women with whom they had vaginal intercourse; Kalutwo was ostracized by other Sambians as a "rubbish man" and his unwillingness or inability to move on to heterosexual marriage led Stoller and Herdt to conclude he was a homosexual and thus different from other Sambian males; see Robert J. Stoller and Gilbert Herdt, "Theories of Origins of Homosexuality," *Archives of General Psychiatry* 42 (1985): 399–404; for the classical sexual inspection reports, see Bronislaw Malinowski, *Sex and Repression in Savage Society* (New York: Harcourt, Brace and Company, 1927) and *The Sexual Life of Savages in North-Western Melanesia* (New York: Horace Liveright, 1929); Margaret Mead, *Coming of Age in Samoa* (New York: William Morrow, 1928) and *Sex and Temperament in Three Primitive Societies* (New York: William Morrow, 1935); Edward E. Evans-Pritchard, *The Nuer* (Oxford: Oxford University Press, 1940); for more contemporary research on sexual and gender diversity, see David D. Gilmore, *Manhood in the Making: Cultural Conceptions of Masculinity* (New Haven: Yale University Press, 1990); Gilbert Herdt, *Third Sex, Third Gender: Beyond Sexual Dimorphism in Culture and History* (New York: Zone Books, 1994) and *Same Sex, Different Cultures: Gays and Lesbians Across Cultures* (Boulder: Westview Press, 1997).

19. The term *Other* is used widely in the humanities to identify groups and individuals defined as alien, exotic, and different; most often Others are from different races, ethnic groups, nationalities, sexualities, or classes; see for instance, bell hooks, "Eating the Other," in her *Black Looks: Race and Representation* (Boston: South End Press, 1992), 21–39.

20. I extend Halberstam's argument about masculinity to sexuality, adding the terms *hypersexual* and *hyposexual*; she argues that masculinity is seen as the sole legitimate sphere of men, a social definition she contests; see Judith Halberstam, *Female Masculinity* (Durham: Duke University Press, 1998); see also Yen Le Espiritu, *Asian American Men and Women: Labor, Laws, and Love* (Thousand Oaks, CA: Sage Publications, 1997), 90–95; David L. Eng, *Racial Castration: Managing Masculinity in Asian America* (Durham: Duke University Press, 2001).

CHAPTER 1

ETHNOSEXUAL FRONTIERS
Cruising and Crossing Intimate Intersections

Ethnicity and sexuality are strained, but not strange bedfellows. The territories that lie at the intersections of racial, ethnic, or national boundaries are ethnosexual frontiers—erotic locations and exotic destinations that are surveilled and supervised, patrolled and policed, regulated and restricted, but that are constantly penetrated by individuals forging sexual links with ethnic Others across ethnic borders. Ethnosexual frontiers are the borderlands on either side of ethnic divides; they skirt the edges of ethnic communities; they constitute symbolic and physical sensual spaces where sexual imaginings and sexual contact occur between members of different racial, ethnic, and national groups.

Some of the sexual contact across ethnic boundaries is by "ethnosexual settlers" who establish long-term liaisons, join and/or form families, and become members of ethnic communities "on the other side." Some sexual contact is by "ethnosexual sojourners" who arrange for a brief or extended stay, enter into sexual liaisons, but eventually return to their home communities. Some sexual contact is by "ethnosexual adventurers" who undertake expeditions across ethnic divides for recreational, casual, or "exotic" sexual encounters, often more than once, but who return to their sexual home bases after each excursion. Some sexual contact is by "ethnosexual invaders" who launch sexual assaults across ethnic boundaries, inside alien ethnic territory, seducing, raping, and sexually enslaving ethnic Others as a means of domination and colonization. Ethnosexual frontiers are sites where ethnicity is sexualized, and sexuality is racialized, ethnicized, and nationalized.

All sexual ethnic boundary crossing has the capacity to generate controversy since ethnic groups almost always encourage members to "stick to your own kind," and since ethnic ideologies often contain negative stereotypes of outsiders. Thus, ethnosexual travelers of any type or motivation are seldom welcomed with open arms. Despite a number of similarities among all four categories of ethnosexual contact, settling and sojourning differ from adventuring and invading in a number of ways.

ETHNOSEXUAL SETTLERS AND SOJOURNERS

Ethnosexual settlers and sojourners migrate across the globe or simply travel across town to make social, emotional, and sexual contact with local populations. Settlers and sojourners often try to blend into the ethnic community in which they establish sexual liaisons. These individuals can be seen to "go native," discarding an old ethnicity or nationality for a new one. They often adopt local customs, seek acceptance by local people, attempt to "pass" as members, and seek to establish lasting relationships with locals.

Sexual contact is a major means of cultural transmission and often opens the door to assimilation.[1] Thus, assimilation—the incorporation or integration of an individual or group into another group or society—can be seen as a live sex act, though it is seldom discussed in sexual terms. The intense interpersonal involvement associated with sexual intimacy pulls willing partners toward one another on many social and cultural fronts, blending their lives and biographies, creating conditions conducive to assimilation. The most institutionalized form of sustained ethnosexual contact is intermarriage which, by definition, involves members of two different racial, ethnic, or national groups. When one of the partners moves into the ethnic community of the other that person becomes an ethnosexual settler or sojourner—a permanent or long-term resident in another ethnic setting. As a result of extended contact over time, ethnic settling or sojourning can lead to "ethnic conversion" or "ethnic switching"—instances where an individual changes ethnicity.

The most common form of ethnic switching is religious conversion: a non-Jew marrying a Jew and converting to Judaism, a non-Muslim marrying a Muslim and converting to Islam, a non-Catholic marrying a Catholic and converting to Catholicism. Language change is another form of ethnic conversion, where an individual learns the language of the partner and in essence linguistically migrates into a new ethnic community. There are less recognized, sometimes more subtle forms of ethnic conversion. Mary Kelly describes the non-Lithuanian American spouses of Lithuanian Americans in Kansas City and Seattle who learned Lithuanian cooking, attended folk dancing and language classes, and who traveled to their adopted ethnic "homeland" after Lithuania gained independence from Soviet rule in the early 1990s. One frequent factor in these and other ethnic conversions is the de-

cision to raise a mixed couple's offspring with knowledge of the religion, traditions, language, and/or identity of one partner's ethnicity. As one Lithuanian ethnic convert told Kelly:

> I wanted to visit the country from which my husband's parents emigrated, to
> get to know the people and to dance with them, and to share cultural ideas. I
> felt this would help my children to more fully appreciate their heritage.[2]

Ethnic conversion or passing are not "ethnic options" for everyone.[3]
Some ethnic boundaries are more permeable than others. Race often serves
as a solid barrier to assimilation. In the United States the practice of "hypodescent" or the "one drop rule," for instance, classifies all people with
African ancestry as "black" whether they are race identified or not.

> This is the way the American system works: if you have one parent or an-
> cestor with African origins, you are black. You are not a member of the
> white family that might also claim you. . . . You are in the black family, as
> will be all of your children and your grand children and your great-grand-
> children. It is by thus redefining "family" to exclude their black family mem-
> bers that white americans keep themselves and their "family" white . . .
> "family" stops where "black" begins.[4]

The contradictions, tensions, and sometimes the absurdities resulting from
hypodescent classification schemes have generated debates about racial data
collected by the U.S. Census Bureau, in particular about the decision to include a "biracial" category for individuals of mixed African, European, Asian,
Native American, or other "racial" backgrounds in the 2000 Census.[5] The
existence of individuals of mixed racial ancestry is the direct result of ethnosexual contact, but the *meaning* and *classification* of such individuals involve the politics of color and continuing controversies associated with sexually crossing the U.S. color line.

Rigid racial classification systems are not the only reason that migration
does not always result in ethnic assimilation. In some cases ethnic identities
are strengthened in immigrant communities, and ethnic boundaries become
effective barriers to extensive intimate contact. For instance, the influx of ethnically distinct migrants into a neighborhood or region can create new ethnic
awareness on both sides of an ethnic boundary. Rather than assimilating, immigrant groups can become new ethnic groups when they settle into a neighborhood and establish ethnic associations such as churches and restaurants.
Locals in host communities can develop ethnic consciousness in response to
the presence of new migrants and their different religions, languages, and cultures. Researchers have documented, for instance, an ethnic political economy
in the south Florida Cuban American/Latin American ethnic enclave, including the Latinoization of Miami culture (music, food, religion) and social life,

and a non-Latino (Anglo, African American) reaction to this new ethnic community.[6] The presence of large numbers of Cuban and Latin Americans, many of whom are bilingual, some of whom speak Spanish exclusively, contributed to the rise of an official English language, "English Only," or "English First" movement in Florida in the 1980s that reflected heightened ethnic awareness by resident Anglos—both black and white.[7]

Despite tensions associated with immigration, interethnic sexual contact remains an inevitable feature of migration. One reason for this is the gendered character of much international migration. Although the migration of entire families occurs, until the recent upsurge in women's international migration, most intra- and international migrants have been men, often young men. This gender imbalance in immigration has resulted in a shortage of co-ethnic women in destination communities. Even when migrant men have wives and children back home, sexual relationships that cross ethnic boundaries are often established in immigrant settings.[8] Another reason for both short-term and sustained ethnosexual contact is the ethnic character of sexual desire and desirability. Individuals gazing across racial, ethnic, and national boundaries are often attracted by what they see. Like all sexual attractions, the desire for intimate contact with ethnic Others may not last, but when it develops into a long-term relationship it is likely to contribute to reshaping ethnic identities.

Yet another factor contributing to ethnosexual settling and sojourning, even where there are co-ethnic partners available, is generational. The children of immigrants—second generation and beyond—are considerably more likely than their parents to cross local ethnic boundaries to establish amorous alliances. Intergenerational ethnosexual drift frequently is defined as a threat to ethnic group vitality and survival. For instance, Jews in the United States marry outside their religion more than any other religious group.[9] In order to strengthen the ties to Judaism and to Israel among members of the Jewish diaspora, ties that are presumed to have been weakened by intermarriage, in 1999 the Israeli government in partnership with Jewish philanthropists and communities abroad launched "Birthright," a $210 million project to fund ten-day visits to Israel for American Jewish college students in the hopes that they would "return home with a heightened awareness of their Judaism"[10]—an awareness that might reduce the frequency of Jewish ethnosexual settling and sojourning across religious ethnic borders.

ETHNOSEXUAL ADVENTURERS AND INVADERS

Sexual contact across ethnic boundaries is not always a long-term affair, and it is not always a welcome advance. Recreational sex with and sexual abuse of members of other ethnic groups are the specialties of ethnosexual adventurers and invaders. These forms of hit-and-run ethnosexuality, especially adventuring because of its relative ease and casualness, are at least as common, possibly even more common, historically than are ethnosexual settling and sojourning for several reasons. First, ethnosexual adventurers and invaders are less likely to be penalized or stigmatized for having sex with sometimes reviled ethnic Others since they often keep their border crossings a secret, they deny their liaisons, or their acts officially are overlooked or approved. These are in contrast to the situations faced by ethnosexual settlers or sojourners whose interethnic intimacies are public, and who can encounter family resistance and social disapproval. Secrecy, deniability, and official approval are especially important in interethnic sexual relations because intimate encounters across ethnic boundaries have been historically and remain quite likely to be sources of gossip, disapproval, or condemnation, and in some cases ethnosex is against the law.

One telling example of both the frequency, but also the controversy associated with ethnosexual adventure and invasion in U.S. history is the long-standing debate over the paternity of the offspring of Sally Hemings, an enslaved woman owned by President Thomas Jefferson. Sexual contact between slaves and their owners throughout antebellum U.S. history was both common and coerced. Despite its prevalence, slaveowners' sexual exploitation of slaves either was denied outright or ignored in "polite society" because of the disreputability of black-white sexual intimacy. The Hemings/Jefferson relationship was no exception. Hemings's descendants and many historians long have identified Jefferson as Hemings's lover and the father of her children. Their claims were scientifically investigated in the 1990s when DNA from Jefferson's descendants was compared with DNA from Hemings's descendants and was found to be compatible. Those defending Jefferson's "honor" argued that another male relative of Jefferson's could have been the father of Hemings's children. The combined DNA and historical record, however, pointed to Thomas Jefferson. Despite this evidence, so important was the deniability of this sexual breach of proper color conduct, that more than two centuries later, Jefferson's descendants continued to refuse to allow Hemings's descendants to become official members of the Jefferson family kinship organization or be buried in the family grave site.[11]

Ethnosexual adventuring and invasion also are more common than settling or sojourning because they are relatively easier and more convenient. Ethnosexual adventures and invasions are short-term and noncommittal enterprises, involving little investment of time or resources. Even in highly segregated settings, adventurers easily can find different-raced partners since the ethnic geography of sexuality generally permits opportunities for mixing—in entertainment areas, "red light" prostitution districts, or border towns. Illicit interethnic encounters are made possible in these liminal spaces situated in the borderlands between racial, ethnic, or national communities.[12] For instance, Julia Davidson argues that race and eroticism are important intertwined features of international "sex tourism." She quotes from a sex travel "guidebook" written by a Western male "professional" sex tourist who describes Bangkok, Thailand, as a hypersexualized, racialized space in which he fancies himself a kind of sexual social worker:

> Bangkok is sexy, lusty, sleazy. . . . It's sad to see these girls with no choice in life, waiting for their next customer. It's amazing that they seem to have fun and put a smile on their faces. Many Arabs and Europeans are known to abuse these girls. As an American you are the preferred customer . . . in the Orient women are second class citizens, often treated in dehumanizing ways. There's nothing you can do to change it, but you can still be one of the kind and generous ones who helps.[13]

Both ethnosexual adventuring and invasion often are "wink and nod" activities associated with masculine coming-of-age or solidarity rituals. Ethnosexual adventurers can be socially defined simply as young men "sowing their wild oats" or displaying evidence of sexual bravery or *sangfroid*. For example, a visit to a brothel staffed by members of a different racial, ethnic, or nationality group might be accepted or even applauded, where a "dating" relationship across ethnic boundaries would be censured. Ethnosexual invasion, in particular, is a highly institutionalized feature of many racial, ethnic, and nationalist conflicts. The rape and sexual enslavement of ethnically distinct women in wartime generally is a collective enterprise, part of the camaraderie and solidarity of military units, and a collateral campaign associated with military operations. Gang rape of "enemy" women and patronage of wartime brothels run or protected by military authorities and filled with women who are abducted, economically desperate, or displaced by war have been throughout history among the spoils of war and the perquisites of victors.

Ethnosexual adventuring and invasion are common features of political economies of desire which depend on stereotypes of the sexual talents or characteristics of members of particular races, ethnicities, or nationalities. Assertions of the impurity, inferiority, or hypersexuality of ethnic Others often are used to justify ethnosexual invasions including rape, forced sexual servitude, and trafficking in women or children for sexual purposes.[14] Part of the allure of commercial sex destinations is the alleged ethnically specific sexual features of those working there. Such ethnosexual mythologies include visions of Others with large or exotic genitals who are possessed of unusual sexual prowess or skill or who are exceptionally attractive or beautiful. The promise of exotic sex offered for sale by men, women, and children of different races, ethnicities, and nationalities is a main attraction of sex tourism around the world.[15]

Ethnosexual frontiers have been controlled, cruised, and crossed around the world throughout history. In the next section we will visit several sexually forbidden frontiers in the United States and abroad, in the past and the present. The cases presented here will provide a broad sense of the style of inquiry we will be using in this book. The following seven accounts of close encounters in racial, ethnic, and national sexual spaces answer in more detail the question posed at the beginning of this book: what's sex got to do with race, ethnicity, and nationalism?

ETHNOSEXUAL ENCOUNTERS

The first example of the connection between ethnicity and sexuality is detailed in a report from the ethnosexual front in the Protestant-Catholic battleground in Northern Ireland. This 1979 poem by Linda Anderson is a cautionary tale about the heavy price to be paid by women who cross the line and violate the partisans' rules of celibacy or of giving aid or comfort to ethnic Others while "their men" are in prison for their part in the ethnic conflict. In such cases, an individual's decision when and with whom to have sex ceases to be a personal choice, but becomes an ethnically loaded public act which others in the community claim the right to define, judge, and punish. The woman in this poem pays a high price for what most of us consider a private decision.

GANG BANG, ULSTER STYLE
by Linda Anderson
Broken Belfast Street,
Grey and dingy,
Sealed off with barbed wire
To stop murderous neighbours.
You lived in that trap,
Suffocating.
He was in another prison
Called Long Kesh.

> Sleepwalking woman,
> You shuttlecocked
> From jail to jail
> On dutiful visits,
> Your eyes were old
> They did not match
> The bright hair
> That made men watch you
> Avidly.

You met him—
Another starved somnambulist.
Two living corpses clung together,
Thawed each other for a while.
But they found out.
They dragged you to their playroom.
Now you lie limp,
Face down,
Dumped in a ditch.
Routine policemen come
Accustomed, stony-faced
'Turn her over, see the damage'.

　　O, poor adventuress—
　　In the name of virtue,
　　They cut off your flaxen hair,
　　Defiled your lovely breasts,
　　Before degutting you.[16]

Anderson's poem illustrates how the inspection and regulation of sexuality can be used to forge and maintain ethnic solidarity, but not always in predictable ways. David McKittrick and his associates have compiled accounts of more than 3,600 deaths associated with the Northern Irish "troubles" during the period 1966–1999. Many of the deaths are variations on the story in Anderson's poem. One famous case is the 1972 Irish Republican Army's (IRA) abduction and killing of Jean McConville, a widow with ten children. McConville was raised a Protestant, but converted to Catholicism when she married a Catholic man who died of cancer a year before she disappeared. Although the reasons for her disappearance were never entirely clear, a frequently suggested explanation is that she "angered the IRA by comforting a [British] soldier who had been seriously injured outside her door."[17] After her disappearance McConville's children were placed in orphanages, but came back together as adults in search of their mother's body.

The IRA's murder of McConville and other female sexual "collaborators" and those suspected of sexual disloyalty had mixed consequences for the maintenance of Protestant/Catholic ethnic boundaries and intragroup solidarity. While such killings no doubt struck fear in the hearts of men and especially women considering violating ethnosexual rules, excesses associated with such rules and their enforcement also mobilized opposition and motivated the building of bridges across ethnic divides. In the case of Jean McConville, her adult children's continuing search for her remains became a cause celebre in the Northern Irish peace movement of the 1990s and contributed to the formation of "Families of the Disappeared," an organization established in Northern Ireland in 1994 with the objective of having all bodies returned to families for burial.[18]

Our next ethnosexual destination exposes some interesting contradictions in the U.S. racial-sexual cosmology. Interracial sexual contact has been a hallmark of American history, but so has the sexual demonization of members of various racial groups, especially African Americans, mainly by those who have come to define themselves as "white."[19] The U.S. sexual color line constantly has been crossed, but it also continuously has been policed—both formally (e.g., laws against miscegenation) and informally (e.g., lynchings and castrations). In spite of an established pattern of interracial sexual intimacy made quite visible by large numbers of racially mixed Americans, U.S. history has been punctuated by "discoveries" of racial sexual threats and associated ethnosexual panics and hysteria (e.g., the white slavery panics of the early twentieth century).[20] American discourses of ethnosexual danger most often are articulated as threats to the purity and safety of white women by sexually menacing nonwhite men. This is especially ironic since white men have posed constant and serious threats of sexual violence against women of all colors throughout United States history.[21]

Despite the prevalence of sexual race-baiting in American social, cultural, and political discourse, it turns out that not all interracial contact is depicted in the U.S. media or in the popular imagination as racial pollution or sexual threat. Indeed, some members of some races are not only secretly desired, they are openly eroticized. In such cases, invitations to cross sexual boundaries and to enter ethnosexual frontiers are commodified and marketed to interested sex consumers. This is especially true in the case of Asian women and white men.

The Internet is a symbolically rich domain for cruising sites of ethnosexual desire. There are many websites that promote interracial, intercultural, and international exchanges of various sorts, including sexual exchanges. Examples include "Euro-Japanese Virtual Encounters," "Asia Friend Finder," "The Pacific Century Club," "Brides by Mail," and "Soulmates International," a website designed to put "Western men" in touch with "quality Asian ladies" from the Philippines for virtual and real relationships.[22] These sites reveal a sexualized and gendered face to interracial fantasies. For instance, note the word "Brides"; there are no "Husbands By Mail" sites, and the point of these sites is seldom to put Asian men in touch with quality Western ladies. The following bit of ethnosexual confessional testimony can be found on the "Soulmates International" website; among the tips and advice given in response to FAQs (frequently asked questions) are:

WHY DO YOUNG FILIPINA WOMEN WANT AN OLDER MAN 30 TO 60? Filipino women are looking for a life partner. . . . They are smart and realise that men 20–30 are not stable, don't have definite goals for their life, and do not treat women with the same respect as an older man.

ARE THESE WOMEN LOOSE WOMEN OR PROSTITUTES? No. These women are not bar girls or prostitutes. Many of these women from 17–25 are virgins.

DO FILIPINA's MAKE GOOD WIVES? They are taught that marriage is a life long commitment. . . . When you ask questions of a Filipino woman like how many children would you like to have, or would you like to be a working wife, or a housewife, her answer will always be that is up to my future husband to decide.

DO THEY LOOK AFTER THEIR BODIES? If you like a petite woman, then you will be pleased with a Filipina. They have very little body hair. They are fanatically clean about their personal hygiene and appearance. . . . Basically a 15 year old Filipino girl has more class than the average 25 year old American girl.

SHOULD YOU WESTERNISE A FILIPINO WIFE? No. You pick this girl because of the fine characteristics they have. If you're foolish enough to want to turn her into an Westernised woman shame on you![23]

This depiction of Filipina women reflects a long tradition in Western societies, stretching back before colonialism, in which Asian women are characterized as exotic, submissive, and sexually available.[24] It is not only on the Internet that we can find evidence of this stereotype of Asian women. In a special issue published in the fall of 1993, *Time Magazine* ran a cover story that played on the cluster of attractive sexual characteristics often attributed to Asian women to ease the blow of their predictions about the changing racial composition of the U.S. population from predominantly "white" to "nonwhite." The cover photo, shown in Plate 1 of the color insert, was a "composite" picture of America's racial future—a lovely young woman, only ever-so-slightly oriental, only ever-so-slightly brown. It is revealing, but not surprising, that *Time*'s editors chose to computer simulate a woman's face, not a man's face, and that the "racial mixing" that produced the *Time* composite American was essentially a pretty, young white woman. Someone any man—or woman—would be proud to bring home to the family.[25]

Ethnosexual cosmologies of desire and desirability are not found only in popular media and interpersonal communications, they can also be found in demographic data. Our next example comes from the U.S. Census Bureau, a government agency with an abiding interest in race and sex. Every month the Census Bureau conducts the Current Population Survey (CPS), gathering data on a sample of the United States population in order to track trends between the official census of the population that is conducted every ten years. In 2001 the Census Bureau issued a report on "America's Families and Living Arrangements" based on March 2000 CPS data. A variety of characteristics of American families was reported: ages of family members, earnings, education levels, number of children, races of married couples. The data showed that race matters in American marriages. Of the CPS estimated 56.5 million marriages in the United States in 2000, the overwhelming majority (53.6 million, or 94.6 percent) were between members of the same race in the U.S. "racial pentagon"—black, white, brown, yellow, red.[26] This means that when Americans marry, fewer than 10 percent of those unions involve partners of different races.

If race matters in American marriages, some races matter more than others. The CPS report contained data on rates of intermarriage between various races in 2000: in 93.9 percent of marriages involving whites, both partners were white; in 89.1 percent of marriages involving blacks, both partners were black; in 73.7 percent of marriages involving Asian Americans, both partners were Asian American; in 73.1 percent of marriages involving Hispanics both partners were Hispanic; and in 33.0 percent of Native American marriages, both partners were Native American.[27]

By deconstructing these data according to the gender of the partners involved in interracial marriages, we can see that not only does race matter in patterns of ethnosexual attraction (or not), gender matters too. There is an ethnosexual factor at work in the intimate economies of marriage markets. When blacks and whites intermarry, gender matters a great deal. It will be no surprise to most Americans that three-quarters of marriages between blacks and whites involve a black husband and a white wife. The opposite gender trend can be seen in marriages between Asian Americans and whites. Again gender matters, and again most Americans would not be surprised to learn that two-thirds of marriages between Asians and whites involve an Asian wife and a white husband. Table 1 shows the race of spouses in marriages involving blacks and whites and Asian Americans and whites in the United States in 2000.[28]

As we can see from Table 1.1, the race of husband and wife in black-white intermarriage is a gendered mirror image of the race of husband and wife in Asian-white intermarriage. Out of 655,000 marriages between Asian Americans and whites, 452,000 or 69.0 percent are between an Asian American woman and a white man; in contrast, out of 363,000 marriages between blacks and whites, 268,000 or 73.8 percent are between a black man and a white woman. These numbers reflect a clear gender reversal in race of marriage partners in these two types of interracial marriage.[29] What this table illustrates is the power of ethnosexual imaginings and ideologies to drive the intimate choices involved in decisions if and whom to marry. If gender did

Table 1.1 Asian-White and Black-White Intermarriage by Race of Opposite-Sex Spouse, 2000 in thousands

	RACE OF SPOUSE			
	ASIAN		BLACK	
	Number	Percent	Number	Percent
White Wife	203	31.0	268	73.8
White Husband	452	69.0	95	26.2
Total	655	100.0	363	100.0

Source: U.S. Bureau of the Census, Current Population Survey, "America's Families and Living Arrangements, March 2000," Table FG3: Married Couple Family Groups, by Presence of Own Children Under 18, and Age, Earnings, Education, and Race and Hispanic Origin of Both Spouses: March 2000 (http://www.census.gov/population/socdemo/hh-fam/p20-537/2000/tabFG3.txt)

not matter in racial intermarriage, the percentages in these tables would be 50 percent in all cases. Instead, the table shows that in black-white marriages, the odds are 3 to 1 that the the wife will be white, and in Asian-white marriages, the odds are 2 to 1 that the husband will be white. These Census Bureau data provide us with statistical evidence of the workings of race in the choice of marriage partner.[30] It is no coincidence that the black-white and Asian-white ethnic boundaries are perhaps the most sexually loaded in U.S. society, past and present.

Our fourth ethnosexual narrative involves ethnicities confronting sexualities. Tim Davis recounts the queer saga of the struggle over the sexual meaning of Irish Americanness that surrounded the question of who should be permitted to march in the Boston St. Patrick's Day parade, also known as the "Evacuation Day" parade in commemoration of the ouster of British and loyalist troops from the city in 1737. In 1992, "three Irish-American women involved in Queer Nation/Boston formed the Irish-American Lesbian, Gay, and Bisexual Pride Community, later known as GLIB."[31] GLIB sought the right of its members to participate in the annual St. Patrick's/Evacuation Day parade, which was organized by the South Boston Allied War Veterans Council. The Veterans Council objected and the case ended up in court. Boston City Councillor James Kelly, who represented the district in South Boston where the march was organized, opposed GLIB's inclusion in the march:

> GLIB, the gay, lesbian, and bisexual group of trouble makers who hate the Catholic Church and its teachings, are not welcome in South Boston's Evacuation Day Parade. If parading is so important to them, let them raise their own money, organize their own parade, and apply for a permit to march in downtown Boston to express their sexuality.[32]

Scholars studying the dispute argue that the resistance to the inclusion of GLIB in the march exposed an assumption about the heterosexuality of Irishness. GLIB challenged the notion that all Irish Americans were straight and that nationality itself had an implicit sexual orientation. Carl Stychin characterized the subsequent court battle as a dispute that "centers directly on the *sexuality* of national identities and speaks to *both* the construction of the sexuality of an Irish American and to an American identity."[33] While the Massachusetts state courts permitted GLIB to march in the parade in 1992 and the next few years because the parade received public funding, in 1995 the U.S. Supreme Court ruled against GLIB (*Hurley and South Boston Allied War Veterans Council v. Irish-American Gay, Lesbian and Bisexual Group of Boston* 1995), arguing that the parade was a private function of the Veterans Council who could exclude organizations and individuals if they wished. What is interesting about this case is that it reveals what is often a hidden feature of ethnicity or nationality—its presumed heterosexuality. Part of the reason for this heteroassumptivity is the close connection between family and community in ethnic, racial, and national groups. Homosexuality does not fit easily into ideologies stressing traditional family life as the cornerstone of ethnic community. Thus, homophobia is a common feature of racial, ethnic, and nationalist ideologies and programs of social control. Unlike racism and prejudice that seek targets *outside* ethnic boundaries, homophobia can be directed *inside* ethnic communities as well, and used to create an internal sexual boundary that excludes or "disqualifies" a group's own members.

To visit the next intersection of ethnicity and sexuality, we must travel to the war zone of Bosnia-Herzegovina in the former state of Yugoslavia in the early 1990s. Following the collapse of the Soviet Union in 1990, waves of ethnic conflict swept across the former Soviet republics and Eastern Europe. Despite decades of peaceful coexistence among diverse national, religious, and linguistic groups, there were many ethnic conflicts in Yugoslavia during this time as politicians fanned nationalist flames and jockeyed for geopolitical position by making claims of ethnic purity and sounding alarms against internal ethnic threats.

As it often does, sex became a weapon of war in these conflicts. Perhaps the most notorious, though by no means the only example of sexual assault during this period was the ethnosexual violence by Orthodox Christian Serbian men against Catholic and Muslim Bosnian women, many of whom had been their neighbors for years. Alexandra Stiglmayer interviewed Bosnian women rape victims, including a forty-five-year-old Muslim woman who described her rape one night around midnight in May 1992, when four men forced their way into the house where she was staying with her mother-in-law and three children. Please be forewarned, these accounts of rape in war may be very disturbing to some readers:

> One of them grabbed hold of me; his last name is Todorevic. . . . I recognized them . . . they were our neighbors. They . . . took me into the house of my husband's uncle who had been shot. Four young women were there already; one of them was my daughter-in-law. They dragged us one after the other into the room, and what all didn't they do with us there! They beat us, tortured us, raped us—they did whatever came into their heads.[34]

Serbs and many other groups involved in Yugoslavia's ethnic nightmares of the 1990s not only killed and raped their neighbors, they rounded up many men and women and interned them in concentration camps; not only Muslims were victims:

> One ethnic [Catholic] Croat woman was detained in a Serb-controlled camp with 34 other women and a large number of men. She reported that all 34 women in the camp were raped. "There were so many killings, torture. Death became very familiar. All of the women were begging to be killed, to be shot, not to be tortured. . . . " Another ethnic Croat woman was detained in a "special house" where she was raped by several men every night for approximately two months. Every night she could hear screams and cries of other women. She reported that, while raping her, the men were shouting: "you will have a Serb child."[35]

In Bosnia the use of rape and sexual torture was an extremely aggressive means of reestablishing an ethnic boundary separating Serbs from Croats and Muslims, an ethnic distinction that had blurred during the decades following World War II when members of the ethnic communities had intermarried and established residential, social, and sexual connections especially in urban areas such as Sarajevo. By choosing which women to rape, men from one ethnic group designated who was and was not a protected, respected member of their community. Like armed conflict between men, rape was used to draw an ethnic line in the sand separating one group from another, designating who had rights and who did not. The use of intimate acts to create ethnic distance reveals an interesting paradox in ethnosexual connections. There is an inherent contradiction in having sex with someone defined as an impure outsider since it can involve the violation of sexual taboos (having sex with polluted Other women). Ironically, sexually crossing an ethnic boundary often is used to build and reinforce the walls that divide ethnic groups.

For our sixth troubling tale of race and sex, we must travel back to the United States and to November 1987, when an African American teenager,

Tawana Brawley, who had been missing for four days, reported being abducted, abused, and raped by a group of white police officers. Her case became the center of a controversy in which she was defended by supporters and defamed by skeptics. The case was investigated by a New York Grand Jury that concluded she had fabricated the story. The Tawana Brawley case both parallels and diverges from several other instances of sexualized racial violence in the United States during the 1980s and 1990s, including the O. J. Simpson murder case in California, the New York Central Park jogger case, and the New York Howard Beach assault and murder case.[36]

In contrast to these three examples where nonwhite men were accused of attacking or seeking sexual contact with white women, the Tawana Brawley case involved a racial gender reversal of the victim and her accused assailants—a black woman who accused white men of attacking her. Thus, the Brawley case harkened back to centuries of U.S. history in which enslaved black women were the sexual property and therefore the sexual quarry of white men. The sexual side of slavery is not well known although the magnitude of the sexual abuses that occurred during slavery remains one of the greatest scandals in U.S. history. The sexual exploitation of African-ancestry women and the sexual mutilation of African-ancestry men by mainly European-ancestry men seldom are chronicled in the American national story. These scenes in U.S. race relations are often unspoken or whispered, *sotto voce* asides in the more widely and loudly disseminated historical and contemporary ethnosexual scripts, which tend to feature pure white women threatened by dangerous dark men and defended by provoked white men. The fact that Brawley's charges challenged the usual scenario of victimized white womanhood and valorized white manhood no doubt contributed to the uproar, denunciations, and polarization that characterized the case.

The voices speaking out from the Brawley case echo a broader conversation that can be heard at past and present stops on the ethnosexual frontier running along the U.S. black-white color line:

> This case began with a young, black fifteen-year-old girl who was kidnapped, raped, sodomized. "KKK" and "NIGGER" were inscribed on her body—and feces. She was then placed in a plastic garbage bag and dumped on the road for dead. (C. Vernon Mason, attorney for Tawana Brawley)[37]
>
> If Tawana was a white girl, you wouldn't make us prove how the crime happened. But because she's black she's got to prove herself. You know it . . . and I know it. The fact that you've got five hundred black people in this room and every one of them has got a different complexion means that white rape is a reality in the United States. (Reverend Al Sharpton)[38]
>
> Based upon all of the evidence that has been presented to the grand jury, we conclude that Tawana Brawley was not the victim of a forcible sexual assault by multiple assailants over a four-day period. There is no evidence that

any sexual assault occurred. The grand jury further concludes that there is nothing in regard to Tawana Brawley's appearance on November 28 that is inconsistent with this condition having been self-inflicted. (New York Grand Jury report)[39]

My name is Tawana Brawley. I am not a liar, and I'm not crazy. I simply want justice, and then I want to be left alone. My family and I thought we couldn't get any justice, so we decided not to cooperate. We had no *New York Times* to leak to, so we got Alton Maddox, C. Vernon Mason, and the Reverend Al Sharpton to fight for us. . . . I wish to thank God for sparing my life. . . . He holds my hand, and He let me live. He'll stop the cover-up once and for all. I have not deceived my family, my advisers, and most of all, my people. I trust in God, and He will see me, and my Mom, and my family, through.[40]

Although the veracity of Brawley's charges of sexual abuse has been questioned repeatedly inside and outside several courts of law, the capacity of the case to elicit outrage and sympathy on both sides of the U.S. color line dramatizes the volatility of ethnosexual matters. The following analysis by two journalists covering the story reveals how much credibility depends on resonance with established historical and cultural ethnosexual expectations:

Imagine if the first story about the alleged gang rape of Tawana Brawley had been different in a few crucial details. What if she was a talented and pretty *white* teenager from a modest middle-class family in Dutchess County, a girl who loved to read, a cheerleader? What if *that* teenager was found wrapped in a large plastic garbage bag, shivering and nearly unconscious, covered in excrement, missing one shoe, wearing ripped and burned jeans. . . . What if anti-white racial epithets had been written on her clothing and torso; and if in the hospital, in answer to the question, "were you raped?" she'd scribbled the words "a lot," and in answer to the question "Who did it?" she'd scrawled "black cop." (Mike Taibbi and Anna Sims-Phillips)[41]

This imagined racially reversed scenario illustrates the racially loaded nature of sexuality and the sexually loaded nature of race. Sexuality gives a special power and meaning to ethnic and racial tensions; the introduction of race into a charge of sexual assault can be explosive, reminding us once again that sex and race are a volatile mixture.

Our last example involves a more subtle, but equally powerful marriage of ethnicity and sexuality than those described above. This ethnosexual encounter is located in a different combat theatre from the ethnic war fronts of Northern Ireland or Bosnia. This is a voice from the Vietnam war of the 1960s and 1970s. Like those other two conflicts, the Vietnam war was staged in a gendered, sexualized battle theatre. The war was a site of masculinities in conflict as various raced, classed, and ideologically divided American manhoods engaged other raced, classed, and ideologically divided Vietnamese,

Laotian, and Cambodian manhoods. During the war there were also sexual encounters between American GIs and Asian women in the brothels and clubs of Saigon, Bangkok, and other military "rest and recreation" destinations as well as in the combat zones of the war.[42]

Arno Karlen describes the disdain of some GIs for American men who opposed the war and who tried to convince others to join them in resisting the draft and U.S. involvement in Southeast Asia. Gendered and sexualized contempt for war protesters can be heard in the following comment by a U.S. Non-Commissioned Officer (NCO):

> In 1968 pacifists set up coffee houses to spread their word near military bases. A Special Forces NCO said to a *Newsweek* reporter, "We aren't fighting and dying so these goddam pansies can sit around drinking coffee."[43]

This NCO's reference to draft resisters and war protesters as "pansies" reflects not only the masculinist character of war, but also the heterosexual, heteronormative nature of what Robert Connell refers to as "hegemonic masculinity"—a dominant form of masculinity often associated with nationalism, patriotism, and manly codes of honor.[44] "Real men" fight wars, and they often fight them against pansies and perverts. During times of war enemy men commonly are depicted either as wimps or rapists, and they are hypo-, homo-, or hypersexualized. The link between war and manhood and the notion of our men as virile and their men as degenerate (and our women as pure and their women as sluts) illustrates often hidden, but powerful sexualized assumptions about the nation, its citizens, its defenders, and its enemies. Good citizenship relies on appropriate sexual behavior and proper gender performance. Good citizens are heterosexual, valiant (in the case of men), and virtuous (in the case of women). Sexuality and gender, thus, are important building blocks of the nation.[45]

CONCLUSION

What could a poem about a woman in Northern Ireland possibly have in common with an internet advice column's description of Filipina women's suitability as partners for American men, or with U.S. Census Bureau data on the races of married couples, or with a dispute over the inclusion of non-heterosexuals in a Boston St. Patrick's Day parade, or with the testimony of Bosnian women raped by Serbs, or with the controversy over the reported rape and abuse of a black teenager by white police, or with the complaint of a U.S. soldier about draft resisters? These are very different tales, told at different times, in different places, and most importantly, touching on many different subjects. Or are they?

While these narratives are spoken by a multitude of voices reflecting multiple positions and perspectives, there is a similar set of themes linking them to one another across time and space. These accounts portray racialized, ethnicized, and nationalized scenes of manliness and womanliness. They are pictures of potent and impotent men and of ruled and unruly women, descriptions of male strength and weakness and of female seductive power and vulnerability, depictions of masculine sexual desire and feminine sexual desirability. We see gender and sexuality as a series of similar and different images sketched out across ethnic, racial, and national canvases. These stories illustrate the boundaries that divide male and female, romantic longing and reviled loathing, the reputable and the disreputable. They present racial, ethnic, and national sexual images of us and them. They detail real and imagined sexualized and gendered differences between races, ethnic groups, and nations.

In later chapters of this book we will examine in more depth many ethnosexual frontiers in many national and international spaces: the United States black-white color line, American Indian–white relations, nationalist conflicts and movements in the United States and around the world, in war and military zones, in tourist destinations, and in workplaces in the global economy. To prepare for our explorations, in Chapter 2 we will outfit ourselves with a conceptual map and a set of analytical tools for rethinking and reenvisioning ethnicity and sexuality. Thus reoriented and theoretically armed, we will begin a more in-depth exploration of the intimate intersections and forbidden frontiers where ethnicity and sexuality converge.

NOTES

1. For a discussion and critique of the concept of assimilation, see Yetman, *Majority and Minority*, 227–71.

2. Mary E. Kelly, "Ethnic Conversions: Family, Community, Women, and Kinwork," *Ethnic Studies Review* 19 (1996): 81–100, 91; see also Mary E. Kelly, "Ethnic Pilgrimages: People of Lithuanian Descent in Lithuania," *Sociological Spectrum* 20 (2000): 65–91; the transmission of an ethnic heritage to one's children occurs more widely than in cases of ethnic conversion; for instance, in cases of "ethnic recovery," where an individual was not raised in the family tradition, the desire to pass on one's ancestral religion, traditions, heritage commonly produces a kind of "reverse cultural transmission," where the adult becomes "more ethnic" as a result of child rearing; see M. Herbert Danzger, *Returning to Tradition: The Contemporary Revival of Orthodox Judaism* (New Haven: Yale University Press, 1989).

3. Mary Waters, *Ethnic Options: Choosing Identities in America* (Berkeley: University of California Press, 1990).

4. Judy Scales-Trent, *Notes of a White Black Woman* (University Park: Pennsylvania State University Press, 1995), 62–63.

5. Margo J. Anderson and Stephen E. Feinberg, *Who Counts? The Politics of Census-Taking in Contemporary America* (New York: Russell Sage Foundation, 1999); for a discussion of similar, but interestingly different issues in the Canadian census, see Monica Boyd, Gustave Goldmann, and Pamela White, "Race in the Canadian Census," in *Race and Racism: Canada's Challenge*, ed. Leo Driedger and Shiva S. Halli (Montreal: McGill/Queen's University Press, 2000), 33–54; Melissa Nobles, *Shades of Citizenship: Race and the Census in Modern Politics* (Stanford: Stanford University Press, 2000).

6. Alejandro Portes and Alex Stepick, *City on the Edge: The Transformation of Miami* (Berkeley: University of California Press, 1993); Maria de los Angeles Torres, "Encuentros y Encontronazos: Homeland in the Politics and Identity of the Cuban Diaspora," *Diaspora* 4 (1995): 211–38; David Rieff, *The Exile: Cuba in the Heart of Miami* (New York: Simon and Schuster, 1993); Guillermo J. Grenier and Lisandro Perez, "Miami Spice: The Ethnic Cauldron Simmers," in *Origins and Destinies: Immigration, Race, and Ethnicity in America*, ed. Silvia Pedraza and Reuben G. Rumbaut (Belmont, CA: Wadsworth, 1996), 360–72; Silvia Pedraza, "Cuba's Refugees: Manifold Migrations," in *Origins and Destinies* (Belmont, CA: Wadsworth Publishing Company, 1996), 263–79; Silvia Pedraza, "Cuba's Revolution and Exodus, " *The Journal of the International Institute*, University of Michigan 5 (1998): 8–9; for a discussion of the dynamic character of Chicano culture, see Jose David Saldivar, *Border Matters: Remapping American Cultural Studies* (Berkeley: University of California Press, 1997); and for a discussion of Asian American cultural politics (as distinct from cultural production), see Lisa Lowe, *Immigrant Acts: On Asian American Cultural Politics* (Durham: Duke University Press, 1998).

7. It was not only South Florida that the issue of English as the national language in the United States became a political issue, although the politics of English only was more likely to emerge in states with significant immigrant populations, English as an official language became part of the discourse of American nationalism in general during the 1980s; see Dennis Baron, *The English-Only Question: An Official Language for Americans?* (New Haven : Yale University Press, 1990); similar restrictive language policy movements have occurred in other countries and regions, including Sri Lanka, France, Puerto Rico, and Quebec; some of these take the form of backlashes against immigrants, some are reflections of heightened ethnic nationalism; see Mark Cooray, *Changing the Language of the Law: the Sri Lanka Experience* (Québec: Presses de l'Université Laval, 1985); Amílcar A. Barreto, *Language, Elites, and the State: Nationalism in Puerto Rico and Quebec* (Westport, CT: Praeger, 1998).

8. Hsiu-hua Shen, "Crossing the Taiwan Strait: The Gender and Sexual Politics of Identity Construction in the Global Economy" (Ph.D. diss., University of Kansas, 2003); Ann Stoler, "Sexual Affronts and Racial Frontiers: European Identities and the Cultural Politics of Exclusion in Colonial Southeast Asia," *Comparative Study of Society and History* 24 (1992): 514–51.

9. Ellen Jaffe McClain, *Embracing the Stranger: Intermarriage and the Future of the American Jewish Community* (New York: Basic Books, 1995).

10. Joel Greenberg, "Trips to Renew Jewish Ties Set Off Debate over Costs," *New York Times* (January 8, 2000): 1.

11. Dinitia Smith and Nicholas Wade, "DNA Tests Offer Evidence That Jefferson Fathered a Child with His Slave," *New York Times on the Web* (November 1, 1998) (http://www.shamema.com/dna-jeff.htm); see also Annette Gordon-Reed, *Thomas Jefferson and Sally Hemings: An American Controversy* (Charlottesville: University Press of Virginia, 1997); in 2000 the Monticello Association, a Jefferson descendant organization, released an interim report on the question of whether to open membership and burial rights to Hemings's descendants:

> The Executive Committee of the Association did not wish to be rushed into making a hasty decision . . . [and announced in 1999] the formation of a Membership Advisory Committee to recommend to the Executive Committee and the Association membership the criteria that should be used for determining if a person is, or is not, a descendant of Thomas Jefferson. . . . The committee was to have prepared its recommendations by the annual meeting in May 2000. (James J. Truscott, "Statement on the Interim Report issued by the Membership Advisory Committee of the Monticello Association," May, 2000, 2; http://www.monticello-assoc.org/interim.html)

In May 2002 the Monticello Association membership voted 74–6 "to bar the kin of slave Sally Hemings from joining the family organization" (Leef Smith, "Jefferson Group Bars Kin Of Slave: Hemings Family Remains Unshaken," *Washington Post* [May 6, 2002]: B1).

12. See Kevin J. Mumford, *Interzones: Black/White Sex Districts in Chicago and New York in the Early Twentieth Century* (New York: Columbia University Press, 1997); David Bell and Gill Valentine, eds., *Mapping Desire: Geographies of Sexualities* (New York: Routledge, 1995).

13. Julia O'Connell Davidson, *Prostitution, Power, and Freedom* (Ann Arbor: University of Michigan Press, 1998), 179; Davidson refers to Cassirer's statement as "vintage sex tourist twaddle . . . in which Cassirer, like many sex tourists I have interviewed, manages to construct himself as esteemed and honourable by contrasting himself favourably against other 'abusive' and ungentlemanly prostitute users" (Ibid.); see also Ryan Bishop and Lillian S. Robinson, "How My Dick Spent Its Summer Vacation: Sex and the Commerce of Global Communication," *Genders* (2002); Ryan Bishop and Lillian S. Robinson, "Travelers' Tails," in *Prostitution in a Global Context,* ed. Susan Thorbeck (London: Zed, 2002).

14. See Anne Llewellyn Barstow, *War's Dirty Secret: Rape, Prostitution, and Other Crimes Against Women* (Cleveland: Pilgrim Press, 2000); Siriporn Skrobanek, Nattaya Boonpakdee, and Chutima Jantateero, *The Traffic in Women: Human Realities of the International Sex Trade* (London: Zed Books, 1997).

15. See Kamala Kempadoo, *Sun, Sex, and Gold: Tourism and Sex Work in the Caribbean* (Lanham, MD: Rowman and Littlefield, 1999).

16. Linda Anderson, "Gang Bang Ulster Style," in *Pillars of the House: An Anthology of Verse by Irish Women from 1690 to the Present,* ed. Angeline A. Kelly (Dublin: Wolfhound, 1988), 144–45. I am grateful to Linda Anderson, Department of Creative Writing, Lancaster University, UK, for her permission to reprint this poem; I wish to thank Katie Conrad, University of Kansas, Department of English, for bringing the poem to my attention.

17. David McKittrick, Seamus Kelters, Brian Feeney, and Chris Thornton, *Lost Lives: Stories of the Men, Women, and Children Who Died as a Result of the Northern Ireland Troubles* (Edinburgh: Mainstream Publishing, 1999), 301; my thanks to

Barry Shank, Ohio State University, Division of Comparative Studies, for bringing this book to my attention. See also Tom Inglis, "Sexual Transgression and Scapegoats: A Case Study from Modern Ireland," *Sexualities* 5 (2002): 5–24.

18. Ibid., 302.

19. See Lipsitz, *The Possessive Investment in Whiteness*.

20. For example, Brian Donovan documents the history of panics and legislation against "white slavery" in the United States in "The Sexual Basis of Racial Formation: Crusades Against 'White Slavery,' " (Ph.D. diss., Northwestern University, 2001); admonitions about and disdain for racial mixing come from both sides of the black-white color line and scholars report that disapproval of mixed race couples is not limited to European Americans, but is expressed by African Americans as well; see Michele Wallace, *Black Macho and the Myth of the Superwoman* (London: Verso, [1979] 1990), 9–10 and Micaela di Leonardo, "White Lies, Black Myths: Rape, Race, and the Black 'Underclass,' " in *The Gender Sexuality Reader: Culture, History, Political Economy*, ed. Roger N. Lancaster and Micaela di Leonardo (New York: Routledge, 1997), 53–68.

21. See Saidiya Hartman, *Scenes of Subjection: Terror, Slavery, and Self-Making in Nineteenth-Century America* (New York: Oxford University Press, 1997); Albert L. Hurtado, *Intimate Frontiers: Sex, Gender, and Culture in Old California* (Albuquerque: University of New Mexico Press, 1999); Angela Davis, "Rape, Racism, and the Capitalist Setting, *Black Scholar* 9 (1978): 24–30 and *Women, Culture, and Politics* (New York: Random House, 1989).

22. The Soulmates International homepage is http://www.soulmatesinternational.com/; there are dozens of such sites, including: "The Pacific Century Club" (http://www.pacificcentury.com/), "Euro-Japanese Virtual Encounters," (http://www.daopian.com/ejve/), "Get Married Now" (http://www.getmarriednow.com/), "Asia Friend Finder" (http://asiafriendfinder.com/welcome/), and "Brides by Mail" (http://www.bridesbymail.com/); I would like to thank Hsiu-hua Shen for pointing out these ethnosexual websites to me. Not all of the international websites are devoted to arranging communication between Western men and Asian women; some are simply interested in sexual crossings of national boundaries, for instance, at http://www.one-and-only.com, I searched through some personal ads posted by men from outside the United States looking for women in the United States. The heading, "Looking for hot married womans!!!!!!" caught my eye; when I looked it up, I saw in fact that it was posted by a man who described himself as "36, 5'9" blue green eye dark hair" and was signed, "Love john."

23. See http://www.tmx.comau/webads/faq.htm

24. See Edward Said, *Orientalism* (New York: Pantheon Books, 1978); Margaret Jolly, "From Point Venus to Bali Ha'i: Eroticism and Exoticism in Representations of the Pacific," in *Sites of Desire, Economies of Pleasure: Sexualities in Asia and the Pacific*, ed. Lenore Manderson and Margaret Jolly (Chicago: University of Chicago Press, 1997), 99–122; Lisa Lowe, *Critical Terrains: French and British Orientalisms* (Ithaca: Cornell University Press, 1991); see also Espiritu, *Asian American Women and Men*; Jennifer P. Ting, "The Power of Sexuality," *Journal of Asian American Studies* 1 (1998): 65–82. For a less sanguine view of Asian and Asian American women's stereotypes, see Leslie Bow, *Betrayal and Other Acts of Subversion: Fem-*

inism, *Sexual Politics, Asian American Women's Literature* (Princeton: Princeton University Press, 2001). For a discussion of printed mail order Asian bride catalogues, see Ara Wilson, "American Catalogues of Asian Brides," in *Anthropology for the Nineties: Introductory Readings*, ed. Johnetta B. Cole (New York: The Free Press, 1988), 114–25.

25. Scholars report that the racial composition of the composite woman on the *Time* cover did not reflect a perfect racial demographic projection, but rather the image was ethnically "weighted" toward Mediterranean features that editors felt readers would find more palatable and appealing; see Lauren G. Berlant, *The Queen of America Goes to Washington City: Essays on Sex and Citizenship* (Durham: Duke University Press, 1997), 192–211; David R. Roediger, *Colored White: Transcending the Racial Past* (Berkeley: University of California Press, 2002), Chapter 1; my thanks to Charles Gallagher for bringing this book to my attention.

26. Hollinger, *Postethnic America.*

27. The much higher percentage of American Indians marrying non-Indians is part of a historical trend toward exogamy among indigenous Americans; see C. Matthew Snipp, *American Indians: The First of This Land* (New York: Russell Sage Foundation, 1989); the percentages for white and black marriages are for "non-Hispanic" whites and blacks since the "race" question in the CPS does not include "Hispanic" (which is asked in a different question); figures for Asian Americans and Native Americans do include Hispanics; "Asian American" includes a broad array of national origin groups and is categorized by the Census Bureau as "Asian/Pacific Islander;" Native Americans also include a broad array of tribal groups and is categorized by the Census Bureau as "American Indian/Alaska Native"; see U.S. Census Bureau, Population Division, Fertility & Family Statistics Branch, "America's Families and Living Arrangements, March 2000" (June 29, 2001); data are from Table FG3: "Married Couple Family Groups, by Presence of Own Children Under 18, and Age, Earnings, Education, and Race and Hispanic Origin of Both Spouses: March 2000," http://www.census.gov/population/socdemo/hh-fam/p20–537/2000/tabFG3.txt; my thanks to Larry Hoyle and Steven Maynard-Moody, Policy Research Institute, University of Kansas for helping me locate these census data.

28. See http://www.census.gov/population/socdemo/hh-fam/p20–537/2000/tabFG3.txt.

29. Ibid.

30. I wish to thank to David Ekerdt, Department of Sociology and Gerontology Center, University of Kansas, for his help in interpreting these data; gendered racial differences also can be seen in other categories of interracial marriage (e.g., between Asians and blacks, Hispanics and non-Hispanics), but the black/white and Asian/white cases show the most dramatic ethnosexual patterns; to examine other patterns of gender and race in interracial marriage, see http://www.census.gov/population/socdemo/hh-fam/p20–537/2000/tabFG3.txt.

31. Tim Davis, "Diversity of Queer Politics and the Redefinition of Sexual Identity and Community in Urban Spaces," in *Mapping Desire*, 297.

32. Ibid., p. 301.

33. Carl F. Stychin, *A Nation by Rights: National Cultures, Sexual Identity Politics, and the Discourse of Rights* (Philadelphia: Temple University Press, 1998), 41.

34. Alexandra Stiglmayer, "The Rapes in Bosnia-Herzegovina" in *Mass Rape: The War against Women in Bosnia-Herzegovina*, ed. Alexandra Stiglmayer (Lincoln: University of Nebraska Press, 1994), 104; see also Ruth Seifert, "War and Rape: A Preliminary Analysis," in *Mass Rape*, 54–72.

35. Beverly Allen, *Rape Warfare: The Hidden Genocide in Bosnia-Herzegovina and Croatia* (Minneapolis: University of Minnesota Press, 1996), 73.

36. O. J. Simpson was a black man formerly married to a white woman whom he was accused of murdering in June 1994; he was found not guilty by a mainly black jury in a criminal trial in October 1995, but found responsible for the murder by a mainly white jury in a later civil proceeding. In June 1989, a white woman was jogging in Central Park when she was raped and beaten nearly to death by a group of nonwhite teenaged boys, several of whom were found guilty of the attack. In December 1986 in Howard Beach, New York, three black men were attacked and one, Michael Griffith, was killed by a passing car as he was chased by a white male mob who were said to be "defending" their neighborhood from the presence of black men; in particular, one precipitating factor was a local woman who was thought to be involved in a sexual liaison with a black man; the men were found guilty in a trial in 1988, but the verdict was reversed a year later; for a discussion of the O. J. Simpson criminal trial as a racial soap opera, see Linda Williams, *Playing the Race Card: Melodramas of Black and White from Uncle Tom to O.J. Simpson* (Princeton: Princeton University Press, 2001).

37. Robert D. McFadden, Ralph Blumenthal, M.A. Farber, E. R. Shipp, Charles Strum, Craig Wolff, *Outrage: The Story Behind the Tawana Brawley Hoax* (New York: Bantam Books, 1990), 218.

38. Ibid., 310

39. Ibid., 367.

40. Mike Taibbi and Anna Sims-Phillips, *Unholy Alliances: Working the Tawana Brawley Story* (New York: Harcourt Brace Jovanovich, Publishers, 1989), 368–69.

41. Ibid., xi–xii.

42. For a discussion of the rape of Vietnamese women by U.S. soldiers, see Daniel Lang, *Casualties of War* (New York: McGraw-Hill, 1969).

43. Arno Karlen, *Sexuality and Homosexuality: A New View* (New York: W.W. Norton, 1971), 508.

44. Robert W. Connell, *Masculinities* (Berkeley: University of California Press, 1995); see also Robert A. Nye, *Masculinity and Male Codes of Honor in Modern France* (New York: Oxford University Press, 1993); George L. Mosse, *The Image of Man: The Creation of Modern Masculinity* (New York: Oxford University Press, 1996).

45. See George L. Mosse, *Nationalism and Sexuality: Middle-Class Morality and Sexual Norms in Modern Europe* (Madison: University of Wisconsin Press, 1985); Andrew Parker, Mary Russo, Doris Sommer, Patricia Yaeger, eds., *Nationalisms and Sexualities* (New York: Routledge, 1991).

CHAPTER 2

CONSTRUCTING ETHNICITY AND SEXUALITY
Building Boundaries and Identities

Anthropologists Chris Hann and Ildiko Beller-Hann visited the Caucasus region between Russia and Turkey in 1992–1993 shortly after the disintegration of the Soviet Union had relaxed tensions between the two countries and made international travel easier. As Russians crossed the border into Turkey, Hann and Beller-Hann observed an intensification and sexualization of the color line between "dark" Muslim local residents and "white" Orthodox Christian Russian visitors. The influx of Russians tourists and traders into northern Turkey selling Soviet-era manufactured goods and underselling local businesses created a competitive ethnic atmosphere between the Russians and the Turks; the presence of Russian women selling their whiteness to local Muslim men generated a "moral panic" that further heightened ethnic tensions:

> The consequences of the trade and prostitution for images of the [Turks'] self and of the [Russian] Other were considerable. People used metaphors of military invasion and occupation. . . . Assessments of the [Russian] women themselves were revealing. Many people in [the small Turkish towns of] Rize and Artvin, men and women, agreed that some of the foreign women were genuinely attractive. According to this aesthetic the pale, blonde Slav women were much preferred to the darker women from [the Caucasus region]. . . . We later realized that this conforms to the traditional positive associations of whiteness in Turkish Islamic culture.[1]

Hann and Beller-Hann reported that as local men increasingly crossed the ethnosexual boundary to purchase the services of these "white" prostitutes, the Russian women's presence caused a moral uproar. Local men began sexually harassing all foreign women, and local women increasingly veiled themselves so as not to be mistaken for foreigners. The anthropologists reflected on the changes that had occurred in the Caucasus region in the decade since their first visit:

> Whereas in 1983 a foreign woman could walk around the small towns . . . without being hassled in any way, by 1993 the risk of molestation was ever-present. Men who did not threaten women physically were nonetheless likely to express their aggression in other ways: patronising or making fun of them when they entered shops, and proclaiming loudly as they left that all foreign women were *pis* (filthy).[2]

Despite their assessment of the Russian women's cleanliness, local men spent a good deal of time and money pursuing them:

> Older men spoke in sorrow about the behavior of sons who had sold their last gold chain in order to consort with a foreign woman. . . . Some older women spoke with anger about their husbands' behavior, and everyone seemed to agree that the divorce rate had risen sharply. . . . Other women attempted to organize petitions and letters of protest to the provincial governor.[3]

What caused the ethnic crisis in these Caucasus communities in the 1990s? History alone cannot explain the deterioration in interethnic civility documented by Hann and Beller-Hann. Russians and Turks long have viewed one another as ethnically distinct, so the changes in interethnic relations between 1983 and 1993 did not occur simply because the two groups had a history of ethnic difference. Something caused the rise in ethnic animosity. The magnification of the ethnic differentness and tensions observed by the researchers were the results of increased intergroup economic and sexual contact and competition. The lesson we should draw from this example is that ethnicity is not a fixed, unchanging feature of social landscapes or individual biographies. Rather, the *extent* and *meaning* of ethnic differences are socially defined, historically and situationally changeable, and sexually loaded.

THE SOCIAL CONSTRUCTION OF ETHNICITY

Most people think about an individual's race, ethnicity, or nationality as an inherited feature of biography and genealogy. It is both skin deep and deeper—in the blood. Ancestry matters, but how much? The ethnic differences between dark Muslim Turks and light Christian Russians certainly are related to their ancestry. As Hann and Beller-Hann's research shows, however, the importance and volatility of those differences change over time and depend on economic, political, and social patterns in the interaction between the two groups. Consider some examples closer to home: Americans who just moved to Chicago, but who are from Nigeria or China or Mexico or Ireland or the Navajo nation in Arizona. What are the racial, ethnic, national meanings of the ancestry of such individuals? Are they "African Americans," "Asian Americans," "Latinos," "European Americans," and "Native Americans" respectively? Or are they Nigerians, Chinese, Mexicans, Irish, and Navajo/Dine? The answer depends, in part, on where they are. In the United States these individuals represent the "colors" of the American racial pentagon—black, yellow, brown, white, red.[4] But in their respective homelands (Nigeria, China, Mexico, Ireland, Navajoland), their ethnicity, if they have one, would depend on other social characteristics, such as their religion, kin or clan affiliation, region or town of origin, or native tongue.

For instance, the Nigerian in Nigeria doesn't have an ethnicity based on skin color. Ethnicity in Nigeria is more likely to be based on religion, language, region, or community of origin—is the person Muslim or Christian, does the person speak Yoruba or Igbo, is the person from the north or the south, is the person from Oyo or Ilorin.[5] In the United States the same Nigerian is likely to be seen by most Americans (especially white Americans) simply as "black" no matter what the ancestral language, religion, region, or kin group. Religious, linguistic, or regional internal distinctions so important in Nigeria collapse into a single racialized color category in the United States.[6]

Ethnic constructions, whether they are based on religion, language, region, or color, inevitably are imbued with meanings and stereotypes: who is hardworking, who is lazy; who is clean, who is dirty; who is rational, who is emotional; who is smart, who is stupid; who is reliable, who is undependable; who is moral, who is immoral; who is modest and virtuous, who is vulgar and promiscuous. Such glorifications and denigrations appear to be very close to cultural universals in ethnic systems—some peoples are defined as "good" and others are labeled as "bad." The features attributed to the ethnic good or the ethnic bad are remarkably consistent as one listens to ethnic discourses around the world: our purity versus their filth, our honesty versus their chicanery, our chastity versus their debauchery. We should note that much of this discourse involves matters of sexuality and gender.

In situations of interethnic tensions these kinds of conflicting claims and accusations confront one another in finger pointing back and forth across ethnic boundaries, in arguments over who is to blame for ethnic segregation, ethnic inequality, and ethnic conflict. There is a familiar resonance in the similar accusations and animosities exchanged by partners in many different cases of ethnic conflict and persistent segregation around the world: between Palestinians and Israelis in the Middle East, Catholics and Protestants in

Northern Ireland, blacks and whites in the United States, Muslims and Hindus in India, indigenous groups and mestizos in Mexico, Malays and Chinese in Malaysia, Tamils and Sinhalese in Sri Lanka, Francophones and Anglophones in Canada, aboriginal and settler populations in Australia.

The questions and examples, differences and similarities, tensions and contradictions listed above paint a complex picture of racial, ethnic, and national boundaries and their definitions. Nothing is clear and nothing is simple about ethnicity. Like real estate, the meaning of ethnicity is a matter of location, location, location. Where are you, what is your "subject position," what is the subject position of the person viewing and categorizing you?[7] By subject position, I mean what do you think you are ethnically and what perspective do you hold because of the skin you (think you) are in? And what about those whom you encounter as you move through the social world—what do they think you are, what perspective do they hold because of the skin (they think) you are in and the skin they (think they) are in? Jerry Kang describes the view of ethnic Others that we each have as a result of our subject position as "racial mapping."[8] Our fears, desires, prejudices, and preferences for the company of members of various ethnic groups are shaped by the racial maps we and others carry in our heads; sometimes those maps are not the same.

For instance, your father is an Irish Catholic and your mother is a Nigerian Muslim. What are you? Are you Irish? Or white? Or Nigerian? Or black? Or African? Or African American? Or biracial? Or Catholic? Or Muslim? Or American? And does it matter what *you* think you are? Or does it matter what *they* (the social audiences you encounter, the people you meet) think you are? Do you get to decide, or does someone else decide for you which of these possible ethnicities you *really* are? And does that opinion about what you are ethnically change as you move through the day into and out of different situations each with its different set of spectators inspecting and speculating about your ethnicity? What are you in your racially integrated university lecture hall in the morning? Then what are you in the St. Patrick's Day parade where you play in the "Sons and Daughters of Erin" marching band? Then what are you at your Friday Muslim prayers or your Sunday Catholic church service? Then what are you at your third-generation German Jewish romantic partner's family dinner? Finally, does it matter if you are a man or a woman, or if your partner is same sex or opposite sex?

Do you change ethnicities as you encounter these different ethnic opinion groups in different places? Where and when are you black, white, Muslim, Catholic, Nigerian, Irish, American? And who gets to decide in each of these settings? What are you really when you are whatever it is you really are? In whose opinion—yours, theirs, and which "they" truly matters—your classmates, other Irish band members/marchers, fellow Muslims, fellow Catholics, your date's family? Are all of these opinions equally valid—yours and (which of) theirs? Do they all combine to make the *real* you. What if they conflict with one another or with your personal or family definition of your ethnic situation? Opinions differ. Can you really be a composite person? How much choice do you have? Can you be both black and white, both Nigerian and Irish, both Muslim and Catholic? Do you have the choice *not* to have a race or ethnicity?

Where and how does your sexuality fit into these ethnic niches? Does your mixed racial ancestry raise any questions or conjure up any stereotypes about your sexual desirability or desires? If you're a man, what does your race (whatever they think it is) imply about your sexuality to your classmates, or to the Irish band members, or fellow Muslims, or Catholics, or your date's family? Are you seen to be asexual, virile, safe, dangerous, respectable, undesirable and by which of these audiences? And if you're a Nigerian Irish woman—what are the sexual meanings and attributes others assign to you as you stand before them? Do their definitions of your race generate any "feelings" in them (and you) about your sexual purity, activity, desirability, suitability as a friend, coworker, lover, spouse? If you're a homosexual Nigerian Irish, Muslim Catholic does your sexual orientation make any difference to these various ancestry groups (Nigerians, Irish, Muslims, Catholics) or to the others whom you encounter in your daily life? And what about your gender—does it matter if you're a Nigerian Irish gay man or a lesbian? Of course these same questions can be posed again if you're a heterosexual.

Just for the sake of "clarity," let's add to this mix of people with opinions about you another audience representing yet another subject position: some skinheads looking for an opportunity to beat up a nonwhite. What are you, our Irish Nigerian friend, as you walk alone down a dark street one evening and run into this crowd? Whose opinion matters? Which part of you will they attack—only the Nigerian part, but not the Irish part, only the black part, but not the white part? What happens to your ethnic choices and beliefs about yourself in this situation? And will your safety from this group of racists be enhanced or diminished if you are walking with someone of a different ethnicity—say, your white romantic partner? Will the darkness of your skin and the lightness of your date's complexion make an attack more likely or less likely? Will your genders matter and the presumed message about your sexuality that those genders carry?

The previous discussion might leave the impression that all of this talk of ethnicity and sexuality applies simply to nonwhites, that only "people of color" have an ethnicity, and that the rest of us white folks are just, well, just "people." This is, of course, far from the case. Race is an official fact in the United States as reflected in documents such as birth certificates, driver's licenses, and eventually on death certificates. Being white in the United States has important consequences, and for most of U.S. history in most places whiteness has been a source of comfort and privilege. In the segregated South, being white meant being free and safe in a way that being black simply did not. Similarly, being white today means one is less likely to be profiled by police or followed around with suspicion in department stores, and more likely to be served in restaurants or granted credit.[9] But being white also means that in some situations one can be viewed with dislike and contempt or even threatened with violence. For instance, a white person can be seen as an unwelcome intruder by nonwhites during situations of racial tension, and a white who crosses the color line, say by kissing or holding the hand of a nonwhite, can become a target of hostility or attack by racist whites and viewed with suspicion by some nonwhites. So, like blacks, whites have a race; it's the meaning and consequences of their color that can vary across time, place, and audience.[10]

Ethnicity is not merely a feature of one's ethnic ancestry. The social definition of an individual's race, ethnicity, and nationality is decided and given meaning through interactions with others. An individual's ethnicity is as much the property of others as it is the person's making the ethnic claim. An Irish Nigerian might check off "biracial" on a race questionnaire, but in the United States that person is quite likely to be defined as "African American" or "black." A blond, blue-eyed Cherokee might identify as an American Indian, but others looking for stereotypical native characteristics such as dark hair or skin, might challenge such an ethnic self-definition and consider the person "white."

Ethnicity is, then, the result of a dialectical process that emerges from the interaction between individuals and those whom they meet as they pass through life. An individual's ethnicity is a negotiated social fact—what you think is your ethnicity versus what others think is your ethnicity. Individuals can have a portfolio of ethnic identities, some of which are more or less salient in various situations and vis-à-vis various audiences. As settings and spectators change, the socially defined array of ethnic options open to us changes: white, Irish, Catholic, black, Nigerian, Muslim, Indian, Navajo. A person's ethnicity is, thus, a matter of structure and power: which ethnic categories are available in a society to be sorted into, and who gets to do the sorting.

For instance, researchers report that Africans and Caribbean Island immigrants living in the United States often view themselves as ethnically and culturally distinct from African Americans.[11] This distinction is one that is seldom seen or shared by whites and other American ethnic groups because of the "one drop rule" classifying all Americans with any degree of African ancestry as black. This racial cosmology renders the internal boundary dividing African Americans from Africans or Caribbean Islanders on the basis of national origin virtually invisible and meaningless to whites and other nonblacks. These distinctions (Jamaican, Kenyan, African American), however, can be quite noticeable and very important to those enclosed inside the "black" ethnic boundary.[12] Does that mean the native-born/foreign-born boundary inside African America is not real or important in U.S. society? The answer is another question—"real" or "important" to whom—to African Americans, African or Caribbean immigrants, nonblack Americans? The relative importance of this ethnic boundary to different ethnic constituencies and audiences illustrates how structure (recognized ethnic categories) and power (whose opinion matters) work together to map ethnicity.

ESSENTIALLY SPEAKING[13]

The constructionist model being used here argues that biographical and biological characteristics such as native language or skin color are the building blocks of ethnicity, not its inherent essence.[14] An individual's race or ethnicity is not biological in any social sense; it is a socially negotiated, constructed fact. Despite this admonition to beware of our assumptions about what is "biological" and "natural" about race and ethnicity, it is easy to slip into comfortable, everyday essentialist thinking about ethnic differences as genuine, factual, physiological, and "real" in their own right, and not dependent on social conventions and constructions in order to give them social life. For instance, when we speak of the U.S. racial pentagon of black, brown, red, yellow, and white, it is important to recognize that these are completely fictive, constructed categories. No serious scholarship in the humanities, social sciences, or natural sciences argues that races exist, have consistently measurable boundaries, or that humans reliably can be differentiated in any meaningful way on the basis of skin color, hair texture, physical characteristics, or other usual indicators commonly associated with Western notions of "race." Nevertheless, this ethnic sorting device resides deep in the minds of many Americans (and others). Even those who disagree with the categories and question which groups should be included in them often slip into essentialist thinking about race. Racial distinctions "feel" right and seem to many to be accurate reflections of U.S. ethnic reality. We believe them to be real, and so they are. But that reality is a socially constructed one.

The "intuitive" appeal of U.S. racial categories is evidence of the hegemonic power of such ethnic constructions. That such categories seem obvi-

ous and genuine illustrates how widely held and deeply imbedded these social definitions of race are in U.S. society and culture. It is difficult to think
past these powerful essentialisms. That is our challenge. In order to describe
and expose racial, ethnic, and national constructions and to show their intersections with sexuality, we will have to suspend our belief in them. However, we must try simultaneously to talk about racial, ethnic, national, and
sexual categories as if they were real, while maintaining a constructionist
skepticism about them. We will have to remind ourselves continually to ask:
how did these racial categories come to be and how did they become such es-
sentialized, hegemonic, naturalized, comfortable assumptions about the social world?

Constructing Ethnic Boundaries

Ethnicity is not only situational, negotiated, and constructed, it can be seen
as external to the individuals being defined in a particular ethnic way. Ethnicity can be thought of as a series of moving boundaries that crisscross populations, shifting to divide people into different categories at different times
by different people. The notion of ethnic boundaries as a way to see ethnic
differences in a society is one way to pull back from the racial hegemonies
that so easily seem to dominate casual thinking about ethnicity. Ethnic
boundaries are also a way to think about ethnicity separate from the cultural,
social, or physical characteristics of individuals or groups. The ethnic boundary model was developed in the early work of anthropologist Fredrik Barth.
Barth began a conceptual "deconstruction" of ethnicity in the late 1960s by
drawing scholarly attention away from the cultural content that many anthropologists saw as the central core of ethnicity and by redirecting researchers' gaze toward the borders that mark the edges of ethnic communities.[15] He argued that it was not simply culture (dress, customs, language,
religion) that defined and divided individuals ethnically. He pointed out the
importance of ethnic boundaries as markers in both physical and symbolic
space that signify who is and who is not a member of an ethnic group.[16] According to this view, ethnicity is a matter of who is inside and who is outside an ethnic boundary.

Conceiving of ethnicity as a system of boundaries that divide a population into different groups provides a way to think about ethnicity in terms
of its structure rather than its content, that is, its presumed genetic or cultural bases. Instead of assuming that ethnic differences inevitably lead to segregation or conflict, we can ask questions about the conditions under which
ethnic boundaries will be erected and defended versus the conditions pro-
moting ethnic integration and tranquility. We can ask questions about why

particular group characteristics (language, religion, appearance) become the building blocks for barriers that separate us from one another. When we see violence erupt between ethnic groups, we can think of explosions occurring along particular ethnic boundaries, and we can ask when boundaries will become volatile. When we see people reaching over walls, making connections across ethnic boundaries—intermarrying, forming friendships, moving in next door to one another, we can ask about the conditions that weaken ethnic boundaries, allowing individuals to pass through, over, or around these dividing walls. When we see people pull away from one another, speaking words and enacting deeds of hatred and intolerance, we can envision them peering suspiciously over ethnic boundaries, taking aim and tossing grenades over the walls that separate ethnic groups. The notion of ethnic boundaries allows us to imagine ethnic police guarding ethnic borders, patrolling ethnic frontiers, erecting ethnic checkpoints, demanding ethnic identification, and turning away or rounding up nonmembers, and once again we can ask when this will happen and when it will not.

If we return to the example at the beginning of this chapter describing the strengthening of ethnic boundaries between Turks and Russians in the Caucasus, and the increase of tensions and animosities along that ethnic boundary, now we can speak of economic and sexual processes that promoted the fortification and defense of that Turkish/Russian, Muslim/Christian, dark/light ethnic boundary. Now we also can describe the ethnosexual adventuring that occurred across the boundary and the controversies those crossings generated. As this example and others we will encounter in this book will illustrate, sexuality, then, is an important factor in the erection and defense of ethnic boundaries.

The boundary model suggests a kind of ethnic cartography is possible in which we can chart the ethnic landscape by tracing lines in the geographic, legal, cultural, social, economic, political, or sexual sand.[17] These lines are marked by ethnic insiders and outsiders, and both the lines (ethnic boundaries) and the terrain they surround (the membership and meaning of various ethnicities) are social constructions. The boundary trope permits us to survey the ethnic world through a number of different lenses. We can envision ethnic boundaries as *spatial* boundaries—the borders of national states in the global system or of ethnocultural regions enclosed within or spanning national borders, or spatial boundaries can mark the edges of ethnic neighborhoods or ghettos in segregated cities. We also can see ethnic boundaries imbedded in the law, *legal* boundaries—in formal definitions of who is and is not a member, citizen, white, black, and as a result, who has which rights, and who is subject to what kinds of treatment. Ethnic boundaries are detectable as *cultural* markers—seen in tastes in food, fashion, furnishings, film, music, art, and other forms of recreational consumption, as well as in styles of demeanor and talk marked by body language, accents, dialects, jargon, and linguistic differences. Ethnic boundaries are evident in *institutional* affiliations such as religion, education, clubs, and organizations. Ethnic boundaries also are *social*—reflected in patterns of friendship and association, *economic*—seen in business transactions, investments, partnerships, and *political*—revealed in patterns of support for political candidates, policies, or positions. Ethnic boundaries are *ideational,* imaginary, in the mind, in the consciousness—reflected in notions of self and others, in the texture of feelings, intuitions, comfort levels, trust, affinity, and in the sense one has of connectedness, familiarity, safety, membership, of being "home" or "among friends." Finally, and most important for the agenda of this book, ethnic boundaries are *sexual*—manifesting themselves in patterns of dating, childbearing, marriage, and sexual relations, including sexual assault, rape, and sexual slavery, as well as in sexual cosmologies—theories of ethnosexual attributes, practices, preferences, and perversions.

CONSTRUCTING SEXUAL BOUNDARIES

The same insights about the socially constructed aspects of ethnicity can be applied to sexuality. Just as we can conceptualize ethnicity as a series of boundaries dividing a population according to various characteristics such as language, religion, culture, or color, sexuality can be seen as a set of boundaries dividing a population according to sexual practices, identities, orientations, desires. In any society we can identify divisions of the population along sexual lines. We can observe differences in levels of sexual activity (celibate, active, occasional, promiscuous), types of sexual partners (same, opposite, both), kinds of sexual desire, practice, intensity (fetishists, exhibitionists, sado-masochists, monogamists, experimentalists), sorts of sexual identities (gay, straight, bisexual, transgendered). Sometimes these differences are benign and unimportant. But sometimes they can become the basis for discrimination, conflict, and violence. Sexuality, like ethnicity, is a highly charged aspect of personal and collective life. Individual and group sexual characteristics are the subjects of strong moral judgments and strict social control.

Virtually all aspects of sexuality—objects and types of sexual desire, frequency, styles, times, and places of sexual activity, methods of reproduction (or not), choices of partners—are deeply controversial and are both formally and informally scrutinized and regulated. For instance, what is the point of sex? Procreation, recreation, interpersonal connection, personal actualization, emotional fulfillment, political expression, identification, rebellion, experimentation? What *is* sex exactly? A basis of group membership, an individual or collective right, a cultural construction, an occupation, an addiction, a moral choice, a means to an end, or an end in itself? Is sexuality primarily a behavior, an identity, or a desire? What constitutes "having" sex versus "doing" sex versus "being sexual?"[18] Is sex physical, emotional, spiritual, something else, or all of the above? Who are appropriate partners for sexual relationships—what should be their gender, ethnicity, age, class?

The questions abound; they are asked and answered in religions, philosophies, courts of law, opinion polls, sex surveys, dorm rooms, and scholarly treatises. The questions and answers change over time and from place to place. Should a man or (more likely) a woman abstain from sex outside of marriage? Does having sex with a member of the opposite sex make one a "heterosexual"? Does having sex with a member of the same sex make one a "homosexual"? Is same-sex or opposite-sex desire or behavior the basis for identity (gay or straight), or simply a desire or behavior in its own right with little or nothing to do identity—what we *do* versus who we *are*? Are people "naturally" bisexual or "omnisexual," or must they be either homosexual or heterosexual?[19] Can sexual orientation (identity, desire, partners) change over the life course, or is one "straight" or "queer" from birth to death? Do all people in all societies at all times have a sexual identity and/or a sexual orientation?

If we approach an analysis of sexuality as a series of boundaries, we obtain a somewhat different set of questions and ultimately a different set of answers from those generated from models of sexuality stressing biology, nature versus nurture, or as a matter of the relative morality of one form of sexuality over another. The sexual boundary model emphasizes and raises some interesting questions about the *spatial* and *temporal* aspects of sexuality. For instance, we can ask where and when sexuality is enacted and accomplished—where are the boundaries of various sexualities and sexual events located in time and space?[20] By mapping sexual boundaries we can chart the placement and timing of sexual practices, sexual desires, sexual identities, and sexual communities.

In any geographic location we can imagine a number of sexual zones—places identified and/or designed for particular sexualities and their enactment. In a city there are "red light districts" for prostitution, "gay districts" for homosexuals, singles bars (presumably for straights), areas zoned for "adult entertainment," neighborhoods that are defined as places for families, or for singles, or for gay men, or for lesbians, places where particular types of sexuality are desired or practiced (leather, sado-masochism, sexual performances). Some of these sex zones are ethnically segregated—separate spaces for sex workers, clients, and sexual contact for different ethnic groups; some of these erotic spaces are integrated and serve as ethnosexual frontiers where members of different ethnic groups meet for sex for profit or recreational sexual interludes.

Sexual boundaries are not only spatial and temporal. Like ethnic boundaries, sexual boundaries can be *cultural,* involving spectacles, music, literature, art, and all of the paraphernalia of cultural production such as gay pride parades and carnivals, sexual contact or performance clubs, sexual websites, straight and queer erotic art, films, and pornography, *legal,* involving the regulation of sexual practice such as laws certifying heterosexual marriage and outlawing sodomy, same sex marriage, divorce, *economic,* involving the production and consumption of sexual products and services such as contraceptives, fashions, sex aids, toys, and pharmaceuticals, prostitution, tourism, *political,* such as restrictions on immigration or debates over discrimination based on sexual orientation or accommodating domestic partners, and *racial, ethnic, or national,* such as sexual stereotypes of particular ethnic groups, the marginalization or exclusion of homosexuals from ethnic communities, nationalist calls for compulsory heterosexuality and sex for procreation—to reproduce the nation.

Like ethnic boundaries, sexual boundaries give the appearance of naturalness and timelessness. They seem inborn, unchanging, and stable. As history and cross-cultural research show us, however, like ethnic boundaries, sexual boundaries are socially constructed, change over time, and individuals can cross sexual boundaries, changing sexual identities and sexualities in the process. Sexual identities (gay, lesbian, bisexual, straight, butch, femme, promiscuous, celibate, monogamous, etc.), like ethnic identities, are negotiated between individuals and audiences, and these can recede or advance in social significance in different situations and throughout the life course. Individuals have portfolios of sexual identities some of which are more or less salient in various situations and vis-à-vis various audiences. As settings and spectators change, the socially defined array of sexual options open to us changes. Shifting definitions of sexual situations can produce a layering of individual and group sexual identities that may or may not resonate with socially recognized or available sexual categories. Not everyone who hears an individual identify as "transgendered" knows what that means, what kind of sexuality is being claimed, or what sexual boundary is being crossed or created.

The social meaning of a person's sexuality, like his or her ethnicity, is a matter of structure and power: which sexual categories are available in the society to be sorted into, and who gets to do the sorting. For instance, before the gay rights movement of the 1970s that opened the closet door for many nonheterosexuals and opened a broader space for expressing and claiming sexualities, homosexual desire or identity in the United States was likely to be defined as simply a personal defect, struggle, or crisis.[21] Definitions of homosexuality remain contested terrain in most societies including the United States, and homophobia still haunts the boundary between heterosexuality and homosexuality. Still, in the past few decades, gay rights' challenges to intolerance toward nonheterosexuals have created more recognized domains for sexually diverse identities and practices.[22]

THE SOCIAL CONSTRUCTION OF SEXUALITY

It is only recently that sexuality scholars have begun to examine heterosexuality in ways that parallel the deconstruction of ethnicity, that is, by peeling away layers of assumptions about ethnic and sexual identity and boundaries. The traditional study of sexuality—"sexology"—has focused primarily on heterosexuality, but not in order to question its naturalness or constructed character. Rather, sexology has confined itself mainly to documenting the practices of heterosexuals (frequency of coitus, orgasm, or masturbation, age at first sexual intercourse, number of sexual partners, etc.), in part to establish the boundaries of "normal" sex.[23] Historically, sexuality studies also have examined "deviant" sexualities (homosexuality, prostitution, unconventional sexual desires, practices, and sites). This interest in the "margins" of normative heterosexuality has reinforced rather than challenged the center. Instead of questioning the assumed naturalness of conventional heterosexuality, both sexology and sexual deviance research have documented and distinguished between the sexually "normal" or the sexually "pathological." Despite the pioneering sexual constructionist work of John Gagnon and William Simon on "sexual scripting" in the early 1970s,[24] as well as much research on the social construction of ethnicity and gender since that time, social constructionism has not been a dominant sociological paradigm for understanding sexuality.

In the past decade or so, however, things have changed. There has been a great deal of research, much of it outside sociology, examining heterosexuality as a social construction, questioning the universality and biological imbeddedness of heterosexual exclusivity, inquiring into the origins of "compulsory heterosexuality,"[25] challenging the norms governing what are defined as acceptable and conventional sexual practices, examining the purposes served by the widespread institutionalization of heterosexuality into the law and into everyday life, and criticizing definitions of proper sexuality and approved sex acts as patriarchal and masculinist.

This work has developed a critical vocabulary: phallocentric, heteronormativity, queer. *Phallocentric* refers to the emphasis on the penis (phallus) and penile penetration as the central pillar of sexuality in theory and practice. *Heteronormativity* refers to the assumption that everyone is heterosexual and the recognition that all social institutions (the family, religion, economy, political system) are built around a heterosexual model of male/female social relations. When queer theorists make the discursive move from "sexuality" to "sexualities," they are *queering* (twisting and turning on its head) heteronormative assumptions and challenging conventional assertions and expectations of universal opposite sex desire and practice.[26] We will use a broad notion of *queer* here to include not only gay and lesbian issues, identities, and communities, but also to refer to other issues, identities, communities situated on the sexual margins, including nonnormative heterosexual practices, identities, and communities of desire such as sado-masochism and nonmonogamy as well as bisexuality, the transgendered, and transsexuality.[27] Queer theory has its work cut out for it since heteronormative, socially approved, "appropriate" enactments of sexuality are perhaps the most embedded and enforced norms in human societies.[28] The challenge is especially great for scholars who contest the validity and universality of the heterosexual/homosexual binary. Such critiques of heteronormativity face deeply held, widespread belief in the naturalness of heterosexuality.

The Historical Construction of Sexualities

One prominent feature of the hegemonic sexual formation in the contemporary West is that sexual practice is expected to be tied to sexual identity. Individuals do not have the choice *not* to have a sexual orientation and identity. One is presumed to be "gay" or "straight," if not in deed, then surely in identity.[29] The connection between sexual behavior and sexual identity, however, has not always been so clear or enforced. Historians have placed the origins of the sexuality/identity nexus in the West sometime in the last two hundred years. For instance, Michel Foucault actually identified the specific moment when homosexuality became something someone *was* rather than something someone *did*—1870:

> [T]he psychological, psychiatric, medical category of homosexuality was constituted from the moment it was characterized—[Carl] Westphal's famous article of 1870 *[Archive fur Neurologie]* on "contrary sexual sensations" can stand as its date of birth—less by a type of sexual relations than by a certain quality of sexual sensibility, a certain way of inverting the masculine and the feminine in oneself. Homosexuality appeared as one of the forms of sexuality when it was transposed from the practice of sodomy onto a kind of interior androgyny, a hermaphrodism of the soul. The sodomite had been a temporary aberration; the homosexual was now a species.[30]

Some historians have placed the date of the construction of homosexuality as a social category and identity somewhat earlier, in the eighteenth century.[31] Whether the transformation of homosexuality from an act into an identity occurred in the eighteenth or nineteenth century, most scholars argue that prior to that time sexuality was a behavior that was socially defined as either good or bad, moral or immoral, whether it was enacted with same sex partners or with opposite sex partners. Thus, before the "invention of homosexuality"[32] sex did not make the man or the woman, and it did not make a person "straight," "bi-," or "queer," but it did "make" an individual "good" or "bad." But haven't there always been people who preferred or had sex exclusively with members of the same or opposite sex or both? The answer is yes. The variety of recorded human sexual activities is vast and diverse. Have people's preference or behavior or orientation always shaped their identities and made them part of sexual communities as is likely today? Not according to scholars of sexuality who would argue that those who lived in and fled Sodom and Gomorrah were not gay or straight, they were moral or immoral according to the standards used to judge them.

SOCIAL CONSTRUCTION, PERFORMANCE, AND PERFORMATIVITY

Whatever the exact time and place that homosexuality became an identity and socially defined a kind of person, the invention of homosexuality led to the crowning of heterosexuality as the "normal" form of sexual desire, identity, and behavior.[33] Like all hegemonies, heterosexuality is not without its detractors and its skeptics. Some of the most interesting recent work deconstructing the nature and content of sexuality is by feminist and queer theorists.[34] Perhaps most intriguing of all is queer theory's challenge to the essentialist sexual *binary* of male/female,[35] and their doubts that men and women are *real*. Feminist social constructionists have consistently acknowledged that the content and meaning of gender roles and gendered bodies vary across time and space. Queer theorists have gone a step farther in their analyses, positing that the male/female binary and the sexed body are utterly unreal except as social conventions or "performatives."

The gendered and sexualized body is a major location for the social construction of men and women, masculinity and femininity, and male and female sexuality. The body is an instrument of *performance* and a site of *performativity*. Gender and sexuality are both performed and performative—conscious and unconscious, intended and unintended, explicit and implicit.[36] These two concepts deserve some attention because of their usefulness in understanding social construction processes in general, for their increasingly common usage among researchers and theorists of gender and sexuality, and for their applicability to other socially constructed roles and categories of interest here, namely race, ethnicity, and nationalism.

The notion of performance in social life was developed by Erving Goffman in the 1950s, and his "dramaturgical" approach has been widely used in sociology and beyond, including in contemporary performance studies.[37] By *performance* I refer to the ways in which we adorn and use our bodies to present ourselves in various roles. Gender and sexuality theorists examine how we perform gender in the ways we walk, talk, sit, defecate, have sex, through our costuming, hair styling, hand gestures, patterns of eye contact, touching, movement, body language in general, topics of conversation, by the cars we drive, jobs we work at, games we play, etc. These are all gendered activities. In U.S. society some are more masculinized (warfare, camouflage patterned clothing, hunting) or feminized (childcare, the color pink, quilting) than others (being a student, wearing blue jeans, swimming), and the gender meanings of all of these vary across time. Whatever the prevailing norms in any time and place, however, these and other gendered behaviors and ways of being are part of the repertoire in the performances we give as men and women, straight and gay as we move through the day and through life. We evaluate, refine, reevaluate, and revise these gender and sexual enactments based on the positive and negative feedback we receive from the audiences we encounter. But gender and sexuality are not only performed, they are also performative and performatively created.

Performativity has its roots outside of sociology in the humanities,[38] and recently has been circulated more widely by queer theorists, in particular by philosopher Judith Butler and those who have used her work.[39] By *performativity* I refer to the ways in which we affirm and reaffirm, construct and reconstruct hegemonic social roles and definitions. We participate, for instance, in performative constructions of gender by our daily repetitive acts of accepted gender performance, by our tacit or implicit approval of the proper gender performances of others, by what we take for granted, assume, expect, demand from ourselves and others in terms of gender appearance and behavior. We become agents of the performative gender order very often without thinking, only noticing when a rule is violated, an expectation is not met, and especially when we unthinkingly are repelled by or shun unsuccessful or unconforming gender performances. Performativity is a powerful mechanism of social construction and social control, all the more so because it tends to go unnoticed, be invisible, operate at the level of intuition. Performatives just seem to *feel* right or wrong. They are difficult to identify or think about because they are so ingrained, presumed, and seemingly "normal." The invisible and comfortable aspects of gender and sexual performatives are major reasons for the durability and pervasiveness of hegemonic gender and sexual regimes.

To emphasize the symbolic, ideational, assumptive nature of performatively constructed gender or racial or sexual systems is not to overlook the importance of material and structural factors in the construction, enforcement, and perpetuation of such social orders. Gayle Rubin refers to a "political economy" of gender and sexuality around the world. She notes that many different types of societies are characterized by the "traffic in women"—in which men exchange women and their productive and reproductive labor (symbolically enacted as a father "giving away the bride").[40] The political economy of gender is both formal (inscribed into law, policies, business protocols) and informal (ingrained in ways of interacting, notions of worth and dignity, and ways of "doing business").

Performance and performativity are both complementary and interdependent. Thus, there is a tension between the performed—concrete, obvious, purposive, deliberate ways gender and sexuality are *enacted,* and the performative—abstract, hidden, unthinking, habitual ways gender and sexuality are *constituted.* This tension reveals the roles of both performance and performativity, for instance, in the gender construction process, the ways they depend on one another for stability *and* for change, and the capacity of each either to support or to subvert the other. Gender performances can fall flat, seem "off," or raise doubts about authenticity if they fail to conform to performative gender rules and expectations. The performative durability of gender regimes depends on constantly being reinforced and reconstituted by encore gender performances. Performative orders can weaken or mutate to the extent that the performances on which they depend are absent, defective, or subversive. Widespread noncompliance with, confusion about, or infiltration from outside traditional gender systems can disrupt gender performances and disturb the performative gender order.

The entry of ever larger numbers of women into the U.S. labor force beginning in the 1970s is an example of how social change can challenge a hegemonic order. Women's increased labor force participation has led to an erosion, albeit somewhat limited, of the gender division of labor in the home (caring for children, housework, cooking, running errands). The strict definition of many household tasks as exclusively "women's work" has loosened somewhat, although women continue to take on a disproportionate share of these duties, and men continue to see themselves as "helping" their working wives rather than redefining what constitutes "men's work."[41] Still, to the extent that these gender roles are changing at all illustrates that while performatives are durable, they are also vulnerable to inconsistent, impossible, or contradictory performances.

It is important to note that most understandings and conceptualizations of performativity stress that it is mainly unconscious and thus inaccessible to us in our everyday actions and thoughts. Social performances arising out of performative orders, whether they are gender, sexual, racial/ethnic, or some other social order (political, economic, cultural, class, age), often are automatic or habitual. Even when such performances are intentional, such as trying to be a sexually attractive man or woman, attempting to display class reputability by speaking or dressing according to expectations, or acting in accordance with norms governing proper racial or ethnic roles such as "being a devout" Jew or Catholic or Muslim, such performances still can reflect little conscious choice since they feel right or comfortable. Social change can occur when a performative becomes problematic. Revolutionary thinking is that which, by definition, exposes and defies performative processes and assumptions. "Black is beautiful." "Workers of the world unite." "The love that dare not speak its name." Such challenges tend to be resisted both consciously and unconsciously, however. As a result hegemonic shifts are rare historical events.[42]

Sexual and Ethnic Performances and Performatives

These observations about the performed and performative aspects of gender and sexuality are equally applicable to race, ethnicity, and nationalism. Skin color, language, religion, or ancestry do not automatically serve as the basis for ethnic identities or groups, result in variations in cultural content, or generate interethnic conflict. Ethnic boundaries are constructed around these differences through both conscious performances and unconscious performatives. Ethnic boundaries are reinforced through intentional ethnic performances such as "acting black" and "acting white" and through boundary recognition and regulation, such as the admonition to "stick to your own kind."[43] Ethnic boundaries are anchored in unintentional performatives such as assumed expectations about ethnic differences, the resonance of certain ethnic stereotypes, the "instinctive" or intuitive appeal of some ethnic groups and aversion to others, or the inconceivable—neighborhoods one doesn't consciously avoid, but where it simply does not even occur to one to look for housing, or the churches, clubs, restaurants, or shops one doesn't *choose* not to visit, but which one simply would never even think to enter.

Just as the presence of female or male bodies does not automatically result in socially meaningful "men" or "women," and just as differences in sexual practice or sexual desire do not always produce stable sexual identities and boundaries, differences in skin color, language, religion, or ancestry do not always generate strong ethnic boundaries. The production of gender and sexual differences requires social and often political recognition, definition, and reinforcement as well as individual and collective assertion and acceptance to become socially "real." The production of ethnic differences has parallel requirements—social and political recognition, definition, and reinforcement as well as individual assertion and acceptance. The gender and sexual identities, meanings, cultures, and social divisions between men and women and heterosexual and nonheterosexual are social constructions, arising out of historical conditions, power relations, and ongoing social processes.[44] The same can be said for the performed and performative nature of race, ethnicity, and nationalism. The connections between gender and sexuality have been extensively documented by feminist and queer theorists. The connections between ethnicity and sexuality and the ways that they aid and support one another remain less charted social space, and thus are the focus of this book.

CONCLUSION: RACING SEX AND SEXING RACE

In the new preface of the 1999 edition of *Gender Trouble,* Judith Butler reflects on the social changes of the 1990s and on responses to, critiques, and extensions of her original work. She comments on what she would have changed had she written the book a decade later:

> If I were to rewrite this book under present circumstances, I would . . . include a discussion on racialized sexuality and, in particular, how taboos against miscegenation (and the romanticization of cross-racial sexual exchange) are essential to the naturalized and denaturalized forms that gender takes.[45]

Butler's ruminations about social change and the intersections of ethnicity and sexuality are central to the journey we are embarked on here. In Chapter 1 we began our discussion of the sexual construction of race, ethnicity, and the nation by describing the terrain inside ethnosexual frontiers and the types of travelers who visit those intimate intersections and by providing a number of examples of the sexual dimensions of ethnic, racial, and national ideologies, identities, and boundaries. Just as ethnicity is sexualized, sex is itself racialized, ethnicized, and nationalized.

Race and sex each reinforce and magnify the other. Sexual descriptions and enactments of race, ethnicity, and nationalism are seductive or threatening depending on the cultural content evoked. Racialized depictions of sexual purity, dangerousness, appetites, desirability, perversion are part of the performative construction of sexual respectability and disreputability, normalcy and deviance. Ethnosexual frontiers are exotic, but volatile social spaces, fertile sites for the eruption of violence. Racial, ethnic, or nationalist defense and enforcement of in-group sexual honor and purity strengthens ethnic boundaries and subjugates members enclosed inside ethnic borders. Both positive and negative stereotypes about the sexuality of ethnic Others reinforce ethnic differences and sustain ethnic segregation. Negative images or accusations about the sexuality of ethnic Others contribute to the creation of disreputable and toxic outgroups and can be used to justify their exclusion, oppression, or extermination.

Ethnic boundaries, then, are both constituted by and constitutive of sexual boundaries. Part of the reason for the enduring color line in the United States is the sexual meaning attached to race. Sexualized racial depictions distinguish blacks from whites. Hegemonic white sexual claims and attributions enhance white sexual self-imaginings and devalue black sexuality, play on white sexual fears of blacks, and reflect white racialized sexual desires. Counterhegemonic black sexual claims and attributions challenge these stereotypes with unflattering sexual images of whites.[46] The sexual ideologies of both heterosexuals and homosexuals contain similar racialized images and stereotypes of erotic others: the sexual anxieties of white men, the sexual submissiveness of Asian women, the sexual looseness of white women, the sexual potency of black men. Heterosexual masculine and feminine performances and performatives constitute gender/sexual regimes that lie at the core of ethnic cultures.

Heteronormative ethnosexual stereotypes are nearly universal depictions of "Self" and "Other" as one gazes across time and space—at the historical landscapes inside different ethnic groups and nations. "Proper" gender roles and sexual behavior are essential to ethnic group membership and ethnic boundaries. Standards of ethnic group honor are created and enforced to support ethnic reproduction agendas. As a result, members of ethnic communities pay a great deal of attention to insiders' sexual demeanor. Ethnosexual expectations are inscribed in both formal and informal rules of conduct governing men and women. Linda Anderson's poem at the start of Chapter 1, "Gang Bang Ulster Style," illustrates the power of a local ethnic community to organize and police its members' sexual behavior and to extract a high price for violations of sexual conduct rules. In the chapters that follow we will explore the racing of sex and the sexing of race in the ethnosexual frontiers in a variety of national and international settings. Our next stop is the "New World."

NOTES

1. Chris Hann and Ildiko Beller-Hann, "Markets, Morality, and Modernity in North-East Turkey," in *Border Identities: Nation and State at International Frontiers*, ed. Thomas M. Wilson and Hastings Donnan (Cambridge: Cambridge University Press, 1998), 251–52; the Russian women were referred to as *Beyaz Rus*; in the local *Lazuri* language, *Beyaz* means "white."

2. Ibid., 253.

3. Ibid.

4. David Hollinger, *Postethnic America: Beyond Multiculturalism* (New York: Basic Books, 1995).

5. David D. Laitin, *Hegemony and Culture: Politics and Religious Change among the Yoruba* (Chicago: University of Chicago Press, 1986).

6. It is important to note that in Nigeria these differences of language, religion, and region are not incidental features of individual biographies with no social consequences; Nigeria's postcolonial history of civil war and political violence followed along these ethnic faultlines, which although they predated colonialism, were exacerbated and institutionalized by British policies of ethnic preference and indirect rule; see William F. S. Miles, *Hausaland Divided: Colonialism and Independence in Nigeria and Niger* (Ithaca: Cornell University Press, 1994).

7. For a discussion of subject positions and standpoint theory, see Nancy C. M. Hartsock, *The Feminist Standpoint Revisited and Other Essays* (Boulder: Westview Press, 1998).

8. Jerry Kang, "Cyber-Race," *Harvard Law Review* 113 (2000): 1131–1208, 1141; Kang is interested in the implications of the Internet and other cyberspaces for race relations since the expectations associated with racial maps are disrupted when an individual's ethnicity is virtually invisible; my thanks to Adalberto Aguirre Jr., for bringing this research to my attention.

9. Whiteness is viewed as quite a valuable commodity by many in the United States; see, for instance, George Lipsitz, *The Possessive Investment in Whiteness: How White People Profit from Identity Politics* (Philadelphia: Temple University Press, 1998); according to Andrew Hacker's informal research, losing their whiteness was estimated to be worth somewhere around $50 million in compensatory damages by white students faced with the hypothetical situation of becoming black (*Two Nations: Black and White, Separate, Hostile, and Unequal* [New York: Scribner's, 1992]); an African American reviewer of Hacker's book did not share this assessment: "My first thought while reading this parable was that $50 million might not be enough compensation if I had to live the next fifty years as a white person" (Gerald D. Geines, "Two Nations but Only One View," *Contemporary Sociology* 22 (1993): 172).

10. Color is not the only dimension of ethnicity that members of the "majority" or "dominant" group often take for granted and attribute to others, but not to themselves, another is language. Although the English language is not an official tongue in most of the United States (yet), for many native English-speaking Americans it is another taken-for-granted, uncontroversial, nonethnic characteristic. If an American speaks English, there's no ethnicity in that. Right? Once again, location and audience matter. If an American English speaker meets with American Spanish-speaking or bilingual or even English-only-speaking Latino community organizers, for instance, or takes a trip to the French-speaking Canadian province of Quebec, that person can quickly discover that an assumed-to-be-neutral linguistic background is an ethnicity imbued with meanings over which the individual has no control and limited knowledge: Anglo or Anglophone.

11. See Milton Vickerman, *Crosscurrents: West Indian Immigrants and Race* (New York: Oxford University Press, 1999); Mary Waters, *Black Identities: West Indian Immigrant Dreams and American Realities* (Cambridge, MA: Harvard University Press, 1999).

12. Although the "one drop rule" is the dominant racial ideology for classifying individuals with any degree of African ancestry in the United States, the *meaning* of blackness is not universally agreed upon by Americans. Once again it depends on who is doing the categorizing. Researchers have found that African Americans born in the United States, for instance, hold diverse opinions about what characteristics and behaviors constitute "authentic" blackness, the social meanings attached to variations in skin tone or social class differences among blacks, and the degree of common interests shared with African-ancestry immigrants from the Caribbean Islands or African continent; see Verna M. Keith and Cedric Herring, "Skin Tone and Stratification in the Black Community," *American Journal of Sociology* 97 (1991): 760–78; Elijah Anderson, "The Social Situation of the Black Executive: Black and White Identities in the Corporate World," in *The Cultural Territories of Race: Black and White Boundaries*, ed. Michele Lamont (Chicago: Russell Sage Foundation, 1999), 3–29; Amy Binder, "Friend and Foe: Boundary Work and Collective Identity in the Afrocentric and Multicultural Curriculum Movements in American Public Education," in *The Cultural Territories of Race*, 222–48; Daryl Williams, "The 'Soul Patrol': Gatekeepers of THE BLACK Identity," presented at the annual meeting of the Midwest Sociological Society, Kansas City, April 1998.

13. For a critique and discussion of the limits of essentialism, see Diana Fuss, *Essentially Speaking: Feminism, Nature, and Difference* (New York: Routledge, 1989).

14. For another discussion of ethnic constructionism, see Stephen Cornell and Douglas Hartmann, *Ethnicity and Race: Making Identities in a Changing World* (Thousand Oaks, CA: Pine Forge Press, 1998).

15. The term *deconstruction* is meant here to be synonymous with "interpreting," "decoding," and "deciphering" underlying meanings and contents of narratives, structures, and actions.

16. Fredrik Barth, *Ethnic Groups and Boundaries* (Boston: Little, Brown, and Company, 1969).

17. Thomas F. Gieryn uses the idea of a "cultural cartography" in his analysis of science and credibility, *Cultural Boundaries of Science: Credibility on the Line* (Chicago: University of Chicago Press, 1999).

18. Laurie Shrage reports that many women sex workers distinguish between "having sex" and "being sexual" on the one hand, and "doing sexuality" on the other hand; the former involve sexual desire and sexual identity, the latter does not; it's just a job, all in a day's or night's work:

> Some sex workers who deny having sex with their clients do fetish work—s/m, exhibitionism, etc.—and do not have sex in any conventional sense with clients, either intercourse or oral sex. Other sex workers who deny having sex at work perform acts that involve genital contact. Yet they argue that they are no more having sex with their clients than an actress playing a sex scene is having sex or a nurse who touches a patient's genitals. The sex worker is merely performing a skilled and highly routinized service. She plays a role that involves certain forms of bodily contact in order to allow her client to satisfy his sexual fantasy or desire. . . . Though it may be a part of the client's fantasy that the sex worker is having sex with him—an illusion the sex worker strives to maintain— she is simply carrying out her job as a skilled and impartial professional completing a business transaction. ("Do Lesbian Prostitutes Have Sex with Their Clients? A Clintonesque Reply," *Sexualities* 2 [1999]: 260)

19. See Carol Queen and Lawrence Schimel, "Don't Fence Me In: Bi-/Pan-/ Omni-Sexuals," in *PoMoSexuals: Challenging Assumptions about Gender and Sexuality*, ed. C. Queen and L. Schimel (San Francisco, Clies Press, 1997), 69.

20. For example, certain buildings and parts of buildings are defined as "appropriate" sexual sites (private residences, bedrooms inside private residences, massage parlors, brothels, motels, hotels), and that sex outside of these designated areas can be risky, illegal, and exciting; similarly time itself can be sexually mapped—when is sexual activity most likely, what are the conventions in any society about when sex should occur—at night, in the morning, in the afternoon, on weekends, during weekdays; should sexual activity and conformity be different during adolescence, young adulthood, middle age, old age?

21. For current theorizing of sexualities, see William Simon, *Postmodern Sexualities* (New York: Routledge, 1996); Diane Richardson, ed., *Theorizing Heterosexuality: Telling It Straight* (Philadelphia, Open University Press, 1996); Gail Hawkes, *A Sociology of Sex and Sexuality* (Philadelphia, Open University Press, 1996); Phoebe Davidson, Jo Eadie, Clare Hemmings, Ann Kaloski, and Merl Storr, eds., *The Bisexual Imaginary: Representation, Identity, and Desire* (London: Cassell, 1997).

22. There is some evidence that Americans are more tolerant of sexual diversity; see Jeni Loftus, "America's Liberalization in Attitudes toward Homosexuality," *American Sociological Review* 66 (2001): 762–82.

23. See Alfred C. Kinsey, Wardell B. Pomeroy, Clyde E. Martin, Paul H. Gebhard, *Sexual Behavior in the Human Male* (Philadelphia: W.B. Saunders, 1948), *Sexual Behavior in the Human Female* (Philadelphia: W.B. Saunders, 1953); William H. Masters and Virginia E. Johnson, *Human Sexual Response* (Boston: Little, Brown, 1966); Edward O. Laumann, John H. Gagnon, Robert T. Michael, Stuart Michaels, *The Social Organization of Sexuality: Sexual Practices in the United States* (Chicago: University of Chicago Press, 1994); Robert T. Michael, John H. Gagnon, Edward O. Laumann, Gina Kolata, *Sex in America: A Definitive Survey* (Boston: Little, Brown, 1994); for a critique of sexology research, see Julia A. Ericksen, *Kiss and Tell: Surveying Sex in the Twentieth Century* (Cambridge, MA: Harvard University Press, 1999).

24. John Gagnon and William Simon, *Sexual Conduct: The Social Sources of Human Sexuality* (Chicago: Aldine, 1973); see also Ann Snitow, Christine Stansell, and Sharon Thompson, eds., *Powers of Desire: The Politics of Sexuality* (New York: Monthly Review Press, 1983).

25. Adrienne Rich, "Compulsory Heterosexuality and Lesbian Existence," *Signs* 5 (1980): 631–60.

26. A further refinement of this discussion distinguishes *heteroconventionality* and *heteronormativity*, where heteroconventionality sets the "standards" for proper straight sex (when, where, how, with whom, etc.) and heteronormativity attempts either to erase or regulate non-heterosexualities (non-straight partners, bodies, behaviors, and desires); for a discussion of these and other sexual technical terms, see Michael Warner, "Introduction," in *Fear of a Queer Planet: Queer Politics and Social Theory*, ed. Michael Warner (Minneapolis: University of Minnesota Press, 1993), vii–xxxi; for an overview of queer theory; Annamarie Jagose, *Queer Theory: An Introduction* (New York: New York University Press, 1996); Steven Seidman, "Intro-

duction," in *Queer Theory/Sociology*, ed. Steven Seidman (New York: Blackwell, 1996), 1–29.

27. Michael Warner summarizes this broader definition of queerness—in practice and research: "For academics and activists 'queer' gets a critical edge by defining itself against the normal rather than the heterosexual" (Warner, "Introduction," xxvi); Warner further describes the queer perspective as resisting "an aggressive impulse of generalization," and embracing the rejection of "a minoritizing logic of toleration or simple political interest-representation in favor of a more thorough resistance to regimes of the normal . . . [so as to] make theory queer, not just to have a theory about queers" (ibid.). In this sense "queering" sexuality and sexuality studies extends to all non-normative, "abnormal" sexualities, not just "homosexuality," and challenges all theories of sexuality, not just theories of "abnormal sexuality" (ibid.); see also Michael Warner, *The Trouble with Normal: Sex, Politics, and the Ethics of Queer Life* (New York: The Free Press, 1999). This is not to presume the equal right of all individuals to claim to be "queer," since the economic, political, social, and personal costs are unevenly distributed across those whose sexuality is more or less controversial, visible, personally optional or recreational, privileged, or socially approved; everyone does not pay the same price to be (a) queer; for a discussion of the costs of queerness, see Judith Butler, "Merely Cultural," *New Left Review* 227 (1998): 33–44.

28. For an amusing heteronormative self-interrogation, see M. Rochlin, "The Heterosexual Questionnaire," in *Men's Lives*, ed. Michael S. Kimmel and Michael A. Messner (Boston: Allyn and Bacon, 1995), 405.

29. There are certainly voices raising doubts about whether these are the only valid choices, but they are less likely to question the notion of sexual identity— whether fixed or fluid; see the essays in Queen and Schimel, *PoMoSexuals*.

30. Michel Foucault, *The History of Sexuality: An Introduction* (New York: Vintage Books, [1978] 1990), 43; Jagose summarizes Foucault's position:

> [A]lthough same-sex acts were condemned in both religious and civil law before 1870, they were regarded as temptations to which anyone might succumb. Sinful and illegal, those forbidden acts were not understood to constitute a certain kind of individual. After 1870 same-sex acts began to be read as evidence of a particular type of person about whom explanatory narratives began to be formed. (*Queer Theory*, 11)

31. See Randolph Trumbach, "Sex, Gender, and Sexual Identity in Modern Culture: Male Sodomy and Female Prostitution in Enlightenment London," *Journal of the History of Sexuality* 2 (1991): 186–203; see also Michel Foucault, *The History of Sexuality*, volumes 1, 2, 3 (New York: Vintage Books, [1976] 1990, [1984] 1990, [1986] 1988); George Chauncey, *Gay New York: Gender, Urban Culture, and the Making of the Gay Male World, 1890–1940* (New York: Basic Books, 1994); Sabrina Petra Ramet, *Gender Reversals and Gender Cultures: Anthropological and Historical Perspectives* (New York: Routledge, 1996).

32. See Siobhan B. Somerville, *Queering the Color Line: Race and the Invention of Homosexuality in American Culture* (Durham: Duke University Press, 2000); Jonathan Ned Katz, *The Invention of Heterosexuality* (New York: Dutton, 1995).

33. The recognition of heteronormativity opens the door to a consideration of the rule structure inside non-heterosexual communities: Is there a *homo*normativity

as well? As Lauren Berlant and Michael Warner note, non-heterosexuals and non-straight communities are not without rules: "To be against heteronormativity is not to be against norms" (Lauren Berlant and Michael Warner, "Sex in Public," *Critical Inquiry* 24 (1998): 547–66, 557); see also Kristen Esterberg, *Lesbian and Bisexual Identities: Constructing Communities, Constructing Selves* (Philadelphia: Temple University Press, 1997) and Christine Robinson, "The Web of Talk: Social Control and the Production of a Lesbian Community" (Ph.D. diss., University of Kansas, 2002).

34. See Diana Fuss, ed., *Inside/Out: Lesbian Theories, Gay Theories* (New York: Routledge, 1991); Roger N. Lancaster and Micaela di Leonardo M., eds., *The Gender/Sexuality Reader: Culture, History, Political Economy* (New York: Routledge, 1997); Seidman, *Queer Theory/Sociology*; Warner, *Fear of a Queer Planet*.

35. See Fuss, *Essentially Speaking*.

36. For discussions of the embodiment and bodily construction of gender and sexuality, see Simon J. Williams and Gillian Bendelow, *The Lived Body: Sociological Themes, Embodied Issues* (New York: Routledge, 1998); Thomas Laqueur, *Making Sex: Body and Gender from the Greeks to Freud* (Cambridge, MA: Harvard University Press, 1990); Emily Martin, *The Woman in the Body: A Cultural Analysis of Reproduction* (Boston: Beacon Press, 1989) and *Flexible Bodies* (Boston: Little Brown, 1994); Jane Gallop, *Thinking Through the Body* (New York: Columbia University Press, 1988).

37. The classical articulation of social performance is Erving Goffman, *The Presentation of Self in Everyday Life* (New York: Doubleday, 1959); for more recent formulations and applications, see Joseph Roach, *Cities of the Dead: Circum-Atlantic Performance* (New York: Columbia University Press, 1996); Peggy Phelan, *Unmarked: The Politics of Performance* (New York: Routledge, 1993); Marvin Carlson, *Performance: A Critical Introduction* (New York: Routledge, 1996); Peggy Phelan and Jill Lane, *The Ends of Performance* (New York: New York University Press, 1998).

38. The early use of "performativity" is attributed to linguist and philosopher J. L. Austin, *How to Do Things with Words* (Cambridge, MA: Harvard University Press, 1975) and is further developed in literary theory by Shoshana Felman, *The Literary Speech Act: Don Juan with J.L. Austin, or Seduction in Two Languages* (Ithaca: Cornell University Press, 1983).

39. Judith Butler, *Gender Trouble: Feminism and the Subversion of Identity* (New York: Routledge, 1990); see also Eve Kosofsky Sedgwick, "Queer Performativity: Henry James's *The Art of the Novel*," *GLQ* 1 (1993): 1–16.

40. Gayle Rubin, "The Traffic in Women: Notes on the 'Political Economy' of Sex," in *Toward an Anthropology of Women*, ed. Rayna R. Reiter (New York: Monthly Review Press, 1975), 157–210; see also Lorber, *Paradoxes of Gender*; Kimmel, *The Gendered Society*.

41. Arlie Russell Hochschild, *The Second Shift: Working Parents and the Revolution at Home* (New York: Viking, 1989).

42. Butler argues that performative orders also can change in small, almost unnoticeable ways, when there are small errors or distortions in the replication of hegemonies; given the power of an overall hegemonic order, it is hard to imagine such errors not being overlooked, corrected in subsequent performances, or disciplined back

into conformity: one is quite unlikely to "forget" to wear one's clothes, though one can forget to wear earrings; thus, the magnitude of errors tends to be self-limiting, and those that do occur tend to be trivial; see Butler, *Gender Trouble*, 163–80.

43. See Todd Boyd, *Am I Black Enough for You? Popular Culture from the 'Hood and Beyond* (Bloomington: Indiana University Press, 1997).

44. Nancy Hartsock, *Money, Sex, and Power: Toward a Feminist Historical Materialism* (New York: Longman, 1983); Sherry Ortner, "Is Female to Male as Nature Is to Culture?" *Feminist Studies* 1 (1972): 5–31 and *Making Gender: The Politics and Erotics of Culture* (Boston: Beacon Press, 1996); Catherine MacKinnon, *Toward a Feminist Theory of the State* (Cambridge, MA: Harvard University Press, 1989); Joan Scott, *Gender and the Politics of History* (New York: Columbia University Press, 1988).

45. Judith Butler, *Gender Trouble: Feminism and the Subversion of Identity*, second edition (New York: Routledge, 1999), xxvi.

46. See bell hooks, "Representations of Whiteness," in *Black Looks*, 165–78; Lorraine Hansberry, *To Be Young, Gifted, and Black* (New York: Signet, 1970); Anna Maria Chupa, *Anne, the White Woman in Contemporary African-American Fiction: Archetypes, Stereotypes, and Characterizations* (Westport, CT: Greenwood Press, 1990); Erica Chito Childs, "Constructing Interracial Couples: Multiple Narratives and Images" (Ph.D. diss., Fordham University, 2001).

CHAPTER 3

SEX AND
CONQUEST

*Domination and Desire
on Ethnosexual Frontiers*

COLUMBIA VERSUS AMERICA: SOOTHED
OR SAVAGE BRAVE NEW WORLD?

Christopher Columbus and Amerigo Vespucci first visited the "New World" within a decade of one another. The impressions of these two Italian explorers could not have been more different. Columbus chronicled his 1492 voyage and first contacts with indigenous people, whom his mistaken geography led him to name "Indians," in a diary he kept for his sponsor, the Spanish monarchy. Columbus recorded his first encounter with native people in an October 11, 1492, entry. He reported that the peoples of the Caribbean islands he and his crew visited on that and subsequent days were affable, attractive, and accommodating:

> [T]o some of them I gave red caps, and glass beads . . . and many other things of small value, in which they took so much pleasure and became so much our friends that it was a marvel. . . . All of them go around as naked as their mothers bore them; and the women also. . . . They are very well formed, with handsome bodies and good faces. . . . They do not carry arms nor are they acquainted with them. . . . They should be good and intelligent servants, for I see that they say very quickly everything that is said to them; and I believe that they would become Christians very easily, for it seemed to me that they had no religion. . . .[1]

Columbus sent a team of explorers inland, and they soon returned with tales of native hospitality and homage which Columbus recounted in his diary on November 5, 1492:

[E]veryone came to see them, men as well as women; and they quartered them in the best houses. The Indians touched them and kissed their hands and feet, marveling and believing that the Spaniards came from the heavens, and so they gave them to understand. They gave them something to eat of what they had. . . . Later the men left, and the women came in and seated themselves . . . around them, kissing their hands and feet and feeling them, attempting to see if they were, like themselves of flesh and bone. They begged them to stay with them for at least five days.[2]

Columbus himself also found the native people he encountered to be welcoming and generous:

So many came that they covered the land, giving a thousand thanks, men as well as women and children. Some of them ran this way, others that way, to bring us bread . . . [and] water in gourds and in clay jugs . . . and they brought us all that they had in the world . . . and all so bigheartedly and so happily that it was a wonder.[3]

Indeed it was a wonder, since at several points of contact Columbus and his men repaid local hospitality by capturing and detaining both native men and women. Columbus's accounts of these kidnappings never questioned the morality of such actions by the "Christians" (as he often referred to his men). For instance,

[T]hey captured one woman . . . in order to treat them courteously and make them lose their fear . . . they brought the woman, who was very young and pretty, to the ship and . . . the Admiral ordered her clothed and he gave her glass beads and bells and brass finger rings and returned her to land very courteously, according to his custom.[4]

Vespucci, who sailed to the New World a few years later, told a different story in his pamphlet, *Mundus Novus*, published around 1504. While Vespucci found indigenous people "well formed and proportioned," he complained that they "destroyed" their "comely countenance":

[Men] bore their cheeks, lips, noses and ears . . . [W]omen do not bore their faces, but their ears only. They have another custom, very shameful and beyond all human belief. For their women, being very lustful, cause the private parts of their husbands to swell up to such a huge size that they appear deformed and disgusting. . . . They marry as many wives as they please; and son cohabits with mother, brother with sister, male cousin with female, and any man with the first woman he meets . . . [T]hey cruelly kill one another, and those whom they bring home captives from war they preserve, not to spare their lives, but that they may be slain for food; for they eat one another, the victors the vanquished.[5]

Figure 3.1, an early-seventeenth-century drawing by Theodor Galle, based on a sixteenth-century work by Jan van der Street, entitled "America," rep-

FIGURE 3.1 "Vespucci 'Discovering' America," Theodore Galle, after Stradanus (Jan van der Street), ca. 1575–1580 (Courtesy of the Burndy Library, Dibner Institute for the History of Science and Technology, Cambridge, Massachusetts)

resents an early illustration contrasting the "civilized" European—a standing Vespucci who is clothed and surrounded by the paraphernalia of technology, with the uncivilized America—a reclining woman who is naked and surrounded by wild animals and cannibals. Vespucci is the modern, masculine scientifically inquisitive traveler, America is the primitive, feminine new world, open to discovery and exploration.[6]

The New World encountered by Columbus was one in which the inhabitants were peaceful, timid, generous, and in awe of Europeans. Columbus praised his men for their Christian kindness in dealing with the natives, kindness that he asserted was "according to [European] custom." Columbus viewed native people as naive and childlike in their nudity, simple in their spirituality, primitive in their technology, and cooperative in their dealings. In contrast to Columbus's Eden, Vespucci's *mundus novus* was more like Sodom and Gomorrah, filled with cruel torturers, depraved cannibals, treacherous men, and licentious women; the inhabitants of the new world were dangerous, duplicitous, promiscuous, and incestuous. The only two points of agreement between the two men's accounts are revealing. Both Columbus and Vespucci found the people they encountered, particularly the women, to be quite attractive, especially those with light skin; and both men congratulated themselves and their crews on their civilized, Christian treatment of the natives.

> Columbus described the inhabitants of two islands his men visited on December 13 and 14, 1492:
>
> And as to their skin, the Christians said . . . that they are whiter than the others [on other islands], and that they saw two young women as white as any in Spain. . . . This king and all the others went about naked as their mothers bore them; and the women did also, without any embarrassment. And they are the most handsome men and women that they had found up to that point: and very white, for if they went about clothed and protected themselves from the sun and wind they would be almost as white as people in Spain.[7]

Vespucci concurred:

> The women as I have said go about naked and are very libidinous; yet they have bodies which are tolerably beautiful and cleanly. Nor are they so unsightly as one perchance might imagine, for, inasmuch as they are plump, their ugliness is the less apparent, which indeed is for the most part concealed by the excellence of their bodily structure. It was to us a matter of astonishment that none was to be seen among them who had a flabby breast, and those who had borne children were not to be distinguished from virgins by the shape and shrinking of the womb, and in the other parts of the body similar things were seen of which in the interest of modesty I make no mention.[8]

Vespucci's rather false modesty is followed by a comment that marks the second point of consensus between Columbus and Vespucci—the Europeans' sexual attraction to native women. For instance, Vespucci and his men apparently were able to set aside their shock at the naked and "libidinous" nature of native women to pursue higher purposes:

> When they had the opportunity of copulating with Christians, urged by excessive lust, they defiled and prostituted themselves.[9]

According to this account only the natives were in possession of "excessive lust" or "prostituted themselves" while Vespucci and his crew simply indulged native women's desires by providing as much "opportunity of copulating" as they could muster. Columbus is less explicit about sex between his men and indigenous women, though he notes that "there are women with very pretty figures," but he stresses that the European men were ordered "to be careful not to annoy anyone in anything and to take nothing from them against their will."[10] Despite Columbus's claims about his men's charitable and restrained treatment of the natives they encountered, in one journal entry just before Christmas in 1492, he reported that in an increasing number of places they visited "all the men make their women hide from the Christians out of jealousy."[11] This comment suggests that native people may have felt they had good reason to become wary of the attention paid to local women by Columbus and his men, a distrust that no doubt set the stage for later interethnic tensions and Euro-indigenous conflicts.

SEX AND CONQUEST: THE WINNING OF THE U.S. WEST

Early European travelers who followed Columbus and Vespucci wrote home describing native men and women as primitive and promiscuous. In his history of the "white man's Indian," Robert Berkhofer reports that the first English language publication about the new world reflected this view:

> These folke lyven lyke bestes without any resonablenes and the wymen be also as common. And the men hath conversacyon with the wymen/ who that they ben or who they fyrst mete/ is she his syster/ his mother/ his daughter/ or any other kyndred. And the wymen be very hoote and dysposed to lecherdnes.[12]

As Berkhofer notes, the new printing press circulated this and similar sensational and graphic reports (this one translated from an early-sixteenth-century Dutch pamphlet) across Europe, and, despite the morally indignant tone of the text, the floodgates opened as Europeans eager to settle this sexually savage, brave New World swarmed across the Atlantic. Certainly these and later lurid accounts of Indian sexual practices and availability held a certain allure to the mostly male European emigrants.

Scholars question the biases and agendas of many European reports about indigenous peoples since they served as justifications for colonial and later American policies of annihilation, "pacification," civilization, and assimilation of Indian populations.[13] Given the loaded nature of sexual matters, sexual descriptions had a special capacity to impress readers and to shape powerful and lasting images of native America. These early sexualized depictions of native peoples combined with those of later colonial and American chroniclers to form a general portrait of "Indian life" as morally and culturally inferior to European and American societies, though still of much interest to writers and their readers.

Ramon Gutierrez, for instance, found early records of Spanish soldiers and Franciscan friars filled with commentary about Pueblo peoples' sexual practices. The Franciscans in particular were prolific in their reports of what they saw as Pueblo "lewd" behavior and sexual promiscuity, including same-sex relations, particularly among those whom some have called "berdache," "two-spirit," "man-woman," or "third sex" individuals.[14] The Franciscans disapproved of sexual intercourse between anyone other than married men and women in anything other than the "missionary position," since as the seventeenth-century theologian Tomas Sanchez stated, this was the "natural manner of intercourse."[15] Despite their condemnation of native sexuality, the Franciscans violated their own vows of celibacy crossing Spanish-Indian ethnosexual boundaries to father many mixed children.[16] Indeed, native/nonnative sexual contact was widely reported across both the North and South American continents, and was reflected in the growth of the "mixed-blood" population.[17] Spanish soldiers and missionaries also reported a pattern of Indian-white sexual negotiations, apparently for purposes of trade for objects or for power, a pattern that is repeated in later accounts of Indian-white contact.

It was not only Europeans from Spain who engaged in sexual contact and commerce with indigenous Americans. The journals of Meriwether Lewis and William Clark, who set out on their westward explorations in 1804, are replete with references to encounters with native peoples along the way; many of these (both the references and the encounters) were of a sexual nature, and many emphasized trade:

> Thursday, November 21, 1805: An old woman & Wife to a Cheif of the Chunnooks came and made a Camp near ours. She brought with her 6 young Squars I believe for the purpose of Gratifying the passions of the men of our party and receiving for those indulgiences Such Small [presents] as She (the old woman) thought proper to accept of. Those people appear to View Sensuality as a Necessary evel, and do not appear to abhor it as a Crime in the unmarried State.[18]

On Christmas eve of that same year, Clark writes again,

> [Cuscalah, a Clatsop] offered a woman to each of us which we also declined axcepting of, which displeased the whole party very much—the female part appeared to be highly disgusted at our refuseing to axcept of their favours &c.[19]

What goes unmentioned in these entries is the frequent willingness of Lewis and Clark's men to enter into native sexual exchanges. In his history of the Lewis and Clark expedition, James Ronda offers some corroboration from a traveler who followed in the wake of the expedition several years later. Henry M. Brackenridge reported this 1811 exchange with an Arikara village chief:

> "I was wondering," said he [the chief], "whether you white people have any women amongst you." I assured him in the affirmative. "Then," said he, "why is it that your people are so fond of our women, one might suppose they had never seen any before?"[20]

While the motives of the whites may have been transparent, what remains unclear is the meaning of these sexual exchanges to the Arikaras or the Clatsops or the Chinooks or the Pueblos. What were these indigenous people thinking when they crossed sexual boundaries; what were the frames of mind and state of affairs on Indian-white ethnosexual frontiers? Ronda provides a clue to solving the mentalities and motivations of various sides in ethnosexual exchanges on the U.S. frontier. It was not only whites with whom native people sought contact. Ronda comments that York, the enslaved African who accompanied his owner, William Clark, was a "central attraction of the Lewis and Clark expedition. . . . York's blackness was viewed by the Arikaras as a sign of special spiritual power. . . . To have sexual contact with York was to get in touch with what seemed awesome spirit forces."[21]

It is important to remember that there are many different frontiers scattered across the time and space being discussed here—different peoples, different eras, different locales, and many different conditions facing native peoples and settler populations. In light of such diversity scholars provide a number of accounts of Indian-white sexual encounters. Ronda offers four reasons why Indians might have been willing to enter into sexual exchanges with white travelers in the early nineteenth century: to trade for European goods (ironware, paint, cloth), to forge commercial links (sealed by sexual relations), to express native hospitality, especially on the plains, and as noted above, to obtain whatever spiritual power non-Indians might possess.[22] Albert Hurtado confirms these several agendas, but he paints a less sanguine portrait of freely given Indian sexual favors. Once again acknowledging wide variation across indigenous communities, conditions, times, and places, Hurtado points out the relative powerlessness of many native women, and reports that sexual exchanges often were coerced, involving rape, forced prostitution, and slavery.[23] Hurtado and Ronda tell a similar story of sexuality and slavery about one of the best known Indian women in history, Sacagawea:

> Sometime in the fall of 1800, the young Lemhi Shoshoni girl, then perhaps twelve or thirteen years old, was camped at the Three Forks of the Missouri with others from her band . . . the party at Three Forks was attacked by Hidatsa raiders. . . . Among the prisoners taken were four boys and several women, including Sacagawea. Sometime between 1800 and 1804, she and one other Shoshoni captive were purchased by Toussaint Charbonneau, a trader. . . . When Lewis and Clark met Charbonneau at Fort Mandan on November 4, 1804. . . . Sacagawea was already pregnant.[24]

The fact that Sacagawea, a Shoshone teenager, was purchased and then impregnated by Charbonneau, a French trader, was sanitized in subsequent references to her by Lewis and Clark and others as Charbonneau's "wife."

This normalized definition of Sacagawea as a willing wife and mother has become an enduring part of the American national narrative, one that was engraved on a U.S. one dollar coin in 2000 shown in Plate 2 of the color insert.

The relationship between Sacagawea and Charbonneau represents one point of contact in the complicated network of ethnosexual frontiers that crisscrossed what Rebecca Faery refers to as the New World's "cartographies of desire."

> The desire of the colonizers for land was conflated with desire for a Native woman who was a representative or stand-in for the land itself; likewise, the effort to "protect" white women from the presumed desire of dark men, both Indian and African, was a coded insistence on the rights of the colonists to territory already taken or not yet taken but desired. The history of Anglo-America, then, is a map of confluent desires, sexual and territorial, that over time produced and consolidated the map of America as we know it today.[25]

Despite their frequent relative powerlessness, Indian women sometimes used whites' sexual desire against them. Kathleen Brown recounts the story of George Cawson, who "met his death after [Powhatan] village women 'enticed [him] up from the barge into their howses' and delivered him to his executioners."[26] She goes on to tell of the sexual trick of a particular Powhatan woman:

> Oppossunoquonuske, a clever werowansqua of another village, similarly led fourteen English men to their demise. Inviting the unwary men to come "up into her Towne, to feast and make merry," she persuaded them to "leave their Armes in their boat, because they said how their women would be afrayed ells of their pieces". . . . Her genius lay in persuading them to rely on other masculine "pieces" . . . [and] the men were easily killed.[27]

Many white sexual advances were not welcomed by native people, but were accepted in acts of desperation. The poverty resulting from forced Indian removals from homelands and the destruction of indigenous economies left many native communities destitute. As a result, some native men turned to thievery and some native women turned to prostitution to survive.[28] In some instances, indigenous populations were so vulnerable that no money changed hands, instead native women simply became sexual prey. Theda Perdue describes the South Carolina Indian trade as

> replete with native complaints of sexual abuse. One trader "took a young Indian against her Will for his Wife," another severely beat three [native] women including his pregnant wife whom he killed, and a third provided enough rum to a woman to get her drunk and then "used her ill."[29]

The rape of Indian women often precipitated Indian-white conflicts, particularly during the Gold Rush, when, according to Hurtado, rapes by whites were widespread and sometimes enacted by federal officials themselves on reservations, where native women were attacked "before the very eyes of their husbands and daughters . . . and they dare[d] not resent the insult, or even complain of the hideous outrage."[30] This sympathetic portrayal of native victims of white sexual assault appeared in an 1856 San Francisco newspaper, but such sympathy was the exception, rather than the rule.

There were many far more critical reports in American media about native life and sexuality, often popularized in the form of Indian captivity narratives where whites were the targets of Indian aggression.[31] Captivity narratives were among the first popular publications written in the new world. Analysts have divided them into several categories. Richard Van Der Beets and Richard Slotkin both describe early captivity narratives, whether based in fact or not, as religious allegories in which white captives undergo redemptive suffering at the hands of Indians and find a path back to godliness upon their return to Christian civilization.[32] Roy Pearce and Rebecca Faery add to this list a political propaganda form of captivity narrative designed to defame either the French or, mainly, the Indians by dramatizing their excesses of brutality, lust, and savagery. These captivity narratives were put to use "making a history, shaping a nation," and fashioning a " 'suitable' national history and identity, one that placed whiteness and masculinity in a superior position to other categories of identity."[33]

A number of analysts identify a third, and probably the most prolific type of captivity narrative—the "penny" or "dime" novel. Like all literature, fictional captivity narratives reflected the customs and assumptions of the times, and since many readers were interested in the tales told by women captives, scholars have read the narratives as morality plays about the proper and improper place of women in American colonial and national society depending on the era in which the narrative was written and edited. Examples of popular nineteenth-century novels featuring women captives include James Fenimore Cooper's *The Last of the Mohicans*. The familiarity of the title of this 1826 novel to contemporary Americans is evidence of the enduring popularity of tales of early American gender, sexuality, and ethnicity.[34]

Whatever the era or genre of the captivity narrative, in cases where sexual assault was reported, most white women captives did not admit to being sexually attacked themselves for fear of public humiliation. Instead they described the sexual assault of other captives by Indians. For instance, Mary Smith and her husband were reportedly captured by Kickapoos and Chickasaws in 1814. In her memoir, *An Affecting Narrative of the Captivity and Sufferings of Mrs. Mary Smith*, she writes that the Indians "ravished, rifled, murdered and mutilated the inhabitants without distinction of age or sex, without any other provocation or incitement than brutal lust and wantonness of barbarity!"[35] Caroline Harris, who was captured by Comanches in Texas in the 1830s, *did* describe her own experiences: "I was doomed to spend eleven months in a state of bondage and misery that beggars description! being not only compelled to cohabit, but to yield to the beastly will of a Savage Brute!"[36]

Despite such graphic and frightening accounts not all captives escaped when they had the chance; in some cases they became members of tribes, migrating permanently across the Indian-white ethnic boundary and changing their ethnicity in the process. So-called "transculturated" or "white Indians" married and chose to stay with their captors. Some did so because of the shame of returning home as sexually "damaged goods,"[37] others because of Indian generosity and sympathy for their plight. For instance, one captive described being moved by a native man's act of kindness: "[a] young Indian, Wechela, brought me a pair of shoes, also a pair of little Mary's. He looked kindly as he laid these articles before me, intimating by his gestures that our lives were to be spared."[38]

Past and present references to Indians as "noble savages" echo the same ambivalency toward native people reflected in many of the above accounts. Faery illustrates the contradictions of simultaneous desire and disgust contained in centuries of white depictions of and interactions with Indians by juxtaposing the ravished image of the white woman captive against the ravishing figure of Pocahantas: the Indian victim in contrast to the Indian princess.[39] Robert Berkhofer summarizes these competing stereotypes of "the white man's Indian":

> [T]he good Indian appears friendly, courteous, and hospitable to the initial invaders of his lands and to all Whites. . . . Along with handsomeness of physique and physiognomy went great stamina and endurance. . . . Modest in attitude. . . . Brave in combat, he was tender in love for family and children . . . the bad Indian [in contrast, marked by] nakedness and lechery, passion and vanity led to lives of polygamy and sexual promiscuity among themselves and constant warfare and fiendish revenge against their enemies . . . thievery and treachery . . . hard slavery of women and the laziness of men.[40]

June Namias analyzed dozens of captivity narratives and reported a dualism in the *white woman's* Indian as well:

> Nineteenth century captivity materials offered mixed messages for women: excitement, possible romantic bliss, but the chance of sexual harassment. The big, dark Indian was pictured simultaneously as a thrill and a sexual threat to white women and consequently a competitive sexual threat to white men.[41]

This dualism is illustrated in Figures 3.2 and 3.3, two nineteenth-century drawings that appeared in captivity narratives.

FIGURE 3.2 "Attempt to Escape, My Capture, and Cruel Treatment," 1782 (Courtesy of the Newberry Library)

FIGURE 3.3   "Miss Lockhart Carried Away by the Camanche Chief," ca. 1780 (Courtesy of the Newberry Library)

THERE'S A METHOD IN THEIR IMAGININGS

Aside from any erotic imaginings[42] aroused by captivity narratives or passions kindled by opportunities for ethnosexual adventures in Indian-white encounters, questions arise: To what uses were put these centuries of sexualized depictions of Indians? What were the social, political, economic, and policy consequences of these many uncomplimentary sexual descriptions of Indians as wanton savages and brutal rapists? How important were depictions of the sexuality of native men and women in defining the boundary between non-Indians and Indians, savage and civilized, noncitizen and citizen?

Certainly the portrayal of Indians as sexually dangerous was a convenient justification for warfare against native societies and for "removing" Indians from areas chosen by whites for settlement. Sherry Smith notes that although no army officer's wife ever was captured by Indians many of those women wrote about the terrors of captivity:

> Woe to the hapless party that fell into the devilish hands of a band of Indians! . . . Babies had their brains dashed out before the eyes of father and mother, powerless to help them. Lucky would the latter have been, had they been treated in the same way; but what she was to endure would have wrung tears from anything but an Indian.[43]

Smith reports, for instance, that Elizabeth Custer, the wife of George Armstrong Custer, "seemed particularly fascinated by the topic" of the fate of white women taken by Indians, and she quotes Mrs. Custer's conclusion that "death would be merciful in comparison."[44] The images and messages contained in comments like these about Indian sexual threats were powerful justifications for eliminating the "Indian problem" by any means necessary.[45]

The sexual observations about native people made by explorers, missionaries, soldiers, traders, settlers, and reformers were not simply prurient preoccupations or voyeuristic reports, though no doubt they served those masters as well. Sexualized depictions of and beliefs about native peoples became part of the imagining of the U.S. West. Real or putative sexual differences between whites and Indians provided a rationale for seizing native resources to "better" manage and use them, and allowed U.S. political and economic interests to paper over their exploitations by launching programs to "improve" Indian individuals and cultures by civilizing and assimilating American Indians.

Reports of Indian depredations and savagery also became a means of justifying white misbehavior and atrocities and provided ample opportunities for white self-aggrandizement. Smith reports that frontier soldiers often described Indian men as skilled warriors, in part to explain a defeat or because "a successful campaign against a formidable foe rather than a weak one could enhance a soldier's reputation back home."[46] The defeat of a strong native opponent also would guarantee continued support for a frontier military presence, a military that sometimes kept itself busy in less than glorious pursuits. Military massacres of Indian women and children were defended by demonizing native women, thus these women whom soldiers sometimes sought as sex partners could be refashioned into suitable adversaries by re-sexing them as men: "[n]ot a gleam of pity entered her feminine breast. She was a cold-blooded, thirsty vulture, only intent upon her prey, as good as the warrior himself."[47]

Another clue to the usefulness of sexualized images of Indians can be found in the labels and meanings assigned to the whites who openly consorted with Indians. From the earliest days of European colonialism well into the nineteenth century, whites who crossed ethnosexual boundaries into Indian country too often or who lingered too long ran the risk of being morally and ethnically redefined. White men who were thought to have too much intimate association with native cultures, and especially with native women, were suspected of disloyalty in native-white conflicts. For instance, one William Baker, a white man who was reported to "Speake much Indian" and to have "turned Indian in nakednes and cutting of haire, and after many whoredomes, is there maried," was believed to have fought alongside the Pequots during the colonial-Pequot war of 1636. The next year authorities used Baker's sexual liaisons against him, and Connecticut officials tried to arrest him "for uncleanness with an Indian squaw, who is now with child by him."[48] Ann Marie Plane describes intimacies between natives and English settlers in colonial New England and catalogs a number of intermarriages and long-term extramarital unions between Christianized Indians and colonists. She notes, however, the tenuous nature of these arrangements, and concludes that native-white conflicts "may have made the official sanctioning of interracial unions virtually unthinkable."[49]

After U.S. independence, white men who consorted with Indian women were seen less as threats to white security than as risks to white morality. Smith comments that "many nineteenth-century men maintained, at least in public statements, that sexual relations with Indian women degraded white men."[50] This was despite widespread sexual contact between native women and male officers and soldiers stationed out west. A good deal of such ethnosexual adventuring no doubt was overlooked, but John D'Emilio and Estelle Freedman report that more enduring Indian-white sexual liaisons, including marriage, were viewed by some whites as a "shame and disgrace to our country."[51] This view was consistent with the negative descriptions of so-called squaw men, white men (often French traders) who lived with Indian women or took Indian wives, and who were sometimes accused by observers of exploiting their relationship with these women's tribes for their own economic gain. For instance, in his 1883 book, *Our Wild Indians*, frontier veteran Colonel Richard Irving Dodge distinguished between pioneering white trappers or traders who married Indian women and the "squaw-men" who "went native," living with their wives' tribes and sending "their squaws to draw rations, buying and selling the same and, even worse, engaging in the clandestine sale of guns and liquor to their native hosts . . . and [having] no compunction whatever about abandoning their families."[52] The denigration of whites residing on the native side of the Indian-white ethnic boundary reinforced stereotypes of indigenous sexual and social disreputability and made their mistreatment easier to overlook.

While whites may have been seen to lose moral and reputational ground by ethnosexual settling or sojourning with Indians, there were some nineteenth-century reformers and "Friends of the Indian" who believed Indians benefited from sustained intimate association with whites, and who advocated racial mixing as a way to improve the Indian race. The mixed offspring of Indian-white marriages were applauded by some reformers as superior to "full-blooded" Indians (if not an improvement over "pure" whites). Herbert Welsh, a well-known member of the Indian Rights Association, a reform organization with mainly white membership, advocated the marriage of white men to native women. In 1892 he met a white schoolmaster and his native wife and was impressed by their relationship and the potential of such unions:

> Welsh cited an [Indian] agency physician who maintained that compared to the full-bloods, the mixed-breeds were "healthier, more intelligent, enjoy life better, are physically stronger, have larger cleaner houses, and approach the domestic condition of the white man."[53]

Some reformers viewed intermarriage as a way to improve and civilize not only native individuals and the race, but native communities and cultures as well. Speaking at an Indian reform conference at Lake Mohonk, New York, in 1897, the Reverend J. A. Lippincott commented, "There is one way to solve the Indian problem: it is the absorption and assimilation of these aborigines into the body of our people."[54] This happy vision of miscegenation fit well U.S. plans to acquire Indian land and resources under the umbrella of policy reform designed to improve the lot of Indians. As it turned out, the offspring of intermarriage and mixed sexual unions sometimes served the economic interests of non-Indians. The "management" of Indian resources was aided by the fact that many of the mixed-blood descendants of these sexual crossings "walked in both worlds"—the native and the white. Such hybrid individuals constituted a potential pool of "middlemen" or cultural brokers between native communities and whites. Mixed bloods could broker deals that served indigenous interests, but their dealings could serve their own personal and family interests as well, and sometimes mixed bloods acted as "servants of power," making deals with whites to the detriment of their tribal relations.[55]

By the beginning of the twentieth century, Indians had been confined to reservations, their economies destroyed, and their lands allotted; native children were undergoing forced acculturation in boarding schools with English-only policies, Christian indoctrination, and training in proper [white] moral, gender, and sexual behavior.[56] As the decades progressed, reservation communities were colonized by the creation of federally linked tribal governments, and programs were designed to eliminate reservations altogether by relocating native people into the cities. The goal of late-nineteenth and early-twentieth-century Indian policy was to dismantle the Indian/non-Indian ethnic boundary and absorb natives into the American "mainstream." Real Indians were to be relegated to history, and the imagined Indian was transformed in whites' minds, if not in native realities, from a hypersexualized savage into a tamed domestic put in service to the American national project. America could now use this new, improved, safely resexualized, and thus truly noble savage to refashion its own image of itself.

WHITE SKIN, RED MASKS

Gender and sexuality played roles not only in whites' imaginings of Indians, but, in a strange twist of cultural history, Indian sexuality and native masculinity also played a role in whites' imaginings of themselves. There is another side to sex and conquest that involves not white men and native women or white women and native men; it involves only men—red and white. This installment in the American chronicle of sex and conquest centers the construction of U.S. nationalism and American manhood out of the ruins and stolen remnants of native nations and masculinities.

White men's attraction to native masculine virility has a long history stretching back to the early days of the American Republic and reaching forward into the present. In *Playing Indian*, Philip Deloria documents that throughout U.S. history Americans, mainly white men, have dressed up and acted in ways they imagined to be Indian. He cites, for instance, the 1773 Boston Tea Party, when white colonists donned costumes and makeup to simulate Mohawks;[57] their "Indian" antics were partly to disguise their identities and partly to intimidate their opponents with feigned Iroquois confederacy fierceness. Whites used native symbolism and simulated "Indian" ceremonies to create solidarity and community in men's fraternal organizations and private clubs such as the nineteenth-century Improved Order of Red Men or the League of the Iroquois,[58] and "the Indian"[59] had a central place in youth organizations designed to build American character and citizenship, such as the Boy Scouts and the Woodcraft Indians.[60] Contemporary Indian play can be witnessed by even the most casual observer today in football stadiums and baseball parks where fans wear "war paint," do "war dances," chant "war songs," and make "Indian" gestures such as "tomahawk chops."[61]

The large-scale appropriation of Indianness, in particular the consumption of Indian virility and potency by mainly white men, began at the turn of the twentieth century when two social trends converged in the United States: the defeat of native nations followed by their internment on reservations and a crisis of confidence in American masculinity as the country moved from an agricultural, rural economy to an urban, industrial society. According to historians, in the late nineteenth century American manhood had lost its moorings.[62] Southern men, despite their tradition of military service and honor, had lost the Civil War to a North whose men they perceived as feminized and weak.[63] Northern white men faced a variety of challenges in the increasingly urban landscapes where they worked and lived: immigrants with their cheap labor and political machines, monopolistic capitalist trusts that controlled wages and prices, boom and bust cycles associated with the unregulated U.S. economy, and women with their demands for political rights and economic opportunities.[64]

Scholars argue that these social, economic, and political changes destabilized American men's sense of independence and efficacy and challenged the historical vision of American strength, adventurousness, and virility.[65] This vision and the challenges it confronted were articulated in 1883 when Frederick Jackson Turner proclaimed the closing of the U.S. frontier and the end of the American frontier spirit. Turner's diagnosis of what was troubling America and his gloomy prognosis about the poor national health of postfrontier America set in motion a search for a tonic to restore American national vision and virility.[66] One place Americans looked, especially American men, for a source of renewal was to the symbol of the frontier—"the Indian," who was now conveniently imprisoned and emasculated on reservations—the better to pose no real threat to the weakened Americans.

Although Indians were thus out of sight (and their total disappearance constantly predicted), they were not out of the minds of Americans. Then as now, the Indian appeared in stories told to a mass public, not only in dime novels and captivity narratives, but also in Wild West shows and early films.[67] Through these endeavors, Americans reinvented and sanitized the Indian to appeal to popular audiences and to serve nostalgic reconstructions of America's frontier days. Whites also used the Indian to reimagine and rebuild American masculinity into an iconic form that has survived into the present.

The contemporary metal of U.S. national manhood was forged out of the collision of native and nonnative masculinities in the country's first major nationalist imperialist project: Manifest Destiny—a vision and set of policies that designed and justified westward expansion as an inalienable right of America and Americans. The westward expansion of the boundaries of the United States at the expense of indigenous individuals and nations is inscribed in American popular culture and popular histories as a series of military events.[68] Colonial images of the Indian warrior in these military encounters were presented first in newspaper accounts, periodicals, and lectures, and later in books, theater, film, and television.[69] Countless scenes in popular media showed brave U.S. frontier soldiers confronting and conquering dangerous but endangered Indian men. The Indians were seen to be clinging to an archaic way of life, making their last desperate, but doomed stand against the superior and inevitable march of civilization across a modernizing western American landscape. The only good Indian was *not* a dead Indian, but rather a subjugated and sanitized Indian—an Indian that could be conquered repeatedly in white men's Indian play.

Imaginings of the Indian as a formidable, but ultimately feckless foe have remained largely undisturbed in the American popular imagination despite the nearly complete eradication of native resistance by 1890–1891 marked by the massacre at Wounded Knee and the murder of Sitting Bull in South Dakota.[70] In his 1894 triumphant rendition of U.S. history, *The Winning of the West*, for instance, Theodore Roosevelt scathingly depicted the Indian not only as brutal, lazy, and incapable of self-motivated productive labor, but also as cruel to men and dangerous to women and children; he argued that white settlers' atrocities against native people were understandable, if not justifiable in light of "the terrible provocations they had endured"[71]:

> [The frontiersman] was not taking part in a war against a civilized foe; he was fighting in a contest where women and children suffered the fate of the strong men. . . . His friends had been treacherously slain while on messages of peace; his house had been burned, his cattle driven off . . . his sweetheart or wife had been carried off, ravished, and was at the moment the slave and concubine of some dirty and brutal Indian warrior.[72]

Roosevelt's Americans drew power from the strength and savagery of their Indian adversaries:

> Their red foes were strong and terrible, cunning in council, dreadful in battle, merciless beyond belief in victory. The men of the border did not overcome and dispossess cowards and weaklings, they marched forth to spoil the stout-hearted and to take for prey the possessions of the men of might.[73]

Roosevelt was not alone in his simultaneous vilification and glorification of native toughness. White soldiers often expressed admiration for native warriors.[74] Francis Paul Prucha recounts the assessment of General George Crook who was in the army at the time of George Armstrong Custer's defeat by Cheyennes and Lakotas in 1876:

> I wish to say most emphatically that the American Indian is the intellectual peer of most, if not all, the various nationalities we have assimilated to our

laws, customs, and language. He is fully able to protect himself, if the ballot be given and the courts of law not closed against him.[75]

Crook described an admirable adversary, someone worthy of respect, even emulation, someone who had something a white man might want.

There is a contradiction and a bitter irony imbedded in the juxtaposition of these opposite realities and images of Indians. On the one hand, there is the destruction of actual native peoples and their societies in the nineteenth-century West. On the other hand, and at the same moment, nonnatives were using imaginary native cultures and people to reinvent themselves as Americans. The reservation system—abject physical and psychological spaces where actual Indians were imprisoned—opened the "West" as a secure space for victorious Americans to settle.

Added to the injuries inflicted on Indians by policies designed to destroy actual native cultures were insults in the form of whites' imitation of what they imagined to be "Indian ways." This supposedly sincerest form of flattery led to an bizarre situation where non-Indians were busy civilizing Indians in an effort to turn Indians into whites, while at the same time non-Indian men were busy emulating, more accurately *simulating* Indian men in an effort to turn themselves into Indians . . . and thereby into true Americans.[76]

Popular media played an important role in spreading the word about the reinvigoration of American manhood. In the modern western novel beginning with *The Virginian* in 1902, for instance, strong, silent men performed heroic acts in the face of overwhelming odds and bloodthirsty foes. In the words of Amy Kaplan, *The Virginian* marked

> the return to an original virile past . . . reopen[ed] the closed frontier and reinvent[ed] the West as a space for fictional representation. . . . There the homeless and nameless Virginian embodie[d] the national essence in his muscular beauty and animal prowess. He defeats a [native] rebellion in a staged theatrical performance before an Eastern audience of travelers, and his physical vigor is composed in the narrator's feminized gaze.[77]

Representations of the Indian as a mirror in which hegemonic masculinity could gaze at itself also were reflected in western landscapes seen off the written page, in theatrical reenactments of the winning of the West. L. G. Moses notes that before the late 1800s "most people who dreamed about the West and longed after excitement and diversion from mundaneness had few places to look except to the printed page—until, that is, the appearance of the Wild West shows."[78] In these touring melodramas and outdoor pageants, men with little patience or ability for reading could find visual images of tough American men overpowering and defeating savage native threats to frontier homes, hearths, and womenfolk: On a May afternoon in 1883,

Colonel William Frederick Cody, better known as "Buffalo Bill," led a group
of Pawnees and locally recruited "cowboys" into the arena at the Omaha,
Nebraska, fairgrounds. The show began, in the words of a Hartford *Courant*
journalist,

> with a pony bare-back riding race between Indians and went on to a climax
> with a grand realistic battle scene depicting the capture, torture, and death
> of a scout by savages; [followed by] the revenge, recapture of the dead body
> and a victory of the government scouts.[79]

Thus, the pageantry of American triumphalism was restaged as a road
show, a traveling circus of Americana playing to different crowds in different venues at different times around the country. And the shows go on. The
Indian wars have continued to provide the props, costumes, and scripts for
whites to play Indians and thus be and become Americans, not only in re-
vivals of the old Wild West shows, but in a variety of settings, past and present: in children's informal play as "cowboys and Indians," on athletic fields
in wars involving teams such as the Cleveland Indians and the Washington
Redskins or the William and Mary Indian Tribe and the Southeastern Oklahoma State University Savages, in films such as John Ford's *The Searchers*
or Kevin Costner's *Dances with Wolves,* and in children's and youth organizations such as the Boy Scouts and the Young Men's and Women's Christian Associations' (YMCA and YWCA) "Indian Guides" and "Indian
Princesses." In these spectacles of nationalism audiences can relive America's
past and dream about the next American century.

The Indian wars are not over. Nor has the boundary disappeared between the Indians and non-Indians who populate the Americas of past and
present. Romanticized, sexualized natives still inhabit the imaginations of
Americans and continue to haunt Americans' images of themselves. Indians
can be found in the same social texts and contexts in which they were captured in the eighteenth and nineteenth centuries, not only on athletic fields
or in romantic and adventure fiction, but in anthropology and history . . .
and sociology, in photography, television, and film, in national parks and
monuments, in the contemporary men's movement, in countless commercial and cultural spaces such as coffeetable picture books, print and visual ad-
vertisements, coins, art, music, holiday pageants and celebrations, and in
clubs, websites, societies, and organizations symbolically and institutionally
designed to constitute and enact America and Americanness.

I invite readers to take a walk down the book aisle in any American dis-
count store, supermarket, or bookstore and to look at the covers of romance
novels. There you will find "the Indian" memorialized in depictions of long-
haired, bare-chested muscular dark and handsome men with lovely, lithe-

some white women swooning in their arms. Plate 3 of the color insert shows one incarnation of this enduring image that appeared on the front cover of *Royal Savage* by Selwyn Anne Grames.[80] A further stroll down the aisle leads to the "true story" adventure novels with their powerful, Indianized white (or "half-breed") men confronting the feminized forces of repression and threats to their rugged individualism, manly autonomy, and inalienable right to freedom: the *Rambos* and *Billy Jacks* of contemporary American adventure fiction and film. In both women's romance and men's adventure fiction, the prominence of sexualized, gendered native images embracing the bodies of white women and worn on the faces of white men, show us that the Indian-white ethnosexual frontier remains an open chapter in the ongoing saga of American culture and identity.

CONCLUSION

This chapter has examined the links between sex and conquest, the role of sexuality in the construction of an enduring ethnic boundary between Indians and non-Indians, and how the sexualization of indigenous peoples has shaped the views of Americans and served the interests of colonial and American governments. The American settling of the U.S. West was not only an epic of competitive positioning by colonial powers, conflicts with indigenous peoples, and spreading settler populations across the continent. The "conquest of the West" involved a series of sexualized encounters between Europeans and Indians that reflected a confrontation of sexualities and sexual systems. This clash of sexualities was an important feature in the development of ideologies that defined each group and the construction of ethnic boundaries that divided them. Definitions of sexual morality distinguished "civilized" Europeans and Americans on the one hand from "savage" Indians on the other.

European colonizers and settlers of the New World had both a practical and prurient interest in the native population—as slaves, guides, emissaries, and sexual partners. Euro-American exploitation of the New World's land and inhabitants was a hallmark of the conquest of the Americas. The settlers who followed in the wake of the early adventurers saw the new land and its peoples through the same set of lenses, and they were driven to satisfy the same kinds of desires. The New World was an exotic and erotic landscape, an imaginary land of milk and honey that lingered in the minds of Europeans throughout the period of colonial settlement and into the era of sovereign state formation on both American continents.

In the United States the vision of America as a place to be colonized and conquered became a central theme in national self-imagining and nation building. The early European explorers' image of themselves as morally superior, benevolent, and called upon to civilize as well as consume the New World was inscribed on the American national identity and institutionalized in the American national state. America's expansionist moral mission grew from the seeds planted at the point of European contact, blossomed into late-nineteenth and early-twentieth-century U.S. imperial control of both continents and regions of the Pacific, and matured into an established perennial American power that has thrived in and dominated the global environment. As the United States has matured from a commercial and political upstart into a mature mercantile and military power, the image of "the Indian" endures as a signifier both of American conquest and the indomitable American spirit.

In the next chapter we will explore the intersection of ethnicity and sexuality in another episode in American history, one that parallels in time the story of sex and conquest chronicled here, but it is a story that is retold as shameful rather than triumphant. Chapter 4 focuses on the sexual dimensions of the black-white color line in America. In that chapter we will reexamine through a sexual lens the enslavement of millions of Africans in the United States from colonial times until the end of slavery in 1865; we will document the role of sexuality in definitions of blackness and whiteness; and we will see how sexuality has contributed to the maintenance of the most durable, violent, and enforced ethnic boundary in America.

NOTES

1. Christopher Columbus, *The* Diario *of Christopher Columbus's First Voyage to America, 1492–1493,* abstracted [and reconstructed] by Fray Bartolome de las Casas, transcribed and translated into English, with notes and a concordance of the Spanish by Oliver Dunn and James E. Kelley Jr. (Norman: University of Oklahoma Press, 1989), 67–69.

2. Ibid., 137.

3. Ibid., 255.

4. Ibid., 219.

5. Robert F. Berkhofer Jr., *The White Man's Indian: Images of the American Indian from Columbus to the Present* (New York: Alfred A. Knopf, 1978), 8–9; see also Amerigo Vespucci, *Mundus Novus, Letter to Lorenzo Pietro di Medici,* translated by George T. Northrup (Princeton: Princeton University Press, 1916).

6. For a detailed interpretation and contextualization of this image and the artists who were involved in its production, see Jose Rabasa, *Inventing America: Spanish Historiography and the Formation of Eurocentrism* (Norman: University of Oklahoma Press, 1993), especially chapter 1.

7. Columbus, *The* Diario *of Christopher Columbus's First Voyage to America,* 225, 233.

8. Berkhofer, *The White Man's Indian*, 9.

9. Ibid.

10. Columbus, *The* Diario *of Christopher Columbus's First Voyage to America*, 255–57.

11. Ibid.

12. Berkhofer, *The White Man's Indian*, 9–10.

13. See Stodola Derounian-Stodola, Kathryn Zabelle, and James A. Levernier, *The Indian Captivity Narrative, 1550–1900* (New York: Twayne, 1993); Berkhofer, *The White Man's Indian*; Kathleen M. Brown, *Good Wives, Nasty Wenches, and Anxious Patriarchs: Gender, Race, and Power in Colonial Virginia* (Chapel Hill: Published for the Institute of Early American History and Culture by the University of North Carolina Press, 1997) and "Brave New Worlds: Women's and Gender History," *William and Mary Quarterly* 50 (1993): 311–28.

14. Ramon Gutierrez, *When Jesus Came, the Corn Mothers Went Away: Marriage, Sexuality, and Power in New Mexico, 1500–1846* (Stanford: Stanford University Press, 1991); the existence and nature of mainly male, cross-dressing "berdaches" is reported in a number of American Indian communities from earliest contact to the twentieth century; see Sue-Ellen Jacobs, Wesley Thomas, and Sabine Lang (eds.), *Two-Spirit People: Native American Gender Identity, Sexuality, and Spirituality* (Urbana: University of Illinois Press, 1997); Walter L. Williams, *The Spirit and the Flesh: Sexual Diversity in American Indian Culture* (Boston: Beacon Press, 1986); Will Roscoe, *The Zuni Man-Woman* (Albuquerque: University of New Mexico Press, 1991); Herdt, ed., *Third Sex, Third Gender*; this is a controversial topic among scholars, and it is difficult to judge the quality and veracity of the research separate from the agendas and sexual identity politics of various supporters and critics; Gutierrez's work, in particular, has generated a great deal of debate; see the special section of *American Indian Culture and Research Journal* 17 (1993): 141ff devoted to critiquing *When Jesus Came, the Corn Mothers Went Away*.

15. Gutierrez, *When Jesus Came, the Corn Mothers Went Away*, 72–73.

16. Ibid., 125.

17. Numbers of Americans of mixed Indian/non-Indian ancestry continue to increase today, partly due to high rates of native/nonnative intermarriage in the United States; for a discussion of American Indian patterns of intermarriage and population trends; see U.S. Office of Technology Assessment, *Indian Health Care* (Washington, DC: Government Printing Office, 1986); Gary D. Sandefur and Trudy McKinnell, "American Indian Intermarriage," *Social Science Research* 15 (1986): 347–71; Snipp, *American Indians*; Karl Eschbach, "The Enduring and Vanishing American Indian: American Indian Population Growth and Intermarriage in 1990," *Ethnic and Racial Studies* 18 (1995): 89–108.

18. Frank Bergon, *The Journals of Lewis and Clark* (New York: Penguin Books, 1989), 324.

19. Ibid., 334.

20. James Ronda, *Lewis and Clark among the Indians* (Lincoln: University of Nebraska Press, 1984), 64; see also Henry M Brackenridge, *Views of Louisiana, Together with a Journal of a Voyage up the Missouri River, in 1811* (Pittsburgh: Cramer, Speer and Eichbaum, 1814).

21. Ronda, *Lewis and Clark among the Indians*, 64.

22. Ibid., 63; see also Kirsten Fischer, *Suspect Relations: Sex, Race, and Resistance in Colonial North Carolina* (Ithaca: Cornell University Press, 2002), especially chapter 2.

23. Albert Hurtado, "When Strangers Met: Sex and Gender on Three Frontiers," in *Writing the Range: Race, Class, and Culture in the Women's West*, ed. Elizabeth Jameson and Susan Armitage (Norman: University of Oklahoma Press, 1997), 122–42; see also Sylvia Van Kirk, "The Role of Native Women in the Creation of Fur Trade Society in Western Canada, 1670–1830," in *The Women's West*, ed. Susan Armitage and Elizabeth Jameson (Norman: University of Oklahoma Press, 1987), 53–62; Patricia Limerick, *The Legacy of Conquest: The Unbroken Past of the American West* (New York: W.W. Norton & Company, 1987), 50ff; Anne M. Butler, *Daughters of Joy, Sisters of Misery: Prostitutes in the American West, 1865–90* (Urbana: University of Illinois Press, 1987), 9ff.

24. Ronda, *Lewis and Clark among the Indians*, 256.

25. Rebecca Blevins Faery, *Cartographies of Desire: Captivity, Race, and Sex in the Shaping of an American Nation* (Norman: University of Oklahoma Press, 1999).

26. Brown, *Good Wives, Nasty Wenches, and Anxious Patriarchs*, 67.

27. Ibid.

28. Sherry L. Smith, *The View from Officers' Row: Army Perceptions of Western Indians* (Tucson: University of Arizona Press, 1990); Butler, *Daughters of Joy, Sisters of Misery*.

29. Theda Perdue, "Native Women in the Early Republic: Old World Perceptions, New World Realities," in *Native Americans and the Early Republic*, ed. Frederick E. Hoxie, Ronald Hoffman, and Peter J. Albert (Charlottesville: University Press of Virginia, 1999), 96–97.

30. Hurtado, "When Strangers Met," 135.

31. For one of the most complete sets of Indian captivity narratives, see *Garland Library of Narratives of North American Indian Captivities*, vols. 1–111 (New York: Garland Publications, 1977).

32. Richard van der Beets, *Held Captive by Indians: Selected Narratives, 1642–1836* (Knoxville: University of Tennessee Press, 1974); Richard Slotkin, *Regeneration through Violence: The Mythology of the American Frontier, 1600–1860* (Middletown, CT: Wesleyan University Press, 1973).

33. Faery, *Cartographies of Desire*, 15; Roy Harvey Pearce, "The Significance of the Captivity Narrative," *American Literature* 19 (1947): 1–20.

34. Especially since film versions are currently available on videotape and DVD; Renee Berland examines the imagined relationships between white women and native men in two novels, *The Last of the Mohicans* and Lydia Marie Child's *Hobomok*; she argues that Childs's tale of an eroticized, romantic encounter between a young Wampanoag man and Mary Conant, a young woman settler, depicts white women as active agents, whereas Cooper's women, Alice and Cora Munro, are more passive and more victimized when they become romantically involved with and are assaulted by native men:

> By the end of the book [*The Last of the Mohicans*] Cora is actually dead, and described as the ghostly bride of an Indian, "transplanted . . . to a place where she would find congenial spirits, and be forever happy." Alice is invisible, borne away within a litter "when low

and stifled sobs alone announced [her] presence." *Hobomok,* on the other hand, allows Mary Conant to transcend her spectrality, and leave behind her angelic purity. She marries Hobomok and gives birth to a son. Later, she divorces him, keeping custody of their child and retaining her own wealth. Her own possession of her body is affirmed when she goes on to marry again.

In both novels, native men simultaneously are sources of white fear and objects of white desire, and in both novels the women pay with their lives (at least once) for acting on their ethnosexual desires; Renee L. Berland, *The National Uncanny: Indian Ghosts and American Subjects* (Hanover: Dartmouth College, 2000), 65. Christopher Castiglia contrasts "typical" popular captivity narratives marked by "savage Indian tormentors and women captives who rely for rescue on [white] masculine financial or military agency," with more nontraditional forms in which

> narrative patterns question the structures the stories elsewhere support, signaling discursive conflicts *within* white culture . . . [where] the captive either fights the Indians in order to avoid capture, or, once captured, uses her own strengths to escape . . . [or where captives] either refuse to return to Anglo-American culture or make clear that their lives among the Indians were no worse than among whites. (Christopher Castiglia, *Bound and Determined: Captivity, Culture-Crossing, and White Womanhood from Mary Rowlandson to Patty Hearst* [Chicago: University of Chicago Press, 1996], 25).

35. Derounian-Stodola and Levernier, *The Indian Captivity Narrative,* 66.

36. Ibid.

37. See James F. Brooks, " 'This Evil Extends Especially to the Feminine Sex': Captivity and Identity in New Mexico, 1700–1846," in *Writing the Range,* 107; June Namias, *White Captives: Gender and Ethnicity on the American Frontier* (Chapel Hill: University of North Carolina, 1993); Derounian-Stodola and Levernier, *The Indian Captivity Narrative,* 73–85.

38. Frances Roe Kestler, *The Indian Captivity Narrative: A Woman's View* (New York: Garland Publishing Company, 1990), 423.

39. Faery, *Cartographies of Desire.*

40. Berkhofer, *The White Man's Indian,* 28.

41. Namias, *White Captives,* 109; see also Gary L. Ebersole, *Captured by Texts: Puritan to Postmodern Images of Indian Captivity* (Charlottesville: University Press of Virginia, 1995).

42. The next two sections of this chapter are based on collaborative work with David Anthony Tyeeme Clark; I wish to thank Tony for introducing me to recent feminist scholarship on the U.S. West and for sharing with me his creative and adventurous work recovering native voices and challenging conventional views of "the Indian" in scholarship and in the American imagination; see David Anthony Tyeeme Clark and Joane Nagel, "White Men, Red Masks: Appropriations of 'Indian' Manhood in Imagined Wests," in *Across the Great Divide: Cultures of Manhood in the American West,* ed. Matthew L. Basso, Dee Garceau, and Laura McCall (New York: Routledge, 2000), 109–30.

43. Smith, *The View from Officers' Row,* 18.

44. Ibid., see also Shirley A. Leckie, *Elizabeth Bacon Custer and the Making of a Myth* (Norman: University of Oklahoma Press, 1993).

45. See Russell Thornton, *American Indian Holocaust and Survival* (Norman: University of Oklahoma Press, 1987).

46. Smith, *The View from Officers' Row,* 148.

47. Ibid., 68.

48. Ibid.

49. Ann Marie Plane, *Colonial Intimacies: Indian Marriage in Early New England* (Ithaca: Cornell University Press, 2000), 37.

50. Ibid., 70.

51. John D'Emilio and Estelle B. Freedman, *Intimate Matters: A History of Sexuality in America* (New York: Harper and Row, 1988), 88.

52. Quoted by David D. Smits, " 'Squaw Men,' 'Half-Breeds,' and Amalgamators: Late Nineteenth-Century Anglo-American Attitudes toward Indian-White Race-Mixing," *American Indian Culture and Research Journal* 15 (1991): 29–61, 39; see Richard Irving Dodge, *Our Wild Indians: Thirty-three Years Personal Experience among the Red Men of the Great West* (New York: Archer House, Inc., [1883] 1959).

53. Smits, " 'Squaw Men,' 'Half-Breeds,' and Amalgamators," 45.

54. Ibid., 43.

55. James Coser, "The Alien as a Servant of Power," *American Sociological Review* 37 (1972): 574–81; for a discussion of the role of mixed ancestry individuals in Indian-white relations, see William E. Unrau, *Mixed-Bloods and Tribal Dissolution: Charles Curtis and the Quest for Indian Identity* (Lawrence: University Press of Kansas, 1989).

56. For a discussion of religious schools' efforts to inculcate "proper" sexual and gender demeanor, see Theda Perdue, *Cherokee Women: Gender and Cultural Change, 1700–1835* (Lincoln: University of Nebraska Press, 1998).

57. Philip Joseph Deloria, *Playing Indian.* (New Haven: Yale University Press, 1999).

58. See Mark C. Carnes, *Secret Ritual and Manhood in Victorian America* (New Haven: Yale University Press, 1989).

59. The notion of "the Indian" is borrowed from the work of Gerald Vizenor, in particular, *Fugitive Poses: Native American Indian Scenes of Absence and Presence* (Lincoln: University of Nebraska Press, 1998).

60. See Jeffrey P. Hantover, "The Boy Scouts and the Validation of Masculinity," in *Men's Lives*, 74–81.

61. For a discussion of Indian sports mascots, see C. Richard King and Charles F. Springwood, *Team Spirits: The Native American Mascot Controversy* (Lincoln: University of Nebraska Press, 2001) and "Fighting Spirits: The Racial Politics of Sports Mascots," *Journal of Sport and Social Issues* 24 (2000): 282–304.

62. This concern over declining masculinity was shared by Europeans. Lieutenant-General Robert Baden-Powell, founder of the Boy Scout Movement in England and author of *Scouting for Boys*, published in 1908, saw scouting as a way to bolster weakening English manhood; see Robert H. MacDonald, *Sons of the Empire: The Frontier and the Boy Scout Movement, 1890–1918* (Toronto: University of Toronto Press, 1993), 18; see also Alan Trachtenberg, *The Incorporation of America: Culture and Society in the Guilded Age* (New York: Hill and Wang, 1982); Michael S. Kimmel, *Manhood in America* (New York: The Free Press, 1996); Joe L. Dubbert, "Progressivism and the Masculinity Crisis," in *The American Man*, ed. Elizabeth H. Pleck and Joseph H. Pleck (Englewood Cliffs, NJ: Prentice-Hall, 1980); Peter G. Filene, *Him/Her/Self: Sex Roles in Modern America* (Baltimore: Johns Hopkins University Press, 1986), 69–93; E. An-

thony Rotundo, *American Manhood: Transformations in Masculinity from the Revolution to the Modern Era* (New York: Basic Books, 1993), 185–93.

63. Nina Silber, *The Romance of Reunion: Northerners and the South, 1986–1900* (Chapel Hill: University of North Carolina Press, 1993).

64. For instance, Jeffrey Hantover argues that in the growing white middle class,

> the professionalization and sanctification of motherhood, the smaller family size, the decline in the number of servants who could serve as buffers between mother and son, and the absence of busy fathers from the home made the mother-son relationship appear threatening to proper masculine socialization. ("The Boy Scouts and the Validation of Masculinity," 75)

65. See Gail Bederman, *Manliness and Civilization: A Cultural History of Gender and Race in the United States, 1880–1917* (Chicago: University of Chicago Press, 1995); John Higham, "The Reorientation of American Culture in the 1890s," in his *Writing American History: Essays on Modern Scholarship* (Bloomington: Indiana University Press, 1978), 78–102; James R. McGovern, "David Graham Phillips and the Virility Impulse of the Progressives," *New England Quarterly* 39 (1966): 334–55.

66. Frederick Jackson Turner, "The Significance of the Frontier in American History," *Annual Report of the American Historical Association for the Year 1893* (Washington, DC: U.S. Government Printing Office, 1894).

67. See Sara J. Blackstone, *Buckskins, Bullets, and Business: A History of Buffalo Bill's Wild West* (New York: Greenwood Press, 1986); Raymond William Stedman, *Shadows of the Indian: Stereotypes in American Culture* (Norman: University of Oklahoma Press, 1982); Berkhofer, *The White Man's Indian*.

68. For an account of the so-called Indian wars as a defensive struggle, see Ward Churchill, "The 'Trial' of Leonard Peltier," preface to Jim Messerscmidt, *The Trial of Leonard Peltier* (Boston: South End Press, 1983).

69. Such images have been seen in Hollywood productions since the earliest days of cinema; for discussions of depictions of the Indian in American popular film, see Peter C. Rollins and John E. O'Connor, eds., *Hollywood's Indian: The Portrayal of the Native American in Film* (Lexington: University Press of Kentucky, 1998); Donald L. Kaufman, "The Indian as Media Hand-Me-Down," in *The Pretend Indians: Images of Native Americans in the Movies*, ed. Gretchen M. Bataille and Charles L.P. Silet (Ames: Iowa State University Press, 1980), 22–34; Alison Griffiths, "Science and Spectacle: Native American Representation in Early Cinema," in *Dressing in Feathers: The Construction of the Indian in American Popular Culture*, ed. S. Elizabeth Bird (Boulder: Westview Press, 1996), 79–95.

70. For an account of the massacre of approximately two-hundred native people, mainly women and children, by the U.S. Seventh Calvary on the Pine Ridge reservation at Wounded Knee, South Dakota in 1890, see Robert Utley, *The Last Days of the Sioux Nation* (New Haven: Yale University Press, 1963); Renee Sampson Flood, *Lost Bird of Wounded Knee: Spirit of the Lakota* (New York: Scribner's, 1995); for an account the murder of Sitting Bull by Indian police and agency personnel on the Standing Rock reservation in South Dakota in 1891, see the letter written by James McLaughlin, Indian Agent at Standing Rock Reservation written on January 19, 1891, to the Indian Rights Association (http://www.pbs.org/weta/thewest/resources/archives/eight/sbarrest.htm).

71. Theodore Roosevelt, *The Winning of the West: From the Alleghenies to the Mississippi, 1769–1776*, volume 1 (Lincoln: University of Nebraska Press, [1894] 1995), 94.

72. Ibid., 95. As Gail Bederman notes, in his writings and speeches Roosevelt "repeatedly contrasts the virile manliness of the Americans to the brutal unmanliness of the Indians . . . the virile white man is both like the Indians and superior to them"; see *Manliness and Civilization*, 181–82.

73. Roosevelt, *The Winning of the West*, 110.

74. Hurtado, *Intimate Frontiers;* Richard Godbeer "Eroticizing the Middle Ground: Anglo-Indian Sexual Relations along the Eighteenth-Century Frontier," in *Sex, Love, Race: Crossing Boundaries in North American History*, ed. Martha Hodes (New York: New York University Press, 1999), 91–111; Jennifer M. Spear, " 'They Need Wives': Metissage and the Regulation of Sexuality in French Louisiana, 1699–1730," in *Sex, Love, Race*, 25–59; Gutierrez, *When Jesus Came, the Corn Mothers Went Away*.

75. Francis Paul Prucha, *The Great Father*, volume 1 (Lincoln: University of Nebraska Press, 1984), 548; another positive assessment of native men is more telling about the usefulness of the Indian, not as a weak, but as a strong adversary; it was a statement about Indian men made by Crook's contemporary, General Nelson A. Miles:

> The art of war among the white race is called strategy or tactics; when it is practised by the Indians, it is called treachery. They employed the art of deceiving, misleading, decoying, and surprising the enemy with great cleverness. The celerity and secrecy of their movements were never excelled by the warriors of any country. They had courage, skill, sagacity, endurance, fortitude, and self-sacrifice of a high order. (ibid)

See also Nelson A. Miles, *Serving the Republic: Memoirs of the Civil and Military Life of Nelson A. Miles* (New York: Harper and Brothers, 1911).

76. See Jean Baudrillard, *Simulacra and Simulation* (Ann Arbor: University of Michigan Press, 1994); in their self-reconstruction endeavors, Americans could find needed "facts" about Indians and Indian manhood in dime novels and in accounts written by army officers, captives, and other "experts"; for a discussion of white "Indian" organizations such as the Improved Order of Red Men, see Carnes, *Secret Ritual and Manhood in Victorian America*.

77. Amy Kaplan, "Romancing the Empire: The Embodiment of American Masculinity in the Popular Historical Novels of the 1890s," *American Literary History* 2 (1990): 659–90, 683.

78. L. G. Moses, *Wild West Shows and the Images of American Indians, 1883–1933* (Albuquerque: University of New Mexico Press, 1996), 4.

79. *Hartford Courant* journalist was quoted in Henry Blackman Sell and Victor Weybright, *Buffalo Bill and the Wild West* (Basin, WY: Big Horn Books, 1979), 135; see also Moses, *Wild West Shows and the Images of American Indians*, 1; Buffalo Bill Cody used actual native people (sometimes "on loan" from the U.S. Department of the Interior) in his Wild West shows; see Blackstone, *Buckskins, Bullets, and Business*, 26, 33.

80. The text on back cover of the book speaks even louder than the image on the cover: "To his own people, he was a traitor with a red man's body and a white man's soul. To the British aristocrats, he was a noble savage who dared to live—and love—as one of their own. To society's beauties, he was an exotic experience, a prize to be won"; Selwyn Anne Grames, *Royal Savage* (New York: Dell, 1980).

CHAPTER 4

SEX AND RACE
The Color of Sex in America

THE HEART AND DARKNESS: SEX AND RACE IN THE PORNO-TROPICS

The opinions and judgments voiced by Christopher Columbus and Amerigo Vespucci about the sexuality and savagery of the indigenous peoples of the Americas were not utterances out of context. Europeans transported with them beliefs about native and tribal peoples as they voyaged from the Old World to the New. Old World "primitives" included groups in the Europeans' own backyard such as the Irish, the Sicilians, and the Samis.[1] No territory, however, was more likely to be seen as barren of civilization and empty of civilized peoples than the "Dark Continent" of Africa.[2] Europeans' casual musings about exploiting and enslaving indigenous Americans were not new notions for the New World. When Columbus boarded the *Santa Maria* and set sail west, the Europeans he left behind had been exploiting and enslaving Africans for at least a century, and much longer if the Greeks and Romans are taken into account, since both of these European-based empires were built on the backs of slave labor and stolen land.[3]

In Europeans' images of Africa and America, both sex and race mattered.[4] Anne McClintock argues that European explorations and colonial exploitations were supported by an ideological apparatus that linked gender, race, and sexuality. Europeans viewed the new peoples they met as racialized, sexually exotic Others:

> For centuries, the uncertain continents—Africa, the Americas, Asia—were figured in European lore as libidinously eroticized. Travelers' tales abounded with versions of the monstrous sexuality of far-off lands, where, as legend had it, men sported gigantic penises and women consorted with apes, feminized men's breasts flowed with milk, and militarized women lopped theirs

91

Europe supported by Africa & America.

London, Published Dec.r 1.st 1792. by J. Johnson, S.t Pauls Church Yard.

FIGURE 4.1 "Europe Supported By Africa and America," William Blake, 1796[5] (courtesy of the United States Library of Congress)

off. Africa and the Americas had become what can be called a *porno-tropics* [emphasis mine] for the European imagination—a fantastic magic lantern of the mind onto which Europe projected its forbidden sexual desires and fears.[6]

Winthrop Jordan traces early writings of racialized hypersexuality in the African porno-tropics to long held and widely circulated theories about the connection between temperature and intemperance:

> In a highly eclectic work first published in 1566, Jean Bodin sifted the writings of ancient authorities and concluded that heat and lust went hand in hand and that "in Ethiopia . . . the race of men is very keen and lustful." Bodin announced in a thoroughly characteristic sentence, "Ptolemy reported that on account of southern sensuality, Venus chiefly is worshipped in Africa and that the constellation of scorpion, which pertains to the pudenda, dominates that continent."[7]

According to Jordan, the European fascination with African sexuality arose in their earliest encounters: "Englishmen . . . fastened upon Negroes a pronounced sexuality virtually upon first sight."[8] Indeed, early in the seventeenth century, William Shakespeare referred to Othello's embraces as "the gross clasps of a lascivious Moor." In fact, Europeans' descriptions of Africans are nearly identical to Columbus's and Vespucci's descriptions of indigenous Americans:

> They are beastly in their living . . . for they have men in women's apparel, whom they keep among their wives . . . they are very greedie eaters, and no lesse drinkers, and very lecherous, and theevish, and much addicted to uncleanenesse: one man hath as many wives as hee is able to keepe and maintaine.[9]

The view of Africa as a site of sensuality continued to engage the European imagination into the seventeenth century as reflected in Francis Bacon's *New Atlantis,* published around 1624. Bacon described a hermit who " 'desired to see the Spirit of Fornication; and there appeared to him a little foul ugly Aethiop.' "[10] The European (and later American) fixation on African male genitalia also reveals itself in these early writings. For instance, Richard Jobson, whom Jordan describes as "a sympathetic observer" of African societies, wrote in 1623 that Mandingo men were "furnisht with such members as are after a sort of burthensome unto them."[11] The anonymous author of *The Golden Coast,* published in 1665, was equally impressed by black men's sexuality and described African men as "very lustful and impudent, especially, when they come to hide their nakedness, (for a *Negroes* hiding his Members, their extraordinary greatness) is a token of their Lust, and therefore much troubled with the Pox."[12] Both Jordan and McClintock quote John Ogilby, who published an adaptation of the travel writings of Olfert Dapper in 1670, and "rather more tactfully informed his readers that west Africans were distinguished by 'large propagators.' "[13]

An interesting counterpoint to this interminable catalog of European prurient fixations and sanctimonious moralism is provided in the autobiography of Olandah Equiano published in 1789. Although there is some scholarly debate about the exact details of his origins, Equiano's memoir situates his birth at around 1745 in West Africa where he describes his capture and enslavement at the age of eleven.[14] During the next four decades, Equiano lived and worked on land and at sea making many voyages to North Amer-

FIGURE 4.2   Olaudah Equiano, 1789 (courtesy of the Kenneth Spencer Research Library, University of Kansas)

ica, the Caribbean, Africa, and Europe. In 1766 he purchased his freedom, worked as a barber and as a sailor, and married an English woman with whom he had two daughters. When he died in 1797, he left his estate to his family with a provision to establish schools in Sierra Leone in West Africa. Equiano's story ends far more happily than do the grim sagas of the millions of other Africans and their descendants who were enslaved by Europeans and Americans. Because of Equiano's success and the subsequent publication of his autobiography, we have an account in which the appraising gaze of Europeans is reversed. In the pages of Equiano's memoir we can read the observations of an African "discovering" Europe and America, and describing his explorations and encounters with the natives. Phillip Morgan's summary of Equiano's reactions to what he saw after being kidnapped provides us some insight into at least one African's assessment of European "civilization."

> In 1756 a confused and frightened Ibo boy . . . kidnapped in the eastern part of the present Benin province and conveyed to the Bight of Biafra coast [of present-day Nigeria], caught his first glimpse of white men. They were British slavers, but the boy knew them only as "white men with horrible looks, red faces, and loose hair." He fainted at the sight. Fearing them as cannibals, the boy grew more anxious as he witnessed their "savage" manner and their "brutal cruelty". . . . [Over the next years] he found much to inspire his wonder. How was it that the British ate with unwashed hands, how could they touch their dead, why were the women so slender and so much less modest than African women?[15]

Equiano's narrative testified to whites' cruelty not only to Africans, but to their own kind: "One white man in particular I saw . . . flogged so unmercifully with a large rope near the foremast, that he died in the consequence of it; and they tossed him over the side as they would have done a brute."[16] The cruelty noted with the most outraged irony by Equiano was whites' treatment of enslaved African women:

> [I]t was almost a constant practice with our clerks, and other whites, to commit violent depredations on the chastity of the female slaves. . . . I have known our mates to commit these acts most shamefully, to the disgrace, not of Christians only, but of men. I have even known them to gratify their brutal passion with females not ten years old. . . . And yet in Monserrat I have a seen a Negro man staked to the ground, and cut most shockingly, and then his ears cut off bit by bit, because he had been connected with a white woman who was a common prostitute; as if it were no crime in the whites to rob an innocent African girl of her virtue, but most heinous in a black man only to gratify a passion of nature, where the temptation was offered by one of a different color, though the most abandoned woman of her species.[17]

This and other Africans' challenges to the Europeans' self-proclaimed superiority in manners and morals were scarcely audible above the strident

din of much more prolific and widely publicized European defamations of
Africans.[18] As we have heard, the European voice was especially loud and
lewd in matters of African sexuality. McClintock reports that a special place
was reserved for African women in the European lexicon of hypersexuality:

> Within this porno-tropic tradition, women figured as the epitome of sexual
> aberration and excess. Folklore saw them, even more than the men, as given
> to a lascivious venery so promiscuous as to border on the bestial. [Around
> 1677] Sir Thomas Herbert observed of Africans, "the resemblance they bear
> with Baboons, which I could observe kept frequent company with the
> Women."[19]

There were, of course, good reasons for these fantasies of African feminine sexual exoticism and masculine sexual excess. The most obvious, of
course, was to justify the Europeans' brutal treatment of both African women
and men, especially their sexual violations of African women. The emphasis
on African sexuality and savagery in the reports of almost exclusively male
Christian European travelers and explorers contributed to a growing and ingrained sexual ethnocentrism among Europeans. Besides serving to develop
a sense of European cultural and technological superiority and to excuse atrocities, there were also clear material motives for depicting Africans as sexually savage and promiscuous. These motives were linked to colonialism and
the slave trade.

It turned out to be easier for Europeans to justify seizing the lands of
savages and enslaving them than it would be to mistreat and violate the rights
of peoples whom Europeans considered their moral equals. Consistent assertions of African savagery rendered them barely human in the European
racial cosmology, and thus in possession of none of the rights reserved for
civilized Christians. And it further turned out to be quite lucrative for the
mercantilistic Europeans to market and sell savages, especially oversexed savages who would "breed" and produce more slaves, and most especially oversexed *female* savages who would hold special salacious appeal to those Christian men who bought and used them. Lurid images of African sexuality served
well the interests of those selling black women to white men. Slavers appealed to their potential customers by portraying African women as willing,
even enthusiastic sexual partners who found white men especially attractive,
and who were

> "hot constitution'd Ladies" possessed of "a temper hot and lascivious, mak-
> ing no scruple to prostitute themselves to the *Europeans* for a very slender
> profit, so great is their inclination to white men". . . . If they can come to
> the Place the Man sleeps in, they lay themselves softly down by him, soon
> wake him, and use all their little Arts to move the Darling Passion.'[20]

Claims (and concerns) about the physical sexual endowments of black men and the sexual appetites of black women circulated back and forth across the Atlantic in the minds and publications of Europeans who settled the Americas. From the early 1500s when the first Africans arrived on the continent as indentured servants (who could theoretically, at least, purchase their freedom), and later into the seventeenth century when these involuntary immigrants were formally enslaved,[21] assertions of African sexual excesses became a foundational component of the black-white racial boundary. Hypersexualized depictions of Africans comprised multiple entries into the cultural ledger of American racialized sexual imaginings, fears, and desires. This long historical record has a familiar contemporary ring. The words of these early Europeans provide us with a revealing and disturbing rhetorical archaeology of the sexual roots of present-day U.S. racist and white supremacist thought and discourse.[22]

The sexual stereotyping of Africans is no doubt more familiar to readers of this book than was the hypersexualized rendering of indigenous Americans described in the last chapter. There are clear parallels, however, in the content and logic of depicting Africans as sexually lascivious and portraying American Indians as inclined toward sexual debauchery. Sexualized images of native peoples in the Americas served to legitimize aggressive colonial and U.S. policies and practices, and to dismiss or at least excuse white sexual predations against native women. Similar characterizations of Africans as oversexed, immoral, and uncivilized served to defend slavery and to camouflage its associated excesses. In particular, the sexual slander of Africans directed attention away from the true scandal of whites' savage sexual treatment of blacks (castration, breeding programs, rape, sexual servitude).

The black-white color line in the United States today constitutes an ethnosexual frontier whose historical roots stretch back to the colonial era. To uncover the sexual foundations of this enduring racial boundary requires spending some time in the uncomfortable historical destination arrived at via the Middle Passage through the Atlantic world. These are the sexual spaces in the slavery system that have been swept aside in American history and everyday consciousness as simply unpleasant and unfortunate. The sexual side of slavery has been ignored in much traditional scholarship as a relatively unimportant aspect of a terrible chapter in U.S. history. Set against the profit motives of slavery, sexual motives might seem only secondary, almost incidental features of that system's political economy of human exploitation. In the next sections of this chapter we will challenge those assumptions by directly confronting sex and slavery and examining how what occurred in that ethnosexual space helped to shape America's estranged yet intimate relationship with race.

SEX AND SLAVERY

Although African sexuality was used by Americans as a rationale for establishing a heavily regulated ethnic boundary separating blacks and whites, it was an ethnosexual frontier that many whites found irresistible. Nowhere was the black-white color line more brutally violated and constantly crossed than during the centuries of American slavery. Abolitionists documented the sexual mistreatment and torture of slaves as part of their campaign to bring an end to what they saw as the cruel and degrading treatment of blacks, but also to stop practices and arrangements that they viewed as corrupting and debasing to whites. The earliest U.S. enunciators of the evils of slavery pointed out the moral cost of slavery to whites. Winthrop Jordan reports, for instance, that in 1762 Quaker theologian John Woolman "linked the Negro's outward condition with the white man's inner corruption; wrongful enslavement of Negroes, he wrote in a telling phrase, 'deprave the Mind in like Manner, and with as great Certainty, as prevailing Cold congeals Water.'"[23] In 1839, the American Anti-Slavery Society published *American Slavery as It Is: Testimony of a Thousand Witnesses.* One of those witnesses was the Reverend Horace Moulton of Marlboro, Massachusetts, who had lived in Georgia for several years, and who argued that the immorality and depravity of slaveowners and overseers was the price they paid for brutalizing others:

> The overseers are *generally loose in their morals.* . . . This daily practice of forcibly robbing others, and habitually living on the plunder, cannot but beget in the mind the *habit* of regarding the interests and happiness of those whom it robs, as of no sort of consequence in comparison to its own.[24]

Testimony of a Thousand Witnesses concludes with a warning about the perilous promise of slavery for its practitioners: "Those who combine to trample on others, will trample on *each other.* The habit of trampling upon *one,* begets a state of mind that will trample upon *all.*"[25]

Testimony of a Thousand Witnesses could well have included the words and warnings of the third president of the United States, Thomas Jefferson. Jefferson owned slaves and fathered mixed-race children with his slave, Sally Hemings.[26] Thus, Jefferson knew whereof he spoke when he declared:

> The whole commerce between master and slave is a perpetual exercise of the most boisterous passions, the most unremitting despotism on the one part, and degrading submissions on the other. Our children see this, and learn to imitate it. . . . The man must be a prodigy who can retain his manners and morals undepraved by such circumstances. And with what execration should the statesman be loaded, who permitting one half of the citizens thus to trample on the rights of the other, transforms those into despots, and these

into enemies, destroys the morals of the one part, and the *amor patriae* of the other. . . . Indeed I tremble for my country when I reflect that God is just: that his justice cannot sleep for ever.[27]

Jefferson may have spoken from experience, but he did not practice what he preached. Jefferson died the owner of slaves, and in 1829 his concubine, Sally Hemings, was listed as a part of the slave inventory of his estate.[28]

Slavery was not only dangerous to the lives of blacks and the morals of whites, it posed a threat to the legal and political order. It was, of course, a major cause of the U.S. Civil War, a conflict that threatened the very survival of the United States as a state and nation. Slavery was also both a peculiar and a perverse institution for the culture and structure of U.S. politics to integrate comfortably. Revered pillars of American political creed and social life, such as the principles of liberty, equality, and the pursuit of happiness, were rendered counterfeit and cynical in the face of slavery's unending misery, forced labor, and lifelong intergenerational servitude. Sexuality magnified these contradictions by complicating slavery in ways that created moral and legal dilemmas for American institutions, ideology, and identity. Slavery's racial, gendered, and sexual dimensions combined to create twisted logics and unconscionable outcomes that strained any credible claims of a fair and just U.S. legal system.

For instance, Kathleen Brown's research on race and rape in colonial Virginia describes the impact of race on the disposition and outcome of legal cases:

> When a white woman accused a black man of rape, her chances of conviction appear to have been much higher. Of eighteen such cases to appear in Virginia's local and General Courts between 1670 and 1767, only two are known to have been dismissed. At least twelve of the nineteen accused black men were executed for their crimes.[29]

White men who were accused of rape did not face such high odds of prosecution and conviction in Virginia. In fact, Brown found no cases brought on behalf of black women rape victims, even free black women, until the late eighteenth century. She attributes this to the fact that black women lacked both the legal and social support needed to bring suit in cases of rape since they were "excluded from the constructs of white female sexual honor and often unprotected by the claims of a husband and father."[30] The exclusion of black women from the moral system that often called for the defense of white women's honor was institutionalized into the laws regulating slavery.

Sharon Block describes two similar cases of rape in the nineteenth century that illustrate the racialization of sex and gender in U.S. jurisprudence and society, and highlight further the contradictions and inequalities that become visible when one makes comparisons across the black-white racial boundary.[31] In both cases, unmarried women servants were raped by their married masters. The juxtapositioning of these two rapes and their aftermaths reveals a hierarchy of race over gender in sexual definitions and dealings in the United States at the time (and, many would argue, continuing into the present).

> Rachel Davis was a fifteen-year-old white indentured servant working in Pennsylvania in 1805 when her master, William Cress, began "making sexual overtures toward her. After months of sexual assaults" Cress's wife had Rachel removed from their home, but Cress continued to pursue her sexually; finally Rachel's father "initiated a rape prosecution against William, who was found guilty and sentenced to ten years in prison."[32]
>
> Harriet Jacobs was a sixteen-year-old black slave working in North Carolina in 1829 when her master, James Norcom, began "making sexual overtures toward her. After months of sexual assaults" Norcom's wife had Harriet removed from their home, but Norcom continued to pursue her sexually; finally Harriet "became a runaway slave, and spent the next seven years a fugitive, hiding in her free grandmother's attic crawlspace."[33]

Women of two different races in nearly identical situations with very different fates. Although both women escaped their master's sexual harassment, "the master of the white servant was sent to prison, while the black slave imprisoned herself to escape her abuser."[34] The contrasting outcomes of these parallel cases leads Block to conclude: "Rape in early America was a crime whose definition was structured by race."[35]

STATE OF MISSOURI V. CELIA, A SLAVE

Cracks in the ideological foundations of democracy in America were continually exposed when the political promise of equality confronted the rude reality of slavery. The contradictions imbedded in the disjuncture between political theory and economic and social practice created everyday dilemmas and ongoing moral crises in slaveholding families and communities. A disturbing and compelling example of how sex and race combined under slavery to subvert so-called civil society led me to Fulton, Missouri, in the summer of 1999. I went to Fulton to look at court documents, to see the nineteenth-century sites of the county jail and courthouse, and to visit the Kingdom of Callaway County Historical Society. I was seeking information about a 144-year-old court case: *State of Missouri v. Celia, a Slave.* Celia was tried and convicted in 1855 for killing her owner, Robert Newsom. Here, briefly are the background and facts of her case.

In his book, *Celia, A Slave,* Melton McLaurin reports that Robert Newsom and his family moved from Virginia to Missouri around 1820.[36] Over the next thirty-five years, until his death in 1855, Newsom became a comfortably prosperous farmer with eight hundred acres on which he raised crops such as wheat, rye, corn, and oats, and grazed livestock—milk cows, beef cattle, swine, and sheep. He achieved this success with the labor of his five male slaves. Newsom had four grown children when his wife died in 1849. His eldest daughter, Virginia, took over as mistress of the household after her mother's death, but Newsom was lacking another kind of mistress, a sexual partner.[37]

Sometime in 1850, a year after the death of his wife, sixty-year-old Robert Newsom set out on the forty-mile trip from Callaway County to neighboring Audrain County to buy a slave. McLaurin argues that Newsom had sex on his mind.[38] In Audrain County Newsom purchased a fourteen-year-old girl named Celia, whom he brought back to Callaway County. He housed her in a cabin about fifty yards behind the family house, separate from the other slavequarters. For the next five years Newsom forced Celia to have sex with him until the night of June 23, 1855. That night when he entered her cabin once again demanding sex, nineteen-year-old Celia hit him on the head with a stick and killed him. By this time Celia had borne two of Newsom's children and was pregnant with a third child. Celia was tried for the murder in the Callaway County court that October. Her stated motive for the killing was that Newsom had raped her frequently, beginning on the day she was purchased. Her testimony was deemed inadmissible in court since slaves were not permitted to testify against whites. The closest Celia came to being able to tell her story in a trial for her life was through the testimony of a local citizen, Colonel Jefferson Jones, who had interviewed her. Jones's account of Celia's story was entered into the court record:

> I went to the jail to converse with Celia (defendant) at the request of several citizens. The object of my conversation was to ascertain whether she had any accomplices in the crime. . . . I asked whether she thought she would be hung for what she had done. She said she thought she would be hung. I then told her to tell the whole matter. She said the old man (Newsom, the deceased) had been having sexual intercourse with her. That he had told her he was coming down to her cabin that night. She told him not to come and that if he came she would hurt him. She then got a stick and put it in the corner. He came down that night. When she heard him coming she fixed the fire to make a little light. There was very little fire in the cabin. She said his face was towards her and he was standing talking to her when she struck him. He did not raise his hand when she went to strike the first blow but sunk down on a stool towards the floor. Threw his hands up when he sunk down. She struck him with one hand, her right hand. The stick with which she struck was about as large as the upper part of a Windsor chair, but not so long. She thought that she did not kill him the first blow at the time of the striking, but thought now that the first blow must have killed him.[39]

After killing Newsom, Celia told Jones that she sat for an hour or so trying to decide what to do, and finally decided she would try to burn Newsom's body.

She put the body on the fireplace, and kindled the fire over and around it with some staves that were made for hogsheads, and were in the yard. She burned the body up, and put some of the bones under the hearth, and under the floor between a sleeper and the fireplace. She said she took out the ashes before day.[40]

To conceal the killing, Celia embarked on a course of action that McLaurin interpreted as evidence of "the depth of her hatred for Newsom and his kin":

The next morning, before the family became alarmed at the absence of Robert Newsom, Celia spied [Newsom's] . . . twelve-year-old [grandson] Coffee Waynescot playing in a cherry tree outside her cabin . . . [S]he asked the boy to come into her cabin and clean out her fireplace. Coffee testified that "she would give me two dozen walnuts if I would carry the ashes out. I said good lick."[41]

Later that day, the family did notice Newsom's absence and authorities' questioning eventually led Celia to confess to the killing.

During the trial four months later, Celia's defense attorney cross-examined Jones and others about Celia's motive for the crime, namely as a defense against Newsom's sexual assaults. Entered into the court record were Celia's statements to Jones that Newsom had raped her at the first opportunity, on the way back from Audrain County on the day he purchased her, and that he continued to do so until his death—rapes that had led to her pregnancies and the births of two of Newsom's children.[42] The court did not recognize in Celia's statements any legal justification for her actions. The rape of enslaved women was covered neither by common law, since slaves were not citizens, nor by the so-called slave codes, which did not prohibit or even speak to the issue of rape.[43] Thus, Celia was not the victim of any crime during her five years with Newsom. Apparently the jurors and the judge saw no moral justification for Celia's actions either. On October 10, 1855, Celia was convicted of murder and two days later the judge sentenced her to death. Some Callaway County citizens who disagreed with either the verdict or the sentence helped arrange Celia's escape from jail less than a week before her November 16 execution date.[44] She was recaptured by the end of the month, however, and after the Missouri State Supreme Court refused to hear her appeal, her sentence was carried out. Celia was hanged in Callaway County on 2:30 P.M. on Friday, December 21, 1855.[45]

THE SEDUCTION OF POWER AND THE POWERLESS SEDUCTRESS

There is an important and complicating fact in the sad tale of racial and sexual terror and injustice embodied in the case of the *State of Missouri v. Celia, a Slave*. That complication can be found in the dilemma facing Celia as she decided how to respond to the repeated sexual abuses of Robert Newsom. It is a complication that may well have made her choose death, which, according to Jefferson Jones's testimony, she expected would be the outcome of her trial. It turns out that Celia faced other pressures in addition to the sexual demands of Newsom. She also had a companion, a partner, a husband—no word works well since under slavery conjugal relationships were neither recognized nor legitimated—his name was George. George sometimes stayed with Celia in her cabin, and when questioned about Newsom's disappearance, George implicated Celia, and then he ran away. In his trial testimony, Jefferson Jones reported asking Celia if George had been involved in the killing:

> I asked her whether she had told anyone that she intended to kill the old man. She said that she never had. I told her that George had run off, and that she might as well tell it if he had anything to do with killing the old man. She said that George need not have run off, for that he knew nothing about it. I asked her if George had advised her to kill the old man. [She] said he never had, [she] said that *George had told her that he would have nothing more to do with her if she did not quit the old man* [emphasis mine].[46]

Saidiya Hartman, who wrote about Celia's case in her book, *Scenes of Subjection*, interprets this last sentence as follows:

> The sexual exploitation of the enslaved female, incredibly, served as evidence of her collusion with the master class and as evidence of her power, the power both to render the master weak and, implicitly, to be the mistress of her own subjection. The slave woman not only suffered the responsibility for her sexual (ab)use but was also blameworthy because of her purported ability to render the powerful weak.[47]

The belief that female sexuality is so powerful as to overwhelm the strongest man is certainly part of the historical mythology of rape as women's responsibility.[48] This view of female erotic power resonates especially strongly with the historical and contemporary view of Others as hypersexualized and seductive. From a hegemonic masculinist standpoint such Others can be understood to include all women, but especially nonwhite women as well as nonwhite men. In this ethnosexual cosmology, white men, despite their legal, social, political, and economic power, are victims of the sexual potency and seductive treachery of women and nonwhites. For instance, Edward Long, a well-known eighteenth-century racist and apologist for slavery, disdained the weakness of white men and lamented the power of black women over them in his *The History of Jamaica*:

> In regard to the African mistress. . . . In well-dissembled affection, in her tricks, cajolements, and infidelities, she is far more perfectly versed, than any adept of the hundreds of [prostitutes of] Drury. She rarely wants cun-

ning to dupe the fool that confides in her; for who "shall teach the wily African deceit?"[49]

Long admonished "white men in the colony . . . [to] abate of their infatuated attachments to black women," and he chastised white women for not making themselves "more companionable, useful, and esteemable, as wives [to white men], than the Negresses and Mulattas are as mistresses."[50] Phillip Morgan summarized Long's claims "that a white man became an 'abject, passive slave' to his black mistress's 'insults, thefts, and infidelities.' "[51]

Long's antiquated assertions about white men's vulnerability to the sexual power of their female slaves survived long after his death. In 1950 Richard Pares published *A West-India Fortune,* an analysis of slavery in the eighteenth-century Jamaica of Edward Long. Despite the vast historical and presumed intellectual gap separating Long's self-interested reflections and Pares's scholarly analysis of Jamaican history, Pares's commentary echoed Long's portrayal of enslaved African women as active agents, if not entirely as controlling seductresses, in white men's ethnosexual crossings. For instance, Pares described as "negrofied," white men who were sexually involved with their black female slaves who "led them by the nose."[52] He also reported that

> [t]he power of sex to persuade the planters to free their property is illustrated by the fact, reported by the legislature of Nevis [Jamaica] in 1789, that there were 5 female slaves to every 4 males slaves, but 9 free negresses to every 4 free negroes.[53]

According to this accounting white men apparently were so weakened by their female slaves' wiles, they were unable to resist enslaved women's desire for liberty, and thus were compelled to free them.

This durable view of enslaved black women as more powerful than their white male owners—owners who enjoyed absolute de jure and de facto control over them, illustrates the powerful social assumptions underlying slavery in general. Assumptions about black women's responsibility not only for their own actions, but for the actions of their white owners, were imbedded in the slavery system and the legal framework supporting it—a framework within which Celia was convicted and hanged. Edward Long's remarks were made nearly a century before Celia killed Robert Newsom and was killed herself; Richard Pares's statements were made nearly a century after Celia's and Newsom's deaths. The words of both men, however, echo across the centuries, resounding as a single voice. That voice and what it communicated about sex, race, and gender could be heard in the comments of Celia's contemporaries, women as well as men.

Fanny Kemble was the English-born wife of a slave owner; her *Journal of a Residence on a Georgian Plantation in 1838–1839* was a favorite of abolitionists because of its sympathetic stance and critical assessment of many aspects of slavery. Fanny recounts how she caught herself blaming the victim in a conversation she had one day with an enslaved woman, Sophy, "who had come to beg for rice."[54] Sophy told Fanny about an incident that occurred when Sophy was giving birth to her second child. Sophy happened to be at the hospital with two other women slaves who were delivering children fathered by a white man, one Mr. K____: "Mrs. K____ came to the hospital, had them all three severely flogged . . . and then sent them to the swamp . . . with farther orders to the drivers to flog them every day for a week."[55] Kemble was appalled at Sophy's story, especially at the recounted actions of the white woman:

> I have thought these details intolerable enough, but this apparition of a female fiend in the middle of this hell I confess adds an element of cruelty which seems to me to surpass all the rest . . . and just conceive of the fate of these unfortunate women between the passions of their masters and mistresses, each alike armed with power to oppress and torture them.[56]

Some of Kemble's horror and outrage at Mrs. K's treatment of Sophy and her two chance companions, however, got redirected toward Sophy when the enslaved woman further disclosed that her own child's father also was white:

> Sophy went on to say that Isaac was her son by Driver Morris, who had forced her. . . . Almost beyond my patience with this string of detestable details, I exclaimed—foolishly enough, heaven knows—"Ah! but don't you know—did nobody ever tell or teach any of you that it is a sin to live with men who are not your husbands?!" Alas, what could the poor creature answer but what she did, seizing me at the same time vehemently by the wrist: "Oh, yes, missis, we know—we know all about dat well enough; but we do any thing to get our poor flesh some rest from de whip; when he made me follow him into de bush, what use me tell him no? he have strength to make me."[57]

Fanny Kemble's questioning revealed, to her chagrin, how strong were her assumptions about black women's seductive complicity in and presumed responsibility for white men's sexual appetites. The power of this hegemony was all the more evident since Kemble, although a white woman, seemed to recognize the powerless and exploited position of enslaved women. Fanny's (un)critical questioning of Sophie shows the power of hegemony to shape our perceptions and perspectives even when we try to see beyond them. Kemble's self-reproach, however, reflected in her comment, "I exclaimed—foolishly enough, heaven knows," provides a ray of hope that by unmasking hegemony, we can begin to discover some of what we take for granted, and thus can begin to see how our own actions and assumptions contribute to the status quo.

Ideological hegemonies do not exist in a material vacuum. There were also many legal and economic incentives for white men to "succumb" to their sexual desire for African women. Black women's lack of social and legal protection against rape made them vulnerable to sexual assault. Enslaved women were especially likely targets of sexual abuse since their rape was rewarded by the possibility of pregnancy, and thus could increase a slaveowner's holdings. This incentive increased in importance after 1808 when the *importation*, but not the *reproduction* of slaves was outlawed in the United States. For the next fifty-seven years until slavery was ended in 1865 with the passage of the Thirteenth Amendment to the U.S. Constitution, a slaveowner's holdings could only be increased by "breeding" slaves. Enslaved black women thus labored for slave owners in all senses of the word—as productive workers in slaveowners' houses, businesses, and fields, and as reproductive workers whose pregnancy, childbearing, and childrearing increased slaveowners' "stock" of slaves. Slave owners had active breeding programs and encouraged and orchestrated sexual contact between enslaved men and women.[58] Male slave owners also had sex with black women to satisfy their sexual appetites and to enlarge their slaveholdings.

Although the law was quite likely to turn a blind eye to sex between white men and black women, especially when the sex was sanctified by slavery, the mixing of race and sex was a breach of law in many states, especially when the partners were black men and white women.[59] For instance, Victoria Bynum studied charges of sexual misconduct in four North Carolina counties during the period from 1850 to 1860; in cases of "fornication" ("women who *gave* rather than *sold* sexual favors" [emphasis mine]),[60] she reported that

> [i]n those indictments of fornication aimed at punishing miscegenation, magistrates prosecuted primarily white women and black men rather than white men and black women. This uneven application of the law reflected the structure of gender and racial relationships. White males claimed the right to govern all women, regardless of race. The sole sexual possession of white women by white men assured perpetuation of the dominant "pure" white race. Possession of a black woman by a white man, whether of her person, labor, or body, demonstrated the powerlessness of the black man. . . . Black women were especially vulnerable. Subjected to sexual exploitation because of their gender, they were denied protection against sexual harassment on account of their race.[61]

Peter Bardaglio's research on the regulation of interracial sex in the South before the end of slavery also finds that antimiscegenation laws did not focus only on the regulation of black male sexuality, but that these laws

> manifested an intense concern with controlling the sexual behavior of white women. [In Maryland], for example, denounced "diverse freeborne Eng-

lishwomen [who were] forgettful of their free Condition and to the disgrace of our Nation doe intermarry with Negro slaves." To discourage "such shamefull Matches," the statute stipulated that any white woman who married a black slave was to serve her husband's master until the slave died.[62]

This last provision of Maryland's antimiscegeny law solved the problem of white women's ethnosexual rule breaking by temporarily reclassifying them as "black." In fact, Bardaglio further argues that the antimiscegenation laws of Maryland and other Southern states were "directed primarily at white women, black men, and their mulatto offspring." This was because of the way in which the racial classification of mixed offspring worked (then and now):

> [A] white woman could give birth to a black child. . . . But . . . a black woman could not give birth to a white child. Such a construction of reproduction clearly served the interests of white men in the South, allowing them to roam sexually among women of any color without threatening the color line.[63]

Antimiscegenation legislation did not officially encourage white men to have sex with black women either, but it provided a clear financial incentive for slaveowners to do so. In Virginia, for instance, local law specified that "the child of a black woman by a white man would be 'bound or free only according to the condition of the mother.' "[64] Bardaglio points out that this provision "ensured that the transgressions of white men would lead to an increase in the population of the slave labor force, providing them with a powerful economic incentive to engage in interracial sex."[65]

Another incentive for white men to have sex with black women was the monetary and symbolic worth of their mixed-race or "mulatto" offspring. Lighter-skinned slaves fetched a higher price at market and occupied a higher status in the cultural system of slaveowning society: they were more likely to be employed in slaveowners' homes rather than in their fields and more likely to be the objects of their male masters' lust. White men's sexual preference for light-skinned enslaved women was no secret to their wives. Marli Weiner's study of plantation mistresses in South Carolina includes the writings of Ella Gertrude Clanton Thomas, a white Georgian and the wife and daughter of plantation owners. Thomas wrote in her journal in 1859 of the sexual exploitation of light-skinned black women who were

> subject to be bought by men, with natures but one degree removed from the brute creation and with no more control over their passions—subjected to such a lot are they not to be pitied. I know that this is a view of the subject that it is thought best for women to ignore but when we see so many cases of mulattoes commanding higher prices, advertised as "fancy girls," oh is it not enough to make us shudder for the standard of morality in our Southern homes?[66]

Thomas personally benefited from the system she deplored and seems motivated at least as much by her concern for Southern white morality, including that of the men in her family who fathered many mixed-race children with their slaves, as by her sympathy with the plight of black women.[67] Whatever her primary concerns, Thomas's observation that light-skinned enslaved women were especially likely to be defined as sexual goods is corroborated by historians. Walter Johnson's study of the nineteenth-century New Orleans "slave market" details the attention given to and relatively higher worth of light-skinned slaves, especially women. Of particular relevance here was the so-called fancy trade in slaves. Johnson quotes a slave dealer, Phillip Johnson's description of a young girl he saw sold in Richmond, Virginia, in 1859: "13 years old Girl, Bright Color, nearly a fancy for $1135."[68] The price, the color, the age, and the gender of the slave were all related:

> The slave market was suffused with sexuality: the traders' light-skinned mistresses, the buyers' foul-mouthed banter, the curtained inspection rooms that surrounded the pens . . . the prices paid for women . . . occasionally reached three hundred percent of the median prices paid in a given year . . . "had those young girls been sold for mere house servants or field hands, they would not have brought half the sum they did."[69]

Johnson argues that the purchase of light-skinned enslaved women was a sexualized transaction between men, where the price paid for a "bright" or "yellow" woman reflected "a contest between white men played out on the body of an enslaved woman."[70] In the words of a former slave, Solomon Northrup: "there were [white] men in New Orleans who would give five thousand dollars for such an extra fancy piece . . . rather than not get her."[71] Thus, the price paid for such a woman "was as much a measure of the buyer as the bought."[72] White men's sexual relations with enslaved black women was common knowledge, if not always openly discussed. Johnson quotes well-known southern diarist Mary Chestnut's comment that sex between white men and black women was "the thing we can't name. . . . Every lady tells you who is the father of all the mulatto children in everybody's household, but those in her own she seems to think dropped from the clouds or pretends so to think."[73]

CONTROLLING BLACK MALE SEXUALITY

Antimiscegenation legislation may have been little concerned with the ethnosexual boundary crossings of white men. But it certainly was used to attempt to control the sexuality of black men. When they were enslaved, black men were depicted sexually more often as overabundant than as dangerous or seductive; which description applied often had to do with the race of their partners. For both enslaved and free black men, sex with white women was mostly a perilous enterprise. Even when their intimate and family relations were with black women, however, black men still could be vulnerable and powerless. Enslaved men and women often were separated from one another and from their children by the vagaries and whims of their owners' commerce and geography—i.e., by being sold away from their kin and loved ones. Further, black men fared no better than black women when they attempted to intervene to stop white men's sexual advances against their women partners and relatives.

Saidiya Hartman recounts such a case that occurred in 1859, only a few years after Celia's execution in Missouri for killing Robert Newsom. Alfred, a slave in Mississippi, was tried for the murder of his overseer, Coleman, who had raped Alfred's wife, Charlotte. The rape was not considered relevant to the murder case partly because, like Celia, the courts did not define Charlotte's rape as legally possible, nor did they recognize her as Alfred's wife. Alfred was found guilty of murder and executed despite the argument of his counsel that all men deserved the protection of law in such cases since they shared the same strong urges to defend their women against sexual assault:

> [T]he humanity of our law . . . regards with as much tenderness the excesses of outraged conjugal affection in the negro as in the white man. The servile condition . . . has not deprived him of his social or moral instincts, and he is as much entitled to the protection of the laws, when acting under their influence, as if he were freed.[74]

It was not only legal status as free or slave, white or black, that shaped the worthiness and rights of victims of sexual assault. Respectability mattered, especially for white women. Despite a notorious history of white retributions against black men for having sex—forced or consensual—with white women, even during the slavery era a black man accused of raping a white woman could escape punishment if the white woman was known to associate with blacks.[75] The devaluation of white women was only part of the equation for estimating the likelihood that black men would be punished for crossing ethnosexual boundaries. It turns out that the valuation of black men also entered into the calculus of retribution. The potential property loss associated with the execution of a male slave, for instance, motivated many slaveowners to argue for leniency and to seek pardons for black men accused or convicted of having sex with white women.[76] Variations in the treatment of black men for real or imagined sexual involvement with white women also was partly determined by the geography and history of slavery, whether an incident occurred in the North or in the South, in which part of the South, and in which historical context or moment of the slavery system.[77]

Prior to the end of the Civil War, black male sexuality, while always potentially troublesome in the minds of whites, had been kept in check by the degradations and total institutional structures of slavery. Perhaps because of the general level of control that slavery afforded and because of the relative rarity of relationships between black men and white women, during the antebellum period from colonial times onward, scholars report that sexual liaisons between white women and black men, while never popularly supported, were somewhat more likely to be tolerated or ignored than later, after the war. For instance, Morgan catalogs numerous instances in contemporaneous accounts and depictions—in memoirs, literature, and art—where white female desire enacted in sexual associations with black men in England and colonial New England went unpunished: "Lemuel Haynes, the first African-American to preach regularly to a white congregation in America, was the child of an African father and white mother and married a white woman himself."[78]

Martha Hodes confirms an occasional surprising tolerance of some black male–white female sexual relations even later in U.S. history, but still prior to the Civil War. She attributes a limited toleration of consensual sexual relations between black men and white women, "in part, to white ideology about the sexual depravity of white women outside the planter classes. . . . Thus could white ideology about lower-class female sexuality overshadow ideas about the dangers of black male sexuality."[79] Apparently, the only thing worse than the dangerousness of black male sexuality was the degeneracy of lower-class white female sexuality.[80] Not only whites turned a scornful eye on white women for their sexual involvement with black men. Hodes found evidence that some black women joined white men in policing the black-white ethnosexual boundary:

> In coastal North Carolina in 1827, for example, a free black woman named Mary Green was sentenced to six months in a dungeon for assaulting a white woman who associated with black men. Mary described the white woman as "of infamous character," and six whites corroborated . . . call[ing] the woman, "one of the lowest of this degraded class of white people" and asserted that Mary should not suffer any more than if she had assaulted another black person (thereby suggesting the equation in white minds between black women and depraved white women).[81]

To whatever limited extent such theories of white women's sexual looseness might have helped to protect black men from whites' retributions for sexually crossing the color line, that protection did not survive the Civil War when freed black men no longer constituted a financial investment. White female lower-class sexuality remained suspect during the postwar period, but whites came to define black men as the greater threat to the racial and sexual order. After the Civil War and the official end of slavery, freedmen became objects of increased sexual suspicion and attack by whites bent on keeping the former slaves in their place even without the apparatus of the slave state. Formal legal means, such as Jim Crow laws that restricted the political, economic, and social rights of free blacks, and informal methods of terror, such as the Ku Klux Klan and lynching, became the machinery of racial sexual social control.[82]

What was it about black men that created such outrage and hysteria in the minds of whites, particularly white men? Sandra Gunning argues that whites, especially Southern whites, feared freed black men would seek retribution for their mistreatment and the abuse of black women under slavery.[83] That same strength and virility that whites had controlled and exploited in enslaved black men took on a new aspect when seen in the bodies and actions of freed black men. David Blight reports an image taken from the letters of Henry McNeal Turner, a Union army chaplain, that must certainly have raised this specter. Turner accompanied his black regiment on the Union army's victorious march across North Carolina at the end of the Civil War. In May 1865, Turner observed the reaction of the white Southerners who watched as his men undressed to keep their clothing dry as they forded a river. He recounts the episode in a letter to the *Christian Recorder*:

> I was much amused to see the secesh [secessionist] women watching with the utmost intensity, thousands of our [black] soldiers, in a state of nudity. I suppose they desired to see whether these audacious Yankees were really men, made like other men, or if they were a set of varmints. [As southern women] thronged the windows, porticos and yards, in the finest attire imaginable . . . brave boys would disrobe themselves, hang their garments upon their bayonets and through the water they would come, walk up the street, and seem to say to the feminine gazers, "Yes, though naked, we are your masters."[84]

Blight describes this scene as "charged with sexual and political symbolism . . . [that] captured a memory that haunted the white South for generations to come: naked black men with muskets, striding out of a river into a town's streets with an audience of white women."[85] The fear that black men's sexuality could be wielded as a weapon of vengeance against white men through sexual assaults on white women was articulated by Philip A. Bruce in *The Plantation Negro as Freeman*:

> He is not content merely with the consummation of his purpose, but takes that fiendish delight in the degradation of his victim which he always shows when he can reek revenge upon one whom he has hitherto been compelled

to fear, and here, the white woman in his power is, for the time being, the representative of that race which has always over-awed him.[86]

Hodes locates white fears of black-white sexual contact not only in the bedroom, but also in the halls of commerce and the chambers of government. In the Reconstruction-era postwar South former slaves could sell and profit from their own labor, open businesses, fraternize with whites, and participate in politics. Freed blacks became active in Republican party politics after the war and confronted white male Dixie Democrats as equals in political arenas. The comeuppance was more than many whites could countenance. Reconstruction had ushered in an era marked by the ascendancy of previously abject, disfranchised black men into the formerly all-white political realm where white men would have to vote alongside, share power with, and even face defeat by blacks. The end of slavery also opened the door to black entry into the economic, social, cultural, and sexual worlds of whites. Something had to be done to stop this overturning of the moral order. The Ku Klux Klan and its campaign of terror against blacks was one response.

Hodes catalogs white justifications for violence against black men in her analysis of the testimony presented before the U.S. Congress in an 1871 inquiry into the conditions in the post–Civil War South and the activities of the Klan. One statement was by a white North Carolina man who testified about the threat he believed black men posed in the postwar South:

> The common white people of the country are at times very much enraged against the negro population. They think that this universal political and civil equality will finally bring about social equality. . . . There are already instances . . . in which poor white girls are having negro children.[87]

Another witness, the postmaster of Meridian, Mississippi, and a Democrat, argued that the Republican strategy of "putting colored men into office, in positions of prominence, will gradually lead them to demand social equality, and to intermingle by marriage with the whites."[88] This bugaboo of white female vulnerability to black male sexuality provided cover for white efforts to stop political and economic competition between whites and blacks, and served as a convenient excuse for white men to reassert their control over black men. Hodes tells the story of Henry Lowther, a married freedman in Georgia, who was visited one night in 1870 by Klansmen seeking to intimidate him for his Republican party activities and economic successes.

> "They said I had taken too great a stand against them in the republican party," Lowther recalled. "I worked for my money and carried on a shop. They got all broke and did not pay me, and I sued them." Lowther concluded, "They have been working at me ever since I have been free. I had too much money." Lowther was jailed on charges of conspiring to murder

another black man but was denied a trial. A white man came to warn Lowther of trouble and asked whether Lowther was "willing to give up your stones to save your life" indicating castration. As Lowther remembered the scene, almost two hundred Klansmen arrived in the middle of the night, and twenty of them carried him away to a swamp. "The moon was shining bright, and I could see them," Lowther recalled; all the men were Democrats. There the Klansmen castrated him.[89]

The Klan claimed its mutilation of Lowther had nothing to do with partisan politics or money, but was because of his sexual disrespect for and illicit relations with white women, a charge heard over and over to justify white depredations on blacks. Even highly visible black male public figures were targets of at least verbal attack when they crossed or were thought to be crossing the color line, even when the crossing took the legally sanctioned form of marriage. David Chesebrough describes the public "clamor" raised against the marriage of African American abolitionist leader Frederick Douglass to Helen Pitts, a white woman, in 1884, a year and a half after the death of his first wife, Anna, who was black:

> The mixed marriage brought a storm of criticism from many quarters. Some blacks accused Douglass of showing "contempt for the women of his own race," and some whites looked upon him as "a lecherous old African Solomon." Douglass's offspring would never become comfortable with the marriage.[90]

Douglass, whose mother had been enslaved, as had he, responded that "my first wife was the color of my mother, and the second the color of my father."[91]

Douglass's marriage to Pitts occurred at a time when violence against black men was escalating, especially in the form of lynching. Although researchers report that charges of "sexual misconduct" accounted for only about one-third of lynchings (accusations of murder were the most common justifications),[92] common understanding of lynching—then and now—was that it was justified by whites who claimed the need to defend white women against black men's sexual aggressions.[93] Underlying this understanding were strong and dangerous assumptions about black men's virulent sexuality.

Challenging these lethal assumptions became the focus of a crusade during the 1890s by one of Douglass's allies in the fight for women's and blacks' civil rights, Ida B. Wells, an African American journalist. Gail Bederman argues that Wells was motivated to dedicate her efforts against the practice of lynching, in part, because of the murder in 1892 of a family friend, Thomas Moss. The reasons for Moss's death were strikingly similar to those given by Henry Lowther for his victimization nearly a quarter-century earlier. Moss and two business associates, Calvin McDowell and Will Stewart, had started a successful Memphis, Tennessee, grocery that was driving an established white-run competitor out of business. The three black men were lynched while awaiting trial for shooting and wounding white men hired by their competitor to terrorize their business. Local authorities expressed indifference to the black men's torture and killing by a white mob, and stood by later while whites looted and destroyed the black men's business.

Wells was outraged by the casual dismissal of this and similar crimes, a casualness displayed not only in the South, but in the North as well, where prevailing notions of lynching depicted it as a "colorful, if somewhat old-fashioned, southern regional custom."[94] In fact, lynchings moved beyond instances of local lawlessness to take on the proportions of large-scale spectacles during the 1890s; they were publicized in advance and attracted large crowds that sometimes numbered in the thousands. An example reported by Grace Hale was the lynching of an African American man, Henry Smith, who was accused of killing a white girl in Paris, Texas, in 1893.[95] Hale argues that spectacles such as this were part of the consolidation of the color line and the construction of whiteness in the postwar U.S. South.

Wells's anti-lynching campaign had little effect in the United States until she traveled to England and lectured on the practice and made lynching a *cause celebre* in Europe and an embarrassment in America. The frequency

FIGURE 4.3   Lynching of Henry Smith, Paris, Texas, 1893 (courtesy of the United States Library of Congress)

of lynchings began a gradual decline after Wells's campaign, but where the practice continued it was with the same sexual excuse repeatedly recited.[96] For instance, nearly four decades after Lowther's ordeal and the Klan's dis-respect-to-white-women defense of its actions, in a 1907 speech, South Car-olina senator Ben Tillman asked the U.S. Congress to suspend due process for blacks accused of sex crimes against white women:

> The white women of the South are in a state of siege. . . . Some lurking de-mon who has watched for the opportunity seizes her; she is choked or beaten into insensibility and ravished, her body prostituted, her purity destroyed, her chastity taken from her. . . . Shall men . . . demand for [the demon] the right to have a fair trial and be punished in the regular course of justice? So far as I am concerned he has put himself outside the pale of the law, human and divine.[97]

The symbolic transformation of black men from emasculated slaves into vengeful rapists during the decades following the Civil War thus set the tone for black-white sexual politics in the twentieth century.[98] Early-twentieth-century concerns about white men's waning social autonomy, personal power, and sexual virility were heightened by biological theories of race pop-ular at the time that supported a view of black men as "hyperpotent."[99] The perceived black male threat to white male hegemony in the United States played itself out not only in economic, political, and social arenas, but in cul-tural venues as well, especially in athletic arenas. Bederman recounts one such racialized match of manhoods, when black Jack Johnson faced the Great White Hope, Jim Jeffries, in the boxing ring:

> At 2:30 on July 4, 1910, in Reno, Nevada, as the band played, "All Coons Look Alike to Me," Jack Johnson climbed into the ring to defend his title against Jim Jeffries. Johnson was the first African American world heavy-weight boxing champion. Jeffries was a popular white former heavyweight champion. . . . [The fight was] a national sensation.[100]

Plate 4 of the color insert is George Wesley Bellows's famous 1907 painting, "Both Members of This Club," of two boxers, one black and one white. Al-though the painting predated the Jackson-Jeffries match by three years, it il-lustrates the contradictions of masculinities—men as partners in an intimate struggle—joined by gender, separated by race.

Jeffries had been reluctant to fight the younger Johnson, but the match had come to have meaning beyond the athletic contest at hand; the Johnson-Jeffries battle developed into a test of white racial dominance. When Jeffries finally agreed to fight Johnson, he explained, "I am going into this fight for the sole purpose of proving that a white man is better than a negro."[101] Be-derman reports that when Johnson trounced Jeffries in bloody rout, race riots broke out in every Southern state, as well as in Illinois, Missouri, New York, Ohio, Pennsylvania, Colorado, and the District of Columbia. . . . In most of the incidents . . . rampaging white men attacked black men who were celebrating Johnson's victory. . . . Even the United States Congress reacted. . . . Within three weeks, a bill suppressing fight films had passed both houses [to avoid repeated showings of the Jeffries defeat].[102]

Retribution against Johnson came in the form of accusations, not of athletic or sportsmanly misconduct, but in an indictment for "white slavery." Johnson's pugilistic skills were perhaps less troubling to white men than his sexual popularity with white women. He had been married to a white woman, and after the Jeffries match, white women pursued him publicly. When Johnson began an affair with Lucille Cameron, a blonde eighteen-year-old, and planned a second marriage to her, her family threatened to have her declared insane and involuntarily committed. Her mother stated that "I would rather see my daughter spend the rest of her life in an insane asylum than see her the plaything of [Johnson]."[103] The courtship created further public outrage, and in 1912 Johnson was charged under the 1910 Mann Act (also known as the "White Slave Traffic Act") with engaging in white slavery (i.e., transporting women across state lines for prostitution).[104] Those initial charges were dropped, but after an inquiry by the U.S. Bureau of Investigation, Johnson was found to have crossed state lines with a white mistress for whom he had purchased gifts; this was sufficient to convict him of white slavery, and in 1913 he was sentenced to a year in prison. He fled the country and lived abroad for seven years, during which time he lost the world heavyweight title to a white boxer, Jess Willard, in Havana in 1915. Johnson returned to the United States in 1920, "an impoverished and greatly humbled former champion."[105]

U.S. efforts to punish black-white social and sexual associations such as those embodied in the Mann Act and the fate of Jack Johnson found their parallel in less official, though similar reactions in England. Although the British had responded supportively and enthusiastically to Ida B. Wells's campaign against lynching in late-nineteenth-century America, they were less charitable about matters of race, sex, and injustice when English women and African men collaborated against British colonialism just a few decades later. Around the time American women finally got the vote in 1920,[106] privileged English women were working with black men in England to support African nationalism. During the interwar period of the 1920s and 1930s anticolonial nationalist movements were building momentum across the African continent, and African nationalists were in Britain agitating for independence. A number of prominent, left-leaning British society women entered into political alliances and sexual relationships with male African nationalists that scandalized British society. Although the women were depicted as sexual adventurers and race traitors, their social position and resources made them valuable, if controversial, allies for African men and the national struggles they represented. White women's bodies also represented a formerly forbidden terrain that no doubt was very tempting to many black men seeking to throw off European colonialism and assert African sovereign power and autonomy. Barbara Bush notes that the sexual dimensions of these political alliances generated an ambivalent response from many of the African nationalists:

> [F]or black male activists this sexual assertion was a "revolutionary act" employed by blacks and Indians to "get their own back in Europe." But they also criticised the "gigolos" and "Europeanised missionary boys" who capitalised on rich white women's "fascination" with black sex ("sexual imperialism") merely for "prestige value."[107]

African American author and black nationalist Marcus Garvey, writing at the time, expressed dismay at the British media's preoccupation with "white women's strange fascination with black men"; many of the latter he considered dilettantes who "gathered in cafes" and seemed to do "no honest work." He complained that the media's focus on these sexual alliances distracted attention from more important issues such as the "frequent moral abuse" of African and Indian women by whites in the colonies.[108] Garvey's contemporary, African nationalist Ras Makonnen, cast a more sympathetic eye on the intimacies between black men and white women in England. He mapped out some of the ways real or imagined interracial sexuality complicated politics, and catalogued the unpleasantries and indignities associated with many black-white relationships, sexual or not:

> All this made us very careful in associating with white women; otherwise you could have terrible things said of them and yourself. Sometimes if you were walking down Piccadilly with a white girl some white drunk would shout "white bastard" at her. Some people would immediately identify this white woman who was walking with you as someone loose, because no outstanding white woman would be seen with a nigger. So against your will you took up a defensive attitude, and managed to let the woman be a little in front of you. . . . One had the same tactics with older women who felt you were a missionary boy, and would take you into coffee shops with some sort of pretentious English smile. Here one could see the great injustice being done, often unconsciously, by many of these fine women who were dedicated to establish Negro rights.[109]

DEFENDING THE SEXUAL COLOR LINE

Despite the passage of much time and history since Europeans began settling North America and importing Africans to enslave for profit and profligacy, there remains in U.S. society today no ethnic boundary more sexualized or scrutinized than the color line dividing blacks and whites. Throughout the

twentieth century black sexuality has remained a preoccupation of white America. In the early decades there were lynchings and castrations of black men and
arrests of both black men and women for sexual misdeeds such as rape, white
slavery, and prostitution.[110] Later in the century there were social controversies over entertainers and public figures who crossed the color line such as
NAACP executive director Walter White in the 1950s or singer Sammy Davis
Jr. in the 1960s. Later there were public policy debates over such issues as welfare expenditures, out-of-wedlock pregnancies, or "youth" crime, that deployed
gendered and sexualized racial subtexts—race-baiting—in electoral politics.
Politicians played the race card in the Republican focus on black felon Willie
Horton during the 1988 U.S. presidential campaign and in their arguments
about affirmative action and racial quotas heard throughout the 1990s.[111]

The black-white ethnosexual frontier is a less deadly danger zone today
than it was a century ago. Even in the face of slowly but steadily increasing
rates of black-white intermarriage,[112] however, the color line remains a controversial intersection where black men and women are still hypersexualized,[113] and where critics of miscegenation speak out from both sides of the
U.S. racial divide.[114] White supremacist and other white racist discourse is
the most vitriolic on the subject of black sexuality and its expression in relationships with whites, particularly white women.[115] There also have been
African American voices, many from the ranks of black women, who report
finding miscegenation objectionable, again and especially when couplings involve black men and white women. For instance, Michele Wallace recounts
the "coming-out of black male/white female couples" at the height of the
U.S. Black Power movement in the late 1960s:

> Black men often could not separate their interest in white women from their
> hostility toward black women. "I can't stand that black bitch," was the way
> it was usually put. Other black men argued that white women gave them
> money, didn't put them down, made them feel like men. And black women
> made no attempt to disguise their anger and disgust. . . . Some black women
> would laugh low in their throats when they saw a black man with a white
> woman and make cracks about his high-water pants or his flat head or his
> walk, anything that might suggest that he was inadequate: "Only the re-
> jects crawl for white pussy."[116]

While the logic behind these black women's disparaging comments might
be different from the critiques of white men, the message is the same—don't
mix sex and race. Wallace observes that black men's involvement with white
women during the 1960s, which she refers to ironically as "white fever," was
a means of asserting black autonomous manhood and of standing up to centuries of white male domination. Chroniclers of the civil rights movement
also report increased sexual contact between blacks and whites during that

era. The movement's challenge to the racial order contributed to an atmosphere in which blacks and whites were allowed and sometimes expected to have sex with one another. Both blacks and whites began to view one another as potential sexual partners through lenses colored by the sexual fantasies, stereotypes, and meanings associated with skin color. For both blacks and whites interracial sexual contact was pregnant with sexual, political, social, and cultural meanings.

Most of the interracial sex reported by historians and participants of the civil rights movement was between black men and white women. Like their black male partners, many white women were infatuated with the notion of sex across the color line, though often for different reasons. For many white women, black men represented exotic and powerful sexuality. For many black men, white women were especially loaded sexual and political signifiers whose meanings were not always flattering. Black men and white women also faced different pressures. Some black men felt pressured to "prove" their manhood by crossing the black-white forbidden sexual frontier. Some white female activists felt pressured to prove their racial liberalism by making themselves sexually available. Mary Rothschild describes the sexual atmosphere for both black and white volunteers in the 1964 "Freedom Summer" Southern voter registration drive and related projects. The Freedom Summer projects opened a space for blacks and whites to confront prevailing taboos against interracial sex, but overthrowing ethnosexual hegemonies was not without its costs:

> While many [white] women volunteers had sexual relationships with black men, there were obviously pressures against such affairs. They were seen as disruptive to the projects and the community . . . [and] women who did not wish to become sexually involved—at least not with several men—faced a classic dilemma. Black men "in search of their manhood" were persistent and aggressive. If a woman refused them, they called her a racist, and she generally became a focus for the hostility of the black men on the project. Furthermore, "racist" was an exceedingly effective epithet: It was, quite simply, the worst thing a volunteer could be.[117]

Whether politically or erotically motivated, Wallace notes that black men's sexual embrace of white women felt to black women like a betrayal, a choice that degraded both black men and black women.

> The black man has not really kept his part of the bargain they made when she [the black woman] agreed to keep her mouth shut in the sixties. When she stood by silently as he became a "man," she assumed that he would subsequently grant her long overdue "womanhood," that he would finally glorify and dignify black womanhood. . . . But he did not. He refused her. His involvement with white women was only the most dramatic form that refusal took.[118]

Patricia Hill Collins directs her critical analysis of black men's sexual involvement white women at white women themselves and "the web of sexual politics that seduce white women with an artificial sense of specialness and vest them with the power to sustain that illusion:"

> For many African-American women, far too few white women are willing to acknowledge—let alone challenge—the actions of white men because they have benefitted from them. . . . One manifestation of white women's privilege is the seeming naivete many white women have concerning interracial relationships with Black men.[119]

Ironically, some critiques of miscegeny, past and present, ally black women with white men as defenders of the black-white ethnosexual boundary. Micaela di Leonardo, an Italian American woman married to an African American, chafes against the stinging criticisms she has received for speaking on the subject of racism and for claiming a degree of integration into her husband's family. Those criticisms are exemplified in this response to her work by a black woman journalist:

> I am not an honorary black person, I'm a real one. Therefore, I have very little patience with people like di Leonardo who feel that they know what our problems are, and how to deal with them. Black people have a historical problem with white people attempting to define them and telling them what to do. . . . We already have to deal with racism. Add white paternalism to that and it's no wonder we can't get together among ourselves and work it out.[120]

Di Leonardo replies that "denying whites the right to speak out against racism just lets them off the hook."[121] She argues that she has sufficient knowledge to speak on racism because of her first-hand experience seeing her husband's and teenage stepson's daily dealings with racism, and because of her own treatment by other whites:

> In the eyes of many whites, I am now, as they say, tarred with the same brush. I, not my husband, was the victim of the sly, sexually insinuating remarks made by male and female faculty at a Southern university where we were being recruited for jobs. And the new racist right has a special place in its heart—and its plans—for me and my intermarrying sisters. William Pierce's The Turner Diaries . . . describes in loving detail the Los Angeles streetscape after the Day of the Rope: miscegenating women hang "from tens of thousands of lampposts" their "grisly forms" hung with placards stating "I defiled my race."[122]

Whatever the potential dangers to whites from their intimate relations with blacks, for most whites most of the time our skin color serves as a passport that we can use to enter exotic worlds of Otherness, remain for a long or short stay as ethnosexual sojourners or adventurers, and then safely pass back into a world of white privilege. In her essay "Eating the Other," bell hooks acknowledges the potential of racial mixing to challenge prevailing racial hegemonies, but is skeptical about the motivations and reflexivity of white ethnosexual travelers and consumers of black (and other nonwhite) cultures and bodies:

> The over-riding fear is that cultural, ethnic, and racial differences will be continually commodified and offered up as new dishes to enhance the white palate—that the Other will be eaten, consumed, and forgotten. . . . Acknowledging ways the desire for pleasure, and that includes erotic longings, informs our politics, our understanding of difference, we may know better how desire disrupts, subverts, and makes resistance possible. We cannot, however, accept these new images uncritically.[123]

RACE AND SEXUALITIES

As the commentaries of Wallace, Collins, di Leonardo, and hooks testify, sexually crossing the color line remains a conspicuous and controversial activity in the United States today. It is not only heterosexual relationships, however, that are shaped by ethnosexual boundaries and the disciplinary regimes that govern them. Lesbian and gay African Americans report that a variation on the admonition not to mix race and sex often greets them in their home communities: don't mix race and sexualities. The cost of queerness to gays and lesbians of color may not be only their sexual respectability, but their racial reputability as well. One important feature of ethnic boundaries involves questions of membership—who *is* and who *is not* a bonifide member of the group; in the case of African Americans, who *is* and who *is not* black.[124]

The struggle over the definition of blackness and the place of sexuality in that struggle came to the fore during the civil rights movement especially during the Black Power era of the late 1960s and early 1970s, when prevailing (mainly white) public definitions of the meaning and rights associated with blackness were challenged by African American activists and intellectuals. The style of Black Power and its contrast to earlier organizations and personae of the civil rights movement (e.g., the Urban League, Dr. Martin Luther King Jr.) were most dramatic and visible in the discourse, dress, and demeanor of the Black Panthers, an activist group founded in 1966 in Oakland, California.[125] One of the Panthers' most effective strategies in the symbolic struggle over the meaning of blackness was their rewriting of the ethnosexual script for African American men. Thomas Wolfe summarized the impact of the Panthers' sexual style on [white] observers at the time:

> [S]he is not alone in her thrill as the Black Panthers come trucking on in. . . . Christ, if the Panthers don't know how to get it all together, as they say, the tight pants, the tight black turtlenecks, the leather coats, Cuban shades, Afros. But real Afros, not the ones that have been shaped and trimmed . . .

but like funky, natural, scraggly . . . wild. . . . *These are no civil-rights* Negroes *wearing grey suits three sizes too big . . . these are* real men![126]

Figures 4.4 and 4.5 illustrate the differences in appearance and styles of manhood between the two phases of the civil rights movement to which Wolfe is referring.

Looking beyond the gaze of white observers to the words of the Panthers themselves, their reinvention and reassertion of black masculinity valorized heterosexuality and racial sexual pride. For instance, in his book *Soul on Ice*, former Black Panther Minister of Information Eldridge Cleaver articulated the meaning of black macho as exclusively heterosexual (and intraracial, despite Cleaver's own ethnosexual travels) when he attacked black author James Baldwin's homosexuality as "somehow un-black."[127] In doing so Cleaver equated black homosexuality with white forced miscegeny and charged gay blacks with participating in a kind of racial suicide:

What has been happening for the past four hundred years is that the white man, through his access to black women, has been pumping his blood and genes into blacks, has been diluting the blood and genes of the blacks—i.e., has been . . . accelerating the Negroes' racial death-wish . . . it seems that many Negro homosexuals [are also] acquiescing in this racial death-wish.[128]

FIGURE 4.4 Memphis Sanitation Workers' Strike, 1968 (Copyright © Bettmann/CORBIS)

FIGURE 4.5 Members of the Black Panther Party, 1969 (Courtesy of Jonathan Eubanks, photographer)

Charles Nero finds support in the work of black scholars for Cleaver's assertions about the incompatibility of blackness and homosexuality, including Frantz Fanon's psychoanalytically based conclusion in *Black Skin, White Masks* that homosexuality was "an attribute of the white race," and did not exist in the Caribbean because blacks there don't experience the oedipal tensions that putatively give rise to same-sex desire.[129] This view of homosexuality as a unique feature of white or Western sexuality has been articulated often by nonwhites and non-Westerners. In the early 1990s, Zimbabwean president Joseph Mugabe justified the exclusion of Gays and Lesbians of Zimbabwe from an international book fair held in Harare, denouncing "homosexuality as a Western corruption imported to Africa through colonization."[130] In 1998, the decennial Anglican Bishops Conference meeting in Canterbury, England, voted to continue church policy that defines homosexuality as incompatible with biblical teachings; those voting to retain the policy were mainly from the ranks of Third World bishops who tended to be more conservative than their colleagues from the West. Some of those casting negative votes argued that the issue was not relevant to their congregations. For instance, the Right Rev. Michael Lugor of Sudan claimed, "In Sudan, we know nothing of homosexuality. We only know the Gospel."[131]

Joseph Beam laments the lack of social and symbolic space available to gay blacks in their own communities in the United States, and describes the feeling of exclusion and invisibility experienced by many black homosexuals:

> When I speak of home, I mean not only the familial constellation from which I grew, but the entire Black community; the Black press, the Black church, Black academicians, the Black literati, and the Black left. Where is my reflection? I am most often rendered invisible, perceived as a threat to the family, or I am tolerated if I am silent and inconspicuous. I cannot go home as who I am and that hurts me deeply.[132]

Black lesbians take their straight sisters to task for their silence on the subject of homophobia in African American communities:

> I am more than a little tired of Black women who say they are political, who say they are feminists, who rely on Black Lesbians' friendships, insights, commitment, and work, but who, when it comes down to the crunch and the time to be accountable, turn their backs. . . . There's nothing to compare to how you feel when you're cut cold by your own.[133]

Collins provides a partial explanation for the reluctance of some black women intellectuals to take up the cause of critiquing heteronormativity and homophobia, namely their wish to avoid being labeled lesbians themselves:

> For Black women who have already been labeled the Other by virtue of our race and gender, the threat of being labeled a lesbian can have a chilling effect on Black women's ideas and on our relationships with one another . . . [since as] Barbara Smith suggests. . . . "Heterosexual privilege is usually the only privilege that Black women have. None of us have racial or sexual privilege, almost none of us have class privilege, maintaining 'straightness' is our last resort."[134]

The homophobia at worst, indifference at best that face lesbians and gays in the black community, combine with the racism of gay whites, to further isolate black homosexuals. Essex Hemphill comments, "The contradictions of 'home' are amplified and become more complex when black gay men's relationships with the white gay community are also examined."[135] He cites as an example of the white gaze that distorts and magnifies black gay sexuality, the work of late gay white photographer Robert Mapplethorpe, in particular his "Man in a Polyester Suit." The photograph features a black male torso in a business suit, his pants unzipped and his large, flaccid, uncircumcised penis exposed. Hemphill wonders *who* is the man in the photo and *why* is his head missing?[136] He agrees with Isaac Julien and Kobena Mercer's analysis of the photo as a "colonial fantasy" designed to "service the expectations of white desire."[137]

The writings of Native American, Asian American, and Latino gay men and lesbians resonate with those of African Americans reporting feelings of exclusion both from their home communities and from the white gay world. Lesbians of color express similar experiences of isolation and make similar criticisms of white lesbians and feminists for insensitivity to the differing needs of lesbians of color:

> I think about all the white women I knew in San Francisco. Women with Master's degrees from Stanford University & cars that daddy bought, women with straight white teeth & clear skins from thousands of years of proper nutrition. They chose to be poor. . . . I no longer believe that feminism is a tool which can eliminate racism—or even promote better understanding between different races & kinds of women. . . . Perhaps white women are so rarely loyal because they do not have to be. There are thousands of them to pick up & discard.[138]

CONCLUSION

The sexual history of Africans in America lies at the heart of the social history of race in America. The roots of contemporary racism and racial conflict were planted early in American history in sexual soil, they were fed by sexual fears and desires, and they thrived in an environment of lust, greed, and demeaning sexual stereotypes. To understand contemporary U.S. race relations it is important to understand the role of sexuality in building and supporting U.S. racial boundaries. Sexuality, in particular the sexual exploitation of slaves with its associated intensities of appetite, shame, and denial, was and remains a vital part of the U.S. racial order.

Although its roots can be found in the sexual excesses of the slavery system, even after slavery was outlawed, the demonization of black sexuality remained a convenient excuse to implement and defend continued discrimination, segregation, exploitation (including sexual experimentation), and vilification of African Americans—a pattern that has continued in the twentieth century. Perhaps the most infamous instance of sustained sexual abuse of African Americans after slavery was the so-called Tuskegee experiment in which for forty years black men who were infected with syphilis were not provided treatment for the disease so that the U.S. Public Health Service could study its long-term effects. The "study" began in 1932 and lasted until July 25, 1972, when Associated Press reporter Jean Heller broke the story in the *Washington Star*.[139] On May 17, 1997, President Bill Clinton publicly apologized for the incident on behalf of the United States.

The U.S. government and the American people have yet to apologize for their ancestors' involvement in and support of slavery. Many, if not most, Americans continue to this day to repeat longstanding denials of the extent of the damage done to African Americans by the institution of slavery and continue to refuse to acknowledge the relevance of those past crimes to U.S. race relations today. Part of the pattern of national denial is our comfortable ignorance of the sexual abuses imbedded in slavery and its aftermath in the South and the North.

As we have seen in these first few chapters, whether they are sites of queer or straight intimate connection, ethnosexual frontiers represent real and symbolic spaces where race, gender, and class structures and inequalities routinely are produced and reproduced. Part of the power of ethnosexuality lies in the fact that the intimate intersections that mark the territory where ethnic boundaries meet have the capacity to attract as well as to repel. Ethnosexual crossings involve opposite reactions: longing and loathing, desire and disgust. This allure and ambivalency extends beyond U.S. history and national borders. The presence of ethnosexual boundaries and the dynamics of their construction and crossing are not uniquely American; they are common, I would argue, universal social facts. The remaining chapters in this book gaze outward from the American experience toward international and global ethnosexual frontiers.

NOTES

1. Also known as the "Lapps" of Scandinavia; see Steven G. Ellis, *Tudor Ireland: Crown, Community, and the Conflict of Cultures, 1470–1603* (London: Longman, 1985); Michael Mason, *The Making of Victorian Sexuality* (Oxford: Oxford University Press, 1994); Catherine Hall, "Going A-Trolloping: Imperial Man Travels the Empire," in *Gender and Imperialism*, ed. Clare Midgley (Manchester: Manchester University Press, 1998), 180–99; Desmond Gregory, *Sicily: The Insecure Base. A His-*

tory of the British Occupation of Sicily, 1806–1815 (Rutherford, NJ: Fairleigh Dickinson Press, 1988); Robert Lumley and Jonathan Morris, The New History of the Italian South: The Mezzogiorno Revisited (Exeter: University of Exeter Press, 1997); Lembit Vaba, Juri Viikberg, and Andres Heinapuu, The Endangered Uralic Peoples (http://www.suri.ee/eup/samis.html).

   2. Joseph C. Miller, Way of Death: Merchant Capitalism and the Angolan Slave Trade, 1730–1830 (Madison: University of Wisconsin Press, 1988); Eldred D. Jones, The Elizabethan Image of Africa (Charlottesville: University of Virginia Press, 1971).

   3. For histories of slavery before and after 1492, see Peter Linebaugh and Marcus Rediker, The Many-Headed Hydra: Sailors, Slaves, Commoners, and the Hidden History of the Revolutionary Atlantic (Boston: Beacon Press, 2000); David Eltis, The Rise of African Slavery in the Americas (New York: Cambridge University Press, 2000).

   4. For discussions of how race matters in contemporary America, see Cornel West, Race Matters (Boston: Beacon Press, 1993); Ruth Frankenberg, White Women, Race Matters: The Social Construction of Whiteness (Minneapolis: University of Minnesota Press, 1993).

   5. William Blake's illustration was prepared for J. G. Stedman, Narrative, of a five years' expedition, against the Revolted Negroes of Surinam, in Guiana, on the Wild coast of South America; from the year 1772 to 1777 (London, 1796); for a critical and convincing interpretation of Stedman's narrative and Blake's illustrations, see Marcus Wood, Blind Memory: Visual Representations of Slavery in England and America, 1780–1865 (New York: Routledge, 2000); I wish to thank Jane Rhodes, Department of Ethnic Studies, University of California, San Diego for bringing this book to my attention.

   6. Anne McClintock, Imperial Leather: Race, Gender, and Sexuality in the Colonial Contest (New York: Routledge, 1995), 22; Kathleen Brown argues that although both American Indian and African women were sexualized, "Indian women were much more likely to be described as beautiful and alluring by [early] English writers than were their African counterparts"; Kathleen Brown, "Native Americans and Early Modern Concepts of Race," in Empire and Others: British Encounters with Indigenous Peoples, 1600–1850, ed. Martin Daunton and Rick Halpern (Philadelphia: University of Pennsylvania Press, 1999), 91.

   7. Ibid. It was not only European whites who espoused such notions, so did some of those whom they colonized; Winthrop Jordan quotes from the 1526 writings of Leo Africanus, "a Spanish Moroccan Moor converted to Christianity . . . [who] was as explicit as he was imaginative":

   [T]he Negroes [of Africa] likewise leade a beastly kind of life, being utterly destitute of the use of reason, of dexteritie of wit, and of all arts. Yea, they so behave themselves, as if they had continually lived in a Forrest among wild beasts. They have great swarmes of Harlots among them; whereupon a man may easily conjecture their manner of living. (Winthrop D. Jordan, White over Black: American Attitudes Toward the Negro, 1550–1812 [Chapel Hill: University of North Carolina Press, 1968], 34)

Jordan reports that Africanus's work was translated into English around 1600 (ibid.).

   8. Ibid., 35.

   9. Ibid., 33.

10. Ibid.

11. Ibid.

12. Ibid., 35.

13. McClintock, *Imperial Leather*, 22.

14. See Vincent Carretta, "Olaudah Equiano or Gustavus Vassa? New Light on an Eighteenth-Century Question of Identity," *Slavery and Abolition: A Journal of Slave and Post-Slave Societies* 20 (1999).

15. Philip D. Morgan, "British Encounters with Africans and African-Americans, circa 1600–1780," in *Strangers within the Realm: Cultural Margins of the First British Empire*, ed. Bernard Bailyn and Philip D. Morgan (Chapel Hill: University of North Carolina Press, 1991), 157–59.

16. Olaudah Equiano, *The Interesting Narrative of the Life of Olaudah Equiano, Written by Himself*, ed. Robert J. Allison (Boston: St. Martin's Press, 1995), 55.

17. Ibid., 93–94.

18. For other Africans' narratives, see Philip D. Curtin, ed., *Africa Remembered: Narratives by West Africans from the Era of the Slave Trade* (Prospect Heights, IL: Waveland Press, 1977); my thanks to Tony Clark, American Studies Program, University of Kansas, for bringing this collection to my attention.

19. McClintock, *Imperial Leather*, 22.

20. Jordan, *Black over White*, 35.

21. Scholars differ as to the exact date at which black indentured servants were placed into lifetime servitude, i.e., slavery. Jordan traces the de facto practice of slavery to 1638 when Captain William Pierce of the Salem ship *Desire* brought blacks to New England "from the Providence Island colony where Negroes were already being kept as perpetual servants" (Jordan, *Black over White*, 66–67); Foster argues that the first legal distinction between indentured servants and slaves was made in 1640 in Maryland, followed by the legal recognition of slavery in Massachusetts in 1641 and in Virginia in 1661. William Z. Foster, *The Negro People in American History* (New York: International Publishers, 1954), 37.

22. See Jessie Daniels, *White Lies: Race, Class, Gender, and Sexuality in White Supremacist Discourse* (New York: Routledge, 1997).

23. Jordan, *Black over White*, 274.

24. Theodore Dwight Weld, *American Slavery as It Is: Testimony of a Thousand Voices* (New York: Arno Press, [1839] 1968), 109.

25. Ibid., 210; anti-abolitionists saw a very different set of threats, also sexual, arising not from slavery, but from its abolition; a Southern minister issued this warning about the likely sexual state of affairs in a postslavery South: "Then every negro in South Carolina and every other southern state will be his own master; nay, more than that, will be the equal of you. If you are tame enough to submit, abolitionist preachers will be at hand to consummate the marriage of your daughters to black husbands" (LeeAnn Whites, "The Civil War as a Crisis in Gender," in *Divided Houses: Gender and the Civil War*, ed. Catherine Clinton and Nina Silber [New York: Oxford University Press, 1992], 10).

26. There is debate over the Hemings-Jefferson relationship and the paternity of her children despite recent results of DNA testing confirming that Hemings's descendants are blood relatives of Jefferson; see Smith and Wade, "DNA Tests Offer Ev-

idence That Jefferson Fathered a Child with His Slave." Skeptics admit that while there are definitely Hemingses in the Jefferson family tree and the reverse, they argue that another Jefferson relative besides Thomas could have fathered Sally Hemings's children; Winthrop Jordan reports that "[a]ll the slaves freed by Jefferson were Hemingses, and none of Sally's children were retained in slavery as adults" (*White over Black*, 466); although Jordan, writing in 1968, thirty years before the DNA tests were conducted, considered this evidence of Jefferson's honor and possible innocence against charges of sexually consorting with Hemings, these facts could as easily be read as support for the assertion that Jefferson had a blood relationship with the Hemingses.

27. Thomas Jefferson, *Notes on the State of Virginia*, edited by William Peden (Chapel Hill: University of North Carolina Press, [1787] 1995), 162–63.

28. Sally Hemings was freed after Jefferson's death, though how she obtained her freedom is still debated; Beverly Gray reports that Hemings

> appears on the 1830 census for Virginia along with her two sons and their families. (At least a woman fitting her description does.) The family was listed as white on this census. She is also listed on the special census taken in the state of Virginia, for the purpose of ascertaining the number of free blacks who would relocate in Africa, in 1833 as being free.

See Beverly J. Gray, "The Hemings Family of Monticello," *Ross County Historical Society Magazine Recorder,* February, 1994: 1; see also http://www.angelfire.com/oh/chillicothe/formerslaves.html and Gordon-Reed, *Thomas Jefferson and Sally Hemings.*

29. Brown, *Good Wives, Nasty Wenches, and Anxious Patriarchs,* 209.

30. Ibid., 210. Historians have argued that laws against both rape and interracial sex and marriage are based in notions of white women as the property of white men, in particular, white women's reproductive capacity—to bear, nurture, and rear men's children; Brown cites a rape case tried in Virginia in 1689 to illustrate how the rape of a woman was defined as a violation of a property right attached to her reproductive capacity:

> [Thomas] Seawell claimed to have met up with a "swinishly Drunk" Eliza Farrell at a party. . . . When the "weary" Farrell stumbled to the upper chamber of the house to lie down, Seawell followed her, sexually assaulting her with an ox horn and a lit candle. He brought the incident to Farrell's husband's attention by waving some of Eliza's singed pubic hair in front of his face. Brian and Eliza Farrell did not simply claim damages for the sexual assault or physical injury committed against her, nor was Brian simply interested in defending his violated sense of honor. Rather, the claim of damages against Seawell cited the then-pregnant Eliza's miscarriage as the couple's loss. (Ibid., 207)

31. Sharon Block, "Lines of Color, Sex, and Service: Comparative Sexual Coercion in Early America," in *Sex, Love, Race: Crossing Boundaries in North American History,* ed. Martha Hodes (New York: New York University Press, 1999), 141–63; for a discussion of "racializing sex" in the seventeenth and eighteenth centuries in Virginia, see Brown, *Good Wives, Nasty Wenches, and Anxious Patriarchs,* 207–11.

32. Block, "Lines of Color, Sex, and Service," 141.

33. Ibid.

34. Ibid.

35. Ibid., 143.

36. Melton A. McLaurin, *Celia, A Slave* (Athens: University of Georgia Press, 1991).

37. This account of Celia's life and death are drawn from McLaurin, *Celia, A Slave* and Hartman, *Scenes of Subjection* as well as Callaway County court records.

38. McLaurin, *Celia, A Slave*, 18.

39. Testimony of Colonel Jefferson Jones, *State of Missouri v. Celia, a Slave*, Callaway County Court, October Term, 1855 (Fulton, MO: Callaway County Courthouse).

40. Ibid.

41. McLaurin, *Celia, A Slave*, 31.

42. The third child was stillborn while she was in custody; Ibid., 102–3.

43. For a discussion of rape, slavery, and the law, see Hartman, *Scenes of Subjection*, 79–86.

44. Another enslaved person escaped with Celia, a man named Mat, who was also convicted of murder; both Mat and Celia were recaptured, but Mat escaped again and remained free (McLaurin, *Celia, A Slave*, 104–8); in 1859 the State of Missouri's General Assembly passed an appropriations act

> for the sum of one hundred and eighty-eight dollars and seventy-five cents, in favor of George Bartley, Clerk of the Circuit Court within and for Callaway county, to be appropriated by him in the payment of the costs which accrued in the trial of. . . . Mat, a slave, [who] was indicted, tried, and found guilty of murder in the first degree, in Callaway county; . . . [since] said slave escaped from custody before he was executed. (*Laws of the State of Missouri*, first session, twentieth general assembly, Monday, December 27, 1858 [Jefferson City: C.J. Corwin, Public Printer, 1859], 7)

I wish to thank Susan M. Johnston, Callaway County Circuit Court Clerk for providing me with the transcripts of Celia's and Mat's trials, for sharing local knowledge of the cases with me, and for putting me in contact with the Kingdom of Callaway County Historical Society.

45. McLaurin, *Celia, A Slave*, 114.

46. Testimony of Colonel Jefferson Jones, *State of Missouri v. Celia, a Slave*.

47. Hartman, *Scenes of Subjection*, 87.

48. See Susan Brownmiller, *Against Our Will: Men, Women, and Rape* (New York: Bantam Books, 1975).

49. Edward Long, *The History of Jamaica*, Vols I–III (London: Frank Cass, [1774] 1970), Volume 2, 331.

50. Ibid., 372, 331.

51. Morgan, "British Encounters with Africans and African-Americans," 178.

52. John Pares, *A West-India Fortune* (London: Longmans, Green, and Company, 1950), 134; to be fair to Pares, his use of quotation marks around the word "negrofied" makes it unclear whether he was speaking for himself or simply quoting John Pinney, a plantation owner on whose family records he bases his research; the remainder of Pares's work quoted here, however, appears to be his, not Pinney's analysis; more telling is Pares's uncritical, even generous, analysis of the actions of plantation holder and slaveowner, John Pinney, who

> usually lent himself to . . . [allowing his slaves to purchase their freedom], though he expected his money's worth. . . . Only once does he seem to have refused manumission from any vindictive motive. His manager James Williams had several children by the slave Janetta, *who induced him to waste the substance of the plantation in riotous living* [emphasis mine]. Before these enormities were discovered, John Pinney was willing to free the children upon Williams's giving security for the purchase-money, though he asked him

to think again whether it was wise to add thus to the free coloured population. But when Williams was dead and Janetta's conduct was known, he resolved that her children should be sold, no matter to whom, and she herself relegated to the field gang. (Ibid, 132)

It appears from Pares's analysis, that only Janetta, and not her "manager," John Williams, was guilty of profligacy; Pares goes on to say that "of this last punishment [relegating Janetta to the field gang] he repented, but he still would not let her buy herself freedom, 'as it would be an encouragement for others to act as she had done, to plunder the estate to obtain their freedom' " (Ibid.).

53. Ibid., 354, fn. 36; these figures remind us that slavery, like most social arrangements, was itself complicated by sexuality; for instance, Phillip Morgan reports that in many slave-based societies in the Americas, the offspring of sexual liaisons between slaves and nonslaves were more likely to be freed by their father/owners; see Morgan, "British Encounters with Africans and African-Americans."

54. Frances Anne Kemble, *Journal of a Residence on a Georgian Plantation in 1838–1839* (Chicago: Afro-Am Press, 1969), 227.

55. Ibid.

56. Ibid.

57. Ibid., 227–28; for a general discussion of white women slaveowners' and white wives of slaveowners' views of miscegenation, see George C. Rable, *Civil Wars: Women and the Crisis of Southern Nationalism* (Urbana: University of Illinois Press, 1989), 33ff; Drew Gilpin Faust, *Mothers of Invention: Women of the Slaveholding South in the American Civil War* (Chapel Hill: University of North Carolina Press, 1996), 126–27; Marli F. Weiner, *Mistresses and Slaves: Plantation Women in South Carolina, 1830–80* (Urbana: University of Illinois Press, 1997).

58. See Marie Jenkins Schwartz, *Born in Bondage: Growing Up Enslaved in the Antebellum South* (Cambridge, MA: Harvard University Press, 2000), 177–205.

59. Ibid.

60. Victoria E. Bynum, *Unruly Women: The Politics of Social and Sexual Control in the Old South* (Chapel Hill: University of North Carolina Press, 1992), 94.

61. Ibid., 96–97.

62. Peter W. Bardaglio, " 'Shamefull Matches': The Regulation of Interracial Sex and Marriage in the South before 1900," in *Sex, Love, Race*, 114.

63. Ibid., 115.

64. Ibid.

65. Ibid.

66. Weiner, *Mistresses and Slaves*, 95–96.

67. Ella Thomas was not the only unhappy wife of a planter class man who indulged his sexual appetite with his slaves; James Henry Hammond was a nineteenth-century South Carolina politician and slaveowner who kept detailed records of his property and his life and how he mixed the two together; Carol Bleser describes Hammond's sexual exploits and his wife's response: "Hammond records that he took eighteen-year-old [enslaved] Sally Johnson as his mistress and that he eventually became enamoured of her twelve-year-old daughter Louisa . . . [his wife] Catherine Hammond . . . left him when he refused to give up Louisa" (Carol Blesser, *Secret and Sacred: The Diaries of James Henry Hammond, a Southern Slaveholder* [New York: Oxford University Press, 1988], 19); Hammond eventually sent Louisa away and rec-

onciled with his wife, but before his death he wrote to his son, Harry, making the following chilling arrangements to "care for" his human property:

> In my last will I made I left to you. . . . Sally Johnson the mother of Louisa and all the children of both. Sally says Henderson is my child. . . . Louisa's first child *may* be mine. . . . Her second I believe is mine. Take care of her and her children who are both of *your* blood if not mine. . . . I cannot free these people and send them North. It would be cruelty to them. Nor would I like than any but my own blood should own as Slaves my own blood or Louisa. I leave them to your charge. . . . Slavery *in the family* will be their happiest earthly condition. (Ibid.)

68. Walter Johnson, *Soul by Soul: Life inside the Antebellum Slave Market* (Cambridge, MA: Harvard University Press, 1999), 113; "bright" was a synonym for light-skinned; see also Virginia R. Domínguez, *White by Definition: Social Classification in Creole Louisiana* (New Brunswick, NJ: Rutgers University Press, 1986).

69. Ibid.

70. Ibid.

71. Ibid.; see also Solomon Northrup, *Twelve Years a Slave*, edited by Sue Eakin and Joseph Logsdon (Baton Rouge: Louisiana State University Press, 1968).

72. Ibid.; Hilary Beckles's study of the relationship between slave owners and enslaved women in the Caribbean provides another view of gender dynamics in slavery, one in which enslaved women resisted and challenged the authority of many female mistresses; for instance, slaveowner Mary Hays sent letters from Barbados to Britain between 1814 and 1822 complaining of problems with her women slaves whom she had purchased as a means of living comfortably in colonial society: "They refused to work, lied, stole, ignored instructions and showed contempt for her authority . . . [causing her] 'endless trouble and vexation' [and refusing to respond to her 'gentle and kindly impulses';" see Hilary McD. Beckles, "Taking Liberties: Enslaved Women and Anti-Slavery in the Caribbean," in *Gender and Imperialism*, 153.

73. Ibid., 115; see also D'Emilio and Freedman, *Intimate Matters*, 102–103.

74. Hartman, *Scenes of Subjection*, 84–85.

75. Ibid., 99; see also Fischer, *Suspect Relations*, chapter 4; maligning the respectability and sexual worth of white women who have sex with nonwhite "others" is a common theme in ethnosexual discourse, and is reported widely in a variety of times and places by researchers; see Ortner, *Making Gender*; di Leonardo, "White Lies, Black Myths"; Schutte, *What Racists Believe: Race Relations in South Africa and the United States* (Thousand Oaks, CA: Sage Publications, 1995); Abby L. Ferber, *White Man Falling: Race, Gender, and White Supremacy* (Lanham, MD: Rowman and Littlefield, 1998); Daniels, *White Lies*.

76. Martha Hodes, *White Women, Black Men: Illicit Sex in the Nineteenth Century South* (New Haven: Yale University Press, 1997), 63–65.

77. See, for instance, Joel Williamson, *New People: Miscegenation and Mulattoes in the United States* (Baton Rouge: Louisiana State University Press, 1995); Philip D. Morgan, "Encounters Between British and 'Indigenous' Peoples, 1500–1800," in *Empire and Others*, 65–66; Morgan, "British Encounters with Africans and African-Americans"; my thanks to Barry Shank, Division of Comparative Studies, Ohio State University, for pointing out the importance of regional variations in slavery.

78. Morgan, "British Encounters with Africans and African-Americans," 169.

79. Martha Hodes, "The Sexualization of Reconstruction Politics: White Women

and Black Men in the South after the Civil War," in *American Sexual Politics: Sex, Gender, and Race since the Civil War*, ed. J. C. Fout and M. S. Tantillo (Chicago: University of Chicago Press, 1993), 60.

80. The rage of white Klansmen could be turned against their own race when white women were seen to be consorting or sympathizing with blacks; Hodes reports instances of the raping, beating, shearing the heads, and sexual mutilation of white women known to be the sexual partners of black men; see Hodes, "The Sexualization of Reconstruction Politics," 68.

81. Hodes, *White Women, Black Men*, 43.

82. See Jane Dailey, Glenda Elizabeth Gilmore, and Bryant Simon, *Jumpin' Jim Crow: Southern Politics from Civil War to Civil Rights* (Princeton: Princeton University Press, 2000).

83. Sandra Gunning, *Race, Rape, and Lynching: The Red Record of American Literature, 1890–1912* (New York: Oxford University Press, 1996).

84. David W. Blight, *Race and Reunion: The Civil War in American Memory* (Cambridge, MA: Harvard University Press, 2001), 147, from Henry McNeil Turner's "Army Correspondence," May 15, 1865.

85. Ibid.; my thanks to Melissa Haveman, Department of Sociology, University of Kansas, for bringing this book to my attention.

86. Bruce's retrospective of life under slavery was published in 1889; the contents and timing of the book reflected the power of white Southerners' persistent fears of and viciousness toward black men a quarter-century after the end of the Civil War when white lynchings of black men were at historically high levels; see Gunning, *Race, Rape, and Lynching*, 22. A version of this power/revenge argument was articulated in Black Power discourse nearly a century later: in his book, *Soul on Ice*, published in 1968, Eldridge Cleaver, writing from prison, admits that he became a rapist, first "practicing on black girls," then seeking out "white prey," and argued that

> [r]ape was an insurrectionary act. It delighted me that I was defying and trampling upon the white man's law, upon his system of values, and that I was defiling his women—and this point, I believe, was the most satisfying to me because I was very resentful over the historical fact of how the white man has used the black woman. I felt I was getting revenge. (Eldridge Cleaver, *Soul on Ice* [New York: Dell Publishing Company, 1968], 14)

Whether or not Cleaver's claim that he was "getting even" by raping white women was the sum total of his motivations, in his words we can see ethnosexual contact written as a transaction between men—black and white—with (white) women as the currency in the exchange.

87. Hodes, "The Sexualization of Reconstruction Politics," 71; see also her *White Women, Black Men*.

88. Ibid.

89. Ibid., 64.

90. David B. Chesebrough, *Frederick Douglass: Oratory from Slavery* (Westport, CT: Greenwood Press, 1998), 75.

91. Ibid.; there were some supporters who came to Douglass's defense: white feminists and abolitionists Elizabeth Cady Stanton and Susan B. Anthony were allied with Douglass in the movement to abolish slavery, and Douglass was invaluable as a male supporter of women's rights; their relationship suffered when black men

gained the right to the vote, however, since that was a right that no woman, white or black, would possess until more than a half-century later. Elizabeth Cady Stanton's criticism of this inequity became notorious when she declared in 1868, "it becomes a serious question whether we had better stand aside and see 'Sambo' walk into the kingdom first," and Susan B. Anthony stated that she would "sooner cut off my right hand than ask for the ballot for the black man and not for woman"; Maria Diedrich, *Love across Color Lines: Ottilie Assing and Frederick Douglass* (New York: Hill and Wang, 1999), 289; see also Claire Midgley, "Anti-Slavery and the Roots of 'Imperial Feminism'," in *Gender and Imperialism*, ed. Claire Midgley (Manchester: Manchester University Press, 1998), 161–79.

92. For instance, Stewart Tolnay and E. M. Beck's historical study of Southern lynchings analyzed 2,314 lynchings of African Americans by white mobs during the period from 1882 to 1930 and found that 33.6 percent of these were for "sexual norm violations" including "rape, incest, miscegenation, or improper conduct with a woman"; Stewart E. Tolnay and E. M. Beck, *A Festival of Violence: An Analysis of Southern Lynchings, 1882–1930* (Urbana: University of Illinois Press, 1995), 48.

93. See Stephen Kantrowitz, "White Supremacist Justice and the Rule of Law: Lynching, Honor, and the State in Ben Tillman's South Carolina," in *Men and Violence: Gender, Honor, and Rituals in Modern Europe and America*, ed. Pieter Spierenburg (Columbus: Ohio State University Press, 1998), 213–39; Terence Finnegan, " 'The Equal of Some White Men and the Superior of Others': Masculinity and the 1916 Lynching of Anthony Crawford in Abbeville County, South Carolina," in *Men and Violence*, 240–54.

94. Bederman, *Manliness and Civilization*, 45; see also Vron Ware, *Beyond the Pale: White Women, Racism, and History* (London: Verso, 1992), 167–224; Ida B. Wells-Barnett, *Crusade for Justice: The Autobiography of Ida B. Wells*, edited by Alfreda M. Duster (Chicago: University of Chicago Press, 1970); Wells was not alone in her crusade; the National Organization for the Advancement of Colored People and many other organizations and individuals in the United States and abroad campaigned against lynchings; see for instance, Robert L. Zangrando, *The NAACP Crusade against Lynching, 1909–1950* (Philadelphia: Temple University Press, 1980).

95. Grace Elizabeth Hale, *Making Whiteness: The Culture of Segregation in the South, 1890–1940* (New York: Pantheon Books, 1998); see also Philip Dray, *At the Hands of Persons Unknown: The Lynching of Black America* (New York: Random House, 2002).

96. See Joel Williamson, *The Crucible of Race: Black-White Relations in the American South since Emancipation* (New York: Oxford University Press, 1984).

97. Robin Wiegman, "The Anatomy of Lynching," in *American Sexual Politics*, 237–38.

98. See Angela Y. Davis, "Rape, Racism, and the Myth of the Black Rapist," in *Women, Race, and Class* (New York: Vintage Books, 1981), 172–200; Diane M. Sommerville, "The Rape Myth in the Old South Reconsidered," *Journal of Southern History* 61 (1995): 481–518.

99. See Kevin J. Mumford, " 'Lost Manhood' Found: Male Sexual Impotence and Victorian Culture in the United States," in *American Sexual Politics*, 75–99; Kevin White, *The First Sexual Revolution: The Emergence of Male Heterosexuality in Modern America* (New York: New York University Press, 1993).

100. Bederman, *Manliness and Civilization*, 1.

101. Ibid., 2.

102. Ibid., 3.

103. Kevin J. Mumford, *Interzones: Black/White Sex Districts in Chicago and New York in the Early Twentieth Century* (New York: Columbia University Press, 1997), 9; Cameron was indeed briefly institutionalized, but after her release she and Johnson were married.

104. For historical and recent treatises on "white slavery," see Ernest A. Bell, *Fighting the Traffic in Young Girls or War on the White Slave Trade* (New York: Gordon Press, [circa 1910] 1975); John Dillon, *From Dance Hall to White Slavery: Ten Dance Hall Tragedies* (New York: Padell Book and Magazine Company, 1943); Frederick K. Grittner, *White Slavery: Myth, Ideology, and American Law* (New York: Garland Publishing, 1990); Donovan, "The Sexual Basis of Racial Formation."

105. Bederman, *Manliness and Civilization*, 9; Jack Johnson was among the first Americans to be charged and convicted with "white slavery" in a publicized trial, but he was not the last; along the way another black public celebrity was caught in that racial sexual net: in 1962, rock'n'roll musician Chuck Berry was convicted for bringing a woman he'd met in El Paso, Texas, to his nightclub in St. Louis, Missouri; when he fired her, she went to the police, and Berry was tried twice (the first trial was "so blatantly racist that it was disallowed"), convicted, and sentenced to two years in prison; see Grittner, *White Slavery*, 163; Robert Christgau, "Chuck Berry," in *The Rolling Stone Illustrated History of Rock and Roll*, ed. Jim Miller (New York: Rolling Stone Press, 1976), 58–63.

106. This was two years after English women were granted the right to vote at age thirty; the universal franchise for English women twenty-one years and older was not granted until 1928; in the United States women in Utah had the right to vote from the date of Utah's territorial formation in 1869; it would take another fifty years for the United States to follow that precedent by ratifying the Sixteenth Amendment to the U.S. Constitution (on August 26, 1920), which granted the right to vote to women at age twenty-one; a more recent battle over women's right to vote was in Kuwait, where on July 4, 2000, the Kuwaiti supreme court ruled against cases filed by women who argued that a Kuwaiti electoral law that banned women from voting was unconstitutional; see *Tehran Times*, "Kuwait Court Rejects Women's Right to Vote," July 4, 2000; *Middle East News On-Line*, http://www.middleeastwire.com/kuwait/stories/20000705_meno.shtml).

107. Barbara Bush, " 'Britain's Conscience on Africa': White Women, Race, and Imperial Politics in Inter-War Britain," *Gender and Imperialism*, 216; see also Midgley, "Anti-Slavery and the Roots of 'Imperial Feminism.' "

108. Ibid.; Bush cites Garvey's "Colored Men Who attract White Girls," *News Chronicle* 15 (1937): 4 and *The Black Man* 2 (March to April, 1937): 71–78.

109. Ibid.; bell hooks notes that white women and black men are united in their common oppression by white men and that they sometimes work together to resist white men's rule, but she argues that they also are united in their desire for white men's approval and that in seeking that approval they become unwitting supporters of the patriarchal order. "Doing It for Daddy," in *Constructing Masculinity*, ed. Maurice Berger, Brian Wallis, and Simon Watson (New York: Routledge, 1995), 98–106. It was not only sex between white women and black men that Americans and Euro-

peans found so disturbing and fascinating; Jennifer Terry reports racialized theories of homosexuality were common during the early decades of the twentieth century, and cites the work of psychologists and psychiatrists who describe black women as seducing or corrupting white women, especially in institutional settings like schools or prisons; Jennifer Terry, *An American Obsession: Science, Medicine, and Homosexuality in Modern Society* (Chicago: University of Chicago Press, 1999), 114–17.

110. Brian Donovan, "White Slavery and Race-Making: Crusading against Forced Prostitution, 1887–1917," paper presented at the annual meeting of the American Sociological Association, Washington, DC, 2000.

111. See Bederman, *Manliness and Civilization;* C. J. Cohen, "Punks, Bulldaggers, and Welfare Queens: The Radical Potential of Queer Politics?" *GLQ: A Journal of Lesbian and Gay Studies* 3 (1997): 437–65; Sammy Davis Jr., J. Boyar, and B. Boyar, *Why Me? The Sammy Davis, Jr. Story* (New York: Farrar, Straus, Giroux, 1989); J. Gabriel, *Whitewash: Racialized Politics and the Media* (New York: Routledge, 1997); Paula Giddings, *When and Where I Enter: The Impact of Black Women on Race and Sex in America* (New York: William Morrow, 1984), 253; Gunning, *Race, Rape, and Lynching;* D. M. Hunt, *Screening the Los Angeles "Riots:" Race, Seeing, and Resistance* (New York: Columbia University Press, 1997); Karen Luker, *Dubious Conceptions: The Politics of Teenage Pregnancy* (Cambridge, MA: Harvard University Press, 1996); Mumford, *Interzones;* Wiegman, "The Anatomy of Lynching"; Tali Mendleberg, *The Race Card: Campaign Strategy, Implicit Messages, and the Norm of Equality* (Princeton: Princeton University Press, 2001); Williams, *Playing the Race Card.*

112. The number of black-white marriages has increased from 65,000 in the United States in 1970 to 363,000 in 2000; black-white marriages remain less than 1 percent of all U.S. marriages (U.S. Census Bureau: http://www.census.gov/population/socdemo/ms-la/tabms-3.txt and http://www.census.gov/population/socdemo/hh-fam/p20–537/2000/tabFG3.txt).

113. See Hodes, *Sex, Love, Race;* Earl Ofari Hutchinson, *The Assassination of the Black Male Image* (New York: Touchstone, [1994] 1997); it is not only whites who exploit images of black masculine sexual dangerousness, sometimes blacks do as well, but for different reasons, whether to reaffirm black masculinity or to challenge negative images of African Americans; for instance, see Mark Anthony Neal's discussion of hip-hop in *What the Music Said: Black Popular Music and Black Public Culture* (New York: Routledge, 1998); Susan Gubar's discussion of Nigerian artist, Ike Ude's "racechanged" images in *Racechanges: White Skin, Black Face in American Culture* (New York: Oxford University Press, 1997), 252–56; for an analysis of the dangers of black engagement with phallocentric patriarchy, see also Mark H. C. Bessire and Lauri Firstenberg, *Beyond Decorum: The Photography of Ike Ude* (Cambridge: MIT Press, 2000); bell hooks, *Outlaw Culture: Resisting Representations* (New York: Routledge, 1994), chapters 10 and 11 and *Black Looks,* chapter 6; Robin D. G. Kelley, *Race Rebels: Culture, Politics, and the Black Working Class* (New York: Free Press, 1994), chapter 8.

114. For instance, when the U.S. government accused and convicted Jack Johnson of white slavery in 1913 he had few defenders; his attractiveness and attraction to white women not only threatened and infuriated white men, Mumford reports

that "Johnson's decision to marry white women estranged him from the African-American community; he was caught in between, with neither a white nor a black constituency to support him in a time of crisis" (Mumford, *Interzones*, 9); Jack Johnson would feel right at home in contemporary America were he to hear some of the commentary on racial mixing that is made on both sides of the color line; for views of miscegenation in U.S. history, see Williamson, *New People*.

115. See Daniels, *White Lies*; Betty A. Dobratz and Stephanie L. Shanks-Meile, *"White Power, White Pride!" The White Separatist Movement in the United States* (New York: Twayne Publishers, 1997).

116. Wallace, *Black Macho and the Myth of the Superwoman*, 10.

117. Mary Aickin Rothschild, *A Case of Black and White: Northern Volunteers and the Southern Freedom Summers, 1964–1965* (Westport, CT: Greenwood Press, 1982), 139; Rothschild reports that married women volunteers were less likely to be involved in the sexual politics of the Freedom Summer, and some women adopted a strategy of getting involved with a single man in a "steady" relationship: "I find it's almost a necessity to associate yourself with one person, so the other people will not bother you as much if you have a boyfriend . . . particularly one that's nice and strong, he doesn't want . . . anyone bothering with his girlfriend" (141–42); see also, Sara M. Evans, *Personal Politics: The Roots of Women's Liberation in the Civil Rights Movement and the New Left* (New York: Vintage, 1979); Doug McAdam, *Freedom Summer* (New York: Oxford University Press, 1988).

118. Ibid., 12, 14; for a discussion of black gender relations, see the dialogue between feminist scholar bell hooks and rap singer Ice Cube, in bell hooks, "Ice Cube Culture: A Shared Passion for Speaking Truth," in *Outlaw Culture*, 125–43.

119. Patricia Hill Collins, *Black Feminist Thought: Knowledge, Consciousness, and the Politics of Empowerment* (New York: Routledge, 1990), 190–91.

120. di Leonardo, "White Lies, Black Myths: Rape, Race, and the Black 'Underclass,' " 66.

121. Ibid., 66–67.

122. Ibid., 55.

123. hooks, *Black Looks*, 39.

124. For a discussion of legal and social answers to the question of "who is black?" see James F. Davis, *Who Is Black? One Nation's Definition* (University Park: Pennsylvania State University, 1991).

125. For current reflections and analysis of the Black Panthers and their place in American and African American history, see Kathleen Cleaver and George Katsiaficas, eds., *Liberation, Imagination, and the Black Panther Party: A New Look at the Panthers and their Legacy* (New York: Routledge, 2001); Jane Rhodes, "Fanning the Flames of Racial Discord: The National Press and the Black Panther Party," *Harvard International Journal of Press Politics* 4 (1999): 95–118 and *Framing the Panthers: Media, Race, and Representation in America* (New York: The New Press, 2003); Black Panther cofounder Bobby Seale's homepage is: http://www.bobbyseale.com/

126. Thomas Wolfe, *Radical Chic and Mau-Mauing the Flak Catchers* (New York: Farrar, Straus and Giroux, 1970), 7–8.

127. Clarence Page, *Showing My Color: Impolite Essays on Race and Identity* (New York: Harper, 1996), 101.

128. Cleaver, *Soul on Ice*, 102; not all Panthers were so consistently homophobic; after a meeting between the Panthers and well-known gay French author and philosopher Jean Genet, Black Panthers cofounder Huey Newton published an article calling for an alliance between the black liberation movement and other liberation movements of the 1960s and 1970s, including gay liberation; see Edmund White, *Jean Genet: A Biography* (New York: Vintage Books, 1993); Bobby Seale, *Seize the Time: The Story of the Black Panther Party and Huey P. Newton* (Baltimore: Black Classic Press, [1970] 1991).

129. Charles I. Nero, "Toward a Black Gay Aesthetic: Signifying in Contemporary Black Gay Literature," in *Brother to Brother: New Writings by Gay Black Men*, ed. Essex Hemphill (Boston: Alyson Publications, 1991), 229–52; Nero also cites the work of Asante (1980), A. Poussaint, "What Makes Them Tick," *Ebony* (October 1978); N. Hare and J. Hare, *The Endangered Black Family: Coping with the Unisexualization and Coming Extinction of the Black Race* (San Francisco: Black Think Tank, 1984); see Frantz Fanon, *Black Skin, White Masks* (New York: Grove Press, 1968), 84.

130. Stychin, *A Nation by Rights*, 52; my thanks to Bart Dean, Department of Anthropology, University of Kansas, for bringing this book to my attention.

131. Associated Press, "Anglican bishops condemn homosexual relations" (August 7, 1998) (http://www.amarillonet.com/stories/080798/new_LA0673.shtml); of the 736 bishops who counted at the beginning of the conference, 224 were from Africa, 95 from Asia, and 316 from the United States, Canada and Europe; see also Ed Stannard, "Lambeth Showcases Conservative Anglican World," *Episcopal Life* (August, 1998) (http://www.episcopalchurch.org/episcopal-life/LambOver.html); Stephen F. Noll, "What the Anglican Bishops Said about Sex: The Lambeth Conference's Resolution 1.10, with Introduction and Commentary" (May 28, 2000) (http://www.tesm.edu/writings/nolllamb.htm).

132. Joseph Beam, "Brother to Brother: Words from the Heart," in *In the Life: A Black Gay Anthology*, ed. Joseph Beam (Boston: Alyson Publications, 1986), 231; see also Phillip Brian Harper, *Are We Not Men? Masculine Anxiety and the Problem of African-American Identity* (New York: Oxford University Press, 1996), especially chapter 1; Robert F. Reid-Pharr, *Black Gay Man: Essays* (New York: New York University Press, 2001).

133. Dorothy Smith, "Introduction," in *Home Girls: A Black Feminist Anthology*, Barbara Smith (New Brunswick, NJ: Rutgers University Press, [1983] 2000), xlix.

134. Collins, *Black Feminist Thought*, 195–96; for a discussion of black women's efforts to maintain sexual safety and respectability in the first half of the twentieth century, see Darlene Clark Hine, "Rape and the Inner Lives of Black Women in the Middle West," in *The Gender/Sexuality Reader*, 434–39.

135. Hemphill, *Brother to Brother*, xviii.

136. In a "racechanged" parody of the Mapplethorpe photo, film-maker Ike Ude produced a faux movie poster showing a pink, circumcised penis "that attributes production design to 'Newth Gengrich,' editing to 'Clarence Thomas,' and directing of photography to 'Jessey Elms,' presumably to connect repressive right-wing censorship or self-righteous respectability with shockingly sexualized productions," see Gubar, *Racechanges*, 254.

137. Ibid., xviii; see Isaac Julien and Kobena Mercer, "True Confessions: A Discourse on Images of Black Male Sexuality," *Ten-8* 22 (1986): 6; Mercer provides a revised analysis of Mapplethorpe's work in "Skin Head Sex Thing: Racial Difference and the Homoerotic Imaginary," in *How Do I Look: Queer Film and Video,* ed. Bad Object-Choices (Seattle: Bay Press, 1991), 169–222; my thanks to Sam Joshi, Department of Theatre and Film, University of Kansas. for bringing Mercer's revised discussion to my attention.

138. Chrystos, "I Don't Understand Those Who Have Turned away from Me," in *This Bridge Called My Back: Writings by Radical Women of Color* ed. Cherrie Moraga and Gloria Anzaldua (Watertown, MA: Persephone, 1981), 68–70; see also Gloria Anzaldua, *Making Face, Making Soul: Creative and Critical Perspectives by Women of Color* (San Francisco: Aunt Lute Foundation, 1990); Russell Leong, *Asian American Sexualities: Dimensions of the Gay and Lesbian Experience* (New York: Routledge, 1996); Rakesh Ratti, *A Lotus of Another Color* (Boston: Alyson, 1993); Kenneth Plummer, *Telling Sexual Stories: Power, Change, and Social Worlds* (New York: Routledge, 1995); Jacobs et al., *Two-Spirit People.*

139. See James H. Jones, *Bad Blood: The Tuskegee Syphilis Experiment* (New York: Free Press, 1993); Fred D. Gray, *The Tuskegee Syphilis Study: The Real Story and Beyond* (Montgomery, AL: Black Belt Press, 1998); Ann Hickey, "Beyond 'The Deadly Deception': The Influence of Ethnosexual Boundaries in the Tuskegee Syphilis Experiment," paper presented at the annual meeting of the American Sociological Association, Chicago, 2002.

CHAPTER 5

Sex and Nationalism

Sexually Imagined Communities

Sexual Spectacles of Nationalism

In August 1944, U.S. Army photographers documented Allied forces' liberation of France from German Nazi occupation. The image captured in Figure 5.1 is a now-famous picture of two "shorn women" who were accused of sexually collaborating with the Nazis in occupied France during World War II. In the photograph we can see the women's shaved heads, shoeless feet, stripped clothing, and the swastikas tattooed on the women's foreheads. Margaret Weitz interviewed a young Frenchwoman whose father was in the French Resistance; she described the fate of similar French women who were identified as "Nazi collaborators" in the summer of 1944:

> The war was not finished, but in Paris it assumed another form—more perverse, more degrading. . . . The "shorn woman" of rue Petit-Musc . . . walked along with her wedge-soled shoes tied around her neck, stiff like those undergoing a major initiation. Her face was frozen like a Buddha, her carriage tense and superb in the midst of a shouting, screeching mob of faces contorted by hatred, groping and opportunistic hands, eyes congested by excitement, festivity, sexuality, sadism.[1]

This picture was published in a pictorial history of World War II edited by Stephen Ambrose.[2] On the adjacent page of that volume is another photograph. It shows a man on his knees with a blindfold over his eyes; he is just about to be executed with a shot to the head. He is also a French collaborator, but the difference in the images and the treatment of the women and the man speak volumes about the sexualized and gendered nature of patriotism, treason, betrayal, and the relation and relative importance of men and women to the nation.

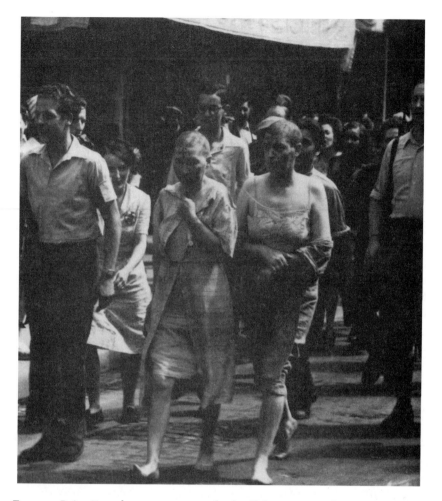

FIGURE 5.1   French women accused of collaborating with Nazis, August, 1944 (Courtesy of the U.S. National Archives)

These images and the above account illustrate several important features about national sexual boundaries, and show how (in this case hetero)sexual behavior on the margins can strengthen hegemonic national sexual orders. First, we can see that national and sexual boundaries are mutually reinforcing. Implicit in the idea of the nation ("who are we?") are certain prescriptions and proscriptions for sexual crossings—what good citizens should and should not do sexually, and whom they should and should not have sex with. In this case, "our" women should not be having sex with "their" (particularly "enemy") men. Second, we can see the ubiquitous double standard that applies to many sexual boundaries: our men can have consensual sex, rape, or even sexually enslave their women and not have their heads shaved and tattooed and be paraded around the town, in fact, men's sexual misconduct in war is seldom prosecuted.[3] On the contrary, in times of war, our women might even want to do their patriotic duty by making themselves sexually available to our men while the sexual police look the other way—as long as internal racial and ethnic boundaries are not violated.[4] Another lesson to be learned from this tale of punishing women sexual collaborators is that their rule breaking was seized as an opportunity to reinforce and reestablish sexual and nationalist hegemony. By disciplining women collaborators, proper sexual demeanor and approved ethnosexual partners were publicly proclaimed.[5] The national sexual order was reinstated: a place for every man and woman, and everyone in their place.

As we know, there are much more familiar images from World War II; the most notorious, of course, is the six-pointed Star of David that Nazis forced Jews to wear—an insignia that reflects the ethnic intolerant face of nationalism. Less familiar than the Star of David is the pink triangle that homosexuals in Germany and Nazi-occupied territories were forced to wear— a stigma that reflects the more hidden heteronormative, sexually intolerant face of nationalism. Pink triangles and Stars of David not only served to distinguish publicly outcast non-Aryan Others from true Aryans, these symbols also reflected potent and degenerate sexual stereotypes of their wearers. In fact, discredited sexuality is an important part of anti-Semitism. For instance, George Mosse reminds us that early-twentieth-century views of female sexuality (consistent with Freudian theory) depicted women's sexual passions as out of control (e.g., hysterical).[6] Thus, male sexual deviants often were considered "feminized" since their urges were seen as feminine failures of self-restraint.[7] Mosse reports that while Jews seldom were described as homosexuals in articulations of fascist and European racism, they were considered nonetheless feminized "sexual 'degenerates'":

> Blacks, and then Jews, were endowed with excessive sexuality, with a socalled female sensuousness that transformed love into lust. They lacked all manliness. Jews as a group were said to exhibit female traits, just as homosexuals were generally considered effeminate.[8]

Not only Jewish men were seen as hypersexual or sexually defective in Nazi discourse, so were Jewish women. Johanna Gehmacher's review of Nazi-era Austrian nationalist propaganda documents a similar denigration of Jewish women's sexuality, and a depiction of Jewish women as procurers of Aryan victims for their men's sexual exploits. Gehmacher quotes an early

German National Socialist (Nazi) party propaganda leaflet warning Austrian girls and women of the seductive power of Jews—both women and men:

> Aryan girls, be on your guard against Jewish girls as friends. The Jewish community has ordered them to prepare you for the sin against your blood. They will lead you to dances, bars, etc., that are Jewish contaminated, alien to the Volk, where you will become helpless victims of Jewish playboys and lecherous Jews. You will be lost to your German people from the day you become captivated by those lechers. As women you will beget only Jewish children.[9]

African Americans also were the targets of Nazi World War II propaganda. Plate 5 of the color insert is a World War II Nazi military recruitment poster featuring a racist caricature of an African American soldier in a World War I U.S. Army uniform dragging a white woman by the hair. The German text on the poster reads: "German! Should this once again become a reality?" Robert Moeller described the propagandist's intent: "This Nazi poster was intended to evoke racist memories of black troops, who were among the Allied forces of occupation in the Rhineland after Germany's defeat in the First World War. In the background looms a caricature of a Jew."[10]

Racist and sexualized depictions of Others is a common strategy by all governments, not just extreme nationalists, particularly during times of war. Plate 6 is a 1918 World War I U.S. Army recruitment poster urging citizens to buy U.S. war bonds and admonishing them to Remember Belgium—where German soldiers, referred to derogatorily as "Huns," were reported to have perpetrated widespread rapes. The imagery and threat of rape is a powerful, perhaps the most powerful tool in nationalist repertoires of mobilization.

The Nazis used sexualized racism, homophobia, and misogyny as foils against which to contrast their claims to superior morality and virile, but proper sexuality. Although fascism had a self-denying ascetic ideological strain, it did not advocate sexual abstinence (except for men before battle). Quite the contrary, fascist ideology was imbued with an erotic hypersexuality dedicated to reproducing the Aryan race. In the words of Italian fascist Filippo Tommaso Marinetti, writing in *Democrazia Futurista*:

> We speak in the name of the race, which demands ardent males and inseminated females. Fecundity, for a race like ours, is its indispensable defense in times of war, and in times of peace, its wealth of working arms and genial heads . . . we futurists condemn the spreading feminine idiocy and the devoted imbecility of males that together collaborate to develop feminine extravagance, prostitution, pederasty, and the sterility of the race.[11]

Early-twentieth-century fascism's emphasis on reproducing the race has proved extremely durable and vigorous; its celebration of hyper-heterosexuality can be heard in contemporary fascist and racist ideology. Present-day white supremacists and white nationalists speak a familiar language of virile men and fertile women fervently coming together in the service of their race and nation. In her analysis of white supremacist discourse, Jessie Daniels reprints two images of fascist-approved white female sexuality—one pure and one pornographic. Figures 5.2 and 5.3 illustrate these contrasting, but complementary visions of white femininity. Daniels collected these and many similar drawings from two white supremacist publications, *Thunderbolt* and *War*, and she comments:

> Both images, the first of a sexuality that is chaste and pure, the second of a sexuality that is quasi-pornographic, emphasize the sexual attractiveness of white women. The split image of white women's sexuality is not as clear and simple a division as the classic Madonna/whore imagery, but . . . both categories of women are valued for their sexuality—a sexuality that is implicitly heterosexual and explicitly intended for the pleasure of white men.[12]

FIGURE 5.2 White Supremacist Family Life, 1983 (*Thunderbolt;* courtesy of the Kansas Collection, Kenneth Spencer Research Library, University of Kansas)

FIGURE 5.3   "My Man Is a White Racist," 1987 (*War;* courtesy of the Kansas Collection, Kenneth Spencer Research Library, University of Kansas)

While these images reflect the thoughts and desires of a nationalist fringe, as Homi Bhabha notes, "the margins more and more constitute the center . . . the boundary becomes the place from which *something begins its presencing.*"[13] Thoughts and actions on nationalist peripheries draw their power from their resonance with familiar and acceptable themes in mainstream culture. The perverted articulations of ultranationalists are not conceived in an ideological vacuum. Supremacist discourses are close cousins to more common forms of nationalist ideology in that they espouse traditional nationalist images of home and hearth, love of place and people, and the embrace of commonalities.[14]

In their study of American popular culture during the Cold War's "Red scare," Michael Barson and Steven Heller examine American nationalism under siege by Russian/Soviet "Reds" and "commies." They present written and visual images of the communist threat against the American way of life as it was depicted in films, TV shows, comic books, pamphlets, magazines, and fiction. They note the parallels between anticommunist and anti-Nazi warnings about the sexual dangerousness of national and ideological Others, and comment on the sexual subtext of media depictions of the Red menace:

[for instance] the 1985 movie *Red Dawn* and the 1988 ABC-TV mini-series *Amerika* [were] both about an America overrun by the Russians. This kind of myth[ic threat] was also perpetuated through the pulp magazines which sometimes offered a prurient mix of evil Reds and imperiled babes. Actually, many of the stories in [magazines such as] *Man's, All Male, Men's Stories,* and *Siren* were originally about Nazis, only the uniforms were changed.[15]

The besieged bodies and virtues of American "imperiled babes" were not the only sexual tropes used in U.S. popular media to illustrate the commie threat. During the Cold War, a persona from World War I was recycled into an updated insidious communist sexual threat—that of Margaretha Geertruida Zelle, better known as Mata Hari, the Dutch dancer who was accused and executed in 1917 for spying for the Germans.[16] The seductive power of a politically evil foreign woman and the helplessness of a politically naive American male are dramatized in the 1949 RKO film, *I Married a Communist*, the story of a man trying to overcome his communist past, the loyal woman who loves him, her besotted and beduped brother who is seduced by a shameless communist vamp and agent who later falls for him; this political-sexual quadrangle, illustrated in Plate 7 of the color insert, is resolved by the deaths of everyone but the good, true, and untainted American wife.[17]

Mata Hari, Red scares, shorn women, Nazi and neo-Nazi sexual demons and desires, and other nationalist sexual spectacles and panics illustrate the *moral economy* of nationalism. Nationalism is a system of values and a code of honor that defines who is and is not a *real* American or German or Korean or Brazilian or Iranian. The moral economy of nationalism is gendered, sexualized, and racialized. National moral economies provide specific places for women and men in the nation, identify desirable and undesirable members by creating gender, sexual, and ethnic boundaries and hierarchies within nations, establish criteria for judging good and bad performances of nationalist masculinity and femininity, and define threats to national moral and sexual integrity.

POLICING NATIONAL MORAL BOUNDARIES

What is it about nationalism—mainstream and extremist—that makes imaginings of, judgments about, and the regulation of gender and sexuality such central concerns? Part of the answer to this question can be found in the observations of Emile Durkheim, a sociologist writing at the turn of the last century. Durkheim posed the question: why do all societies have crime? If crime, deviance, and rule breaking are socially universal, then is deviance "normal," and does it serve some important social purpose or function?[18] Durkheim was asking a question about the edges, the periphery, the boundaries of civil society, and about the relationship between activity on the fringe (deviance, rule breaking) and the center ("normal" society). His answer was that both trivial and serious rule breaking are not only common, but useful for societies for several reasons. He argued that rule breaking raises questions about the location of a community's moral boundaries and the content of its core values. Deviance either can challenge the rules (when it becomes widespread), and thus can be a useful means of accomplishing social change, or deviance can reinforce the rules (when deviants are punished), and thus can be a useful means of affirming social hegemony by reminding everyone what is considered right and wrong and what will happen to those who deviate. Durkheim further argued that punishing deviants can create solidarity, a sense of common purpose, and a feeling of renewed community among members who draw themselves together in righteous indignation to pursue and purge deviants.[19]

Nationalist boundaries are a specialized form of the moral boundaries Durkheim described.[20] The margins of nations—ethnic frontiers, gender frontiers, sexual frontiers, ethnosexual frontiers—are all locations where rules about citizenship and proper national demeanor are tested and contested. National symbolic boundaries, like all moral boundaries, are sites for the creation and enforcement of the rules of citizenship, the surveillance, apprehension, and punishment of national deviants or "traitors," and the formation of revised or new definitions of loyalty to the nation. Punishment like that doled out to the shorn women in World War II France reminds everyone in the nation, not just those labeled "deviant," about the presence and power of national boundaries. Questions about core social categories such as gender and sexuality become questions about the nation and what it signifies. Identifying "outsiders" in the nation is part of the process of designating "insiders" and "citizens," and thus of defining the nation itself.

NATIONS, STATES, AND NATIONALISM

Nationalism is an important, ubiquitous, and often virulent form of ethnicity around the world today. Although the notion of the nation has a long history, and most scholars locate the origins of modern nationalism in the last half of the nineteenth century. Researchers note that ideologies of nationhood and nationalism became widely embraced as the preeminent legitimate basis for state building and political claimsmaking in the twentieth century.[21] Like ethnic groups and ethnicity, nations and nationalism can be thought of as a series of boundaries in space and time. National borders divide people and territory, mark who is inside and who is outside the national family, become sites of conflict when challenges to or invasions of the nation are perceived, and require active construction, maintenance, and defense.

By *nation* I refer to a collective identity associated with a region or territory that is sovereign or asserts sovereignty and self-rule (e.g., Portuguese, Americans, French, Quebecois, Navajos, Ogonis, Afrikaners, English, Russians, Chechnians, Iranians). By *nationalism* I refer to an ideology that professes a common history, shared culture, and rightful homeland, and often is marked by ethnocentrism where nationalists assert moral, cultural, and social superiority over other nations and nationalisms.[22] If many of the nations listed above seem unified and historically stable, it is an illusion. Within each of these countries and communities are dominant groups and subordinated groups often with conflicting claims to territory and political rights, engaged in arguments about the authenticity of other groups making such claims and making claims and counterclaims about who and what constitute the nation.

Nationalism can be a means of unifying a people and territory, or it can be a source of conflict and fractionalization. Often it is both. In any country, a dominant group can appeal to nationalism in an effort to control the sovereign state and subjugate minority populations. Subordinate groups can counter with their own nationalist claims using the same language of nationalism to challenge dominant group hegemony, assert collective rights, and/or secede from a state. Thus, it is not unusual for competing nationalisms and nationalists to confront one another inside the same country. In the past decade we have seen conflicting nationalisms in Rwanda, Angola, Yugoslavia, many republics of the former Soviet Union, India, Spain, Israel, and Mexico to name but a few. In all of these countries, ethnic minorities have claimed the status of separate nations and the right either to a sovereign state of their own or to expanded political rights and autonomy.

The global system is composed of many nations (peoples) and many states (countries), and they do not always coincide with one another. The disjuncture between the boundaries of nations and states and/or inequalities among ethnic groups enclosed inside states often lead to nationalist conflicts. Nationalist movements can arise when a national group is stateless (e.g., the Palestinians in the Middle East) or occupies a region of a country from which it seeks independence (e.g., Kashmiris living in India or Basques living in Spain). Nationalism can be irredentist, where a nation is divided into two or more states and where one part seeks to join the other to gain autonomy or independence (e.g., Kurds in Iraq, Iran, and Turkey or Armenians in Azerbaijan).[23]

What is important to note for our purposes here is that very often these seemingly purely political or economic matters become sexualized. As the examples from World War II and the Cold War presented above illustrate, nationalism tends to venerate insiders and vilify outsiders. National self-glorification and Other-defamation have a moral and sexual dimension that should not be underestimated. Calls to defend the sexual honor of those in-

Take a good look at this woman. She was created by a computer from a mix of several races. What you see is a remarkable preview of . . .

SPECIAL ISSUE
TIME
THE NEW FACE OF AMERICA

PLATE 1. *Time* Magazine Cover Girl, 1993   (Timepix)

PLATE 2. Sacagawea U.S. One Dollar Coin, 2000 (Courtesy of the U.S. Mint)

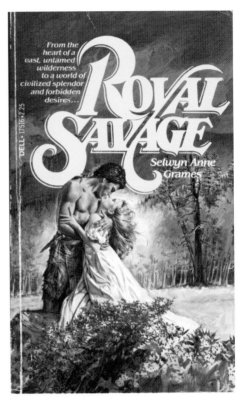

PLATE 3. *Royal Savage* (Copyright © 1980 Selwyn Anne Grames; used by permission of Dell Publishing, a division of Random-House, Inc.)

PLATE 4. "Both Members of This Club," George Wesley Bellows, 1907 (Copyright © Board of Trustees, National Gallery of Art, Washington, DC)

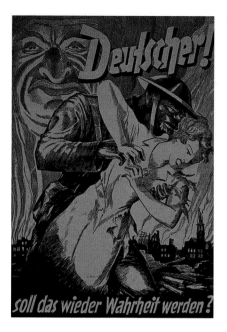

PLATE 5. Nazi World War II Recruitment Poster (Courtesy of the Hoover Institution Archives, Stanford University)

PLATE 6. "Remember Belgium," U.S. World War I "Buy Bonds" Poster (Courtesy of the United States National Archives)

PLATE 7. *I Married a Communist* (Copyright © 1949 RKO Pictures, Inc.; all rights reserved; courtesy of the Margaret Herick Library, Academy of Motion Pictures Arts and Sciences)

PLATE 8. Hula Dancing for the U.S. Navy, 1999 (Courtesy of the U.S. Navy; photographer Gregory Cleghorne)

PLATE 9. "A Portrait of Poedua," John Webber, 1777 (c. 1782) (By permission of the National Library of Australia)

side the nation and insults to the sexual virility and purity of those outside the nation are among the strongest "fighting words" that nationalists can utter. The specification of some groups as superior and others as inferior socially, economically, politically, culturally, morally, and sexually is central to nationalism's power, allure, and mass appeal.

As we have seen in earlier chapters, contemporary ethnosexual meanings and boundaries have their roots in earlier historical periods. The role of sexuality in present-day nationalist practices and discourses also can be traced back in time, in particular to colonialism as a protonationalist precursor of modern nationalism. The sexual strategies of rule pursued by colonial authorities and the contradictions and dilemmas that ethnosexual crossings posed for colonialism set the stage for current national sexual hegemonies and counterhegemonies. The next section describes ethnosexual frontiers in several colonial settings and draws links between past and present nationalisms and sexualities.[24]

SEX AND COLONIALISM

Contemporary states and nations are creations of what Immanuel Wallerstein refers to as the "modern world system,"[25] a global political, economic, social, and cultural system rooted early in the last millennium when a handful of countries, most notably Britain, France, Spain, Portugal, and Holland in Europe and China and Japan in Asia, managed to establish a remarkable colonial and imperial presence that has controlled most of the world's territories, peoples, and commerce for the past several hundred years.[26] Although formal colonialism has been dismantled almost completely, one living reminder of the extent of European global penetration is the number of countries in the world whose citizens speak or who officially have adopted a colonial language. These include Australia and New Zealand, all of the countries of North and South America, including the United States, most of the countries of Africa, and a sizeable number of Asian countries. Out of 209 countries and territories in the world, for instance, 132 have designated English, French, or Spanish as an official language.[27] Despite the obviously European origin of these national languages, their foreign roots often are overlooked or forgotten in debates about official language policy. For example, North American quarrels over national languages tend to be framed as issues of tradition and national purity when actually these are arguments over which *colonial* language will prevail as the "native" tongue: in the United States will it be English only; in Canada will it be English or French?[28]

The history of European colonialism is not only a history of language dominance, it is also a history of sexual dominance. As we have seen, the

conquest of new territories and international slavery involved sexual conquest and sexual trade. The colonies of Asia, Africa, and the Americas were
ethnosexual frontiers visited by European settlers, sojourners, adventurers,
and invaders who left in their wake a legacy of mulatto, mestizo, and meti
populations of mixed European and indigenous offspring. Europe itself became an ethnosexual frontier when the descendants of European-colonial sexual unions came home to live in their (mainly) fathers' European homelands.
Sexual relations in the colonies between Europeans and local peoples shaped
colonial and postcolonial societies around the world. Caste and class systems
based on color emerged in the colonies and wended their way back to the
European continent. In the colonies, European men's affairs with local or imported and enslaved women, and their inclination to make these women their
mistresses and concubines, and even occasionally their wives, produced large
numbers of mixed-race children as the visible evidence of these unions.
European-indigenous sexual arrangements and European sexual excesses and
debauchery were a not-so-secret scandal on the Continent and in European
enclaves in the colonies. Sometimes the sexual appetites and cultures of
European men collided with the sexual appetites and cultures of indigenous
men to create confrontations between masculinities and paroxysms of sexualized violence in the colonies. An example can be found in the role of sex
and violence in colonial India.

India was referred to as the "jewel in the crown" of the British empire
because of the tremendous wealth the British government and its business
partners extracted in gold, silk, cotton, spices, and taxes over more than two
centuries of colonial rule. The blatant nature of British economic and moral
exploitation in India was not lost on social critics of colonialism, which included Karl Marx. In 1853 the *New York Daily Tribune* published one of a
series of articles by Marx condemning British greed and corruption in India:

> The profound hypocrisy and inherent barbarism of bourgeois civilization lies
> unveiled before our eyes, turning from its home, where it assumes re-
> spectable forms, to the colonies, where it goes naked. Did they not, in India
> . . . resort to atrocious extortion, when simple corruption could not keep pace
> with their rapacity? While they prated in Europe about the inviolable sanc-
> tity of the national debt, did they not confiscate in India the dividends of
> the rajahs . . . and did they not, in order to make money out of the pilgrims
> streaming to the temples of Orissa and Bengal, take up the trade in . . . mur-
> der and prostitution . . . ? These are the men of "Property, Order, Family,
> and Religion."[29]

At the time Marx was expressing his outrage over British colonial hypocrisy
and degeneracy, the British East India Company with the help of 200,000 South
Asian troops officered by 40,000 British soldiers ruled India. Most of the thou-

sands of British colonials living in India were men, though by the mid-1800s many English women had emigrated and established families with company and military men. In addition to or instead of European wives, it was common for British men to have Indian mistresses ("Bibis") with whom they set up housekeeping in "Bibighars," homes established outside English compounds in Indian cities. In the British imagination and in their daily lives Indian women were sexualized in ways scholars recognize as the typical colonial gaze: Indian women were defined as seductive, sensual, and exotic. The British view of Indian men also adhered to a colonial sexual script, and they were seen, not as oversexed, but rather as undersexed: passive, feminine, deferential, and incapable of autonomous action.[30] These sexualized stereotypes reflected a British expatriate culture in India that was dissolute and self-indulgent:

> Cawnpore [Kanpur] was not so much a man's as a boy's world. The average regimental officer was "a youngster who makes curry, drinks champagne and avoids the sun." Leaving their Indian troops to the care of Indian officers and British sergeants, European officers became increasingly remote and disdainful. . . . "Sent into exile at an early age, before the traditions of the nursery had been modified by the better influences of education, or by intercourse with cultured minds, the 'cadets' and 'writers' carried the moods of schoolboys into the work of men."[31]

Andrew Ward reports that in the early days of Indian colonialism, the East India Company "prohibited English maidens . . . from emigrating to India, and hoped its officers would seek out Indian brides and mistresses," even providing a "subsidy to marry Indian women."[32] The British paid for their sexual associations with Indian women and their sexual assumptions about Indian men in a number of ways—by scandals at home over English men's consorting with Indian women and by the embarrassing proliferation of mixed-race offspring in India and later in Britain. The biggest price the English paid for their colonial exploits, however, was with their lives . . . and ultimately with their fortunes.

The Sepoy War of 1857 was an Indian soldiers' rebellion that many scholars see as the first major conflict in a century-long battle for Indian independence from British colonial rule.[33] A series of decisions and actions by East India Company and British colonial authorities (including arbitrary imprisonment, widespread mistreatment and torture, excessive taxation, forced labor, prohibition of traditional Muslim and Hindu religious practices, and interference with local political institutions) led to rising unrest among the thousands of Indian subjects, including Indian military troops. British assumptions about the supposedly docile and dutiful Indian military men whom they had armed and trained proved to be their undoing when, on May 9, 1857, Indian troops at Meerut turned their weapons and their rage against their British officers. The rebellion spread across the region during the summer, and became a cause for panic and hysteria in June when more than two hundred English women and children were rounded up, held for several days, and then hacked to death after which their bodies were stuffed down a well at a Bibighar in Kanpur. The British retaliated in a manner that matched the brutality of the Indians at Kanpur, and they tortured and executed hundreds of Indians, some by tying them to the muzzles of cannons that were then shot off.[34] The fighting continued for several months in different cities, and a peace treaty was signed a year later, in July 1858.

It is hard to gauge just how important a role sexuality played in the magnitude and viciousness of the violence by both Indian and British men during the war. Scholars have long and uniformly emphasized the role of the media in reporting Indian men's brutal massacre of English women as a factor contributing to the savagery of English men's retaliations; more recently acknowledged is the relevance of British men's ethnosexual adventuring with Indian women as a factor that heated the outrage and passions of Indian men during the rebellion.[35]

Whatever the role of sexuality in the conflict, scholars define the Sepoy War as a turning point in the history of British colonialism in India. The war led to a British loss of innocence about the depths of their own capacity to act savagely, and revealed their naive and false assumptions about Indian

FIGURE 5.4   British Execution of Indian Soldiers, Sepoy War, 1857 (Copyright © 1998 *Harappa Bazaar*)

men's impotent and tame loyalty to their British "masters." The war also caused a fundamental change in the British view of the Indian colonial subject, summarized by Sangeeta Ray: "The [Sepoy War] marked a crucial shift in the colonial imagining of India as unantagonistically feminine."[36] The war had overturned the British view of India as an open playground for sensual recreation marked by safe and easy access to Indian women and populated by foolish and feminine Indian men.

India was not the only colony where sexuality complicated colonial rule and outraged indigenous colonial peoples. Edward Said has argued that the marriage of the exotic and the erotic has been a common theme throughout history in Western imaginings of the Orient—its lands and its bodies.[37] Ann Stoler's studies of libidinal colonial relations in French Indochina and the Dutch East Indies provides systematic evidence of Said's observations. Stoler documents frequent patterns of sexual contact between Europeans and Asians and a European fascination with ethnosexual matters:

> Colonial observers and participants in the imperial enterprise appear to have had unlimited interest in the sexual interface of the colonial encounter. Probably no subject is discussed more than sex in colonial literature and no subject more frequently invoked to foster the racist stereotypes of European society. The tropics provided a site of European pornographic fantasies long before conquest was underway, but with a sustained European presence in colonized territories, sexual prescriptions by class, race, and gender became increasingly central to the politics of rule and subject to new forms of scrutiny by colonial states.[38]

As Stoler suggests, European-Asian sexual linkages were not without their costs or their consequences. Not only could systems of European and indigenous masculinities run afoul of one another as they did in India, Europeans' sexual indulgences compromised whites' ability to maintain their dignified colonial composure and threatened to expose the fiction of European moral superiority, self-discipline, and libidinal self-control. Thus, while European men may have found Asian women irresistible, a moral and legal crisis developed as a result of the progeny that these unions produced. As the decades of colonialism progressed, the growing number of mixed-race Euro-Asian children raised questions about the stability and purity of French and Dutch national identities in the colonies and in Europe as well. Each colonial power dealt differently at different points in history with the question of how to classify its mixed-race descendants. Would these children be French or Dutch citizens, noncitizens, or something in between; did the gender of the child or of the parent matter in deciding a child's classification?

Part of the dilemma facing European governments as they grappled with the consequences of sexual contact between colonists and natives stemmed from social and scientific theories of the time. Scientific racism in the nineteenth and early twentieth centuries warned about the dangers of "mongrelization" of superior European "races" by the influx of inferior nonwhite blood.[39] In fact, simply *living* in the tropics was considered morally, physically, and sexually dangerous to Europeans:

> Medical manuals warned that people who stayed "too long" were in grave danger of overfatigue, of individual and racial degeneration, of physical breakdown (not just illness), of cultural contamination and neglect of the conventions of supremacy.[40]

Aside from the theoretical issues of what constituted purity of the race or the legal issues associated with classifying mixed-race offspring, European colonial authorities also had to decide on the practical matter what to *do* with the "mixed-blood" children of French, Dutch, and English men and Asian women. Stoler reports that one common practice was to "rescue" mixed Euroasian children and place them in orphanages. This strategy was designed to achieve several ends, all related to European nationalist agendas:

> [M]etis children living in native homes were often *sought out* by state and private organizations and placed in these institutions to protect them against the "demoralized and sinister" influences of native [life and to] . . . keep fair-skinned children from running barefooted in native villages . . . [and] to ensure that the proliferation of European pauper settlements was curtailed and controlled. The preoccupation with creating a patriotic loyalty to French and Dutch culture among children was symptomatic of a more general fear; namely, that there were *already* patricides of the colonial fatherland in the making; that as adult women these children would fall into prostitution; that as adult men with emotional ties to native women and indigenous society they would join the enemies of the state.[41]

Since the United States came as a very late and minor player to international colonialism, the challenge of maintaining the racial purity of Americans arose more out of the country's long history of sexually mixing with the colonized indigenous peoples of North America and the enslaved imported peoples of Africa than from America's limited colonial adventures. Nevertheless, the United States dabbled in colonialism abroad and viewed its colonial subjects using the same sexualized lens through which it peered at Indians and Africans. America's largest-scale undertakings in international colonialism began at the end of the Spanish-American War of 1898, when the United States took control of a number of Pacific and Caribbean territories and peoples, some of them formerly under Spanish rule.[42] The American colonial gaze and the behavior of American men toward colonized women suggests that the United States took the lead of its European cousins. Kevin Santiago-Valles recounts comments made in 1900 by Jacob H. Bromwell, the

Republican representative from Ohio, about the then newly acquired U.S. territory of Puerto Rico:

> Puerto Rico came to us voluntarily and without bloodshed. She welcomed us with open arms. Her adherence to the United States during the Spanish war saved the loss, possibly, of many lives and the expenditure of millions of money. Her people welcomed the armies under [Major General Nelson A.] Miles as deliverers and benefactors.[43]

This verbal characterization of Puerto Rico as feminine and receptive corresponded to turn-of-the-century graphical representations of Puerto Rico as either a helpless child under beneficent U.S. care or a comely damsel embracing American ways and welcoming American travelers. As Santiago-Valles notes, "U.S. travel books and business journalism portraying turn-of-the-century 'Porto Rico' were particularly fond of capturing such maidens—photographically or in writing."[44] He cites as an example Turnbull White's book, *Our New Possessions*, published in 1898, which contained the alluring photograph of "A Colored Belle of Puerto Rico," an image of America's new possession as sexually exotic, but safe, wild, but tame, exotic enough to arouse, but familiar enough to reassure the eager, but anxious traveler (see Figure 5.5). The picture is used to introduce Turnbull's chapter on "Puerto Rico, Its Cities and Its People." It seems clearly intended as an invitation to white readers, stressing the accessibility of the land and its women. The caption under the picture describes the young woman as an "attractive colored girl" and an example of "higher type of that race."[45]

SEXUALLY IMAGINING THE NATION

Colonizers' imaginings and opinions about colonial subjects were not simply exercises in idle curiosity. Europeans and Americans defined who they were as nations in debates about their relationship to colonials. "American" [or "French" or "British" or "Spanish" or "Dutch"] was and is defined as much by what we *are not* as it is by what we *are*. Colonialism provided Americans and Europeans with a set of symbolic and actual places and peoples on which to stage their national dramas of self-discovery and self-invention.[46] The invention of America was set against enslaved, indigenous, and immigrant Others. Part of our national self-construction process was the attribution of moral and sexual characteristics to them and us, the designation of their rights and our rights, the evaluation of their moral and sexual worth in comparison to ours.

In *Imagined Communities* Benedict Anderson argues that all nations are embarked on an ongoing journey of self-invention. He notes, for instance,

FIGURE 5.5 "A Colored Belle of Puerto Rico," 1898 (*Our New Possessions*, Turnbull White)

that there is no more evocative a symbol of modern nationalism than the tomb of the unknown soldier. The illustrative power of this icon lies in the fact that such tombs "are either deliberately empty or no one knows who lies inside them."[47] Thus, they are open to interpretation and waiting to be filled. Like tombs of unknown soldiers, "nations" are empty vessels waiting to be filled by the symbolic work of nationalist founders and defenders. Sexual imaginings are an important part of these national self-construction projects.

Settler states—countries where immigrant populations push indigenous peoples off the land they wish to occupy—frequently employ an especially perverse strategy in their efforts to found a new national identity on the ruins of displaced native cultures. As we saw in Chapter 3, American nationalists used bits and pieces of indigenous cultures and peoples in their symbolic construction of the new American nation. "Playing Indian" in the United States has its counterpart in many settler states where immigrants borrow, revise, and put into service indigenous symbols and cultures in ways their native creators never intended. By reshaping native cultural material in their own imagined image, settlers build the identity, boundaries, and meaning of their new nation. Such [ab]use of indigenousness is not uniquely American. Mexicans also incorporated indigenous cultural material, especially from Indian gender and sexual cultures, for use in constructing the Mexican nation. In Mexico as in the United States, we can see the intersection of ethnicity, gender, and sexuality in nation building.

Like the United States and Canada, Mexico is a settler society that gained independence from European colonial rule. Although Spanish rule was ended in Mexico in 1821, the modern Mexican state was not established until 1910 when the Mexican Revolution overthrew an entrenched post-colonial political and economic elite. In their efforts to create a twentieth-century Mexican national identity, Mexico's Hispanicized mixed-ancestry descendants of mainly Spanish settlers who coupled with Aztec, Mayan, and other indigenous populations undertook a wholesale cooptation of *Indianissimo* or indigenousness in the name of the revolution and a democratic Mexico.

Mexican nationalists of the early twentieth century valorized mixed-race revolutionary heros such as Emiliano Zapata and Pancho Villa to construct and celebrate Mexican national identity.[48] Ironically, while Mexican nationalists were embracing Zapata and Villa and emphasizing and glorifying their Indianness, they were continuing a long history of exploiting and dominating Mexico's indigenous men and women. Indianissimo not only was used to constitute Mexico's mestizo national heroes, Mexican nationalists also incorporated images of and beliefs about indigenous masculine virility into

"Mexican" notions of manliness or *machismo*. The resulting hybrid *Mexicano* was the product of what Ana Maria Alonso refers to as a "militarization of gender."[49] Alonso traces the expropriation of indigenous masculinity and natives' sexual domination by Mexican nationalists in the eighteenth and nineteenth centuries. In a series of "Indian wars" Mexicans conquered native peoples and extracted and distilled their gender and sexual resources:

> Only humiliation could "punish Apache insolence" and "reduce" their extraordinary masculinity. This was to be accomplished by defeating them in warfare and capturing their women, in short, by dishonoring and emasculating them. Such a strategy required that the colonists themselves become the embodiment of heroic masculinity. . . . Paradoxically, in order to constitute themselves as paradigms of heroic masculinity, the men of Namiquipa appropriated the Apache's "nature."[50]

Alonso argues that by emasculating Apaches and other indigenous groups by military means in various conflicts over many decades, mixed-race Mexicans built an ethnic boundary separating themselves from the Indians. Through a series of self-defining military and cultural moves, mestizos made themselves into peasants, ceased to be Indians, and symbolically "whitened" themselves.[51]

The exploitation of real and imagined indigenousness was institutionalized into the ideology of the PRI (Institutional Revolutionary Party), and the success of this symbolic, sanitized Indianissimo contributed to more than seventy years of one-party PRI rule. The PRI's widespread discrimination against and neglect of Mexico's indigenous population, however, ultimately contributed to its undoing. The PRI's corruption and impoverishment of Mexican Indians generated an indigenous uprising in Mexican state of Chiapas in the 1990s that was followed by the party's being voted out of office in 2000.[52]

As the ongoing use of indigenous gender and sexuality in U.S. and Mexican nationalist projects illustrates, the construction of the nation against the foil of its imagined indigenes in its imagined history (and its imagined homeland in the case of settler states) is not unique to the colonial era, nor does it necessarily involve military conflict. Louisa Schein describes a postcolonial instance of national/Other construction in mainland China during the 1980s illustrated by the sexualized simulation of the "tribal" culture of the Miao people, a Chinese indigenous group. "Carefully selected Miao girls would don their best costumes, marks of their beauty and emblems of their difference, and pose as directed for the replication of the images expected and craved by urban [Chinese] consumers."[53] Schein reports that Miao and other "minority" women not only were seen as preserved remnants of an exotic traditional past, but also as "objects of erotic fascination. In many contemporary art and media images, their proportions appeared voluptuous and their expressions were unabashedly inviting. Sometimes their bodies would be more extensively revealed than would be appropriate for a Han woman."[54] Chinese rumors about and "study" of Miao sexual practices, availability, and promiscuity has a familiar resonance to Europeans' fixation on the sexuality of the indigenous populations of America, Africa, and Asia. In fact, Schein argues, like McClintock, Stoler, and Said, that the consumption of "traditional" local Others by Chinese urbanites represents an instance of "internal orientalism," and is part of the cultural construction of Chinese national identity.

GENDER AND NATIONALISM

In countries around the world today there are arguments over the gender or racial or sexual contents of national vessels. What is the proper place for women and men, blacks and whites, gays and straights in the nation: who should vote, be educated, work outside the home, serve in the military, be given a security clearance, run for political office?[55] Such debates are nationalist discussions about the contours and contents of the nation and the places of various gendered, raced, and sexed people in it.

Gender has a particularly important place in the nation-building enterprise. All genders are not socially created as equal partners in nation building, nor do they occupy the same positions on national stages. It turns out that the idea of the nation and the history of nationalism are intertwined with the idea of manhood and the history of manliness. This is not to say that women do not have roles to play in the making and unmaking of states: as citizens, as members of the nation, as activists, as leaders. It is to say that nationalist scripts are written primarily by men, for men, and about men. In these national dramas women are relegated to mainly supporting roles—as mothers of the nation, as vessels for reproducing the nation, as agents for inculcating national culture into new members, and as national housekeepers responsible for maintaining home and hearth for the nation's men who are out and about on important official business—fighting wars, defending homelands, representing the nation abroad, *manning* the apparatus of the state.[56] Thus, the real actors in nationalist productions are men defending their freedom, their honor, their homeland, and their women.[57]

The culture and ideology of hegemonic masculinity go hand in hand with the culture and ideology of hegemonic nationalism.[58] Masculinity and nationalism articulate well with one another, and the modern form of Western masculinity emerged at about the same time and place as modern nationalism. George Mosse notes that nationalism "was a movement which began and evolved parallel to modern masculinity."[59] He describes modern masculinity as a centerpiece of all varieties of nationalist movements:

The masculine stereotype was not bound to any one of the powerful polit-ical ideologies of the previous century. It supported not only conservative movements . . . but the workers' movement as well; even Bolshevik man was said to be "firm as an oak." Modern masculinity from the very first was co-opted by the new nationalist movements of the nineteenth century.[60]

Nationalist politics is a major venue for "accomplishing" masculinity for at least two reasons.[61] First, as noted above, the national state is essentially a masculine institution. Feminist scholars point out its hierarchical author-ity structure, the male domination of decision-making positions, the male superordinate/female subordinate internal division of labor, and the male le-gal regulation of female rights, labor, and sexuality.[62] Second, the culture of nationalism is constructed to emphasize and resonate with masculine cultural themes. Terms such as *honor, patriotism, cowardice, bravery,* and *duty* are hard to distinguish as either nationalistic or masculinist since they seem so thoroughly tied both to the nation and to manhood. My point here is that the "microculture" of masculinity in everyday life articulates very well with the demands of nationalism, particularly its militaristic side. While local mas-culine cultures differ from one another in terms of the class, race, ethnicity, or nation of the men involved, in all societies there are distinct gender cul-tures shaping the lives of boys and girls, of men and women, and it is male gender culture that tends to dominate nationalism. As Cynthia Enloe ob-serves, "nationalism has typically sprung from masculinized memory, mas-culinized humiliation and masculinized hope."[63]

Nationalism, coupled with masculinist heterosexuality, tends to embrace patriarchal forms of social organization that create different and unequal places for men and women in the nation. Such patriarchal systems generally are unsympathetic to feminist efforts to eliminate gender inequality, and see women's rights as secondary and subversive to nationalist goals and strug-gles. Further, standards for national conduct that reflect masculinized het-eronormativity tend also to be homophobic, and thus are intolerant of sex-ual diversity, particularly homosexuality.

The sexist nature of much nationalism has led some scholars to argue that "woman nationalist" is an oxymoron that reflects the historic contra-diction between the goals and needs of women and those of nationalists.[64] Feminists often find themselves attempting to negotiate the difficult, some would say impassable terrain that separates the interests of women and the interests of nationalists. Discussing Hindu and Muslim nationalism in In-dian politics, Zoya Hasan notes the tension between feminist principles and communal religious solidarity: "Forging community identities does not im-ply or guarantee that women will always identify themselves with or adhere to prevailing religious doctrines which legitimise their subordination."[65]

Whatever the problems facing a feminist/nationalist alliance, often women have supported men's nationalist efforts in the name of a united nation, even involving themselves in cadres and military units.[66] Despite their bravery, their taking on of traditional male military roles, or the centrality of their contribution to many nationalist struggles, feminist nationalists often find themselves once again under the thumb of institutionalized patriarchy when national independence is won. A nationalist movement that encourages women's participation in the name of national liberation often balks at feminist demands for gender equality.

> Women who have called for more genuine equality between the sexes—in the [nationalist] movement, in the home—have been told that now is not the time, the nation is too fragile, the enemy is too near. Women must be patient, they must wait until the nationalist goal is achieved, *then* relations between women and men can be addressed. "Not now, later," is the advice that rings in the ears of many nationalist women.[67]

But, waiting is a dangerous strategy, Enloe argues, "every time women succumb to the pressures to hold their tongues about problems they are having with men in nationalist organizations, nationalism becomes that much more masculinized."[68] Women who press their case face challenges to their loyalty, their sexuality, or their ethnic or national authenticity: they are said to be "carrying water" for colonial oppressors, or they are labeled lesbians, or they are accused of being unduly influenced by Western feminism. Third World feminists are quite aware of these charges and share some concerns about the need for an indigenous feminist analysis and agenda; as Delia Aguilar, a Filipina nationalist feminist comments:

> [W]hen feminist solidarity networks are today proposed and extended globally, without a firm sense of identity—national, racial and class—we are likely to yield to feminist models designed by and for white, middle-class women in the industrial West and uncritically adopt these as our own.[69]

Despite efforts to build an indigenous feminism into nationalist movements, many nationalist movements fail to overthrow the patriarchal ancien régime. Indeed, patriarchal, masculinist notions of men's and women's roles often become more entrenched during nationalist mobilizations; an example is the human rights violations of Afghani women by the masculinist nationalism of Afghanistan's former ruling Taliban party. The Taliban government initially was supported widely when it came to power in 1996, partly because it was reputed to provide protection for women who had become targets of sexual abuse under the previous government. The Taliban's draconian measures against women who were required to wear head-to-toe coverings and forbidden to work outside the home or to attend school became an international scandal.[70] Algeria is perhaps the most well-known case of a nationalist movement turning on its female supporters. In 1962 Algeria finally freed itself from French colonial rule. The struggle was a long and bitter one, and the fight for Algerian independence was notable for the involvement of Algerian women. Daniele Djamila Amrane-Minne, who interviewed women veterans of the Algerian liberation movement for her book, *Des Femmes dans la Guerre d'Algérie,* reports that eleven thousand women were active participants in the national resistance movement, and two thousand women were in the armed wing of the movement.[71] Despite this extensive involvement of women in an armed revolutionary movement, once independence was won, Algerian women found themselves pressured to go "back in the kitchen," and to trade their combat fatigues for the *hijab* (traditional Islamic dress) and the veil.[72] Although the new independent Algeria embraced principles of socialism, few gender equality aspects of that doctrine were institutionalized into the formal or informal politics of independence. While women had the vote, their "place" in Algerian society was dictated more by patriarchal traditionalism than by egalitarian socialism. More than four decades after Algerian independence, Algerian women still face the violent enforcement of patriarchal social customs in their daily lives.[73]

The interest of nationalists in "their" women's sexuality is not unique to Algeria, Muslim nationalists, or nationalists in developing countries. Women's sexuality turns out to be a matter of prime national interest around the world for at least two reasons. First, women as mothers are exalted icons of nationalism. In their discussion of Afrikaner nationalism in South Africa, for instance, Deborah Gaitskell and Elaine Unterhalter argue that Afrikaner women appear regularly in the rhetoric and imagery of the Afrikaner "volk" (people), and that "they have figured overwhelmingly as mothers."[74] As Klaus Theweleit summarizes: "woman is an infinite untrodden territory of desire which at every stage of historical deterritorialization, men in search of material for utopias have inundated with their desires."[75]

Women's sexuality is of further concern to nationalists around the world because, as wives, sisters, mothers, and daughters, women often are considered to be the bearers and incarnations of national and masculine honor.[76] For instance, the physical assaults and murders of women suspected of adultery by jealous husbands tend to be taken less seriously or ignored by law enforcement in many countries including the United States.[77] While there are certainly variations across history and around the world in the extent to which such "honor killings" are tolerated, Camilla Fawzi El-Solh and Judy Mabro identify a common connection between men's and family honor and women's sexual respectability as a situation where honor is for men to gain and women to lose: "honour is seen more as men's responsibility, and shame as women's . . . honour is seen as actively achieved while shame is seen as passively defended."[78]

It is not only Third World men whose honor is tied to their women's sexuality, respectability, and shame. Female fertility is valued in the mothers of most nations, but unruly female sexuality is a potential threat to national honor. Mosse describes this duality of purity and fertility in the depiction of women in European nationalist history: on the one hand, "female embodiments of the nation stood for eternal forces . . . [and] suggested innocence and chastity" and most of all respectability.[79] On the other hand, as the white supremacist images above illustrate, the right women need to be sexually available to the right men: "the maiden with the shield, the spirit that awaits a masculine leader [for] the enjoyment of peace achieved by male warriors."[80]

SEXUALITIES AND NATIONALISMS

Just as feminism has the capacity to challenge the stability of the masculinist heterosexual order that underlies nationalist boundaries, so too does homosexuality. Both queers and feminists are problems for nationalists. This is partly because nationalists almost always are traditionalists. Nationalism, even "revolutionary" nationalism is inherently conservative because nationalists tend to fix their gaze backward to real or imagined pasts for their legitimation and to mark their paths to the future. Feminists and homosexuals are among the most vocal critics of these histories, and they oppose many "retraditionalizing" aspects of contemporary nationalist movements since these steps backward usually do not lead to improvements in the rights and options of women and homosexuals.[81] Further, feminists raise questions about the accuracy and justice of patriarchal "golden ages" so often celebrated by nationalist leaders, and homosexuals contradict the core nationalist project of reproducing the nation. Both feminist and homosexuals also tend to be seen by nationalists as potential sources of disloyalty, since their commitment to gender and sexual equality raises doubts in the minds of nationalists about the strength of their allegiance to the nation as the primary unit of identification.

Nationalist preoccupation with homosexuality was not confined to the Nazi targeting of homosexuals during World War II. The Cold War represents another period of "homosexual panic"[82] when many gay men working in Western governments, particularly in the British Foreign Office and U.S. State Department, were fired or reassigned because they were considered to be "security risks." In the United States, Sen. Joseph McCarthy was not only interested in finding and flushing out communists in various arenas of American life; he was also interested in homosexuals, presumably because they were vulnerable to blackmail because of their "lifestyle," and because their weak moral character made them susceptible to communist influence.[83] The fact that one of McCarthy's most vicious lieutenants, Roy Cohn, was a gay man, was one of the McCarthy era's best kept secrets and most ironic breaches of Republican security. Another irony of the focus on homosexuals as likely blackmail targets is that heterosexual misconduct was and is a far more common source of government employee vulnerability, since, as history has shown again and again, people frequently engage in, and frequently go to great lengths to hide, heterosexual affairs.

In recent years lesbian and gay rights groups around the world, but particularly in the West have mounted assaults on ethnosexual exclusionary policies, claiming equal rights to be members of the ethnic community or nation. Chapter 1 included a section on the efforts of gays and lesbians to march in Boston's St. Patrick's Day parade and thus to redefine "Irish" as not exclusively a heterosexual category. During the past few decades both straight and queer sexual rights advocates have asserted equal rights and membership in ethnic and national communities around the world, frequently with more success than in Boston. The integration of Europe is playing an interesting and emerging role in efforts to liberalize conservative nationalism inside European states. In the Republic of Ireland, for instance, both feminist and gay rights groups have appealed *outside* Irish national boundaries, to the European Union, to claim rights within the Irish state. The notorious case of a pregnant Irish teenager denied an abortion in Ireland in 1997 led feminists opposed to Ireland's restrictions on abortions to seek support in the more liberal arenas of European legal and public opinion.[84] Irish gay and lesbian rights groups have appealed to the European Convention on Human Rights to force the decriminalization of same-sex acts between consenting adults in Ireland.[85] In Eastern Europe, there has been pressure on states seeking admission to the Council of Europe to abandon codes outlawing homosexual relations; for instance, in 1993, Lithuania repealed its laws against same-sex acts.[86]

NATIONALIZING SEXUALITY

Despite the common distaste nationalists seem to express for nonheterosexuals two recent studies of sexual micro cultures in urban settings suggest that gay as well as straight, homosexuality as well as heterosexuality can be enlisted in the service of constructing the race, the ethnic group, and the nation. Sasho Lambevski's ethnography of the gay scene in Skopje, Macedonia, describes the way that ethnicity shaped expectations for who should be "top" and who was "bottom," dominant or submissive, giving or receiving in sexual interactions, such as penetrator or penetrated in anal intercourse.[87] Longstanding sexual conventions have led to expectations that Macedonian gay men would be more likely to assume the bottom position despite their frequently superior class and national status vis-à-vis their Albanian partners. Lambevski attributes this ethnosexual positioning, in part, to Albanian Muslim men's tendency to maintain heterosexual identities despite their homosexual activities. Like the "peers" in Albert Reiss's study, Albanian men preferred to be the top/penetrators—a role more consistent with male heterosexual practices and self-conceptions.[88] Macedonian gay men, however, were more willing to identify themselves as gay and thus to be penetrated, sometimes violently in acts of rape. According to Lambevski, both Albanians and Macedonians were constrained by ethnosexual expectations:

> [T]here is a nationalist governance of sex which orders Macedonian homosexuals to avoid Albanians as much as possible when looking for sexual liaisons, while at the same time requiring Albanians to assume the "top" position in their sexual encounters with Macedonians. . . . [but since] there is a number of ethnic Macedonian men who enjoy being sexually dominated by Albanian macho men. . . . The more "Macedonian" the Albanian becomes . . . in gesture, sophistication, dress, social status, etc., the less desirable he becomes in the eyes of the Macedonian.[89]

Lambevski's analysis illustrates the power of ethnosexual microcultures both to reinforce ethnic and national boundaries and to maintain ethnosexual stereotypes and desires.

Petula Sik Ying Ho and Adolf Kat Tat Tsang also examine the role of ethnicity in shaping homosexual encounters in their description of the gay scene in Hong Kong and the different sexual roles of Western and Chinese men.[90] Like Lambevsky, they find ethnonational patterns in ethnic positioning in sexual encounters. This ethnosexual order became unstable in the late 1990s, however, when political changes in Hong Kong created ripples that ran through ideological currents in Hong Kong's gay sexual culture. British colonial rule over Hong Kong ended in 1997. Prior to the transfer of sovereignty from Britain to China, Chinese men more often assumed the colonial (bottom) position with Western men more likely to be on top. When China and Britain changed positions in 1997, so did some Western and Chinese men, with the latter more likely than before to be the top in sexual situations. While not all gay men switched positions, and old habits and desires die hard, Ho and Tsang reported that

> many Chinese gay men had experienced more changes in their relationships with Western partners or more recent changes with new partners. . . . With

regard to anal intercourse, more gay men questioned the stereotype of the Westerner, powerful in terms of wealth, masculinity or attractiveness, being on top while the Chinese partner was at bottom.[91]

Thus, political changes in Hong Kong produced flux in national *and* sexual relations including a greater fluidity of desire and a dilution of the strong ethnic norms governing sexual roles.

The work of Lambevski and Ho and Tsang link varying ethnosexual styles and mores to ethnic and nationalist contexts. But Ho and Tsang also describe a situation of ethnosexual change, where desire, expectations, and practices became fluid when the boundaries dividing Westerners from Chinese were redefined officially. This combination of stability and change seems to typify ethnosexual matters in general, and reflects an inherent contradiction in ethnosexual contact: that individuals can cross ethnic boundaries in the most intimate way, by having sex with one another, yet the ethnic boundary between them remains in place.

CONCLUSION

The historical and contemporary studies of nationalism and its predecessor, colonialism, that we have reviewed here, suggest that building nations and national identities involves inspecting and controlling the sexuality of citizens and condemning the sexuality of noncitizens and those considered outside the sexual boundaries of the nation. The punishment of women inside national borders for disloyal sexual behavior, the sexual exploitation of women considered to be outside the nation, the control of women's reproduction through official policies regulating contraception and abortion, suspicions about the patriotism of homosexuals all reflect the sexualized, indeed, heterosexualized envisioning of the nation.[92]

Contemporary nationalist ideologies define proper places for men and women and valorize the heterosexual family as the bedrock of the nation. This uniformity in sexualized nationalist discourse is a striking feature of the global system of national states. Whether national sexual ideologies are spoken by nationalists from former ruling colonial powers or by nationalists in former ruled colonies, the similarities easily can be heard. In matters involving sex and nationalism, the apparatus of the state is perhaps most visible in its operation. The tendency for national governments around the world to exclude women and homosexuals from what are defined as the most important national institutions, such as those involved in war making and governance, illustrates the gendered, sexualized face of nationalism.

The points of convergence among ethnicity, gender, and sexuality inside nations can be dangerous intersections. The imposition of strict controls on the national meanings and enactments of ethnicity, gender, or sexuality can reinforce national identities and movements, but such ethnosexual disciplinary regimes can generate resistance and can become the nation's undoing. Masculinist heterosexuality is a core component of the bedrock upon which nationalist boundaries rest. Feminism, unruly female sexuality, and homosexuality are three cracks in that foundation. Contemporary states must manage both their international frontiers as well as their internal ethnic, gender, and sexual frontiers. Calming restlessness on ethnosexual frontiers represents one of the most controversial challenges facing contemporary nations in the global system.

NOTES

1. Margaret Collins Weitz, *Sisters in the Resistance: How Women Fought to Free France, 1940–45* (New York: John Wiley and Sons, 1995), 277.

2. Stephen Ambrose and Charles L. Sulzberger, eds., *American Heritage New History of World War II*, revised edition (New York: Viking Press, 1997), 492.

3. I have found few instances of men being punished for having sex with enemy women, though this may be beginning to change—in spring 2000, the UN convened an *International Criminal Tribunal for the Former Yugoslavia* in The Hague, Netherlands, to investigate and prosecute war crimes in the former Yugoslavia; see Carlotta Gall, "Milosevic Is Given to U.N. for Trial in War-Crime Case," *New York Times*, June 29, 2001: 1; prior to the twenty-first century, there were sometimes prosecutions for rape during war; see Brownmiller, *Against Our Will*.

4. Kay Saunders, "In a Cloud of Lust: Black GIs and Sex in World War II," in *Gender and War: Australians at War in the Twentieth Century*, ed. Joy Damousi and Marilyn Lake (Cambridge: Cambridge University Press, 1995), 178–90; Graham Smith, *When Jim Crow Met John Bull: Black American Soldiers in World War II Britain* (New York: St. Martin's Press. 1988); Walter A. Luszki, *A Rape of Justice: MacArthur and the New Guinea Hangings* (Lanham, MD: Madison Books: 1991).

5. See Emile Durkheim, *The Rules of the Sociological Method* (New York: The Free Press, 1938) for a classical articulation of this social fact.

6. Mosse, *Nationalism and Sexuality;* note the etymology of the word "hysteria," which is derived from both Greek *(hystera)* and Latin *(hyster-)* referring to the uterus or womb.

7. Depicting "others" as feminine is often used in other ways: to delegitimize or trivialize grievances or dissent (see Brown, *Good Wives, Nasty Wenches*), to denigrate or dismiss opponents or colonized people (men) (see Timothy Sweet, "Masculinity and Self-Performance in the *Life of Black Hawk*," *American Literature* 65 [1993]: 475–99; Kiril Petkov, *Infidels, Turks, and Women: The South Slavs in the German Mind, circa 1400–1600* [New York: Peter Lang, 1997]), or as a critical discourse act against a dominant group (see M. Mac An Ghaill, "The Making of Black English Masculinities," in *Theorizing Masculinities*, ed. Harry Brod and Michael Kaufman [Thousand Oaks, CA: Sage Publications, 1994], 183–199).

8. Mosse, *Nationalism and Sexuality,* 36; for a discussion linking the effeminization of Jews to the resurgence of masculinist heteronormativity in late nineteenth-century Europe, see Daniel Boyarin, *Unheroic Conduct: The Rise of Heterosexuality and the Invention of the Jewish Man* (Berkeley: University of California Press, 1997); for a detailed, albeit heavily psychoanalytic, discussion of the Nazi preoccupation with sexuality and homosexuality, see Klaus Theweleit, *Male Fantasies,* volume 1, translated by Stephen Conway (Minneapolis: University of Minnesota Press, 1987).

9. Johanna Gehmacher, "Men, Women, and the Community Borders: German-Nationalist and National Socialist Discourses on Gender, 'Race,' and National Identity in Austria, 1918–1938," in *Nation, Empire, Colony: Historicizing Gender and Race,* ed. Ruth R. Pierson and Nupur Chaudhuri (Bloomington: Indiana University Press, 1998), 206; although this pamphlet warned Austrian women and girls against association with Jewish women and girls, it was firmly planted in heterosexual dangers—that Jewish females would lead Austrian females into sexual relationships with Jewish men, *not* lesbians.

10. Robert G. Moeller, *Protecting Motherhood: Women and the Family in the Politics of Postwar West Germany* (Berkeley: University of California Press, 1993), 109.

11. Barbara Spackman, *Fascist Virilities: Rhetoric, Ideology, and Social Fantasy in Italy* (Minneapolis: University of Minnesota Press, 1996), 12; see also Filippo Tommaso Marinetti, *Democrazia Futurista,* in *The Untameables/F.T. Marinetti,* trans. Jeremy Parzen (Los Angeles: Sun & Moon Press, 1994); *Democrazia Futurista* originally was published in 1919.

12. Daniels, *White Lies,* 40, 60–61; see also Abby L. Ferber, *White Man Falling: Race, Gender, and White Supremacy* (Lanham, MD: Rowman and Littlefield, 1998).

13. Homi Bhabha, "Life at the Border: Hybrid Identities of the Present," *New Perspectives Quarterly* 14 (1997): 30–31, 30; Bhabha is quoting from Martin Heidegger: "a boundary is not that at which something stops, but . . . from which something begins its *presencing.*"

14. Research on the construction of whiteness as a unified and preferred racial category in the United States and Europe, for instance, suggests that white supremacist ideology serves not only to build group solidarity among and within extreme white supremacist or neo-Nazi groups; Charles W. Mills argues that white racial superiority is part of national identities in most of the states of Europe and the Americas although few politicians would publicly admit this (*The Racial Contract*). There are important differences in how whiteness defines the various nations on these three continents, but the place of skin color on the nationalist palettes of most of these states is widely documented in popular culture (debates about which films, music, art, literature comprise national canons), public opinion surveys (on friendship patterns, intermarriage, standards of beauty), intersections of class and race where each defines the other ("money whitens," "if you're black, get back"), historical controversies over military service and patterns of political participation or office holding (which groups should serve, in what capacity, be sent to the front, vote, be nominated for office, be elected); see Lipsitz, *The Possessive Investment in Whiteness;* Ruth Frankenberg, ed., *Displacing Whiteness: Essays in Social and Cultural Criticism* (Durham: Duke University Press, 1997); Ware, *Beyond the Pale* and "Island Racism," *Feminist Review* 54 (1996): 65–86.

15. Michael Barson and Steven Heller, *Red Scared: The Commie Menace in Propaganda and Popular Culture* (San Francisco: Chronicle Books, 2001), 12.

16. For a revisionist look at Mata Hari, see Julie Wheelwright, *The Fatal Lover: Mata Hari and the Myth of Women in Espionage* (London : Collins & Brown, 1992).

17. Barson and Heller, *Red Scared*, 76.

18. Durkheim, *The Rules of the Sociological Method*.

19. Of course, punishment does not always reflect widespread community consensus, often there is public indifference to deviance and its punishment, and sometimes there is public opposition to particular punishments, such as the controversy surrounding the death penalty in the United States (see Herbert H. Haines, *Against Capital Punishment: The Anti-Death Penalty Movement in America, 1972–1994* (New York: Oxford University Press, 1996).

20. For a more recent discussion of moral boundaries, see Kai T. Erikson, *Wayward Puritans: A Study in the Sociology of Deviance* (New York: Wiley, 1966).

21. See, for instance, Hobsbawm, *Nations and Nationalism since 1780;* Connor, "When Is a Nation?" and Ernest Gellner, *Nations and Nationalism* (Oxford: Blackwell, 1983).

22. I distinguish nations from races or ethnic groups by their claims to political autonomy or independence and by their territoriality. Nationalists also often claim the nation is racially or ethnically (linguistically, religious, culturally) pure and descended from common racial or ethnic roots.

23. For recent compendia of classical and contemporary conceptual and empirical work on nationalism, see David McCrone, *The Sociology of Nationalism* (New York: Routledge, 1998); John Hutchinson and Anthony D. Smith (eds.), *Nationalism* (New York: Oxford University Press, 1994); Geoff Eley and Ronald G. Suny (eds.), *Becoming National: A Reader* (New York: Oxford University Press, 1996); Alexander J. Motyl (ed.), *Encyclopedia of Nationalism* (San Diego: Academic Press, 2000).

24. For a groundbreaking collection of essays on this topic, see Parker et al., *Nationalisms and Sexualities*.

25. Immanuel M. Wallerstein, *The Modern World System: Capitalist Agriculture and the Origins of the European World-Economy in the Sixteenth Century* (New York: Academic Press, 1974).

26. See Mills, *The Racial Contract*.

27. Other much more minor contenders are Dutch and Portuguese; Japan is the official language in only two places: Japan and Angaur in the Palauan Islands; for most of the twentieth century Russian vied for a place among the world's colonial languages as it was an official language in the republics and territories of the former Soviet Union; with the collapse of Soviet rule in the 1990s and the independence of the former republics, now only three countries list Russian as an official language: Russia, Kazakhstan, and Kyrgyzstan; for a listing of the world's countries and territories and their official languages, see http://www.webofculture.com/worldsmart/languages.html

28. The colonial wars continue in the twenty-first century in the form of language policy campaigns: "English First" assaults on Spanish in the United States and the longstanding conflict between Anglophones and Francophones in Canada.

29. Karl Marx, *New York Daily Tribune*, (July 22, 1853; see http://www.emory.edu/ENGLISH/Bahri/Mutiny.html; see also *Karl Marx and Frederick Engels* (New

York: International Publications, 1985), Volume 15, 305–31; my thanks to Robert Antonio, Sociology, University of Kansas, for bringing to my attention this source containing Marx's extended comments on British colonialism in India during the period of the Sepoy War.

30. See, for instance, Mrinalini Sinha, *Colonial Masculinity: The 'Manly Englishman' and the 'Effeminate Bengali' in the Late Nineteenth Century* (Manchester: Manchester University Press, 1995); Indrani Chatterjee, "Colouring Subalternity: Slaves, Concubines and Social Orphans in Early Colonial India," *Subaltern Studies* 10 (1999): 49–97; Revathi Krishnaswamy, *Effeminism: The Economy of Colonial Desire* (Ann Arbor: University of Michigan Press, 1998).

31. Andrew Ward, *Our Bones Are Scattered: The Cawnpore Massacres and the Indian Mutiny of 1857* (New York: Henry Holt and Company, 1996), 10–11.

32. Ibid., 13.

33. See Ward, *Our Bones Are Scattered*; Ainslee Thomas Embree, *1857 in India: Mutiny or War of Independence?* (Boston: Heath, 1963); Tapti Roy, *The Politics of a Popular Uprising: Bundelkhand in 1857* (New Delhi: Oxford University Press, 1994); C. A. Bayly and D. H. A. Kolff, eds., *Two Colonial Empires* (Boston: M. Nijhoff, 1986); Henry Scholberg, *The Indian Literature of the Great Rebellion* (New Delhi: Promilla and Company, 1993).

34. Ward, *Our Bones Are Scattered*, 451–52; many other atrocities were committed by the British who turned Hindu and Muslim prisoners' religious beliefs against them:

> Soldiers . . . forced beef down the throats of the Hindu captives, pork down the throats of the Moslems. Prisoners were daubed with animal fat; some Moslems were even sewn into pig skins before hanging. Sweepers were employed to execute Brahmin prisoners, many of whom were first smeared with cow's blood. (Ibid., 442).

35. See Chatterjee, "Colouring Subalternity"; Nancy L. Paxton, "Mobilizing Chivalry: Rape in British Novels about the Indian Uprising of 1857," *Victorian Studies* 36 (1992): 5–30; Jenny Sharpe, *Allegories of Empire: The Figure of Woman in the Colonial Text* (Minneapolis: University of Minnesota Press, 1993), 57–82; Sangeeta Ray, *En-Gendering India: Woman and Nation in Colonial and Postcolonial Narratives* (Durham: Duke University Press, 2000), 51–89; Rudrangshu Mukherjee, " 'Satan Let Loose upon Earth' " The Kanpur Massacres in India in the Revolt of 1857," *Past and Present* 128 (1990): 92–116; Barbara English and Rudrangshu Mukherjee, "Debate: The Kanpur Massacres in India in the Revolt of 1857," *Past and Present* 142 (1994): 169–89; my thanks to Ross H. Frank, Ethnic Studies Department, University of California, San Diego, for bringing to my attention the debate between Rudrangshu Mukherjee and Barbara English in *Past and Present*.

36. Ray, *En-Gendering India*, 19, see also 51–89.

37. Said, *Orientalism*; the European sexual gaze was not confined to Asia, but extended to Africa and the America where Europeans consorted with those under colonial rule and produced telltale mixed offspring; Joseph Boone summarizes this broadening of Said's insight: "In transforming the nonwestern world into a fantasized image of sexual promise and excess, the orientalist project has most often relied . . . on a set of metaphors equating the Anglo-European colonizer with phallic conquest and the colonized other with stereotypes of feminine receptivity, fecundity,

and availability"; Joseph Allen Boone, *Libidinal Currents: Sexuality and the Shaping of Modernism* (Chicago: University of Chicago Press, 1998), 358.

38. Ann Stoler, "Making Empire Respectable: The Politics of Race and Sexual Morality in 20th-Century Colonial Cultures," in *Imperial Monkey Business: Racial Supremacy in Social Darwinist Theory and Colonial Practice*, ed. Jan Breman (Amsterdam: Vu University Press, 1990), 37; see also Stoler, "Sexual Affronts and Racial Frontiers" and *Capitalism and Confrontation in Sumatra's Plantation Belt, 1870–1979*, second edition (Ann Arbor: University of Michigan Press, 1995).

39. Somerville, *Queering the Color Line.*

40. Stoler, "Making Empire Respectable," 54.

41. Ibid., 58. Indigenous people were no less troubled by the genetic and cultural hybridity that resulted from indigenous-European sexual contact, but their concerns were different, for instance, in the United States, many members of Indian nations were suspicious of the loyalty of so-called mixed bloods, some of whom had entered into economic and political agreements with whites to the detriment of their native kin.

42. After the war new U.S. possessions included Guam, Hawaii, and the Philippines in the Pacific, and Cuba and Puerto Rico in the Caribbean.

43. Kevin Santiago-Valles, "The Sexual Appeal of Racial Differences: U.S. Travel Writing and Anxious American-ness in Turn-of-the-Century Puerto Rico," in *Race and the Production of Modern American Nationalism*, ed. Reynolds J. Scott-Childress (New York: Garland Publishing, 1999), 127.

44. Ibid., 130.

45. Turnbull White, *Our New Possessions: Four Books in One (The Philippine Islands, Puerto Rico, Cuba, The Hawaiian Islands)* (Chicago: Monarch Book Company, 1898), 357.

46. Japanese ethnosexual colonial and imperial exploits will be discussed in Chapters 7 and 8.

47. Benedict Anderson, *Imagined Communities: Reflections on the Origin and Spread of Nationalism* (London: Verso, 1991), 9.

48. There is a Mexican gendered, sexualized negative national narrative of indigenous weakness and betrayal reflected in the story of "Malinche," an Aztec woman baptized as Dona Marina and a consort of Spanish conquistador Hernando Cortes; she is mythologized in Mexican nationalist discourse as a figure of feminine national betrayal and the mother of mixed-race Mexicans; see Sandra Messinger Cypress, *La Malinche in Mexican Literature from History to Myth* (Austin: University of Texas Press, 1991).

49. Alonso, Ana Maria, *Thread of Blood: Colonialism, Revolution, and Gender on Mexico's Northern Frontier* (Tucson: University of Arizona Press, 1995), 94; Jan Rus, "The 'Communidad Revoluctionaria Institucional': The Subversion of Native Government in Highland Chiapas, 1936–1968," in *Everyday Forms of State Formation: Revolution and the Negotiation of Rule in Modern Mexico*, ed. Gilbert M. Joseph and Daniel Nugent (Durham: Duke University Press, 1994), 265–300.

50. Alonso, *Thread of Blood*, 94; see also, Daniel Nugent and Ana Maria Alonso, "Multiple Selective Traditions in Agrarian Reform and Agrarian Struggle: Popular Culture and State Formation in the *Ejido* of Namiquipa, Chihuahua," in *Everyday Forms of State Formation*, 209–46.

51. Alonso, *Thread of Blood*, 71, 102.

52. The devalued nature of Mexico's Indian ancestry is reflected in Latino racial self-identification in the U.S. census; for instance, in both 1990 and 2000 only around one percent of respondents who identified themselves as Hispanic listed "Indian" as their race, despite the fact that many if not most Americans of Mexican, Caribbean, and Latin American ancestry have family trees with indigenous roots; see Clara E. Rodriguez, *Changing Race: Latinos, the Census, and the History of Ethnicity in the United States* (New York: New York University Press, 2000); http://www.census.gov/prod/2001pubs/c2kbr01-1.pdf.

53. Louisa Schein, "Multiple Alterities: The Contouring of Gender in Miao and Chinese Nationalisms," in *Women Out of Place: The Gender of Agency and the Race of Nationality* ed. Brackette F. Williams (New York: Routledge, 1996), 79–102, 82.

54. Ibid.

55. While some of these questions might seem quaint leftovers of another time or the antiquated agendas of ultra conservatives, there are contemporary debates in virtually all countries about whether or not mothers' time is best spent in childrearing or in work outside the home; whether or not women or homosexuals should qualify for military education or service; whether or not various racial or ethnic groups truly fit the national ideal or are truly disadvantaged in society; the overwhelmingly male heterosexual gender composition of current governments around the world, including (especially, and we can add "white" in the case of) the United States, suggests that issues of gender, race, and sexuality in the modern nation are far from settled, rather, they remain in flux, contested, and a central preoccupation of nationalists in many states.

56. See Floya Anthias and Nira Yuval-Davis, eds., *Racial Boundaries: Race, Nation, Gender, Colour and Class and the Anti-Racist Struggle* (London: Routledge, 1992); Nira Yuval-Davis and Floya Anthias, eds., *Woman-Nation-State* (New York: St. Martin's Press, 1989); Sylvia Walby, "Woman and Nation," in *Ethnicity and Nationalism*, ed. Anthony D. Smith (New York: E.J. Brill, 1992), 81–99; Kumari Jayawardena, *Feminism and Nationalism in the Third World* (London: Zed Books, 1986); Neyereh Tohidi, "Gender and Islamic Fundamentalism: Feminist Politics in Iran," in *Third World Women and the Politics of Feminism*, ed. C. T. Mohanty, A. Russo, and L. Torres (Bloomington: Indiana University Press, 1991), 251–65; Julie Skurski, "The Ambiguities of Authenticity: *Dona Barbara* and the Construction of National Identity," *Poetics Today* 15 (1994): 605–42; Paulette Pierce and Brackette F. Williams, " 'And Your Prayers Shall Be Answered through the Womb of a Woman," in *Women Out of Place: The Gender of Agency and the Race of Nationality*, ed. Brackette F. Williams (New York: Routledge, 1996), 186–215.

57. There are, of course, exceptions to this—women who become leaders of nationalist movements, resistance movements, and states, but that list is short and the same names appear again and again; as Roger Horrocks notes when discussing male dominance in public life: "The exception—Margaret Thatcher—proves the rule"; Roger Horrocks, *Masculinity in Crisis: Myths, Fantasies, and Realities* (New York: St. Martin's Press, 1994), 25.

58. For a discussion of various models of masculinity, including a definition of hegemonic masculinity, see Connell, *Masculinities*; Mike Donaldson, "What Is Hege-

monic Masculinity?" *Theory and Society* 22 (1993): 643–57; Bederman, *Manliness and Civilization*; Kimmel and Messner, eds., *Men's Lives*; Fred Pfeil, *White Guys: Studies in Postmodern Domination and Difference* (London: Verso, 1995); Rotundo, *American Manhood*; Michael Schwalbe, *Unlocking the Iron Cage: The Men's Movement, Gender, Politics, and American Culture* (New York: Oxford University Press, 1995).

59. Mosse, *The Image of Man*, 7.

60. Ibid.; other political ideologies of that time, in particular colonialism and imperialism, also resonated with contemporary standards of masculinity; see Roslyn Wallach Bologh, *Love or Greatness: Max Weber and Masculine Thinking—A Feminist Inquiry* (London: Unwin Hyman, 1990); John M. MacKenzie, "The Imperial Pioneer and Hunter and the British Masculine Stereotype in Late Victorian and Edwardian Times," in *Manliness and Morality: Middle-Class Masculinity in Britain and America, 1800–1940*, ed. J. A. Mangan and J. Walvin (Manchester: Manchester University Press, 1987), 176–98; James Walvin, "Symbols of Moral Superiority: Slavery, Sport, and the Changing World Order, 1900–1940," in *Manliness and Morality*, 242–60; Sinha, *Colonial Masculinity*; Seth Koven, "From Rough Lads to Hooligans: Boy Life, National Culture, and Social Reform," in *Nationalisms and Sexualities*, 365–91; Hobsbawm, *Nations and Nationalism since 1780*.

61. Robert Connell, *Gender and Power: Society, the Person, and Sexual Politics* (Stanford: Stanford University Press, 1987).

62. See Connell, *Masculinities*; Suzanne Franzway, Dianne Court, and Robert W. Connell, *Staking a Claim: Feminism, Bureaucracy, and the State* (Cambridge: Polity Press, 1989); Judith Grant and Peta Tancred, "A Feminist Perspective on State Bureaucracy," in *Gendering Organizational Analysis*, ed. Albert J. Mills and Peta Tancred (Newbury Park, CA: Sage Publications, 1992), 112–28.

63. Cynthia Enloe, *Bananas, Beaches, and Bases: Making Feminist Sense of International Politics* (Berkeley: University of California Press, 1990), 45; for a current discussion of gender and nationalism, see Tamar Mayer, "Gender Ironies of Nationalism: Setting the Stage," in *Gender Ironies of Nationalism: Sexing the Nation*, ed. Tamar Mayer (New York: Routledge, 2000), 1–12.

64. See McClintock, *Imperial Leather*; Enloe, *Bananas, Beaches, and Bases*; Craig Calhoun, "Social Theory and the Politics of Identity," in *Social Theory and the Politics of Identity*, ed. Craig Calhoun (Cambridge, MA: Blackwell, 1994), 9–32 and "Nationalism and Civil Society: Democracy, Diversity, and Self-Determination," in *Social Theory and the Politics of Identity*, 304–35, 326.

65. Zoya Hasan, "Introduction: Contextualising Gender and Identity in Contemporary India," in *Forging Identities*, xv; see also Hasan, *Quest for Power*; for a discussion of "Islamic feminism," see Haideh Moghissi, *Feminism and Islamic Fundamentalism: The Limits* (London: Zed Books, 1999), 125–48.

66. Jayawardena, *Feminism and Nationalism in the Third World*; Rosemary Sayigh and Julie Peteet, "Between Two Fires: Palestinian Women in Lebanon," in *Women and Political Conflict*, ed. R. Ridd and H. Callaway (New York: New York University Press, 1987), 106–37; Marie-Aimee Helie-Lucas, "The Role of Women during the Algerian Liberation Struggle and After: Nationalism as a Concept and as a Practice towards Both the Power of the Army and the Militarization of the Peo-

ple," in *Women and the Military System*, ed. T. E. Isaksson (New York: St. Martin's Press, 1988), 171–89; Homa Nategh, "Women: Damned of the Iranian Revolution," *Women and Political Conflict*, 45–60; Stephanie Urdang, *And Still They Dance: Women, War, and the Struggle for Change in Mozambique* (New York: Monthly Review Press, 1989).

67. Enloe, *Bananas, Beaches, and Bases*, 54.

68. Ibid., 60.

69. Ibid., p 64; for a discussion of Third World indigenous feminisms, see Kumari Jayawardena, "Introduction," in *Feminism and Nationalism in the Third World*; Chilla Bulbeck, *Re-Orienting Western Feminisms: Women's Diversity in a Postcolonial World* (New York: Cambridge University Press, 1999).

70. See Ahmed Rashid, *Taliban: Militant Islam, Oil, and Fundamentalism in Central Asia* (New Haven: Yale University Press, 2000); Deborah Ellis, *Women of the Afghan War* (Westport, CT: Praeger, 2000); Jan Goodwin and Jessica Neuwirth, "The Rifle and the Veil," *New York Times On-Line*, October 19, 2001; see also, Jan Goodwin, *The Price of Honor: Muslim Women Lift the Veil of Silence on the Islamic World* (Boston: Little, Brown, 1994); Michael Griffin, *Reaping the Whirlwind: The Taliban Movement in Afghanistan* (Sterling, VA: Pluto Press, 2001).

71. Chris Kutschera, "Algeria's Fighting Women," *The Middle East* (April 1996): 40–41.

72. Elise Boulding, *Women in the Twentieth Century World* (Beverly Hills: Sage Publications 1977), 179; see also Anissa Helie, "Between 'Becoming M'tourni' and 'Going Native': Gender and Settler Society in Algeria," in *Unsettling Settler Societies*, ed. Daiva Stasiulis and Nira Yuval-Davis (Thousand Oaks, CA: Sage Publications, 1995), 263–91; Meyda Yegenoglu, *Colonial Fantasies: Towards a Feminist Reading of Orientalism* (Cambridge: Cambridge University Press, 1998), 136–44.

73. Algerian women have paid a high price for their resistance in recent years. Following the suspension of the results of the 1992 elections, whose outcome would have installed a pro-Islamic government, Islamic militants have escalated their armed opposition, and women, particularly those who do not wear the *hijab*, have become targets of their violence:

> Crimes against women included abduction, torture, rape, gang rape and killing, crimes which were common by mid-1995. . . . Feminist, militants, female journalists and teachers are particularly targeted, some of them forced to lead a clandestine life, having to hide from the bullets of the killers and their knives by constantly changing addresses and covering their tracks. (Malika Mehdid, "En-Gendering the Nation-State: Woman, Patriarchy and Politics in Algeria," in *Woman and the State: International Perspectives*, ed. S. M. Rai and G. Lievesley [London: Taylor and Francis, 1996], 93–94)

For news accounts of these attacks, see Ibrahim M. Youssef, "Bareheaded Women Slain in Algiers: Killings Following Islamic Threats," *New York Times*, March 31, 1994:A3; Peter Steinfels, "In Algeria, Women Are Caught in the Cross-Fire of Men's Religious and Ideological Wars," *New York Times*, July 1, 1995:8, 10.

74. Deborah Gaitskell and Elaine Unterhalter, "Mothers of the Nation: A Comparative Analysis of Nation, Race, and Motherhood in Afrikaner Nationalism and the African National Congress," in *Woman-Nation-State*, 60.

75. Theweleit, *Male Fantasies*, 294.

76. See Julie Peteet, "Gender and Sexuality: Belonging to the National and Moral

Order," in *Hermeneutics and Honor: Negotiating Female "Public" Space in Islamic/ate Societies*, ed. Asma Afsaruddin (Cambridge, MA: Center for Middle Eastern Studies of Harvard University, Harvard University Press, 1999), 70–88.

77. Lynette Feder, *Women and Domestic Violence: An Interdisciplinary Approach* (New York: Haworth Press, 1999); Jody Raphael, *Saving Bernice: Battered Women, Welfare, and Poverty* (Boston: Northeastern University Press, 2000).

78. Camilla Fawzi El-Solh and Judy Mabro, "Introduction: Islam and Muslim Women," in *Muslim Women's Choices: Religious Belief and Social Reality*, ed. Camilla Fawzi El-Solh and Judy Mabro (Providence, RI: Berg Publishers, 1994), 8; although El-Solh and Mabro are specifically discussing men's and women's honor in Islamic cultures, Dorothy Thomas discusses the phenomenon and defense of "honor killing" in Brazil, Dorothy Q. Thomas, *Criminal Injustice: Violence against Women in Brazil—An Americas Watch Report* (New York: Human Rights Watch, 1992); see also Sueann Caulfield, *In Defense of Honor: Sexual Morality, Modernity, and Nation in Early-Twentieth-Century Brazil* (Durham: Duke University Press, 2000); Lyman L. Johnson and Sonya Lipsett–Rivera, *The Faces of Honor: Sex, Shame, and Violence in Colonial Latin America* (Albuquerque: University of New Mexico Press, 1998); Ann Twinam, *Public Lives, Private Secrets: Gender, Honor, Sexuality, and Illegitimacy in Colonial Spanish America* (Stanford: Stanford University Press, 1999); Amani M. Awwad, "Gosship, Scandal, Shame, and Honor Killing: A Case for Social Constructionism and Hegemonic Discourse," *Social Thought and Research* 24 (2002): 39–52; Dilek Cindoglu and Murat Cemrek, "Honor Crimes in the Middle East: Contested Boundaries through Women's Bodies," paper presented at the annual meeting of the American Sociological Association, Chicago, 1999; for a discussion of "honor rape," see Shahla Haeri, "Women's Body, Nation's Honor: Rape in Pakistan" in *Hermeneutics and Honor*, ed. Asma Afsaruddin (Cambridge, MA: Center for Middle Eastern Studies of Harvard University, 1999), 55–69.

79. Mosse, *Nationalism and Sexuality*, 98; these images of acceptable female sexuality stood in contrast to female "decadents" (prostitutes or lesbians) whose actions are "unpatriotic, weakening the nation" and dishonoring the nation's men; Ibid., 109.

80. Ibid., 98; there are some exceptions to this; for instance, in the many socialist revolutions in the Second and Third World, women were granted constitutionally equal rights, though in practice this complete de jure gender equality generally fell short of the mark; nonetheless, the legal challenges to patriarchal customary and official law brought about by socialist gender policies often represented quite a radical break with tradition, though this radicalism was sometimes short-lived; for a discussion of patriarchal notions of men's and women's sexuality in post-revolutionary Cuba, see Lois M. Smith and Alfred Padula, *Sex and Revolution: Women in Socialist Cuba* (New York: Oxford University Press, 1996), especially 178–80; Helen I. Safa, *The Myth of the Male Breadwinner: Women and Industrialization in the Caribbean* (Boulder: Westview Press, 1995), 125–68.

81. For a discussion of "retraditionalization," see Joane Nagel, *American Indian Ethnic Renewal: Red Power and the Resurgence of Identity and Culture* (New York: Oxford University Press, 1996), 193.

82. Eve Kosofsky Sedgwick, *The Epistemology of the Closet* (Berkeley: Univer-

sity of California Press, 1990), 184–85; Judith Butler, *Bodies that Matter: On the Discursive Limits of "Sex"* (New York: Routledge, 1993), 126.

83. Barbara Epstein, "Anti-Communism, Homophobia, and the Construction of Masculinity in the Postwar U.S.," *Critical Sociology* 20 (1994): 21–44; see also Cindy Patton, "To Die For" in *Novel Gazing: Queer Readings in Fiction,* ed. Eve K. Sedgwick (Durham: Duke University Press, 1997), 330–52; Albert Fried, *McCarthyism* (New York: Oxford University Press, 1997); Robert J. Corber, *Homosexuality in Cold War America: Resistance and the Crisis of Masculinity* (Durham: Duke University Press, 1997); L. J. Moran, "The Uses of Homosexuality: Homosexuality for National Security," *International Journal of the Sociology of Law* 19 (1991): 149–70.

84. The Irish Supreme Court did permit the thirteen-year-old girl, who was raped, to travel to England to have an abortion in December 1997; see James E. Clarity, "Top Irish Court Lets Girl, 13, Have Abortion in England," *New York Times,* December 2, 1997:A6–7; see also Katie Conrad, "Domestic Queers: Home and Nation in Ireland," paper presented at the Hall Center for the Humanities, University of Kansas, September 14, 2000.

85. Stychin, *A Nation by Rights,* 137.

86. Saunders, "In a Cloud of Lust," 82.

87. Sasho A. Lambevski, "Suck My Nation—Masculinity, Ethnicity, and the Politics of (Homo)Sex," *Sexualities* 2 (1999): 397–419.

88. Reiss Jr., "The Social Integration of Peers and Queers."

89. Lamberski, "Suck My Nation," 410.

90. Petula Sik Ying Ho and Adolf Kat Tat Tsang, "Negotiating Anal Intercourse in Inter-Racial Gay Relationships in Hong Kong," *Sexualities* 3 (2000): 299–324.

91. Ibid., 313.

92. See Parker *et al., Nationalisms and Sexualities;* Stychin, *A Nation by Rights;* Matthew C. Gutmann, *The Meanings of Macho: Being a Man in Mexico City* (Berkeley: University of California Press, 1997).

CHAPTER **6**

SEX AND WAR

Fighting Men, Comfort Women, and the Military-Sexual Complex

Several years ago a student came to see me during office hours to discuss a research project he was planning for that semester. He said he wanted to write a paper on Korean prostitution in Junction City, Kansas. I looked at him blankly, thinking there was some kind of miscommunication between us. He was an international student, and perhaps we were having a language problem. Either I did not understand his description of the project or he did not understand the assignment. What would Koreans (especially Korean prostitutes) be doing in a small town 150 miles west of Kansas City? As we discussed his project further, I began to understand what this Korean student already knew—that both South Korea and Kansas are ethnosexual destinations where the global meets the local in the pursuit of racialized sex and romance.

The next three chapters of this book will explore the global economy of desire, looking for ethnic and sexual connections in places we might not necessarily think of as libidinal locations—war fronts, peacekeeping missions, economic development projects, export processing zones, travel and tourist destinations, housekeeping and childcare work. This chapter will focus on the geopolitics of ethnicity and sexuality mainly in the twentieth century, and will examine the ethnosexual dimensions of international conflicts, civil wars, the Cold War, and the post-Soviet "new world order." We will survey the ways that sexuality is deployed in military missions and the uses of sexual technologies in making war and keeping the peace.

SEX AND THE MILITARY MAN

Since the Korean War of 1950–1953 hundreds of thousands of U.S. armed services personnel have been stationed on dozens of military bases and installations in South Korea. For instance, in 2001 U.S. Forces in Korea officials reported that there were ninety-five military bases and installations of various sorts in South Korea, forty-one of which were "major sized bases/installations" staffed by approximately thirty-seven thousand troops and service personnel.[1] Some of these troops are based stateside in Junction City, Kansas, home of the U.S. Army's First Infantry Division—"The Big Red One." While they are stationed in South Korea many American servicemen frequent hundreds of bars and brothels surrounding military bases, some of which were set up and are inspected by U.S. and Korean authorities. These Americans sate their sexual desire and spread their sexual seed among thousands of Korean and other mainly Asian prostitutes servicing these servicemen. For instance, Katharine Moon estimates that

> [s]ince the war, over one million Korean women have served as sex providers for the U.S. military. And millions of Koreans and Americans have shared a sense of special bonding, for they have together shed blood in battle and mixed blood through sex and Amerasian offspring.[2]

GIs in Korea do not simply have sex with local women, some marry Korean women who return with them to the United States when the men complete their tours of duty. Moon reports that "from the early 1950s to the early 1990s, over 100,000 Korean women have immigrated to the United States as wives of servicemen."[3] Some of these marriages are, no doubt, affairs of convenience arranged for profit or immigration purposes, and some are matches made for love or romance. Some marriages last, some do not.

In the United States, Korean women from dissolved unions often find themselves strangers in a new land, attempting to establish an independent life, possessing only a limited knowledge of English and few job skills, competing for employment in local labor markets primarily oriented to providing services to the military base. These women have easy access linguistically and culturally to already established Korean businesses catering to soldiers, and many find work as waitresses, bargirls, dancers, masseuses, and prostitutes. This combination of military, marriage, and migration accounted for what initially seemed to me to be the unlikely presence of Korean prostitutes in Junction City, Kansas.

The number of Korean prostitutes in Junction City is no doubt small and represents a tiny proportion of the number of American prostitutes working near U.S. military bases across the United States. Korean prostitutes in Junction City are, of course, only a tiny fraction of the number of Korean and other Asian prostitutes working near U.S. military bases in Korea, and still a smaller fraction of German and other European prostitutes working near U.S. military bases in Germany, or the number of Japanese, Okinawan, and other Asian prostitutes working near U.S. military bases in Japan,[4] or Filipino prostitutes who worked near U.S. military bases in the Philippines until those bases were closed in 1992,[5] or Panamanian and Latin American prostitutes who worked near bases in the former U.S. Canal Zone before the canal was turned over to Panama in 1999. These are to name but a few of the ethnosexual work zones surrounding U.S. and other countries' military bases around the world. These militarized ethnosexual frontiers are collateral creations of the global defense and warfare system.

An important aspect of Korean prostitution in Korea and Kansas involves the place of Asian women in Western erotic meaning systems. Lynn Thiesmeyer argues that the imaginary construction of Asian women's sexuality is accomplished by "discourses of seduction" in which the Asian female body is characterized by servile sexual availability. She argues that this longstanding, performative Western sexual stereotype of Asian women works to silence dissident discourses and mask inconvenient realities of Asian women's physical abuse, forced servitude, and sexual exploitation by both Western and non-Western men.

> The western image of the Asian female, the Asian body, and Asian sexuality has been reproduced, yet scarcely updated for centuries. As a late twentieth-century representative body of cultural feudalism and exoticism, the Asian/Asian-American woman has no parallel in the fantasies of the West. Wendy Chapkis points out that "advertisements using Asian women, for example, are evocative not only of the sexual mystery but also the docility and subservience supposedly 'natural to the oriental female'. . . . These women thus become metaphors for adventure, cultural difference, and sexual subservience."[6]

Thus, for American servicemen the sexual recreation areas that surround U.S. military bases, especially in Asia, are ethnosexual sites where Western fantasies of Asian female sexuality meet material manifestations of Asian women, and where the marriage of geopolitics and racial cosmologies is consummated nightly.

Although the presence of U.S. bases provides the customer base for the local and immigrant prostitutes, the bars and brothels that ring military installations are owned and regulated by a variety of economic players. Aida Santos argues that there are many local groups and actors directly or indirectly involved in the sex industry: local club owners, organized crime rings, politicians and party officials, law enforcement; she also cites local patriarchal cultural patterns, especially "male political privilege that underlies the institutionalized use of women's bodies."[7] Saundra Sturdevant and Brenda Stoltzfus's discussion of the bar system in Olongapo that was situated near the Subic Bay U.S. military base in the Philippines described a similar local/foreign partnership:

> The bar owners are Filipinos, Chinese, and American ex-Navy men who either have married a Filipina or have a front in order to own a bar. They are community members active in the Lion's and Rotary Clubs. The mayor also owns several clubs. The club owners have an association, which enables them to control what happens in the bar system.[8]

There are many interests served by the sexual service industry. There is money to be made, troops to be entertained, tensions to be released, strategic interests to be protected, and masculinity to be militarized. Cynthia Enloe argues that militaries and military operations depend on

> particular presumptions about masculinity in order to sustain soldiers' morale and discipline. Without a sexualized "rest and recreation" (R&R) period, would the U.S. military command be able to send young men off on long, often tedious sea voyages and ground maneuvers? Without myths of Asian women's compliant sexuality would many American men be able to sustain their own identities of themselves as manly enough to act as soldiers. Women who . . . work as prostitutes around American bases in Asia tell us how a militarized masculinity is constructed and reconstructed in smoky bars and in sparsely furnished boardinghouses. If we only look at boot camps and the battlefield—the focus of most investigations into the formation of militarized masculinity—we will not be able adequately to explain just how masculinity is created and sustained in the peculiar ways necessary to sustain a military organization.[9]

Enloe is joined by a number of critics of the U.S. global military presence who argue that the military mobilization of masculinity to serve national interests—economic and geopolitical, foreign and domestic—is not without its costs—to the men themselves and to the country as a whole. The presence of the U.S. military is deeply resented in many countries, not the least because of the local presence of American culture and consumers, especially sexual consumers. Chalmers Johnson argues that

> [f]ew Americans who have never served in the armed forces overseas have any conception of the nature or impact of an American base complex, with its massive military facilities, post exchanges, dependents' housing estates, swimming pools, and golf courses, and the associated bars, strip clubs, whorehouses, and venereal disease clinics that they attract. . . . They can extend for miles, dominating localities and in some cases whole nations.[10]

In such cases, the American presence can be experienced by locals as an occupation by foreign men, women, equipment, vehicles, buildings, war machinery and materiel, as an invasion of Western culture, ideas, and desires, and as a source of pollution and corruption. Johnson links anti-American sentiment and actions, such as attacks on U.S. military and civilian targets, to the "blowback" from America's international presence and foreign policy that, he argues, are hidden from average Americans or conveniently denied by informed Americans and their government.[11]

FIGHTING MEN AND COMFORT WOMEN

As Enloe notes, sexuality has always been an important, though often disregarded aspect of all militaries and military operations. Throughout history women have been among "camp followers" providing services such as laundry, nursing, companionship, and sex to soldiers on military missions during peace and war.[12] Sometimes these women have been wives, relatives, or girlfriends, but always among their ranks have been prostitutes as well. Women who have had sex with servicemen around the world, however, have not always been volunteers. Throughout history local women have been involuntarily "drafted" in the sexual service of militaries as rape victims and sexual slaves.[13]

Rape in war is at its core an ethnosexual phenomenon. Whether a war is fought across national borders or inside state boundaries, the military front is typically an ethnosexual frontier. Differences in nationality, race, or ethnicity separate the combatants and identify the targets of aggression in military operations. Whether violence in war is from combat or sexual attack, and whether it is guns or bodies that are used as weapons, those who are physically or sexually assaulted almost always are different in some ethnic way. Men at war do not, as a rule, rape their "own" women unless, of course, those women are suspected of disloyalty, especially sexual disloyalty or "collaboration."

Sexual exploitation and abuse are important weapons of war, and rape is perhaps the most common component of war's sexual arsenal. Susan Brownmiller documents the routine practice of rape, especially gang rape, in war.[14] Moving or occupying armies use the rape of "enemy" women and girls as both a carrot and a stick: raping local women is a spoil of war for the troops to enjoy, and rape is also a technique of terror and warfare designed to dominate and humiliate enemy men by sexually conquering their women. Rape in war, as in many other ethnosexual settings, is best understood as a transaction between men, where women are the currency used in the exchange. Sexually taking an enemy's women amounts to gaining territory and psychological advantage. In countries around the world, rape often is defined as a polluting action, a way to soil the victim, her kin, and her nation physically and symbolically. Sexual warfare can extend beyond the moment of violation in situations where victims are reputationally smeared, physically mutilated, or when pregnancies or births result from sexual assaults. For instance, the widespread rape of mainly Muslim and some Croatian women by Serbian men in Bosnia in the early 1990s was partly intended to impregnate the women so that they would bear Serbian babies, "little Chetniks."[15] In order to guarantee that these rape victims could not obtain abortions, the Serbs set up concentration camps where pregnant women were imprisoned until they gave birth.[16]

Probably the best-known instance of rape in war is the so-called Rape of Nanking that occurred during the Japanese invasion of China in the winter and spring of 1938–1939, when Japanese soldiers raped an estimated eighty thousand Chinese women and girls.[17] A less well-known instance of Japanese wartime sexual exploits was the sexual enslavement of thousands of mainly Asian women by the Japanese Imperial Army during World War II. Sexual slavery in war is a variation on the theme of wartime rape. Slavery extends the tactic of rape as a short-term strategy of a military mission into a permanent feature of military operations. The Japanese military established camps of so-called military comfort women (Jugun Ianfu) in Japan and other countries where Japanese troops were stationed. While there were some mainly lower-class Japanese women forced into sexual slavery, most of the estimated 200,000 women enslaved by the Japanese army were ethnic or national Others brought from Korea, China, Taiwan, Indonesia, Malaysia, and the Philippines to sexually service the troops.[18] Kazuko Watanabe reports that in such settings a woman's worth as a sexual commodity was based on her class and her ethnicity:

> The Japanese Imperial Army divided comfort women into a hierarchical order according to class, race, and nationality. . . . .Korean and most other Asian women were assigned to lower-class soldiers. Japanese and European women went to high-ranking officers. Most of the European women were Dutch [often of mixed ancestry] who were imprisoned in a prisoner of war camp in the Netherlands East Indies.[19]

Soldiers' rankings of and preferences for women of particular races and nationalities enslaved in rape camps were not unique to the Japanese military.[20] Japan was not the only country that established large-scale organized operations of forced sexual servitude during World War II. The Nazis used concentration camps in Germany and other occupied countries for more than industrial and war-related labor, their program of genocide against the Jews, and the mass deportation and killing of Roma (gypsies) and other "non-Aryan" peoples. Sexual labor was also demanded of women internees, and both men and women prisoners were used for sexual experimentation by Nazi scientists and physicians. German concentration camps were sites of forced prostitution and sexual assault, and as was the case with Japan, not all women in the German camps were treated as "equal" when it came to sexual abuse. A woman's age, youth, and physical appearance made her more or less likely to be the target of Nazi sexual aggression.[21] And, as in so many areas of social life, even (especially) in wartime concentration camps, ethnicity mattered. There were official prohibitions against German soldiers having sex with Jewish women, though these rules often were not enforced. Many Jewish women survivors reported extensive sadistic sexual torture, as well as rape, and these assaults often were accompanied by a barrage of racial and anti-Semitic verbal abuse.[22]

The Allies also were involved in sexual violence and exploitation during World War II. Some was in the form of mass rapes, such as those committed against German women by the Soviet army.[23] In other cases, sexual abuse and exploitation resulted when military personnel capitalized on the vulnerability of women who faced economic hardship, malnourishment, or starvation because of the war's disruption of local economies and food production. Many women in occupied or liberated countries found sexual liaisons or prostitution preferable to the grim alternatives available for themselves and their dependent families. U.S. troops also committed rapes during the war and the occupation that followed. In her examination of U.S. Army records, Brownmiller found 947 rape *convictions*, not simply charges or trials of American soldiers in Army general courts-martial during the period from January 1942 to July 1947.[24]

Wartime rape did not stop at the end of World War II, nor did its ethnosexual character change after 1945. The practice of rape in war extended into major and minor conflicts during the second half of the twentieth century—in civil wars, wars of independence, and military invasions, interventions, and operations in countries and regions around the world including Bangladesh, Vietnam, Iraq, Kuwait, Bosnia, Croatia, Serbia, Rwanda, Liberia, Kashmir, and Sierra Leone.[25] The logic of rape in war is always the same: rapes are committed across ethnosexual boundaries, and rape is used by both sides for the familiar time-honored reasons—to reward the troops, to terrorize and humiliate the enemy, and as a means of creating solidarity and protection through mutual guilt among small groups of soldiers. Ethnic loyalty and ethnic loathing join hands in rape in war.

In the post-Soviet era East European nationalist conflicts the use of rape as a weapon of war has begun to move from the shadows more fully into view. For instance, during the 1990s warfare occurred along a number of ethnic and national borders in the former Yugoslavia—between Croats and

Serbs, Christians and Muslims, and against Roma, among others. The most notorious of these ethnic conflicts was in Bosnia; the conflict's notoriety stemmed in part from its sexual character, especially the mass rape of Bosnian Muslim women by Orthodox Christian Serbian men. Many of these men and women were former neighbors. Muslims and Christians had lived side by side in the city of Sarajevo and elsewhere in Bosnia for decades and many had intermarried. That peace was shattered in 1992 when "ethnic cleansing" began.

Ethnic cleansing, or the removal of one ethnic group from a territory claimed by another, followed a common pattern across the region. Groups of armed Serbian men (sometimes uniformed troops and sometimes "irregulars" who were not officially in the military and not in uniform) roamed Bosnian towns and villages in groups, opportunistically looting and pillaging houses and businesses, raping and killing mainly unarmed Muslims they encountered along the way. Survivors reported that the Serbs came through the same towns several times in waves. During the first wave, typically, some of the Muslim men were killed and the rest were rounded up to be killed later or to be interned in concentration camps. Muslim women, children, and the elderly were left behind. It was during the next waves of Serbs passing through the towns that they raped local non-Serbian girls and women.

Munevra was a forty-eight-year-old widow with three sons ranging in age from fourteen to twenty-four, ages that made them targets for the Serbs to kill or deport to concentration camps. She kept the young men hidden in the cellar as small groups of armed Serbian men repeatedly came through the town. In the spring of 1992, two men came to her house and sexually assaulted her. Please note, Munevra's account of her abuse and the testimony of other rape victims below may be very disturbing to some readers.

> I was afraid my sons would hear me. I was dying of fear 'cause of my sons. They're decent people. . . . Then this man touched my breasts. He pulled up my blouse and took out my breasts. . . . He said, "For a woman your age your breasts aren't bad." Then they brought me to the other room. . . . I begged him and cried, and I crossed my legs. Then he took out his thing, you know, and he did it and sprayed it on me. When he was done the other one came and did the same thing. . . . When they left, my sons came out and . . . they asked me what happened: "What'd they do to you?" I said, "Nothing." I couldn't tell them about it. . . . I'd rather die than have them find out about it.[26]

Women's and families' shame about such incidents were part of the process of victimization and violation.[27] Munevra's experience occurred relatively early in the nationalist conflict; far worse sexual violations were in store for women as the war escalated.

The scene in Serbian so-called rape camps was a longer, more brutal nightmare for Muslim and other non-Serbian women and girls. Twenty-six-year-old Ifeta was arrested by Serbian soldiers, most of whom she knew, and taken to a women's camp in Doboj:

> Three drunken [Serbian army] soldiers . . . dragged her into a classroom . . . here she was raped by all three men "at the same time," says Ifeta, point-ing to her mouth and backside. "And while they were doing it they said I was going to have a baby by them". . . . After that the rapes were a part of Ifeta's daily life. . . . It was always a gang rape, they always cursed and hu-miliated her during it, and the rapists very frequently forced her to have oral sex with them.[28]

Another camp internee, Kadira, described the weeks she spent at Doboj:

> "They pushed bottle necks into our sex, they even stuck shattered, broken bottles into some women. . . . Guns too. And then you don't know if he's going to fire, you're scared to death". . . . Once she was forced to urinate on the Koran. Another time she and a group of women had to dance naked for the Serbian guards and sing Serbian songs. . . . She has forgotten how many times she was raped.[29]

The same pattern of sexual terror, torture, and rape used by the Serbs in their campaigns of ethnic cleansing and warfare in Bosnia was repeated in Kosovo, Yugoslavia, in 1998–1999. Once again groups of Serbian men—po-lice, soldiers, irregulars—swept through villages invading homes and raping Kosovar Albanian (mainly Muslim) female occupants, sexually attacking Kosovar Albanian women refugees fleeing combat zones, and sexually as-saulting Kosovar Albanian women who were being held hostage or detained. The Kosovo conflict ended when NATO troops entered Kosovo in June 1999.[30]

In spring 2000, the UN convened the *International Criminal Tribunal for the Former Yugoslavia* in The Hague, Netherlands, to investigate and prosecute those ordering mass killing and mass rape in the various ethnic conflicts in the former Yugoslavia.[31] This investigation raised the issue of whether rape and sexual slavery are "crimes against humanity." Enloe ar-gues that this question reflects a new awareness and public airing of what has been a long hidden history of sexual assault, torture, and exploitation of women during war:

> [T]he rapes in Bosnia have been documented by women's organizations . . . [that] have helped create an international political network of feminists who are making news of the Bosnian women's victimization not to institution-alize women as victims, not to incite men to more carnage, but to explain anew how war makers rely on peculiar ideas about masculinity . . . [F]emi-

nist reporters are using news of wartime sexual assaults by male soldiers to rethink the very meanings of both sovereignty and national identity. . . . If they succeed, the construction of the entire international political arena will be significantly less vulnerable to patriarchy.[32]

As the reports of human rights hearings and organizations document every year, it is not only enemy women who are the targets of sexual abuse and torture in war. I have not seen reported the establishment of rape camps with men as sexual slaves, however, men often are assaulted sexually as part of intimidation, torture, and combat in international conflicts and wars, as well as in military or paramilitary operations against internal political or ethnic insurgents. For instance, in Bosnia, there were numerous reports of cases in which Muslim and Croatian men were castrated or forced to castrate one another:

> In villages, towns, cities, the countryside, and concentration camps, male and female adults and children are raped as part of more extensive torture. Many of the atrocities committed are centered on the genitalia . . . [T]estimonies of castrations enforced on Bosnian-Herzegovinian and Croatian prisoners, and in particular of orders under threat of death that they castrate each other with various instruments and at times with their teeth, are widely available, as the [United Nations] Bassiouni Report makes clear.[33]

Men also can be vulnerable to sexualized warfare in more indirect ways. In her critique of Japan's patriarchal Confucianist view of all women and racist treatment of non-Japanese men and women, Kazuko Watanabe also identifies a danger for men. She argues that in many countries men are trapped in masculinist roles, and forced to act out patriarchal and sexual scripts that commodify and endanger them as well as the women they victimize:

> Men's bodies and sexualities are also victims of militarist and consumerist capitalist societies. Men are, supposedly, unable to control their sexual impulses and are in need of prostitutes. [In World War II] Male soldiers were dehumanized to make them good fighters then stimulated by sexual desire that was fulfilled by comfort women. . . . Both the soldiers who were forced to die for the emperor on the battlefields and today's businessmen who die for their companies from *karoshi* (overwork) have often been rewarded with prostitutes.[34]

Watanabe's analysis suggests that although they are perpetrators of the rape and sexual abuse of both women and other men in times of war, men pay a psychological, social, and physical price for their complicity in patriarchal masculinist systems of sexual and ethnosexual violence. For instance, many soldiers display varying degrees of post-traumatic stress or "shell shock" following combat. Michael Kimmel reports that during World War I officers and doctors tended to view such disorders as "failures to conform to gender demands":

> Most psychiatric treatments for shell shock involved treating the disease as the result of insufficient manliness. T. J. Calhoun, assistant surgeon with the Army of the Potomac, argued that if the soldier could not be "laughed out of it by his comrades" or by "appeals to his manhood," then a good dose of battle was the best "curative."[35]

Although modern-day soldiers suffering from post-traumatic stress are viewed with more sympathy than their historical counterparts, many, including those working in the health care industry, still view soldiers exhibiting symptoms arising from combat and military operations with some suspicion, as malingerers, frauds, or weaklings.[35]

SEX AND PEACE

A state of war is not a necessary condition for the militarization of sex. Even in peacetime or as part of a "defense" strategy, the presence of military troops, operations, or bases creates a convenient and lucrative market for the sex industry, and occupying or peacekeeping troops find ample opportunity for sexual associations with and sexual attacks against local women and girls. It is the scale of military operations, not the occurrence of actual combat, that determines the amount and intensity of sexual action—commercial, congenial, and coercive—on the ethnosexual frontiers surrounding military installations and troops. For instance, the Cold War changed the character of military-related prostitution, which was already operating on a large scale at the end of World War II. After the war, the Allied powers established permanent military bases in former hostile states (e.g., Germany, Japan, Italy) and in many friendly countries as part of the North Atlantic Treaty Organization (NATO) and various mutual defense agreements and treaties (e.g., with the Philippines, Panama, Guam).

During the Cold War, the creation of a global network of military bases and pacts by the U.S. and its allies and by the Soviet Union and its allies greatly expanded the number of armed forces and military installations around the world. These new military consumers generated unprecedented demand for many products and services for military operations and personnel, including sexual services. Military bases became permanent features of the geopolitical landscape in the second half of the twentieth century, and expanded in size and personnel during various Cold War proxy combat engagements such as those in Korea, Vietnam, Central America, and Southern

Africa. Prostitution became a large-scale, stable industry around military bases in many parts of the world. Not just U.S. bases were involved. Soldiers are a diverse set of global ethnosexual adventurers. For instance, Enloe reported during the 1980s there were

> British bases in West Germany, Cyprus, the Falklands and Belize . . . [and] Northern Ireland. . . . The Indian government stationed 45,000 of its soldiers on counter-insurgency duty in Sri Lanka. There have been 50,000 Cuban soldiers stationed in Angola. The Soviet Union maintains bases in Vietnam and Eastern Europe. Vietnamese troops only now are withdrawing from Kampuchea. The French military bases 8,000 of its soldiers in Chad, the Central African Republic, Gabon, Senegal, the Ivory Coast and Djibouti, as well as others in its remaining Pacific and Caribbean colonies. Canada sends troops to its bases in West Germany. Finnish, Fijian, Irish and other men serve overseas as part of United Nations peace-keeping forces.[37]

The sex workers who provided services to these troops typically were ethnically distinct from their clients since soldiers often are stationed in regions of a country with ethnically different populations or in countries where local or immigrant sex workers are of different nationalities from occupying forces. It is important to note in this thus far almost exclusively heterosexual discussion that the sex workers visited by military men are not always women. For instance, U.S. servicemen stationed abroad also seek exotic sexual encounters with Other men. During his tour in the U.S. Marine Corps in the 1980s, former Chief Scout/Sniper David Anthony Tyeeme Clark reported much gossip and bragging by Marines about their sexual exploits with "benny boys"—male sex workers who provided presumably straight Marines with something new and different during their shore "liberty."

> My enlistment was for six years beginning in 1982 . . . [those] years corresponded with the Reagan/Gipper/John Wayne administration . . . when men were men and benny boys provided the best shore leave memories. . . . In my memory of those conversations, guys would insist that benny boys were even better than women (the logic was something like benny boys had insider [sexual] knowledge, something women had to depend on men for learning).[38]

Clark argues that by othering these often gay, ethnically different male sex workers, Marines managed to create the distance they needed to maintain a hypermasculine, hyperheterosexual image of themselves and the Marine Corps. The exotic strangeness they attributed to the benny boys seemed to allow the Marines to camouflage the fact that they were having sex with other men.[39]

The last five decades of postwar global militarization has institutionalized female and male prostitution on an unparalleled scale in the many countries around the world that served NATO and Eastern bloc military operations. The disintegration of the Soviet Union in the early 1990s and the subsequent end of the Cold War changed the logic of many of these military base and personnel placements from superpower competition to international peacekeeping. UN and NATO peacekeeping operations have expanded as has the U.S. military's involvement in peacekeeping. As a result, the international circulation of soldiers remains an important feature of the global system. These new peacekeeping troops are no more celibate than their Cold War predecessors, and the new military missions have generated continuing demand for sexual services. For instance, Judith Stiehm reports that during the United Nations' peacekeeping mission in Namibia in 1989–1990

> some male peacekeepers moved local women into their quarters, UN vehicles were parked in front of brothels, and even high-ranking officials were believed to exploit local women hired by the UN. . . . [In Cambodia in the early 1990s] the abuse of local women and children by UN troops and civilian police was brought to public attention. . . . Apparently the fear of AIDS made "virgins" highly desirable, and younger and younger girls were being recruited for prostitution.[40]

In contrast to the historically casual, even approved links between national armies and sexual service suppliers, Stiehm found that international peacekeeping troops and officials' sexual excursions into local towns and countrysides became controversial as the 1990s progressed. For the first time serious questions were being raised about the taken-for-granted, "boys will be boys" attitude of UN senior officials. Stiehm attributes this change of heart and mind to the presence of women UN workers and peacekeepers and to the involvement of religious NGOs (nongovernmental organizations, such as charitable or relief organizations), both of whom challenged longstanding military men's sexual perquisites.[41] Exposure and criticism of UN troops' ethnosexual appetites and indulgences pressured United Nations officials to design new policies to restrict such behavior. Established ethnosexual practices die hard, however, especially where there is money to be made.

For instance, in April 2000, Kathryn Bolkovac, a United Nations police officer from Lincoln, Nebraska, was fired from her assignment at a UN police post assigned to investigate forced prostitution in Bosnia.

> The official reason: She allegedly falsified a time sheet. Bolkovac's explanation: She filed a report alleging that officers forged documents for trafficked women, aided their illegal transport through border checkpoints into Bosnia, and tipped off sex club owners ahead of raids. . . . The United Nations concedes that two dozen officers with the 2000-member U.N. International Police Task Force, including eight Americans, have been fired for offenses ranging from bribery to sexual impropriety.[42]

Bolkovac was not the only UN police officer who reported sexual misconduct and criminal behavior by UN International Police Task Force (IPTF) personnel in Bosnia. David Lamb, an American UN human rights investigator working in central Bosnia reported in 2001 that

> he and others routinely forwarded evidence of wrongdoing to the [UN] mission's internal affairs unit, only to be told "not to look too deep" . . . he was conducting a major investigation based on information from six women who said they were forced into prostitution. "They gave us a whole list of IPTF people involved. . . . It was just incredible to see the resistance we got from mission headquarters. There was a game being played, and investigators were being intimidated. I was trying to root out the corruption, but I couldn't get any support."[43]

Some Bosnians felt they had little choice but to defend UN laxity and complicity in the illegal sex industry. Journalists William Kole and Aida Cerkez-Robinson interviewed Nezira Samardzic, a twenty-one-year-old university student in Sarajevo, who expressed concerns that such scandals might jeopardize the peacekeeping mission in the ethnically divided, war-torn region: "I can't imagine peace without them. . . . They're only human. I'm afraid that talk about only the bad side might prompt somebody to think the U.N. mission to Bosnia should be terminated."[44]

An important aspect of military-related prostitution, even in peacekeeping settings, is that it illustrates very clearly the links among geopolitics, ethnicity, and sexuality. Even away from war fronts with their direct ethnic and national confrontations, sexual encounters involving foreign military personnel and local people are almost without exception ethnosexual encounters. The women and men providing sexual services to peacetime military and police personnel are invariably racial, ethnic, and national Others. Such sexual encounters often are the only real interactions that occur between locals and foreign soldiers. As a result of this limited, distorted relationship, the commercial sexualized image each has of the other magnifies the stereotypes and prejudices that so often are associated with racial, ethnic, or national differences. The hypersexualization of local women, the commercialization of sexual culture, and the presence of an entrenched sex industry, all of which stem from the militarization of sexuality, often persist long after the wars are over. For instance, Plate 8 of the color insert is posted on the U.S. Navy's website of the Navy Region Hawaii along with advice for new sailors arriving at the Pearl Harbor homeport.[45] The visible wedding of military and ethnosexuality can be seen in the image of a female hula dancer superimposed over that of the Navy frigate, USS Crommelin, moored in the harbor.

THE MILITARY-SEXUAL COMPLEX

Despite the end of the Korean War, Vietnam War, and Cold War, the sex industries they helped to generate and expand have remained permanent niches in many national economies. Besides continuing to service ongoing military operations around the world, a central legacy of the militarized global sex trade is sex tourism.[46] Sex tourism is part of a large sex-for-profit industry which includes, for example, prostitution, pornography, sexual media, materials, and equipment, and nude and exotic dancing. Sex tourism destinations are concentrated commercial sex spaces that provide a wide array of establishments and services to which consumers travel for sex. Sex tourist destinations can draw customers from local populations or from more distant national and international venues. Sex tours often are advertised and arranged by agencies and organizations specializing in sex tourism. Both sex tourism and the broader sex industry of which it is a part are organized commercial operations with legal and illegal components and with some well-paid and some exploited workers.

Sex tourism represents another chapter in the history of sex and war. Sex tourism developed as the international industry it is today with the help of the U.S. military. The strategy of delivering large groups of consumers to commercial sex service destinations began, in part, as a strategy for entertaining the troops during the Vietnam War. Ryan Bishop and Lillian Robinson argue that there is a historical connection between sex-for-sale operations catering to soldiers and sex for sale to tourists: "sex tourism builds on an infrastructure established for military R&R and extended through corporate recreational contracts. . . . "[47] They detail a fascinating link between the U.S. military and the World Bank in the development of the notorious Thai sex industry:

> In 1967, Thailand contracted with the U.S. government to provide "Rest and Recreation" . . . services to the troops during the Vietnam War. Today's customers at the go-go bars spawned by those contracts are not only white Americans but also European and Australian—all *farangs* to the Thais. . . .
> It was in 1971, while the war in Southeast Asia still raged, that World Bank President Robert McNamara, who had been U.S. Secretary of Defense when the R&R contracts with Thailand were signed, went to Bangkok to arrange for the bank's experts to produce a study of Thailand's postwar tourism prospects.[48]

Because of the presence and profitability of the wartime sex industry, the World Bank's advice, which Thailand followed, to specialize in tourism resulted in a large-scale sexualization of the tourist trade. The U.S. military and the World Bank thus became partners in developing what is perhaps the most famous, or infamous depending on one's point of view, sex industry in the world. Phil Williams concurs with Bishop and Robinson's summary of this connection:

> The importance of Thailand in the global sex industry, for example, is generally traced back to the late 1960s and the use of Thailand as a place for "rest and recreation" for American G.I.s in Vietnam. The recommendation by the World Bank in [the 1970s] that Thailand develop "mass tourism" as a means to pay off its debts, encouraged what became, in effect, the peacetime institutionalization of the sex industry in Thailand.[49]

Some scholars argue that historical and cultural aspects of Thai society made it especially suitable for the development of a large-scale sex sector. For instance, although David Leheny agrees with other researchers about the link between Thailand's agreement to provide R&R for U.S. soldiers during the Vietnam war and the burgeoning of its sex industry, he also cites earlier agreements and legislation that set the stage for the present, in particular

> the Bowring Treaty of 1855 which opened Thailand to foreign laborers. Most immigrants were young men from rural South China, planning to earn money for their families by mining tin in Phuket. A large number of Chinese prostitutes accompanied the men, establishing the largest sex centers Thailand had experienced at that time. . . . A 1909 law to prevent the spread of venereal disease effectively legalized prostitution.[50]

Ryan Bishop also supports analyses that identify historical antecedents to contemporary patterns of ethnosexual commerce. He is suspicious of other claims, however, especially those made by sex tourists, that Thai Buddhism and traditions of concubinage provide religious and cultural support for the commercial sex industry:

> It is a bit too neat that "going native" just happens to mesh with one's deepest, darkest desires. . . . [Thailand's] Theravada Buddhism is just as proscriptive about premarital sex, if not more so, than any monotheistic system. In fact, virginity is such an important part of a woman's status as a desirable bride that procurers for the sex trade regularly rape young women, rendering them "damaged goods" and unavailable for marriage.[51]

Kazuko Watanabe sees reflections more of history than of any specific religious or cultural traditions in the present-day sex trade throughout Asia. She argues, for instance, that there are many social, political, and economic parallels between Japan's wartime policy of forcing mainly foreign women into prostitution and its current role as a consumer market for the sex industry, in particular sex tourism, which also involves mainly foreign women as sexual service providers:

Sex tourism to other Asian countries by Japanese men is a contemporary version of the Japanese Imperial Army's sexual exploitation of Asian women. Symbolically, the difference lies only in the way the men dress; instead of military uniforms, they now wear business suits.[52]

CONCLUSION

Ethnicity and sexuality are unlikely but constant companions on war fronts around the world. Ethnosexual exploitation is a common weapon of war and a routine price of peace. In conflicts across and within national borders, differences in language, religion, culture, and color often become justifications for sexual assault; alien ethnic homelands are sighted for sexual strikes and sexual warfare is waged against ethnically defined enemies. Casualties of ethnosexual assaults are not collateral damage associated with military campaigns; they are designated targets of sexual attack; they are victims who are guilty of ethnic Otherness; they are in the wrong skin in the wrong place at the wrong time; they are the sexual means to an ethnic end, a sexual stopover on the path toward a final solution.

The drama of sex and war is not restricted to combat theatres. The post–World War II period with its economic competition and superpower geopolitical rivalry produced a massive military-sexual complex to feed its large-scale manpower's equally large-scale sexual appetites. The militarization of sexuality has outlived the Cold War in the form of an international sex industry that serves military personnel around the world in conflicts and peacekeeping operations and satisfies the growing civilian market for ethnosex. The next chapter looks more closely at the continuing legacies of the military-sexual complex: sex tourism and the global trafficking in women, men, and children.

NOTES

1. Major William H. MacDonald, EUSA/USFK Public Affairs Office, personal communication, July 11, 2001; for a critical view of the U.S. military presence in South Korea, see http://www.apcjp.org/women's_network/skorea.htm

2. Katharine H. S. Moon, *Sex among Allies: Military Prostitution in U.S.-Korea Relations* (New York: Columbia University Press, 1997), 1.

3. Ibid., 175, fn. 42.

4. U.S. military bases were established in Japan during the Allied occupation of the country following the end of World War II; 75 percent of U.S. military bases in Japan are on Okinawa Island; Kazuko Watanabe reports that controversies and demands that the U.S. close its military bases in Japan are the result not only of public opposition to the large sex industry on the island, but also because of the history

of sexual assaults against Okinawan women by U.S. soldiers; see Kazuko Watanabe, "Trafficking in Women's Bodies, Then and Now: The Issue of Military Comfort Women," *Peace & Change* 20 (1995): 501–14. For a discussion of sexual collaboration between U.S. and Japanese authorities during the allied occupation of Japan, see Yuki Tanaka. *Japan's Comfort Women: Sexual Slavery and Prostitution during World War II and the U.S. Occupation* (New York: Routledge, 2002): my thanks to Ayako Mizumura for bringing this book to my attention.

5. Jean Enriquez reports that in recent years since the closing of U.S. bases in the Philippines and the beginning of the Asian economic crisis, "Filipino women have been migrating in flocks to neighboring countries"; many of these women go to South Korea which now "ranks 7th in terms of destination of deployed overseas Filipino workers"; some of these women are willingly recruited and others are unwillingly required to work in the Korean sex industry; see Jean Enriquez, "Filipinas in Prostitution around U.S. Military Bases in Korea: A Recurring Nightmare," *Coalition against Trafficking in Women-Asia-Pacific*, July 11, 2001, http://www.uri.edu/artsci/wms/hughes/catw/filkorea.htm

6. Lynn Thiesmeyer, "The West's 'Comfort Women' and the Discourses of Seduction," in *Transnational Asia Pacific: Gender, Culture, and the Public Sphere*, ed. Shirley G. Lim, Larry E. Smith, and Wimal Dissanayake (Urbana: University of Illinois Press, 1999), 81; see also, Wendy Chapkis, *Beauty Secrets: Women and the Politics of Appearance* (Boston: South End Press, 1986), 53–54; Lisa Lowe argues that there is not a unified Euro-American ahistorical imagining of Asian women, rather there are similarities between regional and historical different "orientalisms"; Lowe, *Immigrant Acts*, 178, n. 7.

7. Aida F. Santos, "Gathering the Dust: The Base Issue in the Philippines," in *Let the Good Times Roll: Prostitution and the U.S. Military in Asia*, ed. Saundra Pollock Sturdevant and Brenda Stoltzfus (New York: The New Press, 1992), 39; Cynthia Enloe provides an even more extensive list of men she argues "contribute to the construction and maintenance of prostitution around any government's military base: husbands and lovers, bar owners, local and foreign, local public-health officials, local government zoning-board members, local police officials, local mayors, national treasury or finance-ministry officials, national-defense officials, male soldiers in the national forces, local male prostitution customers, foreign male soldier-customers, foreign male soldiers' buddies, foreign base commanders, foreign military medical officers, foreign national-defense planners, foreign national legislators" (Cynthia Enloe, "It Takes Two," in *Let the Good Times Roll*, 24–25); see also Cynthia Enloe, *The Morning After: Sexual Politics and the End of the Cold War* (Berkeley: University of California Press, 1993).

8. Saundra Pollock Sturdevant and Brenda Stoltzfus, "Olongapo: The Bar System," in *Let the Good Times Roll*, 46–47.

9. Enloe, "It Takes Two," 23–24.

10. Chalmers Johnson, *Blowback: The Costs and Consequences of American Empire* (New York: Metropolitan Books, 2000), 35; see also Cynthia Enloe, *Maneuvers: The International Politics of Militarizing Women's Lives* (Berkeley: University of California Press, 2000).

11. Ibid., as its 2000 publication date indicates, Johnson's book was written be-

fore the September 11, 2001, attacks on New York and Washington, but he does link the 1996 bombing of the Khobar Towers apartments in Saudi Arabia, an attack that has been attributed to the same suspected perpetrators of the 2001 attacks, to the presence of U.S. military in Saudi Arabia, a presence that was invited by the Saudi government in the early 1990s following Iraq's invasion of Kuwait, but which is resented by "devoutly Muslim citizens of that kingdom [who] see [U.S.] presence as a humiliation to the country and an affront to their religion" (92); my thanks to Norm Yetman, American Studies, University of Kansas, for bringing this book to my attention.

12. See for instance, Butler, *Daughters of Joy, Sisters of Misery.*

13. For a recent overview see Barstow, *War's Dirty Secret.*

14. Brownmiller, *Against Our Will.*

15. Allen, *Rape Warfare,* 96.

16. Ibid., 96.

17. See Iris Chang, *The Rape of Nanking: The Forgotten Holocaust of World War II* (New York: Basic Books, 1997); James Yin and Shi Young, *The Rape of Nanking: An Undeniable History in Photographs* (Chicago: Innovative Publishing Group, 1997).

18. Japan has yet to make satisfactory restitution to Korean and Filipina "comfort women" who were sexually enslaved during the World War II, and some former victims have come forward to demand a public apology and accounting for their treatment; see Seth Mydans,"Inside a Wartime Brothel: The Avenger's Story," *New York Times,* November 12, 1996:A3; Maria Rosa Henson, *Comfort Woman: A Filipina's Story of Prostitution and Slavery under the Japanese Military* (Lanham, MD: Rowman and Littlefield Publishers, 1999); Sangmie Choi Schellstede, *Comfort Women Speak: Testimony by Sex Slaves of the Japanese Military* (New York: Holmes and Meier, 2000); for discussions of Japan's system of brothels, see George L. Hicks, *The Comfort Women: Japan's Brutal Regime of Enforced Prostitution in the Second World War* (New York: W. W. Norton, 1995); Keith Howard, *True Stories of the Korean Comfort Women* (London: Cassell, 1995); Sayoko Yoneda, "Sexual and Racial Discrimination: A Historical Inquiry into the Japanese Military's 'Comfort' Women System of Enforced Prostitution," in *Nation, Empire, Colony: Historicizing Gender and Race,* ed. Ruth Roach Pierson and Nupur Chaudhuri (Bloomington: Indiana University Press, 1989), 237–50; for a discussion of restitution in general and specifically as it relates to the women enslaved by Japan during World War II, see Elazar Barkan, *The Guilt of Nations: Restitution and Negotiating Historical Injustices* (New York: W.W. Norton, 2000), especially chapter 3.

19. Watanabe, "Trafficking in Women's Bodies," 503–504.

20. Both sexual and nonsexual labor were also demanded of women enslaved by the Japanese (ibid., 503); the Japanese also used rape as an instrument of terror and domination, most infamous is the "rape of Nanking" in which thousands of women were raped and killed; see Brownmiller, *Against Our Will,* 53–60.

21. Brownmiller, *Against Our Will,* 61–62.

22. For firsthand accounts of women's treatment in the camps, see Sarah Nomberg-Przytyk, *Tales from a Grotesque Land* (Chapel Hill: University Of North Carolina Press, 1985), 14–20; Livia E. Bitton Jackson, *Elli: Coming of Age in the Holo-*

caust (New York: Times Books, 1980) 59–61; Cecile Klein, *Sentenced To Live* (New York: Holocaust Library, 1988), 73–77; Lore Shelley, *Auschwitz: The Nazi Civilization* (Lanham, MD: University Press of America, 1992).

23. See Cornelius Ryan, *The Last Battle* (New York: Simon and Schuster, 1966); Barstow, *War's Dirty Secret.*

24. Brownmiller, *Against Our Will,* 76–77; these 947 convictions are only part of a much greater universe of sexual assault by U.S. troops for several reasons: most rape is not reported and when it is, convictions are relatively rare even today, much less back in the 1940s during a state of war and/or military occupation; further, these were *convictions* where the soldier was found guilty, and did not include what could only have been a much larger number of charges filed and trials conducted; further still, these records were only for convictions of Army and Air Force personnel, and did not include data on the U.S. Navy or Marine Corps; finally, these records did not include information on charges, trials, or convictions for lesser sexual crimes than rape, such as sodomy or assault with the intent to commit rape or sodomy.

25. See Americas Watch and the Women's Rights Project, *Untold Terror: Violence against Women in Peru's Armed Conflict* (New York: Americas Watch, 1992); Asia Watch and Physicians for Human Rights, *Rape in Kashmir: A Crime of War* (New York: Asia Watch, 1993); Ximena Bunster, "Surviving beyond Fear: Women and Torture in Latin America," in *Women and Change in Latin America,* ed. June Nash and Helen Safa (South Hadley, MA: Bergin & Garvey, 1986), 297–325; Samir al-Khalil, *Republic of Fear: The Politics of Modern Iraq* (Berkeley: University of California Press, 1989).

26. Stiglmayer, "The Rapes in Bosnia-Herzegovina," 101.

27. See Elizabeth Bumiller, "Deny Rape or Be Hated: Kosovo Victims' Choice," *New York Times,* June 22, 1999:1; Peter Finn, "Signs of Rape Sear Kosovo; Families' Shame Could Hinder Investigation," *Washington Post,* June 27, 1999:1.

28. Stiglmayer, "The Rapes in Bosnia-Herzegovina," 117–18.

29. Ibid., 118–19.

30. Human Rights Watch reports that although both sides committed sexual assault during the conflict, rates of rape by Serbian men far outnumbered instances of sexual abuse by Kosovar Albanian men during the conflict; see Human Rights Watch Report, "Kosovo: Rape as a Weapon of 'Ethnic Cleansing' " (March 21, 2000); my thanks to Hsui-hua Shen, Department of Sociology, University of Kansas, for bringing this report to my attention.

31. For early reports on the hearings and judgments of that tribunal, see Marlise Simons, "Bosnian Serb Trial Opens: First on Wartime Sex Crimes," *New York Times,* March 21, 2000:3; John-Thor Dahlburg, "Bosnian Witness Says She Endured Series of Rapes; Courts: Victim No. 50 Testifies in The Hague," *Los Angeles Times,* March 30, 2000:1; Chris Bird, "UN Tribunal Told of Bosnian Rape Camp Horrors," *Guardian,* April 21, 2000:1; Roger Thurow, "A Bosnian Rape Victim Suffers from Scars that Do Not Fade," *Wall Street Journal,* July 17, 2000:18.

32. Cynthia Enloe, "Afterword: Have the Bosnian Rapes Opened a New Era of Feminist Consciousness?" in *Mass Rape,* 219–30; progress continues to be made, slowly, in the shift toward defining rape as a human rights violation and in the prosecution of those responsible for the sexual assaults in the former Yugoslavia: on June

29, 2001, the Serbian government turned over former Yugoslavian president Slobodan Milosevic to the United Nations war crimes tribunal in The Hague, Netherlands; Marlise Simons with Carlotta Gall, "Milosevic Is Given to U.N. for Trial in War-Crime Case," *New York Times*, June 29, 2001:1; it is important to note that at about the same time the rapes and killings were happening in Yugoslavia and Bosnia, millions of men, women, and children were being raped, mutilated, and murdered in Rwanda; while Western governments dithered and delayed responding to both the Yugoslavian and Rwandan massacres and atrocities, and while an international tribunal was established in 1994 to prosecute Rwandans for their war crimes, the issue of rape as a war crime came to the fore in Yugoslavia, but not in the much larger-scale Rwandan case; perhaps it required reports of the mass rapes and sexual enslavement of white women, albeit Muslim white women, for the "civilized" world to take notice of ethnosexual violence in war.

33. Allen, *Rape Warfare*, 78; the "Bassiouni Report" is the result of an October 1992 decision by the Secretary-General of the United Nations to appoint a commission of experts "to examine and analyze information gathered with a view to providing the Secretary-General with its conclusions on the evidence of grave breaches of the Geneva Conventions and other violations of international humanitarian law committed in the territory of the former Yugoslavia" (ibid., 43).

34. Watanabe, "Trafficking in Women's Bodies," 506–507.

35. Kimmel, *Manhood in America*, 133–34.

36. See, for instance, Tracy X. Karner, *Masculinity, Trauma, and Identity: Life Narratives of Vietnam Veterans with Post Traumatic Stress Disorder* (Ph.D. diss., University of Kansas, 1994).

37. Enloe, *Bananas, Beaches, and Bases*, 66.

38. Personal communication, July 22, 2001; Clark was a Corporal in the First Battalion, Seventh Marines, Strategic and Target Acquisition (STA) Platoon.

39. Ibid.; Clark goes on to say:

> It is funny that during a period in U.S. military history when a "good" president restored military "honor," guys were in the Philippines and Thailand receiving oral sex (and who knows what else) from guys—and then talking about it later, giving no indication at all that they might just have participated in sex acts that challenged their masculinity. At the same time, new recruits were being instructed in the "manly" arts of beating up "fags," Naval Intelligence was hunting down "evidence" that guys with HIV and AIDS actually were gay, and Marines having sex with Marines (men) and caught in the "act" were being "punished" with hysterical physical violence in response. (ibid.)

See also Steven Zeeland, *The Masculine Marine: Homoeroticism in the U.S. Marine Corps* (New York: Harrington Park Press, 1996); Tim Bergling, "A Few Good Men," *Genre* (November/December 1997) (http://www.davidclemens.com/gaymilitary/fgm. htm) and Anonymous, "Standby Warning" (http://www.subicbaymarines.com/ Standby.htm).

40. Judith Hicks Stiehm, "United Nations Peacekeeping: Men's and Women's Work," in *Gender Politics in Global Governance*, ed. Mary K. Meyer and Elisabeth Prugl (Lanham, MD: Rowman and Littlefield, 1999), 50–54.

41. Stiehm attributes the "boys will be boys" comment to Yasushi Akashi of Japan, the head of the UN peacekeeping mission in Cambodia; the comment was in response to "a letter signed by more than 180 women [that] was sent to Akashi charg-

ing sexual harassment of staff by UNTAC personnel and harassment of women on the street and asserting that there was no channel for redressing this behavior" (ibid., 54).

42. William J. Kole and Aida Cerkez-Robinson, "U.N. Police Accused of Involvement in Prostitution in Bosnia," Associated Press, July 6, 2001, http://fpmail. friends-partners.org/mailman/listinfo.cgi/stop-traffic

43. Ibid.; peacekeepers on other missions constitute a market for prostitution and the trafficking in voluntary and involuntary sex workers; investigators in Macedonia found the Bosnian situation was reflective of a regional trend:

> [Macedonia's] situation as a transit country for trafficking, and its growing home market for prostitutes—boosted in part by United Nations personnel and NATO-led peacekeepers on leave from nearby Kosovo—illustrate the regionwide problem (Carlotta Gall, "Macedonia Village Is Center of Europe Web in Sex Trade," *New York Times on the Web*, July 28, 2001, http://www.nytimes.com/2001/07/28/international/europe/28TRAF.html

44. Ibid.

45. www.hawaii.navy.mil/NewHomepage/dutyinH.htm

46. Sex tourism is distinct from the general sex industry in that it is the sector of the sex trade that actually provides organized travel and tours to bring sex consumers to concentrated sex service destinations.

47. Ryan Bishop and Lillian S. Robinson, *Night Market: Sexual Cultures and the Thai Economic Miracle* (New York: Routledge, 1998), 248.

48. Ibid., 8–9.

49. Phil Williams, "Trafficking in Women and Children: A Market Perspective," in *Illegal Immigration and Commercial Sex: The New Slave Trade*, ed. Phil Williams (London: Frank Cass, 1999), 154; see also Lisa Law, "A Matter of 'Choice': Discourses on Prostitution in the Philippines," in *Sites of Desire, Economies of Pleasure: Sexualities in Asia and the Pacific*, ed. Lenore Manderson and Margaret Jolly (Chicago: University of Chicago Press, 1997), 233–61.

50. David Leheny, "A Political Economy of Asian Sex Tourism," *Annals of Tourism Research* 22 (1995): 367–84, 373; Annette Hamilton also finds images of a sexualized Thailand in 1950s fiction, images that lead her to argue that Thailand was already a "privileged site" in the "Western masculinist imagination" before the Vietnam War era; she does not conclude, however, that the large-scale commercialization of sex that occurred as a result of the war was irrelevant to contemporary images of a sexualized Thailand; see Annette Hamilton, "Primal Dream: Masculinism, Sin, and Salvation in Thailand's Sex Trade," in *Sites of Desire, Economies of Pleasure*, 157.

51. Ryan Bishop, personal communication, March 16, 2001; see also Bishop and Robinson, *Night Market*, 160–61; see also Thanh-Dam Truong, *Sex, Money, and Morality: Prostitution and Tourism in South-East Asia* (London: Zed Books, 1990); Lenore Manderson, "Public Sex Performances in Patpong and Explorations of the Edges of Imagination," *The Journal of Sex Research* 29 (1992): 451–75.

52. Watanabe, "Trafficking in Women's Bodies," 506. Sex tourism has become a controversial business in many destination and consumer countries. In Thailand, a number of organizations, including "Empower" and "Friends of Women," work directly with women in the sex tourism industry to teach them about AIDS prevention, and "Daughters Education Programme" provides education for village girls to increase their employability outside of sex tourism and to enhance their local status;

Enloe, *Bananas, Beaches and Bases,* 38; June Kane, *Sold for Sex* (Brookfield, VT: Arena, 1998), 122–23. Other international anti–sex trade/sex tourism organizations include the Asian Women's Human Rights Council, ECPAT (End Child Prostitution in Asian Tourism), the Global Alliance Against Traffic in Women, and the Coalition Against Trafficking in Women; see Skrobanek et al., *The Traffic in Women,* 81, 110–16; Kane, *Sold for Sex,* 4; the website for the Coalition Against Trafficking in Women is http://www.uri.edu/artsci/wms/hughes/catw/catw.htm; Julia Davidson reports several demonstrative methods of protesting sex tourism:

> There have been instances of direct action against clients—for example, that organized by Japanese feminist groups at airports, which involved ridiculing and insulting men arriving home from sex tours, and that proposed by the Filipino guerrilla group that adopted the slogan, "Kill a sex tourist a day." Public humiliation has also been used as an instrument to control Taiwanese businessmen caught using prostitutes while in mainland China. (Davidson, *Prostitution, Power, and Freedom,* 198)

Davidson quotes Ren's description of Chinese humiliation techniques:

> Chinese authorities not only sent them to a poultry farm in the outskirts of Bejing for a short period of labor reform, but also sent letters to their employers in Taiwan to inform them of the "repulsive deeds" committed by their employees in China. Hoping that public exposure will deter such behavior, Chinese authorities have also stamped the words "patron of prostitution" on the travel documents of those men who have been found guilty of committing "repulsive deeds." (X. Ren, "China," in *Prostitution: An International Handbook on Trends, Problems, and Policies,* ed. Nanette Davis [Westport, CT: Greenwood Press, 1993], 102–103)

CHAPTER 7

SEX AND TOURISM
Travel and Romance in
Ethnosexual Destinations

Growth in travel and tourism are hallmarks of the post–Cold War period, and ethnosexuality is a feature of the marketing of tourist destinations and products. In the last chapter we saw how the military-sexual complex that emerged during the post–World War II period contributed to the growth of sex industries in many countries such as the Philippines and Thailand and in regions of countries such as Okinawa in Japan and the Panama Canal Zone. Many of these sex sectors expanded their consumer base from military personnel to civilians as international travel and tourism grew, especially during the 1980s and 1990s. In times of peace, as in times of war, sex consumers are drawn to the ethnically exotic sexual encounter. Ethnosex sells in both war and peace, and to cater to customer demand, national tourism bureaus and agencies often market themselves as ethnosexual destinations.

Although our discussion of the commercial expansion of ethnosexuality has focused mainly on the second half of the twentieth century, depictions of distant lands as libidinous locales run through centuries of travel narratives, such as those of Columbus and Vespucci or Lewis and Clark described in earlier chapters. The earliest travelogues written by Westerners visiting the Asia Pacific region contain vivid depictions of peoples and places as erotic and exotic, carnal and carnival—sexualized spectacles of Others and Otherness.[1] For instance, George Forster traveled with his father, Johann Reinhold Forster, on Captain James Cook's second voyage to the Pacific from 1772 to 1775. They described the Polynesian women they encountered in their 1777 and 1778 travel memoirs:

> a beautifully proportioned shape, an irresistible smile, and eyes full of sweetness and sparkling with fire . . . .[and] a charming frankness. . . . The view

of several of these nymphs swimming nimbly all around the sloop, such as nature had formed them was perhaps more than sufficient entirely to subvert the little reason which a mariner might have left to govern his passions.[2]

Plate 9 of the color insert is a portrait of Poedua, the daughter of Orio, a chief of Raiatea in Tahiti, painted by artist John Webber in 1777. The portrait and Bernard Smith's analysis of its origins and meaning illustrate what Anne McClintock refers to as "a long tradition of male travel as an erotics of ravishment:"[3]

> Webber builds upon that image . . . of the Pacific as young, feminine, desirable and vulnerable, an ocean of desire. To her, during the next century, all the nations of Europe will come . . . though it cannot be established entirely beyond doubt, [it is likely that] Webber painted Poedua's portrait during the five days during which she was held hostage in [Cook's vessel] the *Discovery*.[4]

Margaret Jolly notes the historical continuity in images of Pacific Island women presented by the Forsters and those who followed in their wake. Enthusiastic chroniclers of the charms of "native beauties" included women travelers as well, such as journalist Beatrice Grimshaw, who visited Tahiti in the 1890s and early 1900s:

> One exceedingly pretty girl, with a perfect cataract of black hair overflowing her pale green gown, and a pair of sparkling dark eyes that never could be matched outside the magic lines of Cancer and Capricorn . . . has half a dozen French officers around her, enjoying breakfast and flirtation.[5]

The Pacific Islands thus were personified in the imaginations of women and men and in the descriptive discourses of Europeans and Americans as lovely, bare-breasted, beflowered, and deflowered young women.

As we shall see in this chapter, these early accounts of the ethnosexual delights of distant lands resonate with contemporary imaginings of exotic locales and raise an interesting set of issues and questions about the place of ethnicity and sexuality in tourism. What is the role of ethnosexuality in the development of tourist sites, in the marketing of tourist destinations, and in the experience and definition both of being a tourist and of living in and being part of a tourist destination? How do patterns of ethnosexual consumption in tourist markets and the international sex industry mirror and reproduce patterns of domination, inequality, colonization, and imperialism among nations and peoples in the global system? How does consuming the exotic Other through tourism facilitate racial, ethnic, and national self-imaginings and constructions?

SEX AND ECONOMIC DEVELOPMENT

Researchers have noted a number of parallels between sex tourism and other forms of tourism, noting the importance of sex tourism in economic development and the role of commercially organized tours in delivering consumers to sex tourism destinations. Julie Scott identifies a gendered, sexualized side to tourism in general, not just sexual tourism. In her study of the roles of Turkish Cypriot and migrant women in the Cyprus tourist industry, she finds that "[w]hile the participation of Turkish Cypriot women in the tourism labor force has increased in recent years, migrant women are employed primarily in those occupations that are considered 'unsuitable' for local women."[6] She reports, for instance, that the employment of Rumanian women migrants as croupiers in Cyprus' gambling industry is seen as a way to protect local women from being polluted in what is defined as a sexualized work setting.

While it may pose a threat to the virtue of national women and thus require the importation of Other women to work in sexually hazardous occupations, in many developing countries tourism is a major employer and source of foreign revenues.[7] In Third World countries struggling with international debt, such as Tunisia, Puerto Rico, Haiti, Nepal, or the Gambia, tourism has become a larger industry than many traditional exports. While all tourist destinations also are sites of sex commerce, in major sex tourist destinations such as Thailand, the Philippines, Belize, Jamaica, or Sri Lanka, selling local and imported sexuality is an important component of economic development, and some governments even advertise sex tourism.[8] Cofounder of the Coalition Against Trafficking in Women Kathleen Barry links the economics of the sex trade to the economics of development, and Patrick Larvie agrees, arguing, for instance, that "Brazil's tourist industry promotes the country as one which offers sexual attractions as part of the nation's natural and cultural resources."[9]

It is not only government and private tourism promoters who publicize sex tourism, major publishers of tour books such as *Fodor's*, *Frommer's*, *Rough Guide*, and *Lonely Planet* have entered the market, and include sections on night life and gay tourism that refer to the sex trade and offer various bits of advice. For instance, the 1988 and 1991 editions of *Insight Guide* to Thailand explained "how to negotiate the transactions in a massage parlor and how to buy a bar dancer out for the night, advising against taking a prostitute to a first-class hotel."[10] Bishop and Robinson make a connection between sex tourism and tourism in general when they liken sex workers in sex tourist destinations to wildlife and other exotic attractions. They point out that sex tourism produces a "consumer approach to local natural and cultural resources including—semiotically and literally—the sexuality of local women."[11]

Ethnic similarity *and* diversity both are hallmarks of the sex industry and sex tourism. Ethnic similarities can work to facilitate the recruitment of sex workers through ethnic networks that aid in communication and trust and can provide cover for illegal activities by keeping them "in the [ethnic] family." Ethnic differences that separate sex workers and sex industry managers and owners can make exploitation more palatable since it is not one's own people who are being mistreated or coerced. Ethnic differences also characterize the sex worker/client relationship, since sex with an exotic Other is one of the chief attractions for sex tourists, just as dreams of being rescued from poverty is a central fantasy of sex workers. Siriporn Skrobanek and associates interviewed a number of sex workers in Thailand, many of whom walked parallel paths into the sex industry and shared similar dreams of the way out. For instance,

> Noy is 33 and living in Pattaya with an Englishman. She left her village in Roi-et with her sister. . . . They began as go-go girls in a bar. They had no intention of becoming sex workers, but changed their minds because they wanted gold jewelry like other girls there. Noy's sister went to live in Switzerland with her boyfriend, and she sent money home. Noy will take her English boyfriend to visit her home in Roi-et, in the hope he will build her a new house there.[12]

Male sex customers also have dreams and fantasies, often imagining that women sex workers find them especially attractive or exceptionally skilled sexual technicians:

> It's funny, but in England, the girls I fancy don't fancy me and the ones that do fancy me, I don't fancy. They tend to be sort of fatter and older, you know, thirty-five, but their faces, they look forty. But in Cuba, really beautiful girls fancy me. They're all over me. They treat me like a star. My girlfriend's jet black, she's beautiful. . . . Cuban girls don't expect so much. . . . English girls . . . don't want someone like me. . . . If you take a Cuban girl out for dinner, she's grateful.[13]

Kamala Kempadoo's study of the sex trade in Curacao, where the government suspended local laws against brothels and pimping, locates definitions of desire and desirability in longstanding racial hierarchies of superiority and subordination that are rearticulated in contemporary ethnosexual class formations:

> [W]omen who command the better working conditions and pay on the island work as escorts for "VIP's" and are more often than not white European women, mainly Dutch. . . . Migrant sex workers from Colombia and

the Dominican Republic are predominantly "light-skinned," mulatto (mixed African-European) women, while "local" prostitutes who invariably work the streets and ill-paid sectors, are far more likely to be of Afro-Caribbean descent. . . . As one man simply put it, "if she's light-colored, then she is sexually attractive to the population."[14]

Kempadoo links the presence of Curacao's extensive sex industry to global processes—first to colonialism: "[i]n 1944 this island was established by the [Dutch] colonial government as a center in the region for prostitution by migrant women";[15] and more recently to World Bank and International Monetary Fund economic restructuring programs under which both migrating and local "women are increasingly more active in informal economies, which includes sex industries."[16] For some workers, sex work offers wages unmatched in other employment sectors;[17] even when their wages do not meet their expectations, the promise of high wages and the need of many workers to support their entire families draw sex workers from around the world. For instance, Pasuk Phongpaichit argues that "the economic boom in Thailand in the 1980s and early 1990s led to a rapid increase in demand for skilled and unskilled labor" which was filled by poorer neighboring countries, especially Burma, Southern China, Laos.[18] It is not only women, however, who are employed as exotic suppliers of ethnosex in the global sex trade, it is also men.

MEN AT [SEX] WORK

Male sex workers share some of the same motivations, desires, and desperation as women and children working in the sex trade, though they are much less often reported to be enslaved.[19] Like their female counterparts, most male sex workers are poor, and many are hoping for a better life through the money they make hustling or in a rescue relationship. There are also some important differences between men and women working in the sex industry. Unlike their female counterparts—"daughters of joy, sisters of misery"[20]— male sex workers sometimes report using prostitution to gain access to same-sex sexual contact in a local context of forbidden homosexual desire. Male sex workers not engaged in survival sexwork speak of combining "cruising" and recreational sex with prostitution much more frequently than do female sex workers. Dennis Altman interviewed a self-defined gay man in Lima who said he mixed business with pleasure: "When I'm there it's to meet people, and when I meet them I don't think about whether they will pay me or not. . . . If they give me a tip, it's very welcome."[21]

Like women sex workers who may define themselves as straight, bisexual, or lesbians, the reported sexual orientation of male sex workers is not always consistent with their clientele. The issue of *male* sex workers' *real* sexual orientation arises more often in research reports, however, although it is not entirely clear if it is a preoccupation only of the researchers or if the men themselves bring up the subject. In either case, many self-identified straight men have male clients, and gay and bisexual men have sex with women. For instance, Amine Boushaba and associates divide male sex workers in Morocco into *gigolos* and *prostitués homosexuels*. Both groups had mainly male clients, but the *gigolos* defined themselves as heterosexuals and often

> mentioned female partners as well as male clients . . . a few, however, were more ambivalent . . . because sex work allowed them a means of expressing their sexuality [since] society is more tolerant towards a man who has sex with other men for economic need.[22]

Jacob Shifter and Peter Aggleston report that in Costa Rica, although many male sex workers also tend to define themselves as heterosexuals *(cacheros)*, they have sex with men for money; the rule seems to be: "as long as sexual desire continues to be shown towards the opposite sex and behavior is masculine at all times, one is still a [heterosexual] man."[23] Sometimes the attribution of homosexuality is made on the basis of who is the active (penetrator, i.e., heterosexual) and who is the passive (penetrated, i.e., homosexual) partner in the sex act, rather than whether a man is selling sex to a woman or another man.[24]

The distinction between sexual behavior and sexual desire stands in contrast to the essentialist, all or nothing, either gay or straight conception of sexuality characteristic of Western sexual epistemologies. In fact, Shivananda Khan raises questions about the whole hetero/homosexual binary's applicability to non-Western cultures and the extent to which many researchers might simply be finding sexual binaries that exist in their own minds and cultures rather than in the minds of the men they are interviewing:

> In India and Bangladesh (as well as in other countries of the south Asia region), there is a high degree of amorphousness in indigenous frameworks of sexuality and identity. Here identities are mostly based on family and community, as well as to a lesser extent on participation in particular sexual practices, most notably those of penetrator or penetrated. Identity is not based so much on who you are but on what you do, and in what context(s) your social life is constructed.[25]

Some aspects of male sex work parallel findings in studies of women sex workers, not about the issue of sexual orientation, but about workers' interpretations of the meaning of the sex work. It is common to hear both male and female sex workers refer to a paid sexual interlude as a friendship, dating relationship, or something less commercial and more intimate. Fantasies of living a better life or of paid sex developing into a friendship or loving relationship characterize both male and female sex work. One French transvestite *gigolo*[26] reported a long-term intimate relationship with a client:

> He's married. He's a grandfather and lives in the countryside. He's very well known. He comes up once a month to Paris in order to see me. He pays the rent, he pays for the telephone, he gives me 4000 francs a month, jewellery, things like that. He's good luck for me, there's an emotional relationship between us of course. . . . I love him a lot and if we ever broke up, it would make me very upset. . . . He's the father I never had.[27]

Crossing ethnosexual boundaries is a common feature of male sex work as it is for women and children. The racial, ethnic, and national differences between male sex workers and their clients are most clearly revealed by the international character of the sex trade and sex tourism. For instance, Boushaba and associates report that 67 percent of the 172 male sex workers they interviewed in Morocco "sold sex primarily to a non-Moroccan clientele."[28] Michael Tan finds that sex tourism is closely associated with various forms of adult and child male prostitution in the Philippines.[29] Larvie argues that "despite the preponderance of negative images of male sex workers, [hyper-masculine] *miches* are an important attraction for residents and tourists in search of nocturnal diversions in the 'red-light' districts of large Brazilian cities."[30] Antonio de Moya and Raphael Garcia describe Santo Domingo in the Dominican Republic as a burgeoning gay sex tourism destination for North Americans and Europeans during the 1980s before the AIDS epidemic led the government to close down gay hotels and "organized tours stopped coming to the country."[31] As a result, Amalia Cabezas reports that one group of men who were involved in the Dominican gay sex trade, so-called sanky-pankies, have, since the AIDS epidemic, begun to "work mostly with white middle-aged foreign women who seek romance and adventure during their holiday."[32] Thus, while many male sex workers have male clients, not all men sell sex to men. Some sex consumers are women, and their transactions also are likely to involve rendezvous in ethnosexual frontiers.

"ROMANCE" TOURISM

Women's sexual touristic encounters with local Other men most certainly are planted in much earlier sands than those on the beaches of the modern global system. Like all things associated with contemporary globalization, however, the scale and commercialization of women's sexual consumption has increased. Like sex, ethnosex sells, and early in the marketing of Hawaii as a tourist destination, for instance, Jane Desmond notes that "Hawaiian Tourist Bureau ads from the 1920s set up an explicit connection between white women and Native Hawaiian men."[33] She cites a scene at the Royal Hawaiian Hotel described in a 1937 travel book, *Isles of Enchantment:*

> Here an eastern lady of fashion lies prone beneath the sun while a smiling Hawaiian youth anoints her back and legs with coconut oil. . . . Near-by another bronze boy kneels over another fair visitor, kneading and manipulating the muscles in the soothing and relaxing Hawaiian massage.[34]

This quaint depiction of the attractive, attentive, courteous native man servicing the white woman seems much less an explicit hard sell than one would expect in the marketing of contemporary sex tourism, especially that targeting men. Researchers have found, nonetheless, that this image of a safe, but exotic vacation affair has remained a stable feature of women's sex tourism. Although the attitudes and behavior of today's women sex consumers often challenge traditional passive female sexual stereotypes, many contemporary women sex tourists are looking more to be swept away by men than to assert strong control over their paid male partners. These women "romance tourists" are interested in more than a quick sexual encounter; they often establish relationships with the men they "date" while on holiday. For instance, researchers find that it is not uncommon for women romance tourists to establish long-term liaisons with the men they meet on vacation and to correspond, send money, and return year after year to spend time with their offshore "boyfriends."[35]

De Moya and associates studied male sex workers in Puerto Plata, Dominican Republic, in the early 1990s, and found that, like male tourists, female tourists viewed local men through a racialized and sexualized lens, as exotic Others. Many Dominican male sex workers "claimed that for foreign women 'black skin color is the most relevant feature,'" and "long, kinky, and trenched hair, as well as youth, fitness, manliness, and sexiness" were the most sought-after traits of popular male sex workers.[36] Cabezas summarized this view: "The men capitalize on the demand for racialized fantasies of erotic encounters."[37]

Deborah Pruitt and Suzanne LaFont's study of Western women's romance tourism in Jamaica noted the same exoticization of male sex workers, where Jamaican men, especially "Rasta" men wearing dreadlocks, "are constructed [by both white and black women tourists] as more passionate, more emotional, more natural, and sexually tempting" than the men back home.[38] Jamaican men had special appeal for white women since, "Stereotypes of black men and their sexuality" combined with Jamaican "men's displays of

machismo drawn from their cultural gender scripts" to lead white women to
see Jamaican men as "archetypical masculine" men.[39] Pruitt and LaFont also
found that Western women, especially white women, occupied a complementary niche as exotic Others for some Jamaican men:

> Light skin, straight hair and caucasian facial features are highly valued, and
> women who are considered overweight in their own cultures are appreciated
> by many Jamaican men. Thus, foreign women who may not satisfy stan-
> dards of beauty at home find themselves the object of amorous attention by
> appealing to local men.[40]

Although I refer to the local men with whom women tourists enter into
sexual liaisons as "male sex workers," research suggests that this label would
be challenged by many of these working men, just as women sex workers
might argue that they were simply "dating" men who paid them for their
sexual company. Kempadoo finds that

> male sex workers in the Caribbean do not necessarily self-define in the same
> way as women who are in the same position. Instead of being identified . . .
> as prostitute . . . the men tend to be identified as "beach boy," "island boy,"
> "player," "gigolo". . . . Sex with a female tourist who holds the economic
> dominant position in the relationship appears not to threaten or disrupt this
> culturally approved expression of masculinity but rather to enable feelings
> of personal worth and self-confidence.[41]

Nandasena Ratnapala observed a similar definition of the situation in Sri
Lanka among men who offer sex for money to women tourists: "[s]uch men
are found in or near tourist hotels, often operating as tour guides or such in-
nocent-looking jobs . . . in the hotels as bell-boys, waiters, . . . taxi drivers
. . . they often conceal their real work beneath a more socially acceptable
role."[42] And in Peru and the Philippines women find sex for sale not in the
typical venues frequented by male sex customers (e.g., in brothels or massage parlors), but in more "legitimate" spaces such as ballroom dancing stu-
dios or discotheques.[43]

Kempadoo argues that not only do the social and sexual transactions between male prostitutes and women clients tend to uphold the gender order,
but that sex commerce between First World consumers and Third World suppliers reproduces hegemonic racialized and sexualized views of those with
dark skin as hypersexualized and subordinate:

> Racialized male and female bodies in the [Caribbean] region provide . . . a
> stage for First World gendered performances—for European and North
> American men to reenact traditional masculine roles and to reassure them-
> selves of their dominance over women, for European and North American
> women to experiment with, confirm, or expand their gender repertoires.[44]

Instances of these racialized/sexualized North/South narratives can be heard in Vron Ware's recounting of a spate of reports in 1990 in a British tabloid newspaper and women's magazine about the "seduction" of European women by African men. The stories centered on white women traveling to tourist destinations in West Africa, falling in love with local men, and leaving their English husbands. Under the headlines, "Mud-Hut Rat Stole My Wife!" "Gambian Rat Stole My Wife, Too!" and "Love at First Sight," Britain's *Sun* newspaper ran a three-day series, beginning with the saga of thirty-nine-year-old Sandra Anderson who "set up home in a mud hut with a tribal prince after husband Frank took her on a Gambian holiday." The *Sun* articles were accompanied by photos, including one of "eight black men, with dreadlocks, guitars and cheerful smiles, supporting the weight of a horizontal young white woman, all bare legs and arms and smiling happily."[45] The stories detailed a competition that invited the reader to "Test your Marriage in Africa," and promised the winner seven nights in a top Gambian hotel.[46] One *Sun* article began:

> They're tall dark and handsome—and British women just can't resist the magic of Gambian beach boys. The hunky charmers spend their days chatting up the holiday makers and their nights making love to them in the sand.[47]

Ware reports that the women's magazine *Marie Claire* also focused on Gambian sex tourism, emphasizing age differences as well as racial differences between the men and the women. A photograph accompanying a 1990 article entitled, "Seeking Sex in the Gambia," showed "three white women each entwined with a black man," and described them as "a 58-year-old art dealer," "a grandmother," and "62." The article chronicled the tourist experience shared by these and similar women:

> During the day . . . it's common to see women in their fifties and sixties strolling hand in hand with beautiful young men, and on Gambia's long palm-fringed beaches the women go topless and flirt with handsome teenagers.[48]

Figure 7.1 shows one such happy couple. If this image seems something of a "spectacle" to some readers, it serves to remind us of the ways in which race, gender, age, and class serve hegemonic constructions of sexual desirability, respectability, and seemly sexual demeanor.

Sherry Ortner's research on women mountaineers in Nepal is not a study of romance tourism, rather it is a study of romance during tourism—albeit adventure tourism. Ortner's work provides a richly detailed study of gender, race, and class in the construction and maintenance of ethnosexual boundaries, reputations, and normative systems.[49] Mountaineering in Nepal has long been an ethnic frontier where different racial and national masculini-

'We make love on the
beach. Ebu's not that
experienced, so I have
been teaching him'

FIGURE 7.1   Romance Tourism in the Gambia, 1990 *(Marie Claire)*

ties encountered one another on the Himalayan slopes. Western male
climbers always have been accompanied by local climbers referred to gener-
ically as "Sherpas," Nepalese men who also summited, but whose names only
recently have been included in accounts of historical or contemporary climbs.
Beginning in the 1970s, mountaineering became an ethnosexual frontier
when mainly Western women joined the ranks of Western men who had for
decades launched numerous assaults on Mount Everest and other high peaks

of the Himalayas. Ortner focused on what happens when gender gets thrown into this historically exclusively male domain. One thing that happens is that Western women begin having sex with Sherpa men, and all hell breaks loose.

Just as Figure 7.1 illustrates, the world looks different when gender or racial or age roles are reversed, especially when sex is involved. Western male climbers were not reported routinely to have had sex with their Sherpa guides, but many did have sexual relationships with local women in nearby towns. The influence of Western male attitudes toward women and sexuality, and the entry of Western women into this scenario, including their sexual contact with local men on the slopes, disrupted local sexual mores. For example, Ortner describes a deterioration of indigenous sexual etiquette in Sherpa communities throughout the 1960s, 1970s, and 1980s. This deterioration began, she argues, because of the early influence of Western masculinist and sexist views of both sexuality and women, which were adopted by some Sherpa men. The entry of Western women onto the scene and their sexual interest in and availability to Sherpa men seemed to reinforce these Western sexist masculinist stereotypes. As a result of this collision and collusion of masculinities and femininities, Ortner reports that many Sherpa men were more likely to express contempt for all women—Western and local—and they displayed increased disrespect for Western women in general, not just those who were having sex with local men. Ortner also reported that there developed problems of morale and discipline on the climbs and an increase in incidents of sexual harassment of women climbers by local men. For instance, Sherpa men seemed less likely to follow women team leaders' orders, and tensions developed among Western team members—both between women and men and among women—partly because all women's reputations were seen to be damaged by those who were sexually active.

To deal with these problems and tensions, some feminist climbing groups restricted teams only to women climbers (setting aside for the moment the heterosexist assumption that all-women climbing teams guaranteed that no sex would occur). Sherpa women guides were not available to the women climbers, however, so the teams tried to control gender/sexuality issues by agreeing that none of the women would have sex with Sherpa men. Sometimes this worked, but sometimes it did not. When sexual contact occurred, Ortner reported the same problems of discipline and morale developed. Since Sherpa women were never on climbs, there is no basis for comparing what would have happened had Western men been having sex with Sherpa women on the slopes. For instance, would the Sherpa women guides have balked at following Western male team leaders' orders after sleeping with one of the men? Or would the local women have lost respect for the Western men? How would Sherpa men have responded to Western men having sex with

(their) local women guides? Ortner's research reveals that ethnosexual frontiers are nuanced settings where interracial, interethnic, and international
gender definitions and sexual contact rules complicate and confound longstanding and emergent cultural patterns and interpersonal relationships. Even
when ethnosexual contacts in tourist settings are not specifically sexual business transactions, they trouble ethnic, gender, and sexual status quos and reveal the tensions between power based in gender systems and power based
on wealth and class.

Sex and Slavery in the New World Order

The new world order of the twenty-first century with its opening of international borders, increasing international business and leisure travel, and rapidly
growing international communication, has expanded both the supply of and
demand for sex and romance. Many commercial sex providers are migrant
workers who enter the industry through a variety of routes, some legal and
some illegal. Women often knowingly become sex workers, although they may
not be aware of the conditions under which they will labor. Others are more
naive or perhaps too willing to believe recruiters' promises that they will be
simply hostesses, waitresses, or entertainers, and will not be asked to have sex
with clients. Still others are promised jobs outside the sex industry, presumably in factories or as domestic workers, but then find sex work is the only
way they can settle large debts to recruiters or pay off loans their families obtained when they essentially were sold into service. Finally, some sex workers
are coerced by "traffickers" in human beings who locate and force into sexual
servitude migrants or refugees trying to escape poverty or repression.[50]

The United Nations' International Protocol to Prevent, Suppress, and
Punish Trafficking in Persons, Especially Women and Children, Supple-
menting the United Nations Convention Against Transnational Organized
Crime, adopted in November 2000, defines trafficking as:

> the recruitment, transportation, transfer, harbouring or receipt of persons, by
> means of the threat or use of force or other forms of coercion, of abduction, of
> fraud, of deception, of the abuse of power or of a position of vulnerability or
> of the giving or receiving of payments or benefits to achieve the consent of a
> person having control over another person, for the purpose of exploitation. Ex-
> ploitation shall include, at a minimum, the exploitation of the prostitution of
> others or other forms of sexual exploitation, forced labour or services, slavery
> or practices similar to slavery, servitude or the removal of organs.[51]

Sex traffickers often charge fees for transport and then deliver their human cargo to staff the massage parlors, clubs, and brothels of countries around

the world. The trafficked workers then are required to do sex work to repay sex industry managers who have paid off their transport fees. Once they have become sex workers, these migrants are "soiled" symbolically or as a result of contracting diseases such as AIDS, and thus become unfit for other work even after their fees are paid. As Enloe summarizes:

> To succeed, sex tourism requires Third World women to be economically desperate enough to enter prostitution; having done so it is made difficult to leave. The other side of the equation requires men from affluent societies to imagine certain women, usually women of color, to be more available and submissive than the women of their own countries. Finally the industry depends on an alliance between local governments in search of foreign currency and local and foreign businessmen willing to invest in sexualized travel.[52]

Sex work, sex tourism, sex workers, and human trafficking are not only features of Third World and postcolonial landscapes. Gillian Caldwell and associates report that since the break up of the Soviet Union, "Russia and the Newly Independent States, including Ukraine and Latvia, have become primary countries of origin [for sex workers] supplementing and sometimes replacing previously significant sources of women from Asia and Latin America."[53] Eastern European and Russian women's destinations are sex industries in Europe, the Middle East, Asia, and the United States. Their entry into the sex industry is the result of the same combination of forces pushing and pulling women of color into sex work—economics, exploitation, and exoticness, the latter because these white women are "a relative novelty in the sex market."[54] These new sex workers' economic motivations stem from the economic collapse in many former Soviet republics, the consequences of which have been especially harsh for women. Researchers report that in the mid-1990s nearly two-thirds of Russia's unemployed were women, including 70 percent of women graduating from institutions of higher learning.[55]

> For [East European and Russian] women confronting unemployment, sexual harassment, and domestic violence, an offer of good pay for work abroad often seems a magical escape to a better world. . . . Victims of their own hopes and illusions, most trafficked women leave their home country willingly to pursue a seemingly legitimate opportunity, and even those who know they may have to engage in the sex business assume that they will be treated humanely.[56]

Gerben Bruinsma and Muus Meershoek's study of Eastern European women working in the Netherlands' sex industry report similar economic motivations and patterns of exploitation:

> In 1996, in a brothel in the southern part of the country, Dutch police discovered 15 women from Poland, Ukraine, Estonia, and Latvia. Many were

recruited, most of them under false pretenses. Their average age was 21; three of them were minors. The brothel was part of a series, owned by a couple . . . .The prostitutes were not allowed to leave the building and were working 9–19 hours a day . . . [and] sleeping in a dirty, damp cellar. . . . [They] were promised only 25 percent of the earnings. In practice, they did not receive anything. The couple imposed all kinds of fines on them, for example for failing to smile to customers. . . . If a woman somehow succeeded in acquiring a surplus, she was sold by her pimp to another pimp in the same brothel and had to pay back to her new owner the money he had paid for her.[57]

Local nationalist and ethnic conflicts create situations where economic desperation creates a "supply" of women that combines with "demand" from male military personnel to increase rates of trafficking and prostitution— some voluntary, some less than voluntary. Carlotta Gall reports that in 2001, a network of traffickers had spread across the Balkans and into Western Europe:

A decade of conflict in this region and the grinding poverty of post-Communist Eastern Europe, have helped breed this network. Across the Balkans, tens of thousands of women have been caught up by the traffickers and have suffered rape, extreme violence and slavery. . . . Blagoja Stojkovski, the police officer in charge of asylum and immigration in Skopje [Macedonia], said. . . . "They are promised they are going to Italy and some really do go—after two or three months working here they are sold in Albania and taken to Italy. . . . This is a small town. A lady is interesting for just one month."[58]

The United States is also a destination for sex workers from the former Soviet Union and from countries around the world. In a 2001 report on "Trafficking in Persons," the U.S. State Department estimated that

at least 700,000 persons, especially women and children, are trafficked each year across international borders . . . and within countries. . . . The U.S. is principally a transit and destination country for trafficking in persons. It is estimated that 45,000 to 50,000 people, primarily women and children, are trafficked to the U.S. annually. . . . Our understanding is that the problem has broadened [since monitoring began in 1994].[59]

U.S. secretary of state Colin Powell released the report in a July 12, 2001, press conference, expressing shock and dismay:

It is incomprehensible that trafficking in human beings should be taking place in the 21st century . . . trafficking is going on all over the world, in both developed and developing countries, even within the United States. . . . The overwhelming number are women and children who have been lured, coerced or abducted by criminals who trade in human misery and treat human beings like chattel. Deprived of the most fundamental human rights, subjected to threats and violence, victims of trafficking are made to toil under horrific conditions in sweatshops and on construction sites, in fields and in brothels. Women and children, some as young as seven years old, are forced to labor in sex industries where they suffer physical and mental abuse and are exposed to disease, including infection by the HIV virus.[60]

Powell's outrage was certainly appropriate given the details of the report and the magnitude of the problem. He should not have been surprised, however, since in November 1999, his predecessor, Secretary of State Madeline Albright, issued a similar statement about the findings of another U.S. federal government report, the Central Intelligence Agency's (CIA) "International Trafficking in Women to the United States: A Contemporary Manifestation of Slavery and Organized Crime."[61] In fact, the State Department report introduced by Powell quoted figures from the earlier CIA report which was based on a two-year study of illegal trafficking and enslavement of human beings mostly in the sex industry:

> [A]n estimated 45,000–50,000 women and children are trafficked annually to the United States. . . . Examples of this may include Latvian women threatened and forced to dance nude in Chicago; Thai women brought to the US for the sex industry, then forced to be virtual sex slaves; ethnically Korean-Chinese women held as indentured servants in the Commonwealth of the Northern Mariana Islands;[62] and hearing-impaired and mute Mexicans brought to the US, enslaved, beaten, then forced to peddle trinkets in New York City.[63]

A 1995 case illustrates the ethnic and international character of sex trafficking.

> In conjunction with Thai traffickers, Ludwig Janak, a German national who operated a tour guide service in Thailand, recruited Thai women to come to the United States to work. Several of the women were told they would have good jobs working in restaurants. Once in the US, Thai traffickers and a Korean madam forced the women into prostitution. . . . A total of 18 defendants were indicted on charges of kidnapping, alien smuggling, extortion, and white slavery.[64]

Many of the cases recounted in the CIA report involved promises of work outside the sex industry.

> From about February 1996 to March 1998, some 25–40 Mexican women and girls, some as young as 14 years old, were trafficked from the Veracruz state in Mexico to Florida and the Carolinas in the United States. The victims had been promised jobs in waitressing, housekeeping, landscaping, childcare and elder care. Upon their arrival, the women and girls were told they must work as prostitutes in brothels serving migrant workers or risk harm to them-

selves and/or their families. Besides enduring threats, women who attempted to escape were subjugated to beatings. . . . One woman was locked in a closet for 15 days as punishment for trying to escape.[65]

CHILD SEX LABOR

The involvement of children in the commercial sex trade raises questions not obvious when considering adults. While both adult men and women might be enslaved or coerced into sex work, they are capable of informed consent. Children, by definition and international convention those under eighteen, are not considered legally or morally capable of making the decision to sell their bodies. For instance, Heather Montgomery notes the difficulty of determining even what to call children involved in the sex trade: child prostitutes, child sex workers, children exploited by the sex industry. This is because of the volitional assumptions imbedded in the terms *sex worker* or *prostitute*. She cites Ireland's definition of child prostitution as a situation

> where the person selling or hiring their sexuality is under eighteen years of age. . . . All children under the age of eighteen who are in prostitution are considered, *de facto*, to be sexually exploited.[66]

The United Nations Convention on the Rights of the Child also specifies the age of eighteen as the end of childhood, places the responsibility and guilt for child prostitution or pornography squarely on the shoulders of adults involved in any sexual transaction involving children, and defines child prostitution as:

> [T]he act of obtaining, procuring, or offering the services of a child or inducing a child to perform sexual acts for any form of compensation or reward (or any acts that are linked with that offence) (even with the consent of the child).[67]

Montgomery distinguishes between children in the sex industry who are deceived or coerced into situations of forced prostitution from those who "choose" prostitution to escape abusive family situations or to support themselves and their families in situations of economic desperation. Montgomery does not resolve the question of whether it makes sense to talk about "free choice" for those facing extreme poverty. Her question about whether all children must be "saved" and stopped from sex work, however, resonates with the discourse of the prostitutes' rights movement and organizations such as COYOTE (Call Off Your Old Tired Ethics) or those who attended the World Whores' Summit in San Francisco in 1989. Prostitutes' rights discourse emphasizes the hypocrisy present in the simultaneous demand for sex by consumers on the one hand, and the stigmatizing of sex work on the one hand, as well as demands for sex workers' rights to use their bodies as they wish.[68] Scholars are by no means in agreement that children should be included in this logic—that children should have the right to sell their sexuality—because of children's relative vulnerability compared to adults, and because of children's developmental differences from adults. In fact, children are generally seen as a separate and special class needing protection, perhaps at the expense of their rights to be sex workers.[69]

Whatever their sexual rights are or should be, children are reported to be a growing segment of the sex trade because of consumers' fears of AIDS and their often mistaken beliefs that children are less likely to be infected. Williams provides an overview of the illegal global traffic in children for commercial sex, estimating that "the number of child prostitutes world-wide could easily exceed five million."[70] He finds that the same ethnosexual boundaries operate for children as for women in the sex trade generally, and in sex tourism in particular:

> Children are increasingly sold and trafficked across frontiers—between developing and developed countries, among developing countries, and among developed countries. The spread of child prostitution worldwide is part and parcel of the less positive aspects of globalization. The main child trafficking pipelines include those from Nepal to India and from Burma to Thailand. In addition, girls and young women from India and Pakistan are frequently sold to wealthy Middle Eastern men. Abduction, false documentation and sham marriages are all used to facilitate this movement.[71]

Lin Lim also links the sexual exploitation of children to the sex tourism industry, as does the tourism industry itself.[72] For instance, in 1996 the World Tourism Organization passed a resolution condemning organized sex tourism that "denounces and condemns in particular child sex tourism, considering it a violation of Article 34 of the [UN] Convention on the Rights of the Child and requiring strict legal action by tourist sending and receiving countries."[73] The 1999 CIA report on slavery and illegal international trafficking of women and children into the United States describes similar ethnosexual border crossing in the obtaining and moving of children forced into sex work:

> Girls from Asian and African countries, some as young as 9, were essentially sold to traffickers by their parents, "for less than the price of a toaster," one government official said. This mainly happens in cultures where female children are not valued. The girls are smuggled into the United States where, in a typical case, they are forced to work "in an indentured sexual-servitude arrangement."[74]

Conclusion

Gender, class, and politics organize sexual exchanges in macro, international, commercial arenas as well as in micro, national, personal settings. The sex industry today is a lucrative local, national, and international business attracting labor and capital, consumers and workers, entrepreneurs and gangsters. As Watanabe notes, the new warlords of ethnosexuality are less likely to be soldiers than businessmen, less likely to be ethnosexual invaders than ethnosexual traffickers. Although the commercial sex trade still caters to servicemen and still encircles military installations, its clientele and locales have spread well beyond combat zones and military R&R destinations. The sex industry, like other major commercial enterprises, has gone global, with businesses and managers moving from country to country in search of the highest profits, and with workers migrating from villages to cities, from poorer to richer countries in search of the highest wages.

The phenomena of forced sexual slavery and the trafficking of children for sexual exploitation whether in times of war or peace, stand in contrast to the almost festive label, *sex tourism*, or the more neutral term, *sex work*. A reading of summaries of the some of the origins, destinations, and methods of child entry into the sex industry illustrates the ethnosexual character of the trade: girls from Latin America, Asia, Eastern Europe, and Africa are moved to the United States, children are moved from Nepal to India, from Burma to Thailand, from India and Pakistan to the Middle East. These national borders crossed in the trafficking of children parallel the racial and ethnic boundaries that frequently divide those who work in the sex trade from their clients. For both children and adults, race, ethnicity, and nationality are the marks of exploitable and expendable ethnosexual Others.[75]

NOTES

1. See Chris Rojek and John Urry, *Touring Cultures: Transformations of Travel and Theory* (New York: Routledge, 1997).

2. Quoted in Jolly, "From Point Venus to Bali Ha'i," 100–101; see also Johann Reinhold Forster, *Observations Made During a Voyage Round the World on Physical Geography, Natural History and Ethic Philosophy* (London: G. Robinson, 1778); George Forster, *George Forster's Werke—Band 1 [A Voyage Round the World in his Britannic Majesty's Sloop, Resolution]*, ed. Robert L. Kahn (London: B. White, [1777], 1968).

3. McClintock, *Imperial Leather*, 22.

4. Bernard Smith, *Imagining the Pacific: In the Wake of the Cook Voyages* (New Haven: Yale University Press, 1992), 210.

5. Jolly, "From Point Venus to Bali Ha'i," 106; for a discussion of sexuality in

travel literature, see Ian Littlewood, *Sultry Climates: Travel and Sex since the Grand Tour* (London: John Murray, 2001).

6. Julie Scott, "Sexual and National Boundaries in Tourism," *Annals of Tourism Research* 22 (1995): 385–403, 385.

7. See John Urry, *Consuming Places* (New York: Routledge, 1995); Martin Mowforth and Ian Munt, *Tourism and Sustainability: New Tourism in the Third World* (New York: Routledge, 1998).

8. Martin Opperman, *Sex Tourism and Prostitution: Aspects of Leisure, Recreation, and Work* (New York: Cognizant Communications, 1998).

9. Patrick Larvie, "Natural Born Targets: Male Hustlers and AIDS Prevention in Urban Brazil," in *Men Who Sell Sex: International Perspective on Male Prostitution and HIV/AIDS*, ed. Peter Aggleton (Philadelphia: Temple University Press, 1999), 163; Enloe, *Bananas, Beaches and Bases*, 32; Kempadoo, *Sun, Sex, and Gold*.

10. Bishop and Robinson, *Night Market*, 82–91; Bishop and Robinson report that by the 1993 edition of *Insight Guide*, the AIDS epidemic had led editors to moderate the enthusiastic tone of their advice about sex tourism, and to include admonitions such as, "do not be foolish; there is a drugstore just down the street" (84); see also Thiesmeyer, "The West's 'Comfort Women' and the Discourses of Seduction," 73–74.

11. Bishop and Robinson, *Night Market*, 109.

12. Skrobanek et al., *The Traffic in Women*, 40.

13. Davidson, *Prostitution, Power, and Freedom*, 169; for a brief discussion of the resurgence of the sex trade in recent years in postrevolutionary Cuba, see Smith and Padula, *Sex and Revolution*, 178–80; researchers find that a central fantasy for many sex tourists and for some sex workers is that they are "friends" and "dating" rather than engaged in a commercial transaction; sex workers try to establish quick friendships with a returning client in the hopes of developing into a more steady relationship and perhaps something more permanent; for sex customers, there is the illusion of being chosen or special to the sex worker, or of satisfying her sexually; for instance, Davidson quotes a student who was backpacking in Thailand and his explanation of the money he gave to a Thai woman with whom he had sex:

> Basically the thing was, she basically said to me, "I'm going to have to go and sleep with somebody because I need the money." So we were left in this awful situation where . . . she was going to have to sleep with somebody unless I paid her not to. . . . So we talked about it and we agreed, I would give her money. . . . But I'm fairly certain that's not the reason she went off with me. I just don't believe it was. I'm a reasonable judge of character and I wouldn't have gone off with just an out and out girl that was going to be with me just for money. (Davidson, *Prostitution, Power and Freedom*, 177).

14. Kamala Kempadoo, "The Migrant Tightrope: Experiences from the Caribbean," in *Global Sex Workers: Rights, Resistance, and Redefinition*, ed. Kamala Kempadoo and Jo Doezema (New York: Routledge, 1998), 131; see also Safa, *The Myth of the Male Breadwinner*.

15. Kempala, "The Migrant Tightrope," 124.

16. Ibid., 129.

17. For instance, Bishop and Robinson interviewed sex industry workers in Bangkok; a dancer there reported making four times her monthly salary as a maid, and prostitutes could earn ten times that amount and more; Bishop and Robinson, *Night Market*, 157, 165.

18. Pasuk Phongpaichit, "Trafficking in People in Thailand," in *Illegal Immigration and Commercial Sex,* 89; such international migration into Thailand complicated the ethnosexual landscape of the local sex industry; not only were sex consumers and sex workers from a variety of countries, sex workers from the same country were often an ethnically diverse group; for instance, Phongpaichit reports that many refugees from Burma who become sex workers in Thai border towns or in big Thai cities such as Bangkok were Burmese ethnic minorities fleeing discrimination and slavery in Burma: "Mon, Karen, and Shan people [who] prefer to come to Thailand to escape forced labor and other repressive policies imposed on them by the [majority] Burmese government" (ibid., 90); see also Pasuk Phongpaichit, *From Peasant Girls to Bangkok Masseuses* (Geneva: International Labour Organization, 1982); Pasuk Phongpaichit and Chris Baker, *Thailand: Economy and Politics* (Kuala Lampur: Oxford University Press, 1995); see also Yayori Matsui, *Women in the New Asia: From Pain to Power* (New York: Zed Books, 1999).

19. An exception is Ratnapala's discussion of male children who are procured

by local pimps catering for European Paedophiles. Houses are rented out and children are brought there by cheating them, or by using force. In 1995–96, an estimated 1500 children were involved in this kind of work. Of them, nearly two-thirds were boys. . . . Local pimps provide boys according to the particular client's taste. Sometimes, drugs are given to these children in order to arouse them. (Nandasena Ratnapala, "Male Sex Work in Sri Lanka," in *Men Who Sell Sex,* 216–17).

20. Butler, *Daughters of Joy, Sisters of Misery.*

21. Dennis Altman, "Foreword," in *Men Who Sell Sex,* xv; Wim Zuilhof, "Sex for Money between Men and Boys in the Netherlands: Implications for HIV Prevention," in *Men Who Sell Sex,* 23–39.

22. Amine Boushaba, Oussama Tawil, Latefa Imane, and Hakima Himmich, "Marginalization and Vulnerability: Male Sex Work in Morocco," in *Men Who Sell Sex,* 269–70; in 1991 G. Kruks found that 72 percent of males engaging in "survival sex" (for money, food, shelter, protection) in Los Angeles identified themselves as gay or bisexual; G. Kruks, "Gay and Lesbian Homeless/Street Youth: Special Issues and Concerns," *Journal of Adolescent Health* 12 (1991): 515–18; Edward Morse and associates reported that 60 percent of their U.S. sample of male sex workers identified themselves as gay or bisexual; Edward V. Morse, Patricia M. Simon, and Kendra E. Burchfiel, "Social Environment and Male Sex Work in the United States," in *Men Who Sell Sex,* 88.

23. Jacobo Schifter and Peter Aggleston, "*Cacherismo* in a San Jose Brothel: Aspects of Male Sex Work in Costa Rica," in *Men Who Sell Sex,* 143; see also Jacobo Schifter, *Lila's House: Male Prostitution in Latin America* (New York: Harrington Park Press, 1998).

24. Roger Lancaster observes this distinction in Nicaragua as well where *cochon* refers to the male recipient of anal intercourse:

[T]he dominant Anglo-American rule would read as follows. A man gains sexual status and honor among other men through and only through his sexual transactions with women. Homosexuals appear as the active refusenicks of that system. In Nicaragua, the rule is built around different principles. A man gains sexual status and honor among other men through his active role in sexual intercourse (either with women or with other men). Cochones are passive participants in that system. (Roger N. Lancaster, *Life Is Hard: Machismo, Danger, and the Intimacy of Power in Nicaragua* [Berkeley: University of California Press, 1992], 250)

25. Shivananda Khan, "Through a Window Darkly: Men Who Sell Sex to Men in India and Bangladesh," in *Men Who Sell Sex*, 195; even this distinction can be unstable; Ana Louisa Liguori and Peter Aggleton found that although male sex workers in Mexico City made the distinction between heterosexuals and homosexuals, somewhere between 20 and 30 percent of men working any given shift in a brothel might allow themselves to be penetrated; interestingly, penetration was reported by respondents about *other* sex workers, not about the respondents themselves; Ana Luisa Liguori and Peter Aggleton, "Aspects of Male Sex Work in Mexico City," in *Men Who Sell Sex*, 116; see also Gutmann, *The Meanings of Macho;* Carolyn Sleightholme and Indrani Sinha, *Guilty without Trial: Women in the Sex Trade in Calcutta* (New Brunswick, NJ: Rutgers University Press, 1997), 151–53; Dede Octomo, "Masculinity in Indonesia: Genders, Sexualities, and Identities in a Changing Society," in *Framing the Sexual Subject: The Politics of Gender, Sexuality, and Power*, Richard Parker, Regina Maria Barbosa, and Peter Aggleton (Berkeley: University of California Press, 2000), 46–59.

26. A category unlike Moroccan *gigolos* who do not cross-dress, but similar in that both French and Moroccan *gigolos* considered themselves primarily heterosexuals, see Lindinalva Laurindo da Silva, "*Travestis* and *Gigolos:* Male Sex Work and HIV Prevention in France," in *Men Who Sell Sex*, 51.

27. Ibid.; this respondent's closing line suggests that although they were having sex, he chose to emphasize the paternal rather than the sexual aspects and attributes of the relationship, perhaps to include the heterosexual component of his identity.

28. Boushaba et al., "Marginalization and Vulnerability," 266.

29. Michael L. Tan, "Walking the Tightrope: Sexual Risk and Male Sex Work in the Philippines," in *Men Who Sell Sex*, 241–61.

30. Larvie, "Natural Born Targets," 163.

31. E. Antonio de Moya and Rafael Garcia, "Three Decades of Male Sex Work in Santo Domingo," in *Men Who Sell Sex*, 133.

32. Amalia L. Cabezas, "Women's Work Is Never Done: Sex Tourism in Sostia, the Dominican Republic," in *Sun, Sex and Gold* 100.

33. Desmond, *Staging Tourism*, 125.

34. Ibid., 126; see also Clifford Gessler, *Isles of Enchantment* (New York: Appleton-Century, 1937).

35. See Deborah Pruit and Suzanne LaFont, "For Love and Money: Romance Tourism in Jamaica," *Annals of Tourism Research* 22 (1995): 421–40, 437; Beverly Mullings, "Fantasy Tours: Exploring the Global Consumption of Caribbean Sex Tours," in *New Forms of Consumption: Consumers, Culture, and Commodification* (Lanham, MD: Rowman and Littlefield, 2000), 227–50; Davidson, *Prostitution, Power, and Freedom;* Kempadoo, *Sun, Sex, and Gold;* Rory O'Merry reports that men get involved in long-term fantasy relationships with women sex workers as well:

> Some men send money to the girl of their dreams in Thailand. These were the women they had the time of their life with, and were easy to love. They don't feel as if they're sending money to a prostitute, but to a friend who was poor and who lives in a developing country, to help her and her family financially. . . . When he is in town he can have all the sex he can handle—No "I have a headache." The exchange rate makes him a millionaire. Paradise. (Rory O'Merry, *My Wife in Bangkok* [Berkeley: Asia Press, 1990], 139)

36. De Moya et al.'s research is cited and quoted in Cabezas, "Women's Work Is Never Done," 101; see also E. Antonio de Moya, Rafael Garcia, Rosario Fadul, and Edward Herold, *Sosua Sanky-Pankies and Female Sex Workers* (Santo Domingo: Instituto de Sexualidad Humana, Universidad Autonoma de Santo Domingo, 1992).

37. Cabezas, "Women's Work Is Never Done," 101.

38. Pruit and LaFont, "For Love and Money," 437.

39. Ibid.

40. Ibid., 426.

41 Kempadoo, *Sun, Sex, and Gold,* 24.

42. Ratnapala, "Male Sex Work in Sri Lanka," 217.

43. Carlos F. Caceres and Oscar G. Jimenez, "*Fletes* in Parque Kennedy: Sexual Cultures among Young Men Who Sell Sex to Other Men in Lima," in *Men Who Sell Sex,* 190; Tan, "Walking the Tightrope," 244.

44. Ibid., 27.

45. Vron Ware, "Purity and Danger: Race, Gender and Tales of Sex Tourism," in *Back to Reality: Social Experience and Cultural Studies,* ed. A. McRobbie (Manchester: Manchester University Press, 1997), 139; the *Sun* article's author reported that she was "one woman who did not fall under the black magic spell . . . the photographer and I had a job to do."

46. Ibid., 140.

47. Ibid., 139.

48. Ibid., 146–47.

49. Sherry Ortner, "Borderland Politics and Erotics: Gender and Sexuality in Himalayan Mountaineering," in *Making Gender,* 181–212.

50. See Sietske Altink, *Stolen Lives: Trading Women into Sex and Slavery* (London: Scarlet Press, 1995).

51. United Nations, "Assembly Adopts Convention against Transnational Organized Crime and Two Protocols," Press Release GA/9822, November 15, 2000; see http://srch1.un.org:80/plweb-cgi/

52. Enloe, *Bananas, Beaches and Bases,* 36–37.

53. Gilliam Caldwell, Steve Galster, Jyothi Kanicks, Nadia Steinzor, "Capitalizing on Transition Economies: The Role of the Russian Mafiya in Trafficking Women for Forced Prostitution," 42–73 in *Illegal Immigration and Commercial Sex,* 44–47.

54. Ibid., 44.

55. Ibid., 48; see also *Human Rights Country Reports, Russia* (Washington, DC: U.S. Department of State, 1997); Human Rights Watch, "Neither Jobs nor Justice: Discrimination against Women in Russia" (March 1995): 6.

56. Caldwell et al., "Capitalizing on Transition Economies," 50.

57. Gerben J. N. Bruinsma and Guus Meershoek, "Organized Crime and Trafficking in Women from Eastern Europe in the Netherlands," in *Illegal Immigration and Commercial Sex,* 105; see also Donna M. Hughes, "The 'Natasha' Trade: Transnational Sex Trafficking," *National Institute of Justice Journal* (January 2001): 8–15.

58. Gall, "Macedonia Village Is Center of Europe Web in Sex Trade."

59. U.S. Department of State, *Trafficking in Persons Report* (Washington, DC: Government Printing Office, 2001), 1; Caldwell and associates provide a similar definition of trafficking as "the recruitment or transportation of persons within or across

borders [involving] deception, coercion or force, abuse of authority, debt bondage, or fraud for the purpose of placing persons in situations of abuse or exploitation such as forced prostitution, sweatshop labor, or exploitative domestic servitude"; Caldwell et al., "Capitalizing on Transition Economies," 42.

60. U.S. State Department, "Release of the 2001 Trafficking in Person's Report," Press Release, July 12, 2001.

61. Amy O'Neill Richard, "International Trafficking in Women to the United States: A Contemporary Manifestation of Slavery and Organized Crime," Central Intelligence Agency, Center for the Study of Intelligence (Washington, DC: Government Printing Office, 1999).

62. The Northern Mariana Islands, a former colony of Japan, was acquired by the United States at the end of World War II; in 1986 it became a "commonwealth in political union with the U.S." and its people became U.S. citizens; see Central Intelligence Agency, *The World Factbook, 2000* (Washington, DC: Government Printing Office, 2000).

63. O'Neill Richard, "International Trafficking in Women to the United States," iii–v.

64. Ibid., 49.

65. Ibid., 47; the CIA report prompted the introduction of federal legislation and the U.S. House of Representatives also approved extension of federal witness protection programs to the victims of human smuggling and sex slavery; see *The Humanitarian Times* (May 11, 2000):1; my thanks to Norman R. Yetman, University of Kansas for bringing this report to my attention.

66. Heather Montgomery, "Children, Prostitution, and Identity: A Case Study from a Tourist Resort in Thailand," in *Global Sex Workers*, 146; see also, Kevin Ireland, *Wish You Weren't Here* (London: Save the Children, 1993), 3.

67. Lin Lean Lim, "Child Prostitution," in *The Sex Sector: The Economic and Social Bases of Prostitution in Southeast Asia*, ed. Lin Lean Lim (Geneva: International Labor Office, 1998), 171.

68. See Shannon Bell, *Reading, Writing, and Rewriting the Prostitute Body* (Bloomington: Indiana University Press, 1995); Cleo Odzer, *Patpong Sisters* (New York: Blue Moon-Arcade, 1994).

69. See Kane, *Sold for Sex.*

70. Williams, "Trafficking in Women and Children," 160.

71. Ibid., 162–63.

72. Lim, "Child Prostitution."

73. Ibid., 199.

74. *New York Times*, "Once-hidden Slave Trade: A Growing U.S. Problem."

75. It is important to note that most prostitution and sex work by both adults and children do not involve international trafficking, but rather workers and their clients are local; it is the case, however, that much sex work is characterized by racial, ethnic, or class differences between clients and workers; see Kevin Bales, *Disposable People: New Slavery in the Global Economy* (Berkeley: University of California Press, 1999); Kamala Kempadoo and Jo Doezema, eds., *Global Sex Workers: Rights, Resistance, and Redefinition* (New York: Routledge, 1998).

CHAPTER 8

SEX AND GLOBALIZATION

The Global Economy of Desire

They say that when good Americans die they go to Paris.
Indeed? And when bad Americans die, where do they go to?
Oh, they go to America.   (Oscar Wilde, *A Woman of No Importance*)

Oscar Fingal O'Flahertie Wills Wilde was twenty-eight years old in 1882 when he began a lengthy lecture tour of America. When he arrived, he is reported to have told a U.S. Customs officer, "I have nothing to declare but my genius" . . . and, he might have added, his wit. Both were reserved more for exposing the class foibles and hypocrisies of his native Britain[1] than for an America that welcomed Wilde's flamboyant dress and critical repartee with surprising enthusiasm. Wilde's bit of dialogue above was written a decade after his American tour. It provides a glimpse of this sophisticated, though not unfriendly European's assessment of the United States of the late nineteenth century. The comment reflects both familiarity and detachment, an analysis made by someone who was in America, but not of it.

The unique insights and perspective to be gained from outsider observers such as Oscar Wilde suggest that the best way to see America is to leave the country. It is only when traveling beyond U.S. borders that it becomes possible to obtain a broad, more global view of America and Americans. For most Americans, especially those born and raised in the United States, nationality is something we take for granted. Being American is like being white for most European ancestry Americans, it is comfortable and assumed. By leaving the insulated world of home and country we encounter firsthand, often for the first time, the opinions and meanings others attach to our nationality. When repositioned outside the United States, we can catch a glimmer of ourselves seen

through different eyes.[2] Simply crossing those frequently traversed borders that
mark the northern and southern boundaries of the United States, traveling into
Canada or Mexico, transforms Americans into something new: Yanks or Yan-
quis. These nationality monikers often puzzle and offend Americans who are
surprised at the content and intensity of others' beliefs and opinions about them,
and who chafe under their newly assigned identities (though we sometimes are
embarrassed by the behavior of our compatriots traveling abroad).

Nations are imagined as much by outsiders as by insiders. Like ethnic identity, nationality emerges out of an interactive process in which the individual
and others negotiate the symbolic boundaries and content of the nation. Who
is and what it means to be American or French or Thai or Russian or Mexican are defined both outside and inside the nation. Nations and nationalities
are imbedded in a global system of institutions and symbols. That global system is crucial to legitimating a nation's claims to statehood and territory
through processes of formal recognition, such as UN membership, treaties and
alliances, and diplomatic recognition and exchanges. Likewise, the content and
meaning of nations and nationalities are framed by discourses and actors in international and global symbolic spaces, such as world news media, political and
economic forums, and popular culture. Moral and sexual imaginings are part
of the global grammar and technical repertoire of national constructions.

On September 11, 2001, many Americans were surprised to learn how
deeply resented and despised their country was in the opinions and imaginations of some in the global system. The attacks in New York and Washington, D.C., by an international network of Muslim religious extremists and
the anti-U.S. hatred that appeared to have motivated them to such acts
shocked Americans, and led them to ask, "Why do they hate us so?" Americans were not comforted by the fact that these men had been living almost
invisibly for years in the West, mainly in Germany and the United States,
while they planned their suicidal missions. Their exposure to Western societies and education did not temper their distaste for American values and
culture, in fact, familiarity seemed only to have bred further contempt.

In their post–September 11 essay, "Occidentalism" (a play on Edward
Said's and others' discussion of "Orientalism"), Ian Buruma and Avishai
Margalit described the history and content of negative imaginings of the
West. They traced the roots of anti-Westernism back to the colonial era, but
found the ideology especially well articulated in the fascist ideologies of
World War II, in particular in "German-inspired ethnic nationalism and Zen-
and Shinto-based nativism":

> [T]he chief characteristics of this Western enemy would have sounded fa-
> miliar to Osama bin Laden and other Islamic extremists. They are, not in

any particular order, materialism, liberalism, capitalism, individualism, humanism, rationalism, socialism, decadence, and moral laxity.[3]

Buruma and Margalit identify in Occidentalism (and in all religious fundamentalisms, including Christian variants)[4] an antiliberalism that "almost invariably contain[s] a deep hatred of the City . . . [and] urban civilization: commerce, mixed populations, artistic freedom, sexual license, scientific pursuits, leisure, personal safety, wealth, and its usual concomitant, power."[5] They emphasize Occidentalism's disdain for what it considers to be the West's excessive materialism, spiritual bankruptcy, and sexual decadence, and note Occidentalism's resentment of the intrusion of these values into non-Western societies through the West's economic, political, military, and cultural global reach and dominance. They argue that the values of the City are constantly present even in remote destinations because of the ubiquity and allure of Western, especially American mass culture,

> through advertising, television, pop music, and videos. The modern city, representing . . . all the glittering arrogance and harlotry of the West, has found its icon in the Manhattan skyline, reproduced in millions of posters, photographs, and images, plastered all over the world. . . . It excites longing, envy, and sometimes blinding rage.[5]

The extent to which their outrage over Western sexuality and its global marketing played a role in motivating Osama bin Laden and his fellow travelers to violently reshape the Manhattan skyline will never be known. Even a cursory consideration of the gender and sexual policies of bin Laden's protectors, Afghanistan's Taliban regime, suggests that they had a considerable interest in sex and its regulation.[7]

In their preoccupation with the sexuality of Others, bin Laden and the Taliban certainly were not alone. Sexuality plays an ever-present role in macro-level and micro-level international relations. For instance, American Jacalyn Harden discovered the sexual meaning of her race and nationality while she was living and working in Japan in the late 1980s:

> My officemates and I were off to Osaka for our section trip. . . . Kanada-sensei gave me a sympathetic smile, handed me my ticket, and told me that I would be sitting next to Endo-sensei for the two-hour trip. I knew he had a reputation for being *sukebe* (lecherous), especially when he drank. . . . I was only mildly wary. Yet as soon as the train pulled out of Hamamatsu station and the sake bottles appeared, Endo-sensei begged my forgiveness for the sensitive question he was about to ask me: "Why do American teenagers become sexually active so early in life? . . . And by the way, when did you have your first lover?" . . . I asked him if he would talk about sex with a Japanese woman like this. He quickly apologized and said, "Japanese girls are not like black girls or Filipinas . . . they are just different."[8]

Harden found "that Japanese constructions of race and national pride are deeply intertwined with images of women's sexuality, past and present," and although many of the people she encountered during the three years she lived in Japan had met few Americans and still fewer African Americans, many still felt quite confident that they could "identify the differences between the 'real' shy and naive Japanese woman and the 'real' loose and promiscuous American (read, Western) woman."[9] Harden contends, however, that the sexualization of black and white American and Filipina women by Japanese is not unique to Japan or the Japanese view of foreigners. Rather, she argues, "ideas about race, gender, and nationality are both lucrative and commonplace throughout the world today," and are central to the way nations imagine themselves and national Others.[10]

It is not only nationality that emerges when one crosses international borders. As Harden's experience reveals, race and ethnicity also are defined and sexualized by international and global processes. The ways in which the global system and globalization shape ethnosexual boundaries and the intimate intersections among race, ethnicity, nationalism, and sexuality/ies are the focus of this chapter. In the pages that follow we will look at the ways in which race, ethnicity, and nationality are sexualized and the ways in which sexuality is racialized, ethnicized, and nationalized in international trade and commerce and in global entertainment and culture.

THE GLOBAL/SEXUAL [IMAGI]NATION

Globalization is a term that has captured the attention and elicited the skepticism of many commentators, analysts, and observers of international economics, politics, and popular culture. The term often is used to characterize the post–Cold War era and what seems to be a quickening in the pace and a thickening in the density of international communication networks, business transactions, and political, economic, and cultural integration. Scholars debate the origins and newness of the contemporary global system, argue about how long the process of globalization has been underway, and question the extent to which present patterns of globalization are quantitatively and qualitatively different from developments during the past several centuries.[11] However new or old, relatively fast or slow, explicit consideration of the global system and the process of globalization is extremely useful for broadening and internationalizing our understanding the sexual substructure of race, ethnicity, and nationalism.

By *global system* I refer to the networks and flows linking actors and systems across national borders. These networks and flows connect economic, political, cultural, informational, ideological, social, and military actors and systems such as multinational corporations, suprastate organizations, skilled and unskilled work forces and labor organizations, popular culture including books, films, videos, television, music, visual and performance art, fashion, etc., information systems, modes of production, ideas and ideologies, military organizations, alliances, and technologies, trade associations and compacts, immigration and refugee streams and diaspora populations. Examples include the European Union (EU), the United Nations (UN), Cable News Network (CNN), Music Television (MTV), Reuters News Agency, North Atlantic Treaty Organization (NATO), International Ladies Garment Workers Union, the Internet, Palestinians, the Roman Catholic Church, the Organization of African Unity (OAU), the Organization of Petroleum Exporting Countries (OPEC), Cultural Survival, Inc.

By *globalization* I refer to the process whereby these links among national and international actors and systems become more numerous and more tightly connected, and whereby new social, cultural, economic, and political global formations develop. Stuart Hall describes the emergence of "global mass culture" as one instance of a "new kind of globalization":

> Global mass culture is dominated by the modern means of cultural production, dominated by the image that crosses and recrosses linguistic frontiers much more rapidly and more easily and that speaks across languages in a much more immediate way. It is dominated by all of the ways in which the visual and graphic arts have entered directly into the reconstitution of popular life, of entertainment, and of leisure. It is dominated by television, by film, and by the image, imagery, and styles of mass advertising.[12]

Whether the origins of the current global system and its growth and penetration of national spaces are located in the remote or recent past, there is strong evidence that the pace of globalization is speeding up due to technological advances and the opening of markets around the world.[13] Ever more people are coming into ever more frequent contact with one another in real or virtual space as a result of increased international migration, the growing availability of and access to international communications systems, and the accelerated movement of workers and industries around the globe. Globalization connects populations that are distinct from one another in language, religion, appearance, culture, nationality. Since these are the traditional bases upon which ethnic boundaries are built, the world might get smaller as a result of globalization, but it may well become more ethnically divided.[14] Globalization also contributes to both the building of ethnic communities and the breaching of ethnic boundaries through providing increased opportunities for ethnosexual settling, sojourning, adventuring, and invasion. In this way we can think of globalization as an important part of the process whereby race is sexed and sex is raced. Internal and international migration are important mechanisms in ethnic boundary formation and ethnosexual processes.

Fredrik Barth describes an instance of both the enduring and emerging nature of ethnicity in contemporary societies in his discussion of the experiences of a Pakistani family that migrated to Barth's home country of Norway. Many Norwegian institutions such as schools and social service agencies have been successful in fostering a degree of assimilation into Norwegian society in the past three decades since significant Pakistani migration into Norway began. Pakistanis living in Norway, however, maintain a distinctive identity and community, and thus have become a new ethnic group. Barth describes a revealing gendered and sexualized moment when Pakistani assimilation becomes problematic and ethnic boundaries become most visible, fragile, and likely to be defended:

> Let us return to the Pakistani Family in Oslo, and focus on a daughter, born in Norway, to illuminate the processes in identity formation. An important part of her experience will be that of attending school. . . . Physical education, as part of the school curriculum, regularly becomes a painful issue to the Pakistani parents of a daughter. They generally have no objection to the physical exuberance in small girls, but become increasingly concerned . . . as their daughter approaches sexual maturity. . . . Even more threatening, of course, are cross-sexual friendships, romance, and courting, as these develop as a regular part of teenage school life.[15]

If this Oslo Pakistani scenario has a familiar ring, it is because of its parallels to the story I recounted in Chapter 1 of race, sex, and schooling in Cleveland. Oslo in the 1990s, Cleveland in the 1950s—different times, different places, different groups, but similar parental worries about ethnosexual boundaries being crossed by adolescent girls and boys. There are other common elements in the two scenarios. Both involved a migrant ethnic population moving to cities inhabited by a different resident ethnic group. In the case of Norway's Pakistani population, labor shortages in Norway and across Europe the 1970s led to the emigration of "guest workers" out of south Asia where there was a labor surplus and a relatively poorer standard of living. In the case of Cleveland's African American population, labor shortages associated with World War II and the growth of the industrial North led to the emigration of black workers out of the U.S. South where they faced official segregation and a relatively poorer standard of living. There was a global economic dimension to each migration stream as well—the labor shortage in Europe which encouraged Pakistani migration and the wartime labor shortage in northern U.S. cities which encouraged African American migration.[16] In both of these examples we see local and global forces at work in the sexual construction of racial, ethnic, and national boundaries.

The intersection of ethnicity and sexuality and the tensions between local and global rules, structures, and processes is the focus of this chapter. We will examine the sexual dimensions of the global migration of workers, the often hidden sexual aspects of the globalization of production, and the emergence of a sexualized global consumer culture. We will see a link between economies and sexualities outside of the sex industry, and we will observe tensions between local and global sexual standards and images. We will begin looking for ethnosex in the global system in the new denationalized economic spaces created by national governments trying to increase economic development, colonized by international businesses trying to decrease production costs, and populated by workers from rural and poor regions and countries trying to make ends meet.

ETHNOSEXUAL TRADING PARTNERS

Shanghai is the largest city in one of several Chinese "Special Economic Zones" located on the mainland's southern border, one hundred miles across the strait from the island of Taiwan. Shanghai is an industrial and postindustrial boomtown where international capital embraces local land and labor in the pursuit of profit and pleasure. Taiwan is a major economic player in Shanghai and in China's economic development strategy because of its geographic proximity and historical connection to the mainland. The Chinese and Taiwanese populations separated by the Taiwan Strait are both ethnically diverse and nationally divided, yet they share much in common. Both populations speak similar forms of Chinese (Mandarin and Cantonese, among others), and most Taiwanese have recent or past ancestral roots and relatives on the Chinese mainland.[17] The current Chinese/Taiwanese division had its origins in 1949 when Taiwan was taken over by members of the *Kuomintang* (Chinese Nationalist Party) fleeing Mao Zedong's communist revolution on the mainland. The past fifty years of separation have led to the development of major economic, political, social, and cultural differences between China and Taiwan. Many Taiwanese demand independent statehood, but China opposes Taiwanese independence, claiming that the island is a province of China.

Despite strained political relations between China and Taiwan, economic opportunities have led large numbers of Taiwanese companies and entrepreneurs to establish economic ties to the mainland. Taiwanese businessmen working in China have also established intimate ties with mainland Chinese women. The tensions between China's and Taiwan's past and present, thus, are complicated by contemporary ethnosexual liaisons. Hsiu-hua Shen conducted a study of the sexual politics of Taiwanese nationalism. During the period from 1999 to 2001 she interviewed more than one hundred Chinese and Taiwanese women and men about the social and sexual aspects of Taiwanese investments in China. The following composite story is based on the accounts and stories of a number of Taiwanese businessmen stationed in Shanghai:

> Lee is a 40-year-old married Taiwanese manager of a factory producing athletic footwear in one of China's special economic zones on the outskirts of Shanghai. His 35-year-old wife and their two daughters live in a comfortable

apartment in Taipei, Taiwan's capital city. Lee visits his wife and family several times a year for a week at a time, but most of the year he lives in a dormitory paid for by his employer and other Taiwanese corporations whose mostly male managers and executives also live and work in Shanghai. For recreation Lee and his Taiwanese friends to go Shanghai karaoke or dance clubs catering to these expatriates. There they are introduced by the club's matron hostess to mainly mainland Chinese young women or they rendezvous there with Chinese women they've met before. They have drinks in the club's main room, or move into smaller rooms designed for small groups, or perhaps they retire to private bedrooms upstairs. In the past few months Lee has begun spending his evenings with Chiang, a 20-year-old mainland Chinese woman, in her apartment which he pays for; he also pays for her clothes and meals, her brother's school tuition fees, and he gives her a small monthly allowance. The $200 per month that Lee now spends on Chiang instead of in the clubs is not missed by his wife in Taiwan since he continues to send money home on a regular basis. Lee's wife suspects him of having a mistress in Shanghai, but her only alternative is to move the family there, an option that she and Lee have agreed is not feasible because of the quality and kind of schooling their daughters would receive in Chinese schools. At the moment things are going well for Lee, but that will likely change when Chiang tells him about the baby they are expecting, and when the Chinese government's new law takes effect defining Chiang as Lee's common law wife.[18]

The rewards and risks that inhere in such cross-Strait sexual liaisons are reflected in the way Taiwanese businessmen talk about Taiwanese-Chinese ethnosexual boundaries and relationships: the representation of Chinese women as desirable, but economically, politically, socially, and sexually dangerous. Shen recounts a typical cautionary tale she heard circulated in the Taiwanese expatriate community in Shanghai:

Mr. Lin was a rich and married Taiwanese investor who owned seven garment factories and extensive real estate in Taipei and different parts of Taiwan. He took 60 million Taiwanese dollars[19] from Taiwan to invest in Shanghai. Unfortunately, his money was embezzled by his business partner, a Chinese state-operated firm. Lin attempted to make a comeback in Shanghai. He re-opened a firm and registered it under his Chinese girlfriend's name. His girlfriend, however, colluded with another Chinese man to take over his firm and property while he was visiting Taiwan. After he returned to Shanghai, she continued to deceive him and used Lin's Taiwanese passport and visa to obtain a great deal of money in Chinese bank loans. Consequently Lin lost all of his money as well as his Taiwanese identification. He had to be smuggled back to Taiwan on a boat with Chinese illegal immigrants. Lin filed charges in court, but lost his case. His Taiwanese wife, who had led a privileged life, became a maid working for others.[20]

These Shanghai love stories are not isolated international romantic triangles, nor are the dangers warned of in their telling depicted as rare events.[21] Just as historians argue that sexual liaisons and their regulation under colonialism were intimate to the workings of empire both as instruments of rule and as instigators of unruliness, contemporary ethnosexual exchanges between China and Taiwan oil the machinery of international capitalism, facilitating, but also complicating political and economic relations between the two countries. And as we saw in Chapter 5, ethnosexual connections between privileged Europeans and subordinated locals generated both regulations and uproar in colonial Asia. Similarly, the sexual liaisons between privileged businessmen and not-so-privileged local women have become matters of contention on both sides of the Taiwan Strait. In China and in Taiwan, the controversy over Taiwanese businessmen's practice of mixing business and pleasure centers on matters similar to those that vexed colonial authorities: classification and citizenship of mixed offspring, destabilization of national moral and family life, divided national loyalties that result from having sex with and marrying Others. Private ethnosexual contacts thus have become public national concerns involving legislation, law enforcement, and legal actions in both China and Taiwan.[22]

Shu-mei Shih also also found these concerns reflected in Taiwanese and Hong Kong media representations of mainland Chinese women. She argues that media depictions of Chinese women, especially newspaper and magazine stories about mainland women's seductive power, were symbolic reflections of Hong Kong residents' insecurities about the 1997 Chinese takeover of Hong Kong and Taiwanese fears that China will reintegrate Taiwan by force.[23] In Taiwan, Shih found that Chinese women *(dalumei)* are depicted as greedy seductresses who dupe unsuspecting Taiwanese men into giving away their family's money and betraying their nation's trust, and in Hong Kong Chinese women *(biaojie)* are cast as both financial and genetic threats—taking Hong Kong men's money and their sexual seed to recolonize Hong Kong by producing large numbers of mixed offspring:

> [R]epresentations of mainland [Chinese] women in mass media emphasize their cultural difference from the women of Taiwan and Hong Kong and are filled with patriarchal injunctions and eroticizations . . . they are ironically made to become linking agents for the patriarchal "kinship system" in the region [linking China, Taiwan, and Hong Kong] . . . but their "linking" function triggers the fear of contamination in the case of *dalumei,* and in the case of *biaojie,* the fantasy of assimilation.[24]

The stories told by Shen and Shih depict mainly heterosexual affairs since ethnosexual alliances between members of the same sex are less well documented, and the lack of offspring or formal marriage between same sex interethnic international partnerships tends to contribute to their invisibility and deniability. Whether they are heterosexual and homosexual, however, amorous arrangements for love or money in the global economy are not unique to Shanghai or Hong Kong or China. Ethnosexual personal and commercial relationships are a common feature of all international trade and commerce. In her analysis of the "international politics of the banana," Cynthia Enloe finds, for instance, that prostitution has an ethnosexual face in contemporary agricultural production:

> Around some United Brands plantations in Central America brothels are commonplace. They are situated just outside the company gates. While the men on banana plantations are Amerindian, Black and Ladino, the women working in the brothels are overwhelming Ladino.[25]

SEX AND THE WORKING WOMAN

Women are the employees of choice in many low-wage economic settings around the world, not just in the sex industry. The reasons vary: the greater availability of female labor, women's low salaries relative to male workers, notions of women as more compliant workers, managers' desire for opportunities for sexual contact, harassment, or exploitation of women workers, or some theory of women's unique or preferable suitability for the job at hand. In fact, sometimes employers hire women exclusively as workers, though seldom as managers. Saskia Sassen finds that the preference for and availability of women workers from developing countries has produced a historic influx of Third World women into the global wage labor force beginning in the 1980s. Women's international migration into industrial countries and their internal migration from rural to urban or offshore production sites in developing countries have been and continue to be on such a large scale that Sassen concludes that women's migration for work represents "a new phase in the history of women."[26]

Rolando Tolentino examines the role of gender and sexuality in the recruitment of workers in manufacturing sites located in developing country "export processing zones" (EPZs)—sites where international capital engages local labor. As part of a plan to attract foreign investment, the International Monetary Fund and World Bank funded the establishment of EPZs in a number of Third World countries during the 1980s. Tolentino describes the gendered and sexualized spaces for women workers that opened in these new industrial settings:

> [L]ight industries such as food processing and the manufacture of textiles, garments, footwear, tobacco, and phamaceuticals utilize mostly female labor. Women's body parts are idealized, "synergizing" nimble fingers, 20/20 eyesight, and hardy bodies . . . women are preferred for all the stereotypical reasons: lower labor costs, traditional feminine skills, manual dexterity, more productivity, greater tolerance of and better performance in repetitive and monotonous tasks, reliability, patience, low expectations, lack of employment alternatives, a willingness to put up with dead-end jobs, higher voluntary quitting rates . . . young, single, childless women are preferred [because] . . . employers are often reluctant to pay generous maternity ben-

efits; single women are considered more flexible and reliable workers than married women—free to work shift hours and with lower rates of absenteeism caused by child-care problems.[27]

Tolentino goes on to discuss the marketing of Western consumer products and sexual cultural styles to the young single women working in EPZs in the Philippines. Filipino EPZ factories hold cosmetic and Western-style clothing bazaars, beauty contests, and bonuses in the form of gift certificates to department stores that foster the "production of desire for consumer goods" by these young women. The promotion of such consumer goods is part of the development of a Western self-conception and consumer culture among workers, the promotion of cosmopolitan standards of beauty, and a sexualization of the industrial workplace. Tolentino argues that EPZs with their youthful female Western-gazing, consumer-oriented labor force, become locations of culture imbued with a cosmology of global and local sexual desirability where the "still-young female body . . . remains anchored in dreams of modernity, making it refurbishable as a [mail-order] bride transportable to first-world sites."[28]

Making the connection between young Third World women working in Export Processing Zones and interested Western men living and working in industrial countries, or for that matter, between any two individuals separated by culture and geography, has become easier in the modern global system. The romantic pen pal, long-distance arranged marriage, and mail-order bride are longstanding institutions sexually linking individuals across national and international space. Globalization, however, with its facilitated international travel, cosmopolitan cultural production, and improved high speed communications, especially via the Internet, has expanded the number of opportunities for international romantic and sexual contact.

The Internet has made ethnosexual communication quick, easy, and accessible, and it serves as an advertising medium for world sex. Thus, it is not only actual international travel to sexual consumer and sex tourist destinations that spurs the sexual commodification of self and Others around the world, virtual ethnosexual encounters are also part of the cosmopolitan sexual consumer experience. In Chapter 1 I quoted a posting of frequently asked questions from "Soulmates International," a website advising Western men interested in meeting Filipina women. Such websites abound on the Internet, and they are not only dedicated to the mail order bride trade.[29] For instance, the *World Sex Guide* is designed to provide virtual or actual travelers with eyewitness accounts and "reviews" of sex tourist destinations, services, experiences, and providers, and it is only one among many outfitters of global ethnosexual expeditions and flights of ethnosexual fantasy.[30]

Ethnosexual consumers and providers link the West with the East, the North with the South. Brides-by-mail and sex tourism operations represent libidinal commercial spaces where dreams of improving one's own and one's family's fortunes connect with desires for sexual encounters with exotic others. These real and phantasmic exchanges are not unique to Third World settings; ethnosexual frontiers are not only found in the economic borderlands of developing economies designated for investment, enterprise, or export processing. Globalization, especially the migration of workers in pursuit of higher wages, has established ethnosexual beachheads in the developed world as well. Ethnosexual frontiers can be found in industrial countries in factories and agricultural production sites using imported workers, in the growing service sectors of postindustrial economies, and in the informal, grey, or shadow economies of developed countries.

FIRST WORLD ETHNOSEXUAL FRONTIERS

Some sectors in industrial economies have long histories of employing immigrant adult and child labor (e.g., the garment industry, agriculture, domestic service). Gender stratification and sexual exploitation are not new in such work settings, although population growth and economic restructuring has multiplied potential and real workplace problems. Research on recent patterns of immigrant employment in the United States documents the movement of foreign-born workers into businesses and sectors formerly staffed by working class native-born Americans, for example, in food processing, meatpacking, and the service sector.[31] Zaragosa Vargas reports that "Latinos, Blacks, and women are replacing white native-born males as the mainstay of the U.S. labor force. About 2.3 million Latinos have entered the workforce since 1980 and represent one-fifth of the total increase in the nation's jobs."[32]

Language differences, gender hierarchies, and immigration status can combine to create sexually troubled workplaces for many immigrant, especially women, workers. For instance, in February 1999 Tanimura & Antle (T&A), one of the largest lettuce growers and distributors in the United States, reached a $1.9 million settlement with current and former employees who charged California and Arizona T&A supervisors with sexual harassment and retaliation against those who complained. In an announcement following the settlement, William R. Tamayo, an attorney for the U.S. Equal Employment Opportunity Commission commented, "Agribusiness is California's largest industry and employs a million workers each year . . . the Commission has made sexual harassment in the agricultural industry a priority for civil rights enforcement . . . ensuring that these workers, particularly immigrant women who don't speak English, are protected."[33]

Encounters between local employers and migrating global workers are not confined to the public commercial sector. International workers labor in developed countries in job sites out of public view, primarily in private homes, where immigrant women are hired as domestic workers—housekeepers, nannies, and au pairs. While some women always have hired other women to do their housework and childcare, researchers note that as more and more First World women have entered the workplace, growing numbers of Third World women have entered the domestic spaces they vacate to clean their houses and to care for their children, husbands, and elderly parents. Pierrette Hondagneu-Sotelo labels this large-scale movement of mainly women workers the "new world domestic order."[34] The migration of women from their own homes into the homes of others initiates a sequence of female migration from home to home and country to country that Hondagneu-Sotelo calls "transnational motherhood"[35] and Arlie Hochschild describes as a global "nanny chain." Nanny chains have at least three links connecting women and children around the world:

> A typical global care chain might work something like this: An older daughter from a poor family in a third world country cares for her siblings (the first link in the chain) while her mother works as a nanny caring for the children of a nanny migrating to a first world country (the second link) who, in turn, cares for the child of a family in a rich country (the final link).[36]

Rhacel Parrenas interviewed eighty-two Filipina domestic workers in the United States and Italy, and documented similar patterns of migration and transferred caregiving. She argues that through such care chains globalization supports patriarchy by stabilizing the definition of "women's work" (childcare, housework, eldercare), thereby insulating men from domestic duties.[37]

It is not only to industrial countries such as the United States, Britain, France, or Japan that domestic workers travel, it is also to the wealthy economies of the Pacific Rim and the oil-producing Gulf states. For instance, Tolentino notes that "ninety-eight percent of Filipina workers in Hong Kong are domestic helpers."[38] Enloe reports on the difficult conditions facing some of these women, illustrated by the following statement from a former elementary school teacher from Sri Lanka who took a job as a household maid in Saudi Arabia; she describes the loneliness, fear, and coercion she and others experienced on the job:

> Women have no access to leisure or recreation. Uprooted from their cultural environment and left for themselves in an unknown world under very trying working conditions, they experience psychological traumas. Medical facilities are almost absent. The woman can be compelled to do any kind of work, and many of the women are severely abused physically and sexually.[39]

The individual motivations of migrant women and their host families are mainly economic, but there are also social and personal aspects of many domestic labor arrangements. For host women, foreign nannies and housekeepers permit them to pursue career opportunities that provide personal status and meaning; for migrant women, domestic employment offers a chance for travel, adventure, and sometimes escape from dull or abusive family situations. But individual motivations are not all that is driving the push and pull of migrant domestic labor. Enloe argues that the out-migration of women is the result, in part, of the Third World debt crisis brought on by development loan repayment schedules and interest rates:

> When a woman from Mexico, Jamaica, or the Philippines decides to emigrate in order to make money as a domestic servant she is designing her own international debt politics. She is trying to cope with the loss of earning power and the rise in the cost of living at home by cleaning bathrooms in the country of the bankers.[40]

Grace Chang is more specific and more critical in her analysis of the impact of International Monetary Fund and World Bank structural adjustment policies (SAPs) on women's worklives. SAPs routinely require loan-receiving countries to cut government expenditures, lower wages, open markets to imports and investments, devalue local currency, and privatize state enterprises. Chang argues that

> [W]hile SAPs are ostensibly intended to promote efficiency and sustained economic growth in the "adjusting" country, in reality they function to open up developing nations' economies and peoples to imperialist exploitation. . . . [Because of lowered wages and reductions in social services] SAPs strike women in these nations the hardest, and render them most vulnerable to exploitation, both at home and in the global labor market. . . . [M]any have no other viable option but to leave their families and migrate in search of work.[41]

Ultimately, World Bank and IMF policies either will be vindicated for directing developing countries down the road to riches or further vilified for putting already poor countries on the path to increased poverty. In either case, the current policies of international financial institutions, the structure of the global economy, and shifts in the availability of jobs continue to push and pull laboring "postcolonial geobodies"[42] from one home to another and from one country to another.

It is not only money that changes hands in immigrant domestic labor transactions. Hochschild describes a transfer of affection as well. Participants in the nanny chain supply not only their physical labor, but also their emotional labor. Nannies' emotional energies are shifted from the love and caring of their own families and children to the love and caring of their employers' families and children. The shifting of affective resources continues when the nannies' women employers redirect their own emotional energies from their families to their employers and clients. This second transfer is common since many women who are employed in businesses outside the home work in human services jobs often staffed mainly by women (e.g., as nurses, flight attendants, teachers, personnel managers).[43] These are occupations in which "emotion work" and caring for the emotional needs of clients and employees is central to the job, though such duties seldom are included in job descriptions.[44]

Domestic labor can become the locus of ethnosexual boundary crossing because of the intimacies and opportunities that characterize live-in working arrangements. Migrant women work and frequently reside in private homes where wives often spend long hours away at work. The vulnerability of domestic workers to sexual and nonsexual abuse is documented by researchers, and some cases take on the proportions of international incidents.[45] A number of the cases of sexual abuse and slavery reported by the U.S. State Department and Central Intelligence Agency involved domestic workers or women who were promised domestic work, including women imported to the United States to work for foreign diplomats and embassy personnel.[46]

There is a reciprocal tension in economic and emotional transactions. Many of the Filipina domestic workers interviewed by Parrenas reported that the Americans and Italians who hired them grew emotionally attached and sometimes seemed overly dependent on them:

> If you could have only seen them when I was about to go home. In the airport, all the other passengers were looking over at us because one was hugging me, one was tugging me in the right. They were all crying . . . my employers told me that they had to take the children out so that they would not cry. . . . It was such a big drama when I went on vacation. Then when I was in the Philippines, soon after I landed they started calling me long distance. They asked me when I was coming back and I told them I just got there.

Another worker with a similar experience concluded, "I realized then that it is not advisable for your ward to get too attached to you."[47] As these comments reveal, when East meets West and North meets South, both are affected by the interaction, and both can be reshaped by the process of globalization.

RESITUATING THE LOCAL AND THE GLOBAL

The reciprocal character of interactions between local and global, micro and macro, smaller and larger cultures, institutions, and networks often is lost in discussions of globalization, which privilege the global over the local, assume that globalization erases local distinctions and homogenizes local cultural forms into a global masterframe, and argue that change always flows from the center to the periphery. For instance, T. Rajamoorthy questions the indigenous autonomy of the Malay middle class that emerged during the period of vigorous Malaysian economic growth in the 1980s and early 1990s. This local class formation was made possible by the prosperity that resulted from Malaysia's entry and success in the global economy. Rajamoorthy doubts, however, that this new class of Malaysian citizens reflects an authentic "cosmopolitanism"—a balanced blend of local and global cultures. Instead, he argues that the Malaysian new middle class is a global formation that, despite its protestations, is seduced by and wedded to Western consumer culture:

> Unfortunately, for all its pretensions, the developing middle class in Malaysia can hardly be described as truly cosmopolitan. That illusion is fostered by the fact that it is often Westernized, but this is not the same thing as being genuinely cosmopolitan in outlook. With its almost insatiable appetite for Western consumer culture and its penchant for the latest branded goods, it is more likely to be a conduit for such culture rather than the bearer of genuine cross-cultural values.[48]

There is no mistaking the allure of consumer products around the world. Nevertheless, Shirley Lim and Wimal Dissanayake are skeptical about the totalizing effect of Western products and values in local settings. They challenge top-down understandings of the way global processes affect local cultures and societies. They argue that globalization is not an omnipotent, unidirectional force, and that localization can emerge out of global interactions

> that undermine[s] and eventually obliterate[s] localism . . . [rather] localism and globalism are complicated and mutually constitutive. . . . Localism cannot be projected as a counterpoint to the global but is itself a significant dimension of globalization. Paradoxically, globalization has led to a strengthening of local ties, allegiances, and identity politics within different nation-state formations, even though what may emerge is a version of the local that has been thoroughly reshaped by the global.[49]

While Western, First World states may dominate the production of commercial global culture, the effects of these cultural products on local social and cultural systems are not always predictable. Although global culture and the globalization process in general are deeply influenced by Western technologies, ideologies, and material culture, global cultural products and their meanings are reshaped in local settings, and these changes feed back into the global system. It is not simply "Jihad vs. McWorld," as Benjamin Barber summarizes Third World conservative religiosity versus First World commercial secularism.[50] It is Jihad *and* McWorld where both blend into hybrids that can make their presence felt locally and globally.[51]

Images and imaginings of sex and romance represent one sphere where the synergy and even symmetry between global and local cultures can emerge. Sometimes these erotic and amorous hybrids can take the form of surprising, even jarring (at least to Western sensibilities) mixtures of tastes and designs. Louisa Schein describes the wedding of an educated local young couple that took place in 1993 in the market town of Xijiang in the rural

Miao mountains of Guizhou, China—the bride was an elementary school teacher and the groom was the manager of a state-run dry goods outlet:

> The guests are arriving bearing shoulder poles of gifts—pork, sticky rice, homebrewed liquor, quilts, fabric. The bride stays in the nuptial chamber . . . and makes up her face with powder, blush, lipstick, eyeliner, then dresses in Miao finery. . . . Just then a group of city friends arrive, classmates from the days when the couple attended high school in the prefecture seat. . . . [They bring] the *piece de resistance*—a gift borne on shoulder poles. It is an ostentatious yard-long wall hanging behind glass—a photographic decoration slated for the walls of the nuptial chamber. The picture, in a bizarre juxtaposition with or even upstaging of the bride, is of a blonde model in a hot pink g-string bikini lying atop a snazzy racing car. Lovingly, the hanging is given front center placement among the other gifts . . . on display in the nuptial chamber for guests to review. Upon completion of her ethnic adornment, the bride poses with the thing.[52]

Schein tries to make sense of this interjection of a crude cosmopolitan, global image into a traditional, local scene. She speculates on the possible multiple meanings attached to white women in China in the 1990s—as signifiers of "self-possessed independence, . . . or fashionable models of bourgeois consumer expertise, or sultry practitioners of erotic extremity," or as capitalist tools, that is, marketing devices: *"the white woman sells."*[53]

This facsimile of the white woman hanging in Chinese sensual space transmogrifies into a more corporeal manifestation when "the Westerner [is] resituated, with fleshy reality, within the Chinese body" through plastic surgery to widen eyes and raise noses or through other less permanent uses of fashion and cosmetics. Are such Chinese internalizations of the white woman actually local capitulations to global (Western) standards of beauty and desirability? Or do they represent the indigenization and appropriation of what once had been alien and unattainable—the local Chinese consumption of the global white woman? Or are they somewhere in between—a kind of hybrid cultural formation, a fusion of local and global cosmologies of beauty, gender, and sexuality, a polyglot narration of a local/global, "glocal" self that bespeaks neither dominance nor submission, neither colonization nor subversion?[54]

GLOCAL DANCE PARTNERS

In a study of changes in sexual culture during the period of market reform in Shanghai from 1979 to 1996, James Farrer poses similar questions about the place of the local and the global in the production of sexualized youth culture in urban China.[55] One site Farrer explores is Shanghai disco dance clubs in the mid-1990s.[56] Dancing at the disco clubs involved gendered sexual performances (men's athletic break dancing, women's sensual "voluptuous dancing"), which dancers saw as a form of participation in a global dance culture, where foreignness represented the global and, as such, was an especially valued and essential commodity:

> A foreign (often Hong Kong or overseas Chinese) DJ is de rigueur at the biggest discos. International music dominates. . . . The lyrics of the dance songs are typically in English, and Shanghai favorites included the Village People's "YMCA" and Ace of Base's "All That She Wants." . . . [T]he disco is a deliberately engineered space of "foreign" sexual imagery, which Chinese youth appropriate to experiment with alternative sexual styles and sexual self-images. Actual foreigners are props in the exploration of sexual desirability and emotional poise in a global sexual and social marketplace.[57]

Despite the fact that these dance clubs provided opportunities for global self-envisioning, experimental sexual expression, and the occasional ethnosexual encounter, Farrer finds that sexual norms in everyday Shanghai society have remained conservative by many Western standards. For instance, he reports that in a 1990 survey, "80 percent of Shanghai men and women still agreed that 'a woman's chastity was more important than her life.'"[58] This raises questions about the extent of penetration of the global into the local, and whether global culture is mainly confined to symbolic enactments in designated spaces that are segregated from local daily life.

However momentary or circumscribed, the global gaze of participants in the Shanghai disco scene stands in contrast to the more staid local look of another Shanghai dance culture also described by Farrer. He compares the hip, urban disco youth dance scene and its narcissistic, stagy performance-oriented "culture of desirability" with Shanghai's older, more established dance halls and their sociable, formal interaction-oriented "culture of desire." In the dance halls "mostly middle-aged and married factory workers make time in the afternoon to dance romantically in dimly lit warehouses with other married people."[59] Disco dance clubs, Farrer argues, are shaped by and linked to the global, while the dance halls comprise a strictly local scene, albeit one in which Chinese couples waltz and foxtrot Western-style across the floor—spectral reflections of an earlier global moment reinscribed in local dance halls and reinterpreted by the movements and the meanings of the dancers.[60]

Even as Shanghai disco is distant in global and local time and space from Shanghai ballroom dancing, it also distinguishes itself from other Western youth dance cultures, such as "raves," that are conceived as sites of rebellion. As Farrer notes, "Chinese disco is a mass cultural form which represents itself as a site of globality rather than as a site of 'alternative' or 'authentic' sub-cultural difference."[61] Chinese disco is a means to revel in the global, not rebel against it; a way to participate in, not opt out of an imagined global community.

Chinese disco's cultural participation in and consumption of globalization also stands in contrast to another hybrid dance form that emerges out of globalization processes, but that is used to create locality, not to celebrate globality. "Ethnic dance" is one of many borrowed and revised cultural forms (including food, music, art, rituals, celebrations, and customs) used by global migrant groups to recuperate cultural identities and establish ethnic boundaries in host societies. Sanjay Roy describes Indian classical dancing in Britain as one instance of the blending of Eastern and Western cultural forms by South Indian artists and performers in Britain. Through dance and other ethnic performances, immigrants and their descendants construct "imaginary homelands," establishing a home away from home. Roy argues that Indian classical dancing is a cultural practice that provides Indian immigrants with "a positive sense of belonging, not only by symbolising a valorised heritage to which they can lay claim, but also by providing occasions at which they can meet in an 'Indian' context."[62] Roy quotes British-Indian choreographer and dancer Shobana Jeyasingh discussing hybridity in her own work, Making of Maps:

> I suppose the first thing I thought about when I made Making of Maps was the question of heritage. . . . For me, my heritage is a mix of David Bowie, Purcell, Shelley and Anna Pavlova, as it has been mixed as subtly as a samosa has mixed itself into the English cuisine.[63]

Roy defines artists such as Jeyasingh and their South Indian audiences as "inexcluded" since their consciousness and positionality locates them both inside and outside the British nation and culture.[64] In fact, all of these dance scenes—disco and dance halls in Shanghai, raves and Indian classical dance in Britain—are situated in liminal spaces, betwixt-and-between local, national, and global cultures, signifying systems, and social, economic, political, and sexual structures. They are enacted in class borderlands, inside ethnosexual frontiers, and on the edges of multiple meaning systems. These dance scenes, like all artistic, literary, music, and cultural scenes, unite their participants by emphasizing their internal similarities in the face of external differentness. Highlighting commonalities among sometimes quite diverse scene insiders creates a sense of shared culture, and distinguishes scene insiders from mainstream outsiders. Cultural scenes often are marked by insider oppositional cultures of desire and desirability. Their members are united by libidinal bonds and networks of attraction and desire that set them apart from various classed, raced, aged outsiders. These bonds not only create internal solidarities, but can build bridges between local scenes and geographically distant related scenes, thereby creating glocal movements and milieux.[65]

Dance floors and stages are not only locations where dancing enacts the global or reenacts the local, reconstructing individual selves and communities in the process. The staging of dance also is used to represent cultures and places to outsiders—both intranational and international. In some cases dance serves as a constitutive element in the creation of an exotic, ethnosexualized tourist attraction. For example, Yayori Matsui discusses of the marketing of indigenous culture through the medium of dance and the sexualization of "traditional" dancers. Wulai, a tourist spot southeast of Taipei, Taiwan, is visited by half a million mainly urban Asian tourists each year.

> The exotic, beautiful, fair-skinned young girls of an Atayal village nearby are used by the tourist industry as an added attraction. . . . Dropping in at the Atayal Aborigines' Culture Theatre, a stop on the Wulai tourism route, I saw that the hall was filled with Japanese and Korean tourists. Young Atayal girls, dressed in gorgeous traditional costumes, filled the stage, dancing and singing. . . . Mo Na-neng [a poet and aboriginal movement leader] . . . complained to me, "In order to attract tourists, the dancers' skirts have been shortened to make them appear sexy, and the music has been arranged discotheque-style. It has become a show rather than an introduction to the traditional culture of the aborigines."[66]

Dancing exotic Other women have long been a mainstay of travel narratives and tourist destinations. For instance, Jane Desmond describes the visual images that accompanied and complimented written descriptions of the exotic delights of Hawaii, especially those seen in turn-of-the-century postcards and three-dimensional "stereograph" photographs:

> One example, titled "A Hula Dancing Girl," was released some time before 1900. Sold as part of the Keystone "South Sea Islands and Hawaii" set, this stereocard features an oval photo of a young, slender woman in a raffia ["grass"] skirt, posed bare-breasted on the beach. . . . Her hair is pinned up loosely, and she stands, hands on hips, left foot extended—a position apparently made up by the photographer to indicate "dance."[67]

The card's caption further articulates but also moderates its visual message:

> [T]he hula is the national dance. It is a love dance . . . The dancing was done quite as much with the body as with the limbs. There were convulsions of the chest and the entire body . . . No matter how much such a scene was enjoyed by the natives, it was too intense to prove anything but disappointing to civilized people.[68] describes the place of the hula in historical and contemporary tourism in Hawaii: "Long before they disembark from the plane, Hawai'i's visitors have encountered the image of the 'hula girl.' "[69]

Standards of civilization apparently have deteriorated in the last century. Desmond reports that hula dancing lessons are now a widely marketed tourist experience enjoyed by non-Hawaiians. Visitors to the islands no longer are limited to passive, voyeuristic consumption of the hula; they can become hula dancers themselves. Haoles can learn to hula by paying for lessons, taking free classes offered to tourists in shopping malls, or by purchasing "how-to-hula" videotapes to take with them and practice in the privacy of their own homes.[70]

CONSUMING PASSION

The design and marketing of dance as an ethnosexual tourist commodity raises the larger issue of global consumerism in linking ethnicity and sexuality. More specifically, just what is the role of the sexual consumer and consumer culture in the production of ethnosexual frontiers in the global system? How do ethnicity and sexuality combine to shape global consumer demand and products and contribute to the sexualized self-commodification of local actors and markets?

Scholars studying globalization have noted the spread of consumerism as a global value, the desire for Western consumer products as a common feature of the "global village," and the consumer as a unifying force in the construction of a global concept of citizenship.[71] Diane Richardson argues that there has been "a shift in recent years to defining citizenship in terms of consumerism. This representation of the citizen as a consumer is related to the emphasis on individual choice and commercialism associated with the free market economy."[72] The consumer-oriented approach to human relations and human rights (rights to access to a free market and consumer goods) has found its way into the arenas of economic development and the marketing of local human products (culture, labor, sexuality) as a means for economic growth.[73] For instance, in their study of the Thai "economic miracle," Ryan Bishop and Lillian Robinson comment that "shopping increasingly [is] understood as the moral equivalent of sightseeing for the tourist."[74] As we have seen in earlier chapters, for many tourists Thai sexuality is both a major sight to see and commodity to consume.

The spread of consumer culture has resulted not only in increased distribution and demand for Western consumer products globally, but it has had other important consequences for understanding sex and globalization. Western marketing around the world communicates not only information about products, but conveys implicit messages about the kinds of people who consume these products, messages about their modernity and their desirability. As is well documented, sex sells. Thus, the marketing of Western products not only puts sexuality in the service of selling goods, it peddles a specific vision of Western sexuality, lifestyle, and culture to global consumers. The globalization of Western consumer culture is not just the sale of consumer goods in non-Western markets, nor is it simply the generation of demand for Western consumer goods. It promotes the sexualization of consumption and the consumption of sexuality. It markets a libidinal consciousness, an erotic self- and other-imagining, and a particular type of (Western) sexualized world view. For instance, in his discussion of Filipino Export Processing Zones, Tolentino links the Filipino mail order bride market to the sexual and romantic commodification of working Filipinas.[75] As these women compete to win beauty contests and department store shopping sprees, and as they spend their EPZ wages on cosmetics and Western-style clothing, they are reenvisioning, and are being encouraged to view, themselves as potential erotic products for sale and rescue in a global marketplace trading in images of love everlasting, sexual bliss, and the happy family.

Carla Freeman's study of women workers in the offshore information processing industry in the Caribbean identifies a similar connection between women working in the modern economy and the reworking of their conceptions of cosmopolitan femininity and their place in it. "High tech and high heels" go hand in hand for many women "informatics" workers who become part of a local workplace cultural system seen to reflect global modernity, one that combines labor with "lifestyle" and exerts pressure to "dress hard":

> To meet the complex desires and demands of "professional fashion" that are prescribed by company dress codes and, more subtly by peer pressure, women enter into other production/consumption "shifts" beyond their formal workdays. Before and after they work as data processors and on weekends and holidays, they spend their time designing, producing, and purchasing the clothes and accessories that create the "professional feminine" look they and their employers ascribe to informatics. As such, their pink-collar identities are tied not only to their informatics jobs but also to their shopping trips overseas, [and] their clothing design courses.[76]

Many of the women Freeman interviewed dressed for success and were rewarded for their efforts. Margaret was promoted to shift manager in the data processing company where she worked:

> [W]hen we realize that our people are not dressing the way we think they should, we speak with them; we have even gone as far as to ask persons to go back home and change because their attire was not properly suited for the work atmosphere . . . you're governed by a particular code . . . you are being watched. And not only that but, because there are so many young persons, they usually talk about you if you don't look good.[77]

Freeman herself felt the pressure to improve her own appearance, though presumably not in an effort to become Western or modern:

> It seemed both ironic and fitting that fashion and dress played . . . an important role in carrying out my fieldwork. Unexpectedly "skirt suits" and

heels (though I wore simpler, less highly styled suits and lower heels than those that most of the data entry operators wore) became part of my every-day experience, and self-conscious awareness of my own appearance and "ap-propriateness" in dress became a heightened preoccupation.[78]

Leslie Salzinger found similar workplace formal dress codes interfaced with informal expectations linking dressing up according to a certain glocal aesthetic with getting ahead in export-processing factories or *maquilas* in Juarez, Mexico. The clothing worn on the factory floor designated gender and rank (yellow tunics for new workers, light blue for women, dark blue for men, red for female group chiefs); added to these regimented uniforms were the accoutrements of modernity: "lipstick, mascara; eyeliner; rouge; high heels; miniskirts; identity badges."[79] Both Freeman's and Salzinger's work illustrate the ways in which the global and the local work together to promote self-reinvention and self-commodification.[80]

CONCLUSION

The creation of a global consumer culture involves the spread of a whole sys-tem of ideas about what it means to be female and male members of the mod-ern global village, albeit as variously raced and nationalized women and men. Local consumer cultures and identities are shaped by, but also are different from those in the global masterframe. They are both imperialized and indi-genized, subject and sovereign. Global and local consumer cultures are eth-nosexualized as East and West, South and North gaze toward one another through lenses colored by "modern" consumerism. Western sexual com-modification (e.g., the white woman in the string bikini, the Marlboro man, disco and rock 'n' roll, European and American fashion and fashion models) sells a racial, national, and sexual style at home and abroad. Although local and global ethnosexual consumer cultures are a blend of East and West, North and South, First, Second, Third, and Fourth worlds, the power and the loca-tion of the originating message should not be underestimated. Despite the rainbow of skintones in its marketing ads, there is no mistaking the domi-nance of the color white in the United Colors of Benetton.[81]

Although it often goes unacknowledged, sexuality both underpins and un-dermines a variety of processes and institutions in both local and global sys-tems. Sexuality supports gendered, classed, raced, and aged power relations and privileges, and lubricates their smooth operation and reproduction. Sexuality also subverts these same processes and institutions when sexual practices vio-late rules and assumptions about heteronormativity and heteroconventionality. The accelerated, increasing international movement of bodies and business as-sociated with globalization and the global spread of Western consumer culture extend beyond popular culture performance spaces or postindustrial production sites and reach into people's daily lives, interpersonal relationships, and their images of themselves . . . and Others. As globalization links populations in denser, faster, and more complex ways, the political economy of desire will continue to complement and complicate the constantly unfolding global order.

NOTES

1. Wilde was Irish, born in Dublin in 1854, but he was a British citizen as Ireland did not gain its independence from Britain until 1922.

2. See Anthony P. Cohen, "Boundaries of Consciousness, Consciousness of Boundaries," in *The Anthropology of Ethnicity: Beyond "Ethnic Groups and Boundaries,"* ed. Hans Vermeulen and Cora Govers (Amsterdam: Spinhuis, 1994), 70.

3. Ian Buruma and Avishai Margalit, "Occidentalism," *New York Review of Books,* January 17, 2002:4–7, 4; for a description of a much earlier Oriental view of the West, see Frank Dikotter, *The Discourse of Race in Modern China* (London: Hurst and Company, 1992):

> Yu Zhengxie (1775–1840), a major scholar noted for his strong interest in research and his liberal ideas, [who] observed the following differences between the [Western] foreigner and the Chinese:
>
> * Foreign devils had four lobes in the lungs, Chinese had six.
> * Foreign devils had only four chambers in the heart, Chinese had seven.
> * The liver of the foreign devil was located at the right side of the heart, the Chinese liver was situated at the left.
> * The foreign devil had four testicles, Chinese had two.
>
> . . . .Driven by the vigour of his four testicles, the satyr-like foreigner was relentless in his pursuit of sensual pleasures. Anti-Christian leaflets spread the idea that Christians practised sodomy with their fathers and brothers and fornicated with their mothers and sisters. (43)

My thanks to Gwynne Jenkins, Departments of Anthropology and Women's Studies, University of Kansas, for bringing to my attention this early articulation of occidentalism.

4. See Shahin Gerami, *Women and Fundamentalism: Islam and Christianity* (New York: Garland Publishing Company, 1996); for an interesting comparison of parallel criticisms of America and the West by American Christian fundamentalists Jerry Falwell and Pat Robertson and Saudi Muslim fundamentalist Osama bin Laden, see http://funnystrange.com/quiz/index.asp.

5. Ibid.

6. Ibid., 4–5; see also, Melani McAlister, *Epic Encounters: Culture, Media, and U.S. Interests in the Middle East, 1945–2000* (Berkeley: University of California Press, 2001).

7. See Rashid, *Taliban,* especially Appendix 1 for "a sample of Taliban decrees relating to women," 217–19.

8. Jacalyn D. Harden, "The Enterprise of Empire: Race, Class, Gender, and Japanese National Identity," in *The Gender/Sexuality Reader: Culture, History, Political Economy,* ed. Roger N. Lancaster and Micaela di Leonardo (New York: Routledge, 1997), 487.

9. Ibid., 488.

10. Ibid.

11. See Christopher Chase-Dunn, Yuio Kawano, and Benjamin D. Brewer, "Trade Globalization since 1795: Waves of Integration in the World-System," *American Sociological Review* 65 (2000): 77–95; Charles Tilly, "Globalization Threatens Labor's Rights, *International Labor and Working-Class History* 47 (1995): 1–23; Ankie Hoogvelt, *Globalization and the Postcolonial World: The New Political Economy of Development* (Baltimore: Johns Hopkins University Press, 1997); Robert K. Schaeffer, *Understanding Globalization: The Social Consequences of Political, Economic, and Environmental Change* (Lanham, MD: Rowman and Littlefield, 1997); Randall D. Germain, *Globalization and Its Critics: Perspectives from Political Economy* (New York: St. Martin's Press, 2000).

12. Stuart Hall, "The Local and the Global," in *Culture, Globalization and the World System*, ed. Anthony D. King (London: Macmillan, 1991), 19–40; we can update Hall's now decade-old list to include the Internet and telecommunications (faxes, cellphones, high speed information transfer technologies) advances.

13. For a discussion of this and other aspects of globalization, see Robert J. Antonio and Alessandro Bonanno, "A New Global Capitalism? From 'Americanism and Fordism' to 'Americanization-Globalization,'" *American Studies* 41 (2000): 33–78; for an analysis of globalization as a form of "empire" or "global order," see Michael Hardt and Antonio Negri, *Empire* (Cambridge, MA: Harvard University Press, 2000).

14. The global system, thus, is not only central to the formation of new states, globalization tends to promote the development of ethnic differences inside states; see Horowitz, *Ethnic Groups in Conflict;* Susan Olzak, *The Dynamics of Ethnic Competition and Conflict* (Stanford: Stanford University Press, 1992); T. Rajamoorthy, "Globalization and Citizenship in Malaysia," in *Globalization and Citizenship in the Asia-Pacific,* ed. Alastair Davidson and Kathleen Weekley (New York: St. Martin's Press, 1999), 87–93; the strength or weakness of ethnic boundaries also can be affected by global processes; for instance, Takeyuki (Gaku) Tsuda describes a waxing and waning of ethnic boundaries surrounding Japanese immigrants in Brazil during the twentieth century—changes associated with Japan's position in various global developments (World War II, rise in the global economy, Brazil's economic crisis)—return immigration back to Japan; Takeyuki (Gaku) Tsuda,"Japanese Emigration to Brazil," *Ethnic and Racial Studies* 24 (2001): 412–32.

15. Fredrik Barth, "Enduring and Emerging Issues in the Analysis of Ethnicity," in *The Anthropology of Ethnicity*, 11–32, 22. Other researchers report similar sexual tensions facing immigrant families, see M. W. Buitelaar, "Negotiating the Rules of Chaste Behaviour: Re-Interpretations of the Symbolic Complex of Virginity by Young Women of Moroccan Descent in The Netherlands," *Ethnic and Racial Studies* 25(2002): 426–89.

16. Further, in both Oslo and Cleveland ethnic/racial enclaves developed because of "chain migration," where families and communities leave home cities, regions, and countries and reassemble as families and communities in host cities, regions, and countries; this comparison is not intended to erase differences in the history of race relations in the United States and Norway, but it is to point out the importance of sexuality in defending color lines—both by dominant resident groups and by migrant groups.

17. Most of the twenty-one million residents of Taiwan originally are from or descended from people from the Chinese mainland who have migrated to Taiwan for

hundreds of years; there are approximately 300,000 indigenous Taiwanese peoples, however, including the Ami, Atayal, Paiwan, Bunun, Rukai, Puyuma, Tsou, Saisia, Yami (Da-Wu), and Pinpu people; see Leslie E. Sponsel, *Endangered Peoples of Southeast and East Asia: Struggles to Survive and Thrive* (Westport, CT: Greenwood Press, 2000); http://www.indigenouspeople.org/natlit/taiwan.htm

18. Summarized from several cases in Shen, "Crossing the Taiwan Strait."

19. One U.S. dollar was approximately thirty-three Taiwanese dollars in 2001.

20. Hsiu-hua Shen, "Dangerous Liaisons: Representations of Chinese Women across the Taiwan Strait," paper presented at the annual meeting of the American Sociological Association, Anaheim, August, 2001.

21. Sexual liaisons in Shanghai are not restricted to relationships between Taiwanese businessmen and Chinese women; the political economy of desire in China's special economic zones make many Chinese women both inexpensive and willing partners in ethnosexual exchanges with men from around the world, ibid.; see also Anna M. Han, "Holding Up More Than Half the Sky," in *Global Critical Race Feminism: An International Reader*, ed. Adrien Katherine Wing (New York: New York University Press, 2000), 392–408.

22. Shen, "Crossing the Taiwan Strait."

23. Shu-mei Shih, "Gender and a New Geopolitics of Desire: The Seduction of Mainland Women in Taiwan and Hong Kong Media," *Signs* 23 (1998): 287–319.

24. Ibid., 315.

25. Enloe, *Bananas, Beaches, and Bases,* 142; ethnosexual aspects of political and economic enterprises are not new to the contemporary global scene. In a historical study of nineteenth-century colonial-era agricultural plantations in Sumatra, Ann Stoler reports that a combination of sexual harassment by foremen and low wages paid to Javanese women contract workers led many women into prostitution serving a mainly Chinese male worker clientele; Stoler, *Capitalism and Confrontation in Sumatra's Plantation Belt, 1870–1979.*

26. Saskia Sassen, *Globalization and Its Discontents* (New York: The New Press, 1998), 111; see also Bulbeck, *Re-Orienting Western Feminisms,* 167–80; Silvia Pedraza, "Women and Migration: The Social Consequences of Gender," *Annual Review of Sociology* 17 (1991): 303–25.

27. Rolando B. Tolentino, "Bodies, Letters, Catalogs: Filipinas in Transnational Space," in *Transnational Asia Pacific: Gender, Culture, and the Public Sphere,* ed. S. Goek-Lin Lilm, L. E. Smith, W. Dissanayake (Urbana: University of Illinois Press, 1999), 47–48.

28. Ibid., 48; see also Homi Bhabha, *The Location of Culture* (New York: Routledge, 1994).

29. There are dozens of such sites, including: "The Pacific Century Club" (http://www.pacificcentury.com/), "Euro-Japanese Virtual Encounters" (http://www.daopian.com/ejve/), "Get Married Now" (http://www.getmarriednow.com/), "Asia Friend Finder" (http://asiafriendfinder.com/welcome/), and "Brides by Mail" (http://www.bridesbymail.com/).

30. http://www.worldsexguide.com; those visiting this and other such websites should be forewarned, some of the postings are sexually explicit and many readers will find them offensive because of their sexual and their racial, ethnic, and nationalist content; they are quite revealing, however, of ethnosexuality as a global phe-

nomenon; the world sex guide site is not frequently updated, but there are many others for the interested ethnosex consumer.

31. See Colleen Greer, "Ethnicity—It Won't Just Go Away: The Resilience of Ethnicity through Practices of Assimilation: Lao Refugees in a Midwest Community," Ph.D. diss., University of Kansas, 1998; for a recent review of the literature on transnational immigration, see Peter Kivisto, "Theorizing Transnational Immigration: A Critical Review of Current Efforts," *Ethnic and Racial Studies* 24 (2001): 549–77.

32. Zaragosa Vargas, "Rank and File: Historical Perspectives on Latino/a Workers in the U.S.," in *The Latino Studies Reader: Culture, Economy, and Society* (Malden, MA: Blackwell, 1998), 248.

33. Equal Employment Opportunity Commission, news release, February 23, 1999; see http://www.eeoc.gov/press/2-23-99.html

34. Pierrette Hondagneu-Sotelo, Domestica *Immigrant Workers Cleaning and Caring in the Shadows of Affluence* (Berkeley: University of California Press, 2001), 3–28; see also Mary Romero, *Maid in the U.S.A.* (New York: Routledge, 1992).

35. Ibid., 24.

36. Arlie Russell Hochschild, "The Nanny Chain: Mothers Minding Other Mothers' Children," *The American Prospect*, January 3, 2000: 32–36; my thanks to my colleague Norman R. Yetman for bringing this research to my attention.

37. Rhacel Salazar Parrenas, "The Global Servants: (Im)Migrant Filipina Domestic Workers in Rome and Los Angeles," Ph.D. diss., University of California, Berkeley, 1998, 121–25; see also Rhacel Salazar Parrenas, *The Global Servants: (Im)migrant Filipina Domestic Workers in Rome and Los Angeles* (Stanford: Stanford University Press, 2001).

38. Tolentino, "Bodies, Letters, Catalogs," 51.

39. Enloe, *Bananas, Beaches, and Bases*, 193.

40. Ibid., 185.

41. Grace Chang, *Disposable Domestics: Immigrant Women Workers in the Global Economy* (Cambridge, MA: South End Press, 2000); see also Kathryn Kopinak, *Desert Capitalism: Maquiladoras in North America's Western Industrial Corridor* (Tucson: University of Arizona Press, 1996).

42. Tolentino, "Bodies, Letters, Catalogs," 51.

43. A transfer of what she refers to as "surplus love," borrowing from Marx's notion of surplus labor (Hochschild, "The Nanny Chain," 34); Parrenas reports that many immigrant nannies and surrogate caregivers resist investing emotional energy in their emotion work and resent employers' demands for their affection (Parrenas, "The Global Servant," 272–323).

44. See Arlie Hochschild, *The Managed Heart: Commodification of Human Feeling* (Berkeley: University of California Press, 1983).

45. For instance, see Parrenas's discussion of the murder of Delia Maga and the execution for her murder of Flor Contemplacion, both of whom were Filipina domestic workers in Singapore (Parrenas, *The Global Servants*, 414–16).

46. Richard, "International Trafficking in Women to the United States," 28.

47. Parrenas, "The Global Servant," 275; see also Chang, *Disposable Domestics*.

48. Rajamoorthy, "Globalization and Citizenship in Malaysia," 94; see also Timothy Burke, *Lifebuoy Men, Lux Women: Commodification, Consumption, and Cleanliness in Modern Zimbabwe* (Durham: Duke University Press, 1996).

49. Shirley Geok-Lin Lim and Wimal Dissanayake, "Introduction," in *Transnational Asia Pacific*, 4.

50. Benjamin Barber, *Jihad vs. McWorld: How Globalism and Tribalism Are Reshaping the World* (New York: Ballantine Books, 1996); my thanks to Robert Antonio, Sociology Department, University of Kansas, for pointing out the relevancy of this book to my work.

51. All of this is not to underestimate the power of the First World's cultural and commercial presence in the global system; for instance, Frank et al., argue that certain identities, activities, and movements inside states are more likely to be shaped by global processes than others, in particular those tied to the notion of the "nation-state"; they posit that environmentalism and environmental protection and preservation activities and institutions (e.g., national parks, environmental legislation and ministries) inside states are, at heart, global in nature: "when it comes to the natural environment, important aspects of the nation-state form appear to be constituted externally, in the global society" (David John Frank, Ann Hironaka, and Evan Schofer, "The Nation-State and the Natural Environment over the Twentieth Century," *American Sociological Review* 65 (2000): 96–116, 108; see also John Meyer, John Boli, George M. Thomas, and Francisco O. Ramirez, "World Society and the Nation-State," *American Journal of Sociology* 103 (1997): 144–81.

52. Louisa Schein, "The Consumption of Color and the Politics of White Skin in Post-Mao China," in Lancaster and di Leonardo, *The Gender/Sexuality Reader*, 473.

53. Ibid., 475–76; for a discussion of Japanese women's "Occidental longings" for Western societies and peoples whom Karen Kelsky reports they see as less traditionally constraining and sexist, see Karen Kelsky, *Women on the Verge: Japanese Women, Western Dreams* (Durham: Duke University Press, 2001).

54. "Glocal" is a neologism generally used by scholars and those working in international business to refer to places or practices reflecting a meeting or blending of the local and the global; an example would be creole languages in which local languages are combined with an outside, often colonial or imperial language such as French or English; for a discussion of the terms *glocal* and *glocality*, see, Arif Dirlik, "Globalism and the Politics of Place," *Development* 41 (1998); for a discussion of glocal sexual hybridity, see Bulbeck, *Re-Orienting Western Feminisms*, 160–65.

55. James C. Farrer, " 'Opening Up': Sex and the Market in Shanghai," (Ph.D. diss., University of Chicago, 1998; see also James C. Farrer, *Opening Up: Youth Sex Culture and Market Reform in Shanghai* (Chicago: University of Chicago Press, 2002).

56. James Farrer, "Dancing through the Market Transition: Disco and Dance Hall Sociability in Shanghai," in *The Consumer Revolution in Urban China*, ed. Deborah S. Davis (Berkeley: University of California Press, 2000), 226–49.

57. James Farrer, "Disco 'Super-Culture': Consuming Foreign Sex in the Chinese Disco," *Sexualities* 2 (1999): 147–66, 155, 159.

58. Farrer, " 'Opening Up,' " 36; Erwin reports a similar disjuncture between global culture and local practice in Shanghai's private and public telephone "hotlines" (*rexian dianhua*) which proliferated during the 1990s facilitated by an expansion of telecommunications technology; she found that conversation on the hotlines was almost exclusively devoted to sexuality and family matters, which opened wide a new "discursive space" formerly repressed by Communist Party policies, but which Er-

win reports was not paralleled by equally revolutionary changes in behavior; see Kathleen Erwin, "Heart-to-Heart, Phone-to-Phone: Family Values, Sexuality, and the Politics of Shanghai's Advice Hotlines," in *The Consumer Revolution in Urban China*, 145–70; see also, Harriet Evans, *Women and Sexuality in China: Female Sexuality and Gender since 1949* (New York: Continuum, 1997).

59. Farrer, "Dancing through the Market Transition," 227.

60. Another interesting local Chinese dance scene, public tango dancing to recorded music in national monument parks, is briefly described by Richard Kraus, "Public Monuments and Private Pleasures in the Parks of Nanjing: A Tango in the Ruins of the Ming Emperor's Palace," in *The Consumer Revolution in Urban China*, 287–311.

61. Ibid., 162; for discussions of the rave scene, see Maria Pini, "Women and the Early British Rave Scene," in *Back to Reality: Social Experience and Cultural Studies*, ed. Angela McRobbie (New York: Manchester University Press, 1997), 152–69, and "Cyborgs, Nomads, and the Raving Feminine," in *Dance in the City*, ed. Helen Thomas (New York: St. Martin's Press, 1997), 111–29; Georgiana Gore, "The Beat Goes On: Trance, Dance, and Tribalism in Rave Culture," in *Dance in the City*, 50–67; Steve Redhead, *Rave Off: Politics and Deviance in Contemporary Youth Culture* (Brookfield, VT: Avebury, 1993).

62. Sanjay Roy, "Dirt, Noise, Traffic: Contemporary Indian Dance in the Western City; Modernity, Ethnicity and Hybridity," in *Dance in the City*, 74.

63. Ibid., 76; a samosa is a meat or vegetable-filled pastry; see Shobana Jeyasingh, "Imaginary Homelands: Creating a New Dance Language," in *Border Tensions: Proceedings of the Fifth Study of Dance Conference*, (Guildford: University of Surrey, 1995), 193.

64. Roy, "Dirt, Noise, Traffic," 72.

65. For a discussion of libidinal bonds in music scenes, see Barry Shank, *Dissonant Identities: The Rock'n'Roll Scene in Austin, Texas* (Hanover, NH: Wesleyan University Press, 1994); the protests against the 1999 meeting of the World Trade Organization in Seattle, Washington, reflect bridgebuilding between local political and cultural scenes and those in other countries; for a general discussion of local and global movements; see Margaret Keck and Katherine Sikkink, *Activists Beyond Borders: Advocacy Networks in International Politics* (Ithaca: Cornell University Press, 1998) and "Historical Precursors to Modern Transnational Social Movements and Networks," in *Globalization and Social Movements: Culture, Power, and the Transnational Public Sphere*, ed. John. A. Guidry, Michael D. Kennedy, and Mayer N. Zald (Ann Arbor: University of Michigan Press, 2000), 35–53; Douglas Morris, "Internetworked Social Movements: Comparing the Alternative Globalization Movement and Terrorist Networks," paper presented at the annual meeting of the American Sociological Association, Chicago, 2002; Ivana Eterovic, Jackie Smith, and Dawn Wiest, "Surviving in a Changing World: Predictors of Dissolution in the Population of Transnational Social Movement Organizations, 1993–2000," paper presented at the annual meeting of the American Sociological Association, Chicago, 2002.

66. Matsui, *Women in the New Asia*, 114–15.

67. Desmond, *Staging Tourism; Bodies on Display from Waikiki to Sea World* (Chicago: University of Chicago Press, 1999), 41.

68. Ibid., 42.

69. Ibid., 10.

70. Ibid., 3; "Haole" is a generally derogatory term used in Hawaii mainly to refer to whites, but also can include others foreign to the islands; see Hugh D. Mailly, "Haole" in *Encyclopedia Mythica* (http://www.pantheon.org/mythica/articles/h/haole.html).

71. For a general discussion of the postmodern consumer society, see Jean Baudrillard, *The Consumer Society: Myths and Structures* (Thousand Oaks, CA: Sage, 1998).

72. Diane Richardson, "Sexuality and Citizenship," *Sociology* 32 (1998): 83–100, 87; Richardson ties the rise of the global consumer to the nation, noting that the 1991 "Citizen's Charter" in Britain "explicitly defin[ed] citizenship status in terms of the twin responsibilities of consumer and taxpayer" (ibid., 109); see also, David T. Evans, *Sexual Citizenship: The Material Construction of Sexualities* (New York: Routledge, 1993).

73. Cheah puts forth a general critique of human rights not simply as a universalist set of neutrally just principles, but also as a discourse that both reflects and benefits Western interests; she particularly cites human rights tied to market processes and the marketplace:

> [T]he global expansion of intellectual property protection can also be a legalized form of late capitalist theft [in particular] . . . international patent and licensing agreements facilitate a new era of bio-imperialism since they are used by pharmaceutical companies and agribusiness in the North to monopolize the genetic resource of biological diversity in the Third World. (Pheng Cheah, "Posit(ion)ing Human Rights in the Current Global Conjuncture," in *Transnational Asia Pacific*, 25).

74. Bishop and Robinson, *Night Market*, 108.

75. Tolentino, "Bodies, Letters, Catalogs."

76. Carla Freeman, *High Tech and High Heels in the Global Economy: Women, Work, and Pink-Collar Identities in the Caribbean* (Durham: Duke University Press, 2000), 4; my thanks to Eithne Luibheid, Ethnic Studies Department, Bowling Green State University, for bringing this work to my attention.

77. Ibid., 219.

78. Ibid., 220; although Freeman apparently felt the need to keep the height of her fashion and her heels under control, it seems ironic indeed that she was surprised by her compulsion to fit in and by her compliance with local norms to dress "properly," since that was, after all, one of her central observations about the women whose lives she researched; why should a Western professional anthropologist be any less susceptible than local women to what were obviously strong social pressures to conform to certain dress codes?

79. Leslie Salzinger, "From High Heels to Swathed Bodies: Gendered Meanings under Production in Mexico's Export-Processing Industry," *Feminist Studies* 23 (1997): 549–73, 545.

80. This glocal combination led Freeman to argue for an "analysis that explicitly links practices and identities associated with production/consumption and gender/class across local and transnational terrains"; *High Tech and High Heels in the Global Economy*, 4.

81. See Deborah Root, *Cannibal Culture: Art, Appropriation, and the Commodification of Difference* (Boulder: Westview Press, 1996).

CONCLUSION

SEX-BAITING AND RACE-BAITING
The Politics of Ethnosexuality

The central thesis of this book is that sex is a core constitutive element of race, ethnicity, and the nation, and that race, ethnicity, and nationalism are crucial components of sexual and moral boundaries and systems. Sexual images and stereotypes are imbedded in ethnic images and stereotypes. Sexual fears and loathing are endemic to racial terror and hatred. Sexual rules and protocols are inherent in imaginings of the nation. Sexual identities, desires, and practices are defined and constructed by sexualized expectations attributed to one's own and one's partners' racial, ethnic, and national membership. I have argued that there is no more potent force than sexuality to stir the passions and fan the flames of racial tension. Sex-baiting can be as provocative as race-baiting in conjuring up a vision of ethnosexual threat. In fact, sex-baiting is a mechanism of race-baiting when it taps into and amplifies racial fears and stereotypes, and when sexual dangerousness is employed as a strategy to create racial panic. Sex-baiting and race-baiting often are used together by defenders of particular ethnosexual orders to maintain the status quo. It is the sexualized nature of things ethnic, racial, and national that heats up the discourse on the values, attributes, and moral worth of Us and Them, that arouses anger when there are violations of sexual contact rules, that raises doubts about loyalty and respectability when breaches of sexual demeanor occur, that provokes reactions when questions of sexual purity and propriety arise, and that sparks retaliations when threats to sexual boundaries are imagined or detected.

As we have seen in the many examples presented in these pages, there is a sexual message imbedded in ethnic stereotypes and categories, a sexual undercurrent that runs through many ethnic conflicts and controversies, and an ethnosexual subtext in many economic and political debates. I can think of no more potent an image to justify violence and repression than the "rape" of one's homeland or women, and no more convincing an argument for military intervention to civilize or pacify ethnic Others than to accuse them of ethnosexual misbehavior, excesses, or violence. Appeals for protection against sexual threats are extremely durable weapons in the wars of words that accompany conflicts. When those threats are seen to be *ethno*sexual, their power to mobilize a response is greatly enhanced.

On the eve of the January 1991 U.S.-led Gulf war against Iraq for its invasion of Kuwait, for instance, the ethnosexual testimony of a Kuwaiti woman doctor was widely circulated in the news media; she reported numerous rapes of Kuwaiti women by Iraqi soldiers.[1] In what observers described as an "unusually emotional outburst," Sheik Saud Nasir al-Sabah, Kuwait's Ambassador to the United States criticized the lack of direct military intervention to stop the invasion and its accompanying sexual assaults:

> My country is being savaged and destroyed, our women subjected to mass acts of rape, our men and even children are being murdered while these armchair analysts advocate waiting a year or up to 18 months for sanctions to force him [Iraqi leader Saddam Hussein] out.[2]

At the time discrepancies in the estimates of such atrocities led human rights monitors to suspect "that the [President George] Bush Administration and Kuwait and its supporters are relying on reports of atrocities to help counter" arguments against military intervention.[3]

The rape of Afghan women was not a central pillar in the policy that launched the War against Terrorism orchestrated by the second President George Bush in 2001, following the September 11 attack on New York's World Trade Center and the Pentagon building in Washington, D.C. Freeing Afghan women from the repressive and misogynistic rule of the Taliban government in Afghanistan was, however, a goal articulated by Mr. Bush's wife. In a November 17, 2001, national radio address, Laura Bush condemned the Taliban government's oppression of women and its restriction of women's basic rights and freedom:

> The fight against terrorism is also a fight for the rights and dignity of women. . . . I hope Americans will join our family in working to insure that dignity and opportunity will be secured for all the women and children of Afghanistan.[4]

Although most Americans applauded this American stance on women's rights, as history has taught us, gender, sexuality, and nationalism are not always congenial companions. Less than a month after Mrs. Bush's pronouncements, on December 3, 2002, an American soldier serving in the war,

Lt. Col. Martha McSally, the U.S. Air Force's highest-ranking female fighter pilot and the first woman to fly in combat, sued the U.S. Secretary of Defense, Donald Rumsfeld, for the American military's policy of requiring its women military personnel stationed in Saudi Arabia to wear head-to-toe robes *(abayas)* when going off-base. McSally commented: "I can fly a single-seat aircraft in enemy territory, but I can't drive a vehicle. . . . And then I have to sit in the back and at all times I must be escorted by a male . . . that, when questioned, is supposed to claim me as his wife."[5] On January 19, 2002, Gen. Tommy Franks, head of the U.S. Central Command, revoked the policy, stating that it was no longer mandatory that U.S. servicewomen in Saudi Arabia wear *abayas,* but that it remained "strongly encouraged."[6]

Once again, as in so many instances recounted in this book, in the war in Afghanistan we find issues of gender and sexuality intertwined in national political discourse, raising questions about the definition of citizenship and troubling the boundaries dividing "us" and "them." The "rape of Kuwait" by Iraqi men leading up to the Gulf war, the "rape of Nanking" by Japanese men during World War II, the violation of Afghan women's rights by religious extremist Taliban men during the U.S. war in Afghanistan all reflect the specter of sexual abuse as a means to mobilize a population to support military action.

Just as sex-baiting can be a potent weapon for calling troops to arms and making war, it also can be an effective political tool in domestic policy arenas where appeals are made to protect national morality and to uphold the integrity of national borders. As we noted in Chapter 1, immigration can become a site for ethnosexual inspection and a policy arena in which politicians play both race and sex cards to foster a climate of ethnosexual fear and hysteria, to gain political advantage, and to garner support for programs designed to defend racial, ethnic, and national boundaries.[7]

Immigration into the United States and many Western countries has risen in recent decades, in part because of falling birthrates among native-born populations and because of labor shortages. One consequence of these native reproduction decreases, immigration increases, and the relatively larger size of many migrant families, has been a shift in the ethnic composition of many industrial countries. The United States is no exception. The U.S. Census Bureau reported that in 2000 the number of Latinos equaled the number of African Americans in the United States.[8] The Census Bureau also reported that in 2000 whites became a numerical minority in California comprising 46.7 percent of the state's 33.8 million residents; population projections indicated that whites would become a minority in the United States nationally by the mid-twenty-first century.[9]

The changing ethnic composition of the American population has led to something of a common ground for black and white Americans, but for different reasons. Both groups have an interest in the sexual activities of immigrants. The growing nonwhite U.S. population offers an opportunity for alliances between African Americans and other nonwhites to address common concerns such as workplace and housing discrimination and police racial profiling.[10] Those same increases in the nonwhite and/or non-native English-speaking population have generated anti-immigrant legislation and movements in some regions of the United States (e.g., in California, Texas, and Florida) often spearheaded by whites (sometimes with nonwhite support) who hope to restrict immigration, to limit immigrants' access to social benefits including child-related services such as public schooling, medicaid, or nutritional programs, or to pass official English language legislation.[11] Neither those who support nor those who oppose the presence and rights of immigrants speak directly about their rates of reproduction or their sexual practices (frequency of intercourse, use of birth control, sex outside of marriage). Rather, immigration debates tend to focus on the amount of adult legal and illegal immigration and the criminal activities (e.g., human trafficking, drugs) associated with illegal immigration.[12]

Like other ethnosexual preoccupations, the sexual politics of numbers associated with ethnic and immigrant head counts are not uniquely American pastimes. The comings and goings, relative numbers, and birthrates of immigrants and ethnic groups engage the attention of governments and their citizens around the world. For instance, in September 2000, the *Observer* newspaper in England reported a "global watershed" of racial transformation in Britain and many other industrial countries:

> Whites will be an ethnic minority in Britain by the end of the century and in London by the end of the decade . . . it would be the first time in history that a major indigenous population has voluntarily become a minority, rather than through war, famine or disease. . . . The population of ethnic minorities has been growing at between 2 and 4 per cent a year. . . . At the same time, birth rates among white Britons have fallen to negative levels—less than two children per woman.[13]

Britain is not alone in enumerating immigrants and keeping watch over their reproductive activities. Although immigration in Italy is not discussed so much in the language of color as in the rhetoric of culture, Italians are concerned about their dwindling numbers. Italy has among the lowest birthrates in Europe—1.2 children per woman, about half the rate in the United States, and well below the 2.0 rate needed to replace the population. In fact, the birthrate among native-born Italian women is probably even lower since native-born women's average age is increasing and immigrant birthrates are considerably higher.[14] The Italian demographic decline has led to increased immigration into Italy (and many other European countries as well) to fill labor shortages, and has alarmed some Italians:

> "We're talking about the extinction of the Italian race. . . . In 100 years, there won't be any Italians [in Italy] anymore." This is hyperbole, but just barely. If low birth and immigration rates persist, Italy's population would fall to 10 million by the end of the century, according to government estimates . . . as low as today's birth rate is, it may actually be inflated because of a relatively higher [birth]rate among immigrants.[15]

Charting the number of ethnics relative to the native-born population is not the only reason politicians and researchers are interested in ethnosexuality. When social scientists and policymakers search for evidence of any kind of social change relating to race or ethnicity, one of the first places they look is in the bedroom. Sexual contact is the most intimate of ethnic boundary crossings, and intermarriage is perhaps the most controversial ethnosexual act since it tends to be public, officially recognized, and reproductive.

Tracing the rates of intermarriage among different ethnic groups over time in various regions is one way to map the ethnic landscape in a society. Intermarriage rates indicate which ethnic boundaries are strongest and weakest, when in a country's history ethnic boundaries are most defended, or the parts of a country where ethnic boundaries are most relaxed. Intermarriage rates can tell us if race or religion are as important as they used to be as bases for ethnic division in the United States or if the black/white color line in the U.S. South is as strongly defined as in the past or as in the North. International comparisons of intermarriage rates allow us to extend the maps further: Is religion as important an ethnic division in the United States as it is in Canada or Lebanon or Switzerland? How is race defined in the United Kingdom compared to the United States, and is the color line equally fixed in both countries? Sexual contact and intermarriage reveal a great deal about ethnic relations across space and time, and illustrate the power of sexuality to shape racial and ethnic relations.

As we saw in Chapter 1 members of most American racial groups are still quite likely to marry a partner from the same race. Despite this stable pattern of racial endogamy, intermarriage among members of the U.S. racial pentagon has been slowly, but steadily increasing in the past few decades. In 1960 99.6 percent of Americans married within their own race, in 1970 that figure had decreased slightly to 99.3, in 1980 there was a further decline in intraracial marriages to 98.0 percent, in 1990 there was further decline to 95.0 percent, and in 2000, 94.6 percent married within their own race.[16] In Chapter 1 we saw that intermarriage rates vary by ethnic group, ranging in 2000 from 6.1 percent of whites marrying nonwhites, to 10.9 percent of blacks marrying members of another race, to 26.3 percent of Asian Americans out-marrying, to 26.1 percent of Hispanics marrying non-Hispanics, to 67.0 percent of American Indians marrying non-Indians. We also noted in Chapter 1 that interracial marriage is gendered with black male–white female and white male–Asian female marriages the most gender imbalanced interracial couplings.[17] These patterns are consistent with longstanding ethnosexual cosmologies in the United States and the West.

Intermarriage data provide only a limited picture of American patterns of ethnosexual crossing since marriage requires a commitment of time and resources beyond simple cohabitation (living together). David Harris compared 1990 rates of interracial cohabitation with intermarriage, and found cohabitation rates to be considerably higher, leading him to conclude:

> Our findings suggest that there are substantially higher levels of intimate interracial contact than marriage data imply, and consequently that the social distance between racial groups is less than previous work suggests.[18]

Harris's findings combine with the slow, but steady historical increase in American patterns of marital racial exogamy to suggest that while race and gender matter in sex and marriage in the United States, how much they matter may be less than we thought and may be changing. Like all ethnic boundaries, racial boundaries are mutable and flexible. One caveat that should be noted when trying to understand the implications of increased ethnosexual contact for assimilation, however, is the capacity of ethnic boundaries to remain in place despite high rates of sexual contact across them. The stability of the black-white color line is the most dramatic example of this ethnosexual paradox. Another factor not to be underestimated when examining intermarriage rates across time is the elasticity of whiteness. The "white" racial category historically has absorbed many immigrant and ethnic groups once considered as racial Others (Irish, Italians, Armenians, Jews). Rising rates of intermarriage between whites and Latinos, Indians, and Asian Americans raises questions about the stability of the racial classification of some members in these currently nonwhite categories (e.g., middle and upper-class Latinos, mixed-race children of Asian-white couples). The relative stability of the black-white color line in comparison to white absorption of many European groups, reminds us of the power of history to haunt contemporary race relations.

As we discussed in Chapter 4, until the Civil War ended slavery in the United States, white men's sexual access to and exploitation of black women was common and widespread. The diversity of skin tones among African Americans today is visible evidence of those centuries of sexual contact between blacks and whites. It is an interesting and perverse historical fact that sex across the color line has reversed its gender structure in the past century and a half, shifting from sexual contact primarily between white men and black women to sexual contact and marriage primarily between black men and white women. Despite a long history of interracial sex, the color line dividing blacks and whites remains the most stable and dangerous ethnic boundary in American society. Ironically, sex across the color line may do as much or more to strengthen the boundary than to weaken it. This apparent contradiction raises some interesting questions about race and sex: How is it that blacks and whites have had forced and consensual sex throughout U.S. history, yet the color line between these two "races" remains the most visible and volatile American ethnic boundary? Why is it that sex-baiting, especially in the black/white case, seems to retain its strategic power and allure in reinforcing racial boundaries?

The answer to these questions lies in the capacity of ethnicity to sexually attract and repel, in the success of sexuality as an ideology of superiority and inferiority, and in the power of sexuality as an instrument of racial formation—as a means of domination or resistance, as a badge of honor or shame. Having sex with an Other might reflect a heartfelt longing or an act of rebellion or a way to demean and defile another person or group. No motivation is likely to be entirely pure since it is hard to untangle the desire from the disdain. Even when we try to step outside local ethnosexual hegemonies, the racial, ethnic, and national meanings we know that they embody are difficult to ignore. Even when we reach across ethnic boundaries, we remain part of an ethnosexual ideological, legal, and social system that is seldom color-blind, religion-blind, language-blind, or nationality-blind. We may feel that our actions and decisions are our own, but they are imbued with meanings over which we have little control.

Ethnosexual transactions and associations are endlessly fascinating to observers. The burden of this constant scrutiny and surveillance for those who cross ethnosexual boundaries can be difficult to bear. Many interracial relationships manage to survive such social inspection and judgment, but many collapse under their weight. As we have seen, however, there are individuals who will challenge ethnosexual hegemonies and play an ethnosex card of their own, thereby resisting social pressures not to shuffle the deck. Despite the power of ethnosexual regimes to keep us in our proper places and to dictate the ethnic conditions of our intimate relations, there will always be those who challenge the rules and reach across racial and ethnic boundaries to form families and create community. These are the ethnosexual resisters, innovators, and revolutionaries.

NOTES

1. In fact, she reported that she "had treated four cases of rape in three and a half months of work at Maternity Hospital in Kuwait City," and the extent of the rapes was not well documented at the time; see Judith Miller, "Atrocities by Iraqis in Kuwait: Numbers Are Hard to Verify," *New York Times*, December 16, 1990:1, 20, 20.

2 Ibid.; a month earlier similar reports were presented to the United Nations Security Council urging the UN to vote to authorize the use of force against Iraq; see Johanna Neuman, "Fear by Day, Fear by Night," *USA Today*, November 28, 1990:4.

3. Miller, "Atrocities by Iraqis in Kuwait," 1; Kuwait was itself a target of criticism for ethnosexual rape in the summer of 1991 as the Gulf War ended; journalists reported that "more than 100 Filipino women, Sri Lankans and other foreigners have reported being raped or badly beaten in Kuwait City by Kuwaiti soldiers, police and citizens of the emirate" (Jack Kelley, "Kuwait Slow to Deal with Rapes," *USA Today*, July 29, 1991:9); in the spring of 1992, Sheik Saud Nasir al-Sabah, Kuwait's ambassador to the United States, who had argued with passion a year and a half earlier for international intervention into his country to stop rape, articulated an opposite position in a *USA Today* editorial when he declared that the above "alleged beating and raping of women in his country [by fellow Kuwaitis] is a domestic issue, and that human rights are not being violated" (Saud Nasir al-Sabah, "Kuwait's Position," *USA Today*, March 6, 1992:8).

4. http://www.whitehouse.gov/news/releases/2001/11/20011117.html

5. BBC News Online, "US Eases Servicewomen's Dress Code," January 23, 2002 (http://news.bbc.co.uk/hi/english/world/middle_east/newsid_1777000/1777397.stm.

6. Ibid.

7. In the past few years, the term "playing the race card" has been turned on its head, and used by race baiters to criticize people of color who attempt to expose racial injustice; this is not the sense in which I use the term, rather, I refer to playing the race or sex card as equivalent to race or sex baiting, where defenders of particular ethnosexual orders invoke racial or sexual stereotypes to demonize racial and sexual Others and create racial and sexual panics; for examples consistent with this view of the phrase, see Mendleberg, *The Race Card*; Williams, *Playing the Race Card*.

8. There were 35,305,818 Americans who identified their ancestry as "Hispanic or Latino" and 34,658,190 who identified their race as "black or African American"; see http://www.census.gov/Press-Release/www/2001/cb01cn61.html; http://www.census.gov/prod/2001pubs/c2kbr01-1.pdf.

9. John Ritter, "California Racial Data Shifts," *USA Today*, June 19, 2001 (http://usatoday.com/news/census/ca); Anthony Brown, "UK Whites Will Be a Minority by 2100," *The Observer*, September 3, 2000 (http://www.observer.co.uk/uk_news/story/0,6903,363750,00.html); the term "non-Hispanic blacks" has joined "non-Hispanic whites" in the lexicon of racial demography; these terms reflect the flux and ambiguity surrounding Hispanic race in the Census, in the U.S. non-Hispanic population, and among Latinos themselves; very few Hispanics identify their race as "black" (only 2 percent in the 2000 Census) even though many have African ancestry, especially Latinos from the Caribbean (e.g., Cubans, Puerto Ricans, Dominicans); for instance, D'Vera Cohn reported that in 2000 "the Hispanic population

. . . grew nearly 58 percent over the 1990s, catching up to black non-Hispanics and signaling rapid social and political change in this country. Nearly 17 million Hispanics described themselves as white, followed by nearly 15 million who checked 'some other race.'" (D'Vera Cohn, "Shifting Portrait of U.S. Hispanics," *Puerto Rico Herald On-Line,* May 10, 2001 [http://www.puertoricoherald.org/issues/2001/vol5n21/ShiftingPortrain-en.shtml]; see also http://www.census.gov/prod/2001pubs/c2kbr01-1.pdf; for a discussion of the elasticity of whiteness, see Jonathan W. Warren and France Winddance Twine, "White Americans, the new Minority?: Non-Blacks and the Ever-Expanding Boundaries of Whiteness," *Journal of Black Studies* 28 (1997): 200–18.

10. There are potential conflicts of interest as well, such as in federal election districting and resource allocation which can threaten black representation and access to political power and resources; see Genaro C. Armas, "Census Allies Minorities," Associated Press, April 8, 2001 (http://detnews.com/2001/census/0104/27/a05-209146.htm).

11. See Karen E. Rosenblum, "Rights at Risk: California's Proposition 187," in *Illegal Immigration in America: A Reference Handbook,* ed. David W. Haines and Karen E. Rosenblum (Westport, CT: Greenwood Press, 1999), 367–82; Baron, *The English-Only Question.*

12. See many of the papers in Haines and Rosenblum, *Illegal Immigration in America.*

13. Mann, "UK Whites Will Be a Minority by 2100."

14. Bert Roughton Jr., "Incredibly Falling Birth Rate Heralds Changing Face of Italy," Cox Newspapers On-Line, July 25, 2001 (http://www.coxnews.com/washingtonbureau/staff/roughton/11-05-00COXITALYBIRTHSADV051STLD.html); Roughton concludes that the 1.2 child per woman rate will result in a decline of approximately one-third of the Italian population in fifty years (from 57 million in 2000 to 41 million in 2050).

15. Ibid., see also Phillip J. Longman, "The World Turns Gray," *U.S. News and World Report* (March 1, 1999); Michael Specter, "Population Implosion Worries a Graying Europe," *The New York Times,* July 10, 1998:10.

16. For 1960–1990 data, see U.S. Bureau of the Census, "Race by Wife by Race of Husband." (http://www.census.gov/population/socdemo/race/interractab1.txt); for 2000 data, see U.S. Bureau of the Census, Table FG3: "Married Couple Family Groups, by Presence of Own Children Under 18, and Age, Earnings, Education, and Race and Hispanic Origin of Both Spouses: March 2000" (http://www.census.gov/population/socdemo/hh-fam/p20-537/2000/tabFG3.txt).

17. http://www.census.gov/population/socdemo/hh-fam/p20-537/2000/tabFG3.txt.

18. David R. Harris, "Cohabitation, Marriage, and Markets: A New Look at Intimate Interracial Relationships," paper presented at the annual meeting of the Population Association of America, Los Angeles, 2000.

REFERENCES

Allen, Beverly. *Rape Warfare: The Hidden Genocide in Bosnia-Herzegovina and Croatia*. Minneapolis: University of Minnesota Press, 1996.

Alonso, Ana Maria. *Thread of Blood: Colonialism, Revolution, and Gender on Mexico's Northern Frontier*. Tucson: University of Arizona Press, 1995.

Altink, Sietske. *Stolen Lives: Trading Women into Sex and Slavery*. London: Scarlet Press, 1995.

Altman, Dennis. "Foreword. "In *Men Who Sell Sex: International Perspectives on Male Prostitution and HIV/AIDS*, ed. Peter Aggleton, xiii–xix. Philadelphia: Temple University Press, 1999.

Ambrose, Stephen, and Charles L. Sulzberger, eds. *American Heritage New History of World War II*, revised edition. New York: Viking Press, 1997.

Americas Watch and the Women's Rights Project, *Untold Terror: Violence against Women in Peru's Armed Conflict*. New York: Americas Watch, 1992.

Anderson, Benedict. *Imagined Communities: Reflections on the Origin and Spread of Nationalism*. London: Verso. 1991.

Anderson, Elijah. "The Social Situation of the Black Executive." In *The Cultural Territories of Race*, ed. Michele Lamont, 3–29. Chicago: University of Chicago Press, 1999.

Anderson, Linda. "Gang Bang Ulster Style." In *Pillars of the House: An Anthology of Verse by Irish Women from 1690 to the Present*, ed. Angeline A. Kelly, 144–45. Dublin: Wolfhound, 1988.

Anderson, Margo J., and Stephen E. Feinberg. *Who Counts? The Politics of Census-Taking in Contemporary America*. New York: Russell Sage Foundation, 1999.

Anonymous. "Standby Warning" (http://www.subicbaymarines.com/Standby.htm).

Anthias, Floya, and Nira Yuval-Davis, eds. *Racial Boundaries: Race, Nation, Gender, Colour, and Class and the Anti-Racist Struggle*. London: Routledge, 1992.

Antonio, Robert J., and Alessandro Bonanno. "A New Global Capitalism? From 'Americanism and Fordism' to 'Americanization-Globalization.'" *American Studies* 41 (2000): 33–77.

Anzaldua, Gloria, ed. *Making Face, Making Soul: Creative and Critical Perspectives by Women of Color*. San Francisco: Aunt Lute Foundation, 1990.

Armas, Genaro C. "Census Allies Minorities." Associated Press (April 8, 2001) (http://detnews.com/2001/census/0104/27/a05–209146.htm).

Asia Watch and Physicians for Human Rights. *Rape in Kashmir: A Crime of War*. New York: Asia Watch, 1993.

Austin, J. L. *How to Do Things with Words*. Cambridge, MA: Harvard University Press, 1975.

Awwad, Amani M. "Gossip, Scandal, Shame, and Honor Killing: A Case for Social Constructionism and Hegemonic Discourse." *Social Thought and Research* 24 (2002): 39–52.

Bakalian, Anny. *Armenian-Americans: From Being to Feeling Armenian.* New Brunswick, NJ: Transaction Books, 1993.

Balcells, Albert. *Catalan Nationalism: Past and Present.* New York: St. Martin's Press, 1996.

Bales, Kevin. *Disposable People: New Slavery in the Global Economy.* Berkeley: University of California Press. 1999.

Banton, Michael. *Racial and Ethnic Competition.* Cambridge: Cambridge University Press, 1983.

———. *Racial Theories.* Cambridge: Cambridge University Press, 1998.

Barber, Benjamin. *Jihad vs. McWorld: How Globalism and Tribalism Are Reshaping the World.* New York: Ballantine Books. 1996.

Bardaglio, Peter W. " 'Shamefull Matches': The Regulation of Interracial Sex and Marriage in the South before 1900." In *Sex, Love, Race: Crossing Boundaries in North American History,* ed. Martha Hodes, 112–38. New York: New York University Press, 1999.

Barkan, Elazar. *The Guilt of Nations: Restitution and Negotiating Historical Injustices.* New York: W.W. Norton, 2000.

Baron, Dennis. *The English-Only Question: An Official Language for Americans?* New Haven: Yale University Press, 1990.

Barreto, Amílcar A. *Language, Elites, and the State: Nationalism in Puerto Rico and Quebec.* Westport, CT: Praeger, 1998.

Barson, Michael, and Steven Heller. *Red Scared: The Commie Menace in Propaganda and Popular Culture.* San Francisco: Chronicle Books, 2001.

Barstow, Anne Llewellyn. *War's Dirty Secret: Rape, Prostitution, and Other Crimes Against Women.* Cleveland: Pilgrim Press, 2000.

Barth, Fredrik, ed. *Ethnic Groups and Boundaries.* Boston: Little, Brown, and Company, 1969.

———. "Enduring and Emerging Issues in the Analysis of Ethnicity." In *The Anthropology of Ethnicity: Beyond "Ethnic Groups and Boundaries,"* ed. Hans Vermeulen and Cora Govers, 11–32. Amsterdam: Spinhuis, 1994.

Baudrillard, Jean. *Simulacra and Simulation.* Ann Arbor: University of Michigan Press, 1994.

———. *The Consumer Society: Myths and Structures.* Thousand Oaks, CA: Sage, 1998.

Bayly, Christopher A., and D. H. A. Kolff, eds. *Two Colonial Empires.* Boston: M. Nijhoff, 1986.

Beam, Joseph. "Brother to Brother: Words from the Heart." In *In the Life: A Black Gay Anthology,* ed. Joseph Beam, 230–42. Boston: Alyson Publications, 1986.

Bearman, Peter S. "Desertion as Localism: Army Unit Solidarity and Group Norms in the U.S. Civil War." *Social Forces* 70 (1991): 321–42.

Beckles, Hilary McD. "Taking Liberties: Enslaved Women and Anti-Slavery in the Caribbean." In *Gender and Imperialism,* ed. Clare Midgley, 137–57. Manchester: Manchester University Press, 1998.

Bederman, Gail. *Manliness and Civilization: A Cultural History of Gender and Race in the United States, 1880–1917.* Chicago: University of Chicago Press, 1995.

van der Beets, Richard. *Held Captive by Indians: Selected Narratives, 1642–1836.* Knoxville: University of Tennessee Press, 1974.

Bell, David, and Gill Valentine, eds. *Mapping Desire: Geographies of Sexualities.* New York: Routledge, 1995.

Bell, Ernest A. *Fighting the Traffic in Young Girls or War on the White Slave Trade.* New York: Gordon Press, [circa 1910] 1975.

Bell, Shannon. *Reading, Writing, and Rewriting the Prostitute Body.* Bloomington: Indiana University Press, 1995.

Berger, Peter L., and Thomas Luckmann. *The Social Construction of Reality: A Treatise on the Sociology of Knowledge.* Garden City, NY: Anchor Books, 1967.

Bergling, Tim. "A Few Good Men." Genre (November/December 1997) (http://www. davidclemens.com/gaymilitary/fgm.htm).

Bergon, Frank. *The Journals of Lewis and Clark.* New York: Penguin Books, 1989.

Berkhofer Jr., Robert F. *The White Man's Indian: Images of the American Indian from Columbus to the Present.* New York: Alfred A. Knopf, 1978.

Berland, Renee L. *The National Uncanny: Indian Ghosts and American Subjects.* Hanover, NH: Dartmouth College, 2000.

Berlant, Lauren G. *The Queen of America Goes to Washington City: Essays on Sex and Citizenship.* Durham: Duke University Press, 1997.

———, and Michael Warner. "Sex in Public." *Critical Inquiry* 24 (1998): 547–66.

Bessire, Mark H. C., and Lauri Firstenberg. *Beyond Decorum: The Photography of Ike Ude.* Cambridge: MIT Press, 2000.

Bhabha, Homi. *The Location of Culture.* New York: Routledge, 1994.

———. "Life at the Border: Hybrid Identities of the Present." *New Perspectives Quarterly* 14 (1997): 30–31.

Binder, Amy. "Friend and Foe: Boundary Work and Collective Identity in the Afrocentric and Multicultural Curriculum Movements in American Public Education." In *The Cultural Territories of Race,* ed. Michele Lamont, 222–48. Chicago: University of Chicago Press, 1999.

Bird, Chris. "UN Tribunal Told of Bosnian Rape Camp Horrors." *Guardian* (April 21, 2000):1.

Bishop, Ryan, and Lillian S. Robinson. *Night Market: Sexual Cultures and the Thai Economic Miracle.* New York: Routledge, 1998.

———. "How My Dick Spent Its Summer Vacation: Sex and the Commerce of Global Communication." *Genders* (2002).

———. "Travelers' Tails." In *Prostitution in a Global Context,* ed. Susan Thorbeck. London: Zed, 2002.

Bitton Jackson, Livia E. Elli: *Coming of Age in the Holocaust.* New York: Times Books, 1980.

Blackstone, Sara J. *Buckskins, Bullets, and Business: A History of Buffalo Bill's Wild West.* New York: Greenwood Press, 1986.

Blesser, Carol. *Secret and Sacred: The Diaries of James Henry Hammond, a Southern Slaveholder.* New York: Oxford University Press, 1988

Blight, David W. *Race and Reunion: The Civil War in American Memory.* Cambridge, MA: Harvard University Press, 2001.

Block, Sharon. "Lines of Color, Sex, and Service: Comparative Sexual Coercion in Early America." In *Sex, Love, Race: Crossing Boundaries in North American History,* ed. Martha Hodes, 141–63. New York: New York University Press, 1999.

Bogart, Laura M., Heather Cecil, David A. Wagstaff, Steven D. Pinkerton, Paul R. Abramson. "Is It 'Sex'?: College Students' Interpretations of Sexual Behavior Terminology." *Journal of Sex Research* 37 (2000): 108–16.

Bologh, Roslyn Wallach. *Love or Greatness: Max Weber and Masculine Thinking—A Feminist Inquiry.* London: Unwin Hyman, 1990.

Boone, Joseph Allen. *Libidinal Currents: Sexuality and the Shaping of Modernism.* Chicago: University of Chicago Press, 1998.

Boulding, Elise. *Women in the Twentieth Century World.* Beverly Hills, CA: Sage Publications 1977.

Bourdieu, Pierre. *Language and Symbolic Power.* Cambridge, MA: Harvard University Press, 1991.

Boushaba, Amine, Oussama Tawil, Latefa Imane, and Hakima Himmich. "Marginalization and Vulnerability: Male Sex Work in Morocco." In *Men Who Sell Sex: International Perspectives on Male Prostitution and HIV/AIDS,* ed. Peter Aggleton, 263–73. Philadelphia: Temple University Press, 1999.

Bow, Leslie, *Betrayal and Other Acts of Subversion: Feminism, Sexual Politics, Asian American Women's Literature.* Princeton: Princeton University Press, 2001.

Boyarin, Daniel. *Unheroic Conduct: The Rise of Heterosexuality and the Invention of the Jewish Man.* Berkeley: University of California Press, 1997.

Boyd, Monica, Gustave Goldmann, and Pamela White. "Race in the Canadian Census." In *Race and Racism: Canada's Challenge,* ed. Leo Driedger and Shiva S. Halli, 33–54. Montreal: McGill/Queen's University Press, 2000.

Boyd, Todd. *Am I Black Enough for You? Popular Culture from the 'Hood and Beyond.* Bloomington: Indiana University Press, 1997.

Brackenridge, Henry M. *Views of Louisiana, Together with a Journal of a Voyage up the Missouri River, in 1911.* Pittsburgh: Cramer, Speer and Eichbaum, 1814.

Brooks, James F. " 'This Evil Extends Especially to the Feminine Sex': Captivity and Identity in New Mexico, 1700–1846." In *Writing the Range: Race, Class, and Culture in the Women's West,* ed. Elizabeth Jameson and Susan Armitage, 97–121. Norman: University of Oklahoma Press, 1997.

Brown, Anthony. "UK Whites Will Be a Minority by 2100." *The Observer* (September 3, 2000) (http://www.observer.co.uk/uk_news/story/0,6903,363750,00.html).

Brown, Kathleen M. "Brave New Worlds: Women's and Gender History." *William and Mary Quarterly* 50 (1993): 311–28.

———. "Native Americans and Early Modern Concepts of Race." In *Empire and Others: British Encounters with Indigenous Peoples, 1600–1850,* ed. Martin Daunton and Rick Halpern, 79–100. Philadelphia: University of Pennsylvania Press, 1999.

———. *Good Wives, Nasty Wenches, and Anxious Patriarchs: Gender, Race, and Power in Colonial Virginia.* Chapel Hill: Institute of Early American History and Culture, University of North Carolina Press, 1997.

Brownmiller, Susan. *Against Our Will: Men, Women, and Rape.* New York: Bantam Books, 1975.

Bruinsma, Gerben J. N., and Guus Meershoek. "Organized Crime and Trafficking in Women from Eastern Europe in the Netherlands." In *Illegal Immigration and Commercial Sex: The New Slave Trade,* ed. Phil Williams, 105–18. London: Frank Cass, 1999.

Buitelaar, M. W. "Negotiating the Rules of Chaste Behaviour: Re-Interpretations of the Symbolic Complex of Virginity by Young Women of Moroccan Descent in The Netherlands," *Ethnic and Racial Studies* 25 (2002): 462–89.

Bulbeck, Chilla. *Re-Orienting Western Feminisms: Women's Diversity in a Postcolonial World.* New York: Cambridge University Press, 1998.

Bumiller, Elizabeth. "Deny Rape or Be Hated: Kosovo Victims' Choice." *New York Times* (June 22, 1999):1.

Bunster, Ximena. "Surviving beyond Fear: Women and Torture in Latin America." In *Women and Change in Latin America,* ed. June Nash and Helen Safa, 297–325. South Hadley, MA: Bergin and Garvey, 1986.

Burke, Timothy. *Lifebuoy Men, Lux Women: Commodification, Consumption, and Cleanliness in Modern Zimbabwe.* Durham: Duke University Press, 1996.

Buruma, Ian, and Avishai Margalit. "Occidentalism." *New York Review of Books* (January 17, 2002):4–7.

Bush, Barbara. " 'Britain's Conscience on Africa': White Women, Race and Imperial Politics in Inter-War Britain." In *Gender and Imperialism,* ed. Clare Midgley, 200–23. Manchester: Manchester University Press, 1998.

Butler, Anne M. *Daughters of Joy, Sisters of Misery: Prostitutes in the American West, 1865–90.* Urbana: University of Illinois Press, 1987.

Butler, Judith. *Gender Trouble: Feminism and the Subversion of Identity.* New York: Routledge, 1990.

———. *Bodies That Matter: On the Discursive Limits of Sex.* New York: Routledge, 1993.

———. "Merely Cultural. " *New Left Review* 227 (1998): 33–44.

———. *Gender Trouble: Feminism and the Subversion of Identity.* 2nd ed. New York: Routledge, 1999.

Bynum, Victoria E. *Unruly Women: The Politics of Social and Sexual Control in the Old South.* Chapel Hill: University of North Carolina Press, 1992.

Cabezas, Amalia L. "Women's Work Is Never Done: Sex Tourism in Sostia, the Dominican Republic." In *Sun, Sex and Gold: Tourism and Sex Work in the Caribbean,* ed. Kamala Kempadoo, 93–123. Lanham, MD: Rowman and Littlefield, 1999.

Caceres, Carlos F., and Oscar G. Jimenez. "*Fletes* in Parque Kennedy: Sexual Cultures among Young Men Who Sell Sex to Other Men in Lima." In *Men Who Sell Sex: International Perspectives on Male Prostitution and HIV/AIDS,* ed. Peter Aggleton, 179–93. Philadelphia: Temple University Press, 1999.

Caldwell, Gilliam, Steve Galster, Jyothi Kanicks, and Nadia Steinzor. "Capitalizing on Transition Economies: The Role of the Russian Mafiya in Trafficking Women for Forced Prostitution." In *Illegal Immigration and Commercial Sex: The New Slave Trade,* ed. Phil Williams, 42–73. London: Frank Cass, 1999.

Calhoun, Craig. "Nationalism and Civil Society: Democracy, Diversity, and Self-Determination." In *Social Theory and the Politics of Identity,* ed. Craig Calhoun, 304–35. Cambridge, MA: Blackwell, 1994.

———. "Social Theory and the Politics of Identity." In *Social Theory and the Politics of Identity,* ed. Craig Calhoun, 9–32. Cambridge, MA: Blackwell, 1994.

Carlson, Marvin. *Performance: A Critical Introduction.* New York: Routledge, 1996.

Carnes, Mark C. *Secret Ritual and Manhood in Victorian America.* New Haven: Yale University Press, 1989.

Carretta, Vincent. "Olaudah Equiano or Gustavus Vassa? New Light on an Eighteenth-Century Question of Identity." *Slavery and Abolition: A Journal of Slave and Post-Slave Societies* 20 (1999).

Castiglia, Christopher. *Bound and Determined: Captivity, Culture-Crossing, and White Womanhood from Mary Rowlandson to Patty Hearst.* Chicago: University of Chicago Press, 1996.

Caulfield, Sueann. *In Defense of Honor: Sexual Morality, Modernity, and Nation in Early-Twentieth-Century Brazil.* Durham: Duke University Press, 2000.

Central Intelligence Agency. *The World Factbook, 2000*. Washington, DC: Government Printing Office, 2000 or http://www.cia.gov/cia/publications/factbook/geos/cq.html.

Chang, Grace. *Disposable Domestics: Immigrant Women Workers in the Global Economy*. Cambridge, MA: South End Press, 2000.

Chang, Iris. *The Rape of Nanking: The Forgotten Holocaust of World War II*. New York: Basic Books, 1997.

Chapkis, Wendy. *Beauty Secrets: Women and the Politics of Appearance*. Boston: South End Press, 1986.

Chase-Dunn, Christopher, Yuio Kawano, and Benjamin D. Brewer. "Trade Globalization since 1795: Waves of Integration in the World-System." *American Sociological Review* 65 (2000): 77–95.

Chatterjee, Indrani."Colouring Subalternity: Slaves, Concubines, and Social Orphans in Early Colonial India." *Subaltern Studies* 10 (1999): 49–97.

Chauncey, George. *Gay New York: Gender, Urban Culture, and the Making of the Gay Male World, 1890–1940*. New York: Basic Books. 1994.

Cheah, Pheng. "Posit(ion)ing Human Rights in the Current Global Conjuncture." In *Transnational Asia Pacific: Gender, Culture, and the Public Sphere*, ed. Shirley G. Lim, Larry E. Smith, and Wimal Dissanayake, 11–42. Urbana: University of Illinois Press, 1999.

Chesebrough, David B. *Frederick Douglass: Oratory from Slavery*. Westport, CT: Greenwood Press, 1998.

Childs, Erica Chito. "Constructing Interracial Couples: Multiple Narratives and Images." Ph.D. diss., Fordham University, 2001.

Christgau, Robert. "Chuck Berry." In *The Rolling Stone Illustrated History of Rock and Roll*, ed. Jim Miller, 58–63. New York: Rolling Stone Press, 1976.

Chrystos. "I Don't Understand Those Who Have Turned Away from Me." In *This Bridge Called My Back: Writings by Radical Women of Color*, ed. Cherrie Moraga and Gloria Anzaldua, 68–70. Watertown, MA: Persephone, 1981.

Chupa, Anna Maria. *Anne, the White Woman in Contemporary African-American Fiction: Archetypes, Stereotypes, and characterizations*. Westport, CT: Greenwood Press, 1990.

Churchill, Ward. "The 'Trial' of Leonard Peltier." Preface to Jim Messerschmidt, *The Trial of Leonard Peltier*. Boston: South End Press, 1983.

Cindoglu, Dilek, and Murat Cemrek. "Honor Crimes in the Middle East: Contested Boundaries through Women's Bodies." Paper presented at the annual meeting of the American Sociological Association, Chicago, 1999.

Clarity, James E. "Top Irish Court Lets Girl, 13, Have Abortion in England." *New York Times* (December 2, 1997): A6–7.

Clark, David Anthony Tyeeme, and Joane Nagel. "White Men, Red Masks: Appropriations of 'Indian' Manhood in Imagined Wests." In *Across the Great Divide: Cultures of Manhood in the American West*, ed. Matthew L. Basso, Dee Garceau, and Laura McCall, 109–30. New York: Routledge, 2000.

Cleaver, Eldridge. *Soul on Ice*. New York: Dell Publishing Company, 1968.

Cleaver, Kathleen, and George Katsiaficas, eds. *Liberation, Imagination, and the Black Panther Party: A New Look at the Panthers and their Legacy*. New York: Routledge, 2001.

Cohen, Anthony. "Boundaries of Consciousness, Consciousness of Boundaries." In *The Anthropology of Ethnicity: Beyond "Ethnic Groups and Boundaries,"* ed. Hans Vermeulen and Cora Govers, 59–79. Amsterdam: Spinhuis, 1994.

Cohen, C. J. "Punks, Bulldaggers, and Welfare Queens: The Radical Potential of Queer Politics?" *GLQ: A Journal of Lesbian and Gay Studies* 3 (1997): 437–65.

Cohn, D'Vera. "Shifting Portrait of U.S. Hispanics." *Puerto Rico Herald On-Line* (May 10, 2001) (http://www.puertorico-herald.org/issues/2001/vol5n21/ShiftingPortrainen.shtml).

Collins, Patricia Hill. *Black Feminist Thought: Knowledge, Consciousness, and the Politics of Empowerment.* New York: Routledge, 1990.

Columbus, Christopher. *The* Diario *of Christopher Columbus's First Voyage to America, 1492–1493,* abstracted by Fray Bartolome de las Casas, transcribed and translated into English, with notes and a concordance of the Spanish by Oliver Dunn and James E. Kelley Jr. Norman: University of Oklahoma Press, 1989.

Connell, Robert W. *Gender and Power: Society, the Person, and Sexual Politics.* Stanford: Stanford University Press, 1987.

———. *Masculinities.* Berkeley: University of California Press, 1995.

———. "Masculinities and Globalization." *Men and Masculinities* 1 (1998): 3–23.

Connor, Walker. "A Nation Is a Nation, Is a State, Is an Ethnic Group, Is a . . ." *Ethnic and Racial Studies* 4 (1978): 377–400.

———. "When Is a Nation?" *Ethnic and Racial Studies* 13 (1990): 92–103.

Conrad, Katie. "Domestic Queers: Home and Nation in Ireland." Paper presented at the Hall Center for the Humanities, University of Kansas, 2000.

Cooray, Mark. *Changing the Language of the Law: the Sri Lanka Experience.* Quebéc: Presses de l'Université Laval, 1985.

Corber, Robert J. *Homosexuality in Cold War America: Resistance and the Crisis of Masculinity.* Durham: Duke University Press, 1997.

Cornell, Stephen, and Douglas Hartmann. *Ethnicity and Race: Making Identities in a Changing World.* Thousand Oaks, CA: Pine Forge Press, 1998.

Coser, James. "The Alien as a Servant of Power." *American Sociological Review* 37 (1972): 574–81.

Crenshaw, Kimberle, Neil Gotanda, Gary Peller, Kendall Thomas. *Critical Race Theory: The Key Writings That Formed the Movement.* New York: New Press, 1995.

Curtin, Philip D., ed. *Africa Remembered: Narratives by West Africans from the Era of the Slave Trade.* Prospect Heights, IL: Waveland Press, 1977.

Cypress, Sandra Messinger. *La Malinche in Mexican Literature from History to Myth.* Austin: University of Texas Press, 1991.

Dahlburg, John-Thor. "Bosnian Witness Says She Endured Series of Rapes; Courts: Victim No. 50 Testifies in The Hague." *Los Angeles Times* (March 30. 2000): 1.

Dailey, Jane, Glenda Elizabeth Gilmore, and Bryant Simon. *Jumpin' Jim Crow: Southern Politics from Civil War to Civil Rights.* Princeton: Princeton University Press, 2000.

Daniels, Jessie. *White Lies: Race, Class, Gender, and Sexuality in White Supremacist Discourse.* New York: Routledge, 1997.

Danzger, M. Herbert. *Returning to Tradition: The Contemporary Revival of Orthodox Judaism.* New Haven: Yale University Press, 1989.

Davidson, Julia O'Connell. *Prostitution, Power, and Freedom.* Ann Arbor: University of Michigan Press, 1998.

Davidson, Phoebe, Jo Eadie, Clare Hemmings, Ann Kaloski, and Merl Storr, eds. *The Bisexual Imaginary: Representation, Identity, and Desire.* London: Cassell, 1997.

Davis, Angela Y. "Rape, Racism, and the Capitalist Setting." *Black Scholar* 9 (1978): 2–30.

————. "Rape, Racism, and the Myth of the Black Rapist." In *Women, Race, and Class*, 172–200. New York: Vintage Books, 1981.

————. *Women, Culture, and Politics*. New York: Random House, 1989.

Davis, James F. *Who Is Black? One Nation's Definition*. University Park: Pennsylvania State University, 1991.

Davis Jr., Sammy, J. Boyar, and B. Boyar. *Why Me? The Sammy Davis, Jr. Story*. New York: Farrar, Straus, Giroux, 1989.

Davis, Tim. "Diversity of Queer Politics and the Redefinitiontion of Sexual Identity and Community in Urban Spaces." In *Mapping Desire: Geographies of Sexualities*, ed. David Bell and Gill Valentine, 285–303. New York: Routledge, 1995.

Delgado, Richard. *Critical Race Theory: The Cutting Edge*. Philadelphia: Temple University Press, 1995.

Delgado, Richard, and Jean Stefancic. *Critical Race Theory: An Introduction*. New York: New York University Press, 2001.

Deloria, Philip J. *Playing Indian*. New Haven: Yale University Press, 1999.

D'Emilio, John, and Estelle Freedman. *Intimate Matters: A History of Sexuality in America*. New York: Harper and Row, 1988.

Derounian-Stodola, Stodola, Kathryn Zabelle, and James A. Levernier. *The Indian Captivity Narrative, 1550–1900*. New York: Twayne, 1993.

Desmond, Jane C. *Staging Tourism: Bodies on Display from Waikiki to Sea World*. Chicago: University of Chicago Press, 1999.

Diedrich, Maria. *Love across Color Lines: Ottilie Assing and Frederick Douglass*. New York: Hill and Wang, 1999.

Dikotter, Frank. *The Discourse of Race in Modern China*. London: Hurst and Company, 1992.

Dillon, John. *From Dance Hall to White Slavery: Ten Dance Hall Tragedies*. New York: Padell Book and Magazine Company, 1943.

Dirlik, Arif. "Globalism and the Politics of Place." *Development* 41(1998).

Dobratz, Betty A., and Stephanie L. Shanks-Miele. *"White Power, White Pride!" The White Separatist Movement in the United States*. New York: Twayne Publishers, 1997.

Dodge, Richard Irving. *Our Wild Indians: Thirty-three Years Personal Experience among the Red Men of the Great West*. New York: Archer House, Inc., [1883] 1959.

Domínguez, Virginia R. *White by Definition: Social Classification in Creole Louisiana*. New Brunswick, NJ: Rutgers University Press, 1986.

Donaldson, Mike. "What Is Hegemonic Masculinity?" *Theory and Society* 22 (1993): 643–57.

Donovan, Brian. "White Slavery and Race-Making: Crusading Against Forced Prostitution, 1887–1917." Paper presented at the annual meeting of the American Sociological Association, Washington, DC, 2000.

————. "The Sexual Basis of Racial Formation: Crusades Against Forced Prostitution, 1887–1917." Ph.D. diss., Northwestern University, 2001.

Dray, Philip. *At the Hands of Persons Unknown: The Lynching of Black America*. New York: Random House, 2002.

Dubbert, Joe L. "Progressivism and the Masculinity Crisis." In *The American Man*, ed. Elizabeth H. Pleck and Joseph H. Pleck, 303–20. Englewood Cliffs, NJ: Prentice-Hall, 1980.

Durkheim, Emile. *The Rules of the Sociological Method*. New York: The Free Press, 1938.

Ebersole, Gary L. *Captured by Texts: Puritan to Postmodern Images of Indian Captivity*. Charlottesville: University Press of Virginia, 1995.

Eisenstein, Zillah. *Hatreds: Racialized and Sexualized Conflicts in the 21st Century*. New York: Routledge, 1996.

Eley, Geoff, and Ronald G. Suny, eds. *Becoming National: A Reader*. New York: Oxford University Press, 1996.

Ellis, Deborah. *Women of the Afghan War*. Westport, CT: Praeger, 2000.

Ellis, Steven G. *Tudor Ireland: Crown, Community, and the Conflict of Cultures, 1470–1603*. London: Longman, 1985.

El-Solh, Camilla Fawzi, and Judy Mabro. "Introduction: Islam and Muslim Women." In *Muslim Women's Choices: Religious Belief and Social Reality*, ed. Camilla Fawzi El-Solh and Judy Mabro, 1–32. Providence: Berg Publishers, 1994.

Eltis, David. *The Rise of African Slavery in the Americas*. New York: Cambridge University Press, 2000.

Embree, Ainslee T. *1857 in India, Mutiny or War of Independence?* Boston: Heath, 1963.

Eng, David L. *Racial Castration: Managing Masculinity in Asian America*. Durham: Duke University Press, 2001.

English, Barbara, and Rudrangshu Mukherjee. "Debate: The Kanpur Massacres in India in the Revolt of 1857." *Past and Present* 142 (1994): 169–89.

Engstrom, David W. *Presidential Decision Making Adrift: The Carter Administration and the Mariel Boatlift*. Lanham, MD: Rowman and Littlefield, 1997.

Enloe, Cynthia. *Bananas, Beaches, and Bases: Making Feminist Sense of International Politics*. Berkeley: University of California Press, 1990.

Enloe, Cynthia. "Afterword: Have the Bosnian Rapes Opened a New Era of Feminist Consciousness?" In *Mass Rape: The War against Women in Bosnia-Herzegovina*, ed. Alexandra Stiglmayer, 219–30. Lincoln: University of Nebraska Press, 1994.

———. "It Takes Two." In *Let the Good Times Roll: Prostitution and the U.S. Military in Asia*, ed. Saundra Pollock Sturdevant and Brenda Stoltzfus, 22–27. New York: The New Press, 1992.

———. *Maneuvers: The International Politics of Militarizing Women's Lives*. Berkeley: University of California Press, 2000.

Enriquez, Jean. "Filipinas in Prostitution around U.S. Military Bases in Korea: A Recurring Nightmare." *Coalition against Trafficking in Women-Asia-Pacific* (July 11, 2001) (http://www.uri.edu/artsci/wms/hughes/catw/filkorea.htm).

Epstein, B. "Anti-Communism, Homophobia, and the Construction of Masculinity in the Postwar U.S." *Critical Sociology* 20 (1994): 21–44.

Equiano, Olaudah. *The Interesting Narrative of the Life of Olaudah Equiano, Written by Himself*. Edited by Robert J. Allison. Boston: St. Martin's Press, 1995.

Ericksen, Julia A. *Kiss and Tell: Surveying Sex in the Twentieth Century*. Cambridge, MA: Harvard University Press, 1999.

Erikson, Kai T. *Wayward Puritans: A Study in the Sociology of Deviance*. New York: Wiley, 1966.

Erwin, Kathleen. "Heart-to-Heart, Phone-to-Phone: Family Values, Sexuality, and the Politics of Shanghai's Advice Hotlines." In *The Consumer Revolution in Urban China*, ed. Deborah S. Davis, 145–70. Berkeley: University of California Press, 2000.

Eschbach, Karl. "The Enduring and Vanishing American Indian: American Indian

Population Growth and Intermarriage in 1990." *Ethnic and Racial Studies* 18 (1995): 89–108.

Espiritu, Yen Le. *Asian American Men and Women: Labor, Laws, and Love.* Thousand Oaks, CA: Sage Publications, 1997.

Esterberg, Kristen. *Lesbian and Bisexual Identities: Constructing Communities, Constructing Selves.* Philadelphia: Temple University Press, 1997.

Eterovic, Ivana, Jackie Smith, and Dawn Wiest. "Surviving in a Changing World: Predictors of Dissolution in the Population of Transnational Social Movement Organizations: 1993–2000." Paper presented at the annual meeting of the American Sociological Association, Chicago, 2002.

Evans, David T. *Sexual Citizenship: The Material Construction of Sexualities.* New York: Routledge, 1993.

Evans, Harriet. *Women and Sexuality in China: Female Sexuality and Gender since 1949.* New York: Continuum, 1997.

Evans, Sara M. *Personal Politics: The Roots of Women's Liberation in the Civil Rights Movement and the New Left.* New York: Vintage, 1979.

Evans-Pritchard, Edward E. *The Nuer.* Oxford: Oxford University Press, 1940.

Faery, Rebecca Blevins. *Cartographies of Desire: Captivity, Race, and Sex in the Shaping of an American Nation.* Norman: University of Oklahoma Press, 1999.

Fanon, Frantz. *Black Skin, White Masks.* New York: Grove Press, 1968.

Farrer, James C. " 'Opening Up': Sex and the Market in Shanghai." Ph.D. diss., University of Chicago, 1998.

———. "Disco 'Super-Culture': Consuming Foreign Sex in the Chinese Disco." *Sexualities* 2 (1999): 147–66.

———. *Opening Up: Youth Sex Culture and Market Reform in Shanghai.* Chicago: University of Chicago Press, 2002.

———. "Dancing through the Market Transition: Disco and Dance Hall Sociability in Shanghai." In *The Consumer Revolution in Urban China*, ed. Deborah S. Davis, 226–49. Berkeley: University of California Press, 2000.

Faust, Drew Gilpin. *Mothers of Invention: Women of the Slaveholding South in the American Civil War.* Chapel Hill: University of North Carolina Press, 1996.

Feder, Lynette. *Women and Domestic Violence: An Interdisciplinary Approach.* New York: Haworth Press, 1999.

Felman, Shoshana. *The Literary Speech Act: Don Juan with J.L. Austin, or Seduction in Two Languages.* Ithaca: Cornell University Press, 1983.

Ferber, Abby L. *White Man Falling: Race, Gender, and White Supremacy.* Lanham, MD: Rowman and Littlefield, 1998.

Filene, Peter G. *Him/Her/Self: Sex Roles in Modern America.* Baltimore: Johns Hopkins University Press, 1986.

Finn, Peter. "Signs of Rape Sear Kosovo, Families' Shame Could Hinder Investigation." *Washington Post* (June 27, 1999): 1.

Finnegan, Terence. "'The Equal of Some White Men and the Superior Of Others': Masculinity and the 1916 Lynching of Anthony Crawford in Abbeville County, South Carolina." In *Men and Violence : Gender, Honor, and Rituals in Modern Europe and America*, ed. Pieter Spierenburg, 240–54. Columbus: Ohio State University Press, 1998.

Fischer, Kirsten. *Suspect Relations: Sex, Race, and Resistance in Colonial North Carolina.* Ithaca: Cornell University Press, 2002.

Flood, Renee Sampson. *Lost Bird of Wounded Knee: Spirit of the Lakota.* New York: Scribner's, 1995.

Forster, George. *George Forster's Werke—Band 1 [A Voyage Round the World in his Britannic Majesty's Sloop, Resolution].* Edited by Robert L. Kahn. London: B. White, [1777], 1968.

Forster, Johann Reinhold. *Observations Made During a Voyage Round the World on Physical Geography, Natural History, and Ethic Philosophy.* London: G. Robinson, 1778.

Foster, William Z. *The Negro People in American History.* New York: International Publishers, 1954.

Foucault, Michel. *The History of Sexuality,* volumes 1, 2, 3. New York: Vintage Books, [1976] 1990, [1984] 1990, [1986] 1988.

Frank, David John, Ann Hironaka, and Evan Schofer. "The Nation-State and the Natural Environment over the Twentieth Century." *American Sociological Review* 65 (2000): 96–116.

Frankenberg, Ruth. *White Women, Race Matters: The Social Construction of Whiteness.* Minneapolis: University of Minnesota Press, 1993.

Frankenberg, Ruth, ed. *Displacing Whiteness: Essays in Social and Cultural Criticism.* Durham: Duke University Press, 1997.

Franzway, Suzanne, Dianne Court, and Robert W. Connell. *Staking a Claim: Feminism, Bureaucracy, and the State.* Cambridge: Polity Press, 1989.

Freeman, Carla. *High Tech and High Heels in the Global Economy: Women, Work, and Pink-Collar Identities in the Caribbean.* Durham: Duke University Press, 2000.

Fried, Albert. *McCarthyism.* New York: Oxford University Press, 1997.

Fuss, Diana. *Essentially Speaking: Feminism, Nature, and Difference.* New York: Routledge, 1989.

———. *Inside/Out: Lesbian Theories, Gay Theories.* New York: Routledge, 1991.

Gabriel, John. *Whitewash: Racialized Politics and the Media.* New York: Routledge, 1997.

Gagnon, John, and William Simon. *Sexual Conduct: The Social Sources of Human Sexuality.* Chicago: Aldine, 1973.

Gaitskill, Deborah, and Elaine Unterhalter. "Mothers of the Nation: A Comparative Analysis of Nation, Race, and Motherhood in Afrikaner Nationalism and the African National Congress." In *Woman-Nation-State,* ed. Nira Yuval-Davis and Floya Anthias, 58–78. New York: St. Martin's Press, 1989.

Gallop, Jane. *Thinking through the Body.* New York: Columbia University Press, 1988.

———. "Milosevic Is Given to U.N. for Trial in War-Crime Case." *New York Times* (June 29, 2001): 1.

Gall, Carlotta. "Macedonia Village Is Center of Europe Web in Sex Trade." *New York Times on the Web* (July 28, 2001) (*http://www.nytimes.com/2001/07/28/international/europe/28TRAF.html*).

Garland Library of Narratives of North American Indian Captivities, vols. 1–111. New York: Garland Publications, 1977.

Gehmacher, Johanna. "Men, Women, and the Community Borders: German-Nationalist and National Socialist Discourses on Gender, 'Race,' and National Identity in Austria, 1918–1938." In *Nation, Empire, Colony: Historicizing Gender and Race,* ed. Ruth R. Pierson and Nupur Chaudhuri, 205–19. Bloomington: Indiana University Press, 1998.

Geines, Gerald D. "Two Nations but Only One View." *Contemporary Sociology* 22 (1993): 172.

Gellner, Ernest. *Nations and Nationalism*. Oxford: Blackwell, 1983, 1987.

Gerami, Shahin. *Women and Fundamentalism: Islam and Christianity*. New York: Garland Publishing Company, 1996.

Germain, Randall D. *Globalization and Its Critics: Perspectives from Political Economy*. New York: St. Martin's Press, 2000.

Gerson, Judith, and Kathy Peiss. "Boundaries, Negotiation, Consciousness: Reconceptualizing Gender Relations." *Social Problems* 32 (1985): 317–31.

Gessler, Clifford. *Isles of Enchantment*. New York: Appleton-Century, 1937.

Ghaill, M. Mac An. "The Making of Black English Masculinities." In *Theorizing Masculinities*, ed. Harry Brod and Michael Kaufman, 183–99. Thousand Oaks, CA: Sage Publications, 1994.

Giddings, Paula. *When and Where I Enter: The Impact of Black Women on Race and Sex in America*. New York: William Morrow, 1984.

Gieryn, Thomas F. *Cultural Boundaries of Science: Credibility on the Line*. Chicago: University of Chicago Press, 1999.

Gilmore, David. *Manhood in the Making: Cultural Concepts of Masculinity*. New Haven: Yale University Press, 1990.

Godbeer, Richard. "Eroticizing the Middle Ground: Anglo-Indian Sexual Relations along the Eighteenth-Century Frontier." In *Sex, Love, Race: Crossing Boundaries in North American History*, ed. Martha Hodes, 91–111. New York: New York University Press, 1999.

Goffman, Erving. *The Presentation of Self in Everyday Life*. New York: Doubleday, 1959.

Goldstein, Melvyn C. *The Snow Lion and the Dragon: China, Tibet, and the Dalai Lama*. Berkeley: University of California Press, 1997.

Goodwin, Jan, *The Price of Honor: Muslim Women Lift the Veil of Silence on the Islamic World*. Boston: Little, Brown, 1994.

Goodwin, Jan, and Jessica Neuwirth. "The Rifle and the Veil." *New York Times On-Line* (October 19, 2001).

Gordon-Reed, Annette. *Thomas Jefferson and Sally Hemings: An American Controversy*. Charlottesville: University Press of Virginia, 1997.

Gore, Georgiana. "The Beat Goes On: Trance, Dance and Tribalism in Rave Culture." In *Dance in the City*, ed. H. Thomas, 50–67. New York: St. Martin's Press, 1997.

Gotham, Kevin F. *Race, Real Estate, and Uneven Development: The Kansas City Experience: 1900–2000*. Albany: State University of New York Press, 2002.

Grant, Judith, and Peta Tancred. "A Feminist Perspective on State Bureaucracy." In *Gendering Organizational Analysis*, ed. Albert J. Mills and Peta Tancred, 112–28. Newbury Park, CA: Sage Publications, 1992.

Gray, Beverly J. "The Hemings Family of Monticello." *Ross County Historical Society Magazine Recorder* (February 1994).

Gray, Fred D. *The Tuskegee Syphilis Study: The Real Story and Beyond*. Montgomery, AL: Black Belt Press, 1998.

Greenberg, Joel. "Trips to Renew Jewish Ties Set Off Debate Over Costs." *New York Times* (January 8, 2000): 1.

Greer, Colleen. "Ethnicity—It Won't Just Go Away: The Resilience of Ethnicity through Practices of Assimilation: Lao Refugees in a Midwest Community." Ph.D. diss., University of Kansas, 1998.

Gregory, Desmond. *Sicily: The Insecure Base. A History of the British Occupation of Sicily, 1806–1815*. Rutherford, NJ: Fairleigh Dickinson Press, 1988.

Grenier, Guillermo J., and Lisandro Perez. "Miami Spice: The Ethnic Cauldron Simmers." In *Origins and Destinies: Immigration, Race, and Ethnicity in America*, ed. Silvia Pedraza and Reuben G. Rumbaut, Belmont, CA: Wadsworth. 1996.

Griffin, Michael. *Reaping the Whirlwind: The Taliban Movement in Afghanistan.* Sterling, VA: Pluto Press, 2001.

Griffiths, Alison. "Science and Spectacle: Native American Representation in Early Cinema." In *Dressing in Feathers: The Construction of the Indian in American Popular Culture*, ed. S. Elizabeth Bird, 79–95. Boulder: Westview Press, 1996.

Grittner, Frederick K. *White Slavery: Myth, Ideology, and American Law.* New York: Garland Publishing, 1990.

Gubar, Susan. *Racechanges: White Skin, Black Face in American Culture.* New York: Oxford University Press, 1997.

Gunning, Sandra. *Race, Rape, and Lynching: The Red record of American Literature, 1890–1912.* New York: Oxford University Press, 1996.

Gutierrez, Ramon. *When Jesus Came, the Corn Mothers Went Away: Marriage, Sexuality, and Power in New Mexico, 1500–1846.* Stanford: Stanford University Press, 1991.

Gutmann, Matthew C. *The Meanings of Macho: Being a Man in Mexico City.* Berkeley: University of California Press, 1997.

Hacker, Andrew. *Two Nations: Black and White, Separate, Hostile, and Unequal.* New York: Scribner's, 1992.

Haeri, Shahla. "Women's Body, Nation's Honor: Rape in Pakistan." In *Hermeneutics and Honor: Negotiating Female "Public" Space in Islamic/ate Societies*, ed. Asma Afsaruddin, 55–69. Cambridge, MA: Center for Middle Eastern Studies of Harvard University, Harvard University Press, 1999.

Haines, Herbert H. *Against Capital Punishment.* New York: Oxford University Press, 1996.

Halberstam, Judith. *Female Masculinity.* Durham: Duke University Press, 1998.

Hale, Grace Elizabeth. *Making Whiteness: The Culture of Segregation in the South, 1890–1940.* New York: Pantheon Books, 1998.

Hall, Catherine. "Going A-Trolloping: Imperial Man Travels the Empire." In *Gender and Imperialism*, ed. Clare Midgley, 180–99. Manchester: Manchester University Press, 1998.

Hall, Stuart. "The Local and the Global." In *Culture, Globalization, and the World System*, ed. A. D. King, 19–40. London: Macmillan, 1991.

Hamilton, Annette. "Primal Dream: Masculinism, Sin, and Salvation in Thailand's Sex Trade." In *Sites of Desire, Economies of Pleasure*, ed. Lenore Manderson and Margaret Jolly, 145–65. Chicago: University of Chicago Press, 1997.

Han, Anna M. "Holding Up More Than Half the Sky." In *Global Critical Race Feminism: An International Reader*, ed. Adrien Katherine Wing, 392–408. New York: New York University Press, 2000.

Hann, Chris, and Ildiko Beller-Hann. "Markets, Morality and Modernity in North-East Turkey." In *Border Identities: Nation and State at International Frontiers*, ed. Thomas M. Wilson and Hastings Donnan, 237–62. Cambridge: Cambridge University Press, 1998.

Hansberry, Lorraine. *To Be Young, Gifted, and Black.* New York: Signet, 1970.

Hantover, Jeffrey P. "The Boy Scouts and the Validation of Masculinity." In *Men's Lives*, ed. Michael S. Kimrnel and Michael A. Messner, 74–81. Boston: Allyn and Bacon, 1995.

Harden, Jacalyn D. "The Enterprise of Empire: Race, Class, Gender, and Japanese National Identity." In *The Gender/Sexuality Reader: Culture, History, Political*

Economy, ed. Roger N. Lancaster and Micaela di Leonardo, 487–501. New York: Routledge, 1997.

Hardt, Michael, and Antonio Negri. *Empire.* Cambridge, MA: Harvard University Press, 2000.

Hare, N., and J. Hare. *The Endangered Black Family: Coping with the Unisexualization and Coming Extinction of the Black Race.* San Francisco: Black Think Tank, 1984.

Harper, Phillip Brian. *Are We Not Men? Masculine Anxiety and the Problem of African-American Identity.* New York: Oxford University Press, 1996.

Harris, David R. "Cohabitation, Marriage, and Markets: A New Look at Intimate Interracial Relationships." Paper presented at the annual meeting of the Population Association of America, Los Angeles, 2000.

Harris, Marvin. *Patterns of Race in the Americas.* New York: Walker, 1964.

Hartman, Saidiya. *Scenes of Subjection: Terror, Slavery, and Self-Making in Nineteenth-Century America.* New York: Oxford University Press, 1997.

Hartsock, Nancy. *Money, Sex, and Power: Toward a Feminist Historical Materialism.* New York: Longman, 1983.

———. *The Feminist Standpoint Revisited and Other Essays.* Boulder: Westview Press, 1998.

Harvie, Christopher. *Scotland and Nationalism.* London: Allen and Unwin, 1977.

Hasan, Zoya, ed. *Forging Identities: Gender, Communities, and State in India.* Boulder: Westview Press, 1994.

———. *Quest for Power: Oppositional Movements and Post-Congress Politics in Uttar Pradesh.* Delhi: Oxford University Press, 1998.

Hawkes, Gail. A *Sociology of Sex and Sexuality.* Philadelphia: Open University Press, 1996.

Helie, Anissa. "Between 'Becoming M'tourni' and 'Going Native': Gender and Settler Society in Algeria." In *Unsettling Settler Societies* ed. Daiva Stasiulis and Nira Yuval-Davis, 263–91. Thousand Oaks, CA: Sage Publications, 1995.

Helie-Lucas, Marie-Aimee. "The Role of Women during the Algerian Liberation Struggle and after: Nationalism as a Concept and as a Practice towards Both the Power of the Army and the Militarization of the People." In *Women and the Military System,* ed. T. E. Isaksson, 171–89. New York: St. Martin's Press, 1988.

Henson, Maria Rosa. *Comfort Woman: A Filipina's Story of Prostitution and Slavery under the Japanese Military.* Lanham, MD: Rowman and Littlefield Publishers, 1999.

Herdt, Gilbert. *Guardians of the Flutes.* New York: McGraw-Hill, 1981.

———. *Rituals of Manhood.* Berkeley: University of California Press, 1982.

———. *Third Sex, Third Gender: Beyond Sexual Dimorphism in Culture and History.* New York: Zone Books, 1994.

———. *Same Sex, Different Cultures: Gays and Lesbians Across Cultures.* Boulder: Westview Press, 1997.

Hickey, Ann. "Beyond 'The Deadly Deception': The Influence of Ethnosexual Boundaries in the Tuskegee Syphilis Experiment." Paper presented at the annual meeting of the American Sociological Association, Chicago, 2002.

Hicks, George L. *The Comfort Women: Japan's Brutal Regime of Enforced Prostitution in the Second World War.* New York: W.W. Norton and Company, 1995.

Higham, John. "The Reorientation of American Culture in the 1890s." In *Writing American History: Essays on Modern Scholarship,* 78–102. Bloomington: Indiana University Press, 1978.

Hine, Darlene Clark. "Rape and the Inner Lives of Black Women in the Middle West: Preliminary Thoughts on the Culture of Dissemblance." In *The Gender Sexuality Reader: Culture, History, and Political Economy,* ed. Roger N. Lancaster and Micaela di Leonardo, 434–49. New York: Routledge, 1997.

Hobsbawm, Eric J. *Nations and Nationalism since 1780: Programme, Myth, and Reality.* Cambridge: Cambridge University Press, 1985, 1992.

Hochschild, Arlie. *The Managed Heart: Commodification of Human Feeling.* Berkeley: University of California Press, 1983.

———. *The Second Shift: Working Parents and the Revolution at Home.* New York: Viking, 1989.

———. "The Nanny Chain: Mothers Minding Other Mothers' Children." *The American Prospect* (January 3, 2000): 32–36.

Hodes, Martha. "The Sexualization of Reconstruction Politics: White Women and Black Men in the South after the Civil War." In *American Sexual Politics: Sex, Gender, and Race since the Civil War,* ed. John C. Fout and Maura S. Tantillo, 59–74. Chicago: University of Chicago Press, 1993.

———. *White Women, Black Men: Illicit Sex in the Nineteenth Century South.* New Haven: Yale University Press, 1997.

Hollinger, David. *Postethnic America: Beyond Multiculturalism.* New York: Basic Books, 1995.

Holstein, James A., and Gale Miller, eds. *Reconsidering Social Constructionism: Debates in Social Problems Theory.* New York: Aldine de Gruyter, 1993.

Hondagneu-Sotelo, Pierrette. Domestica *Immigrant Workers Cleaning and Caring in the Shadows of Affluence.* Berkeley: University of California Press, 2001.

Hoogvelt, Ankie. *Globalization and the Postcolonial World: The New Political Economy of Development.* Baltimore: Johns Hopkins University Press, 1997.

hooks, bell. *Black Looks: Race and Representation.* Boston: South End Press, 1992.

———. "Eating the Other." In bell hooks, *Black Looks: Race and Representation,* 21–39. Boston: South End Press, 1992.

———. "Ice Cube Culture: A Shared Passion for Speaking Truth." In bell hooks, *Outlaw Culture: Resisting Representations,* 125–43. New York: Routledge, 1994.

———. *Outlaw Culture: Resisting Representations,* New York: Routledge, 1994.

———. "Doing It for Daddy." In *Constructing Masculinity,* ed. Maurice Berger, Brian Wallis, and Simon Watson, 98–106. New York: Routledge, 1995.

Horowitz, Donald. *Ethnic Groups in Conflict.* Berkeley: University of California Press, 1985.

Horrocks, Roger. *Masculinity in Crisis: Myths, Fantasies, and Realities.* New York: St. Martin's Press, 1994.

Howard, Keith. *True Stories of the Korean Comfort Women.* London: Cassell, 1995.

Hughes, Donna M. "The 'Natasha' Trade: Transnational Sex Trafficking." *National Institute of Justice Journal* (January 2001): 8–15.

Human Rights Watch. "Neither Jobs nor Justice: Discrimination against Women in Russia." *Human Rights Watch Report* (March 1995).

———. *Slaughter among Neighbors: The Political Origins of Communal Violence.* New Haven: Yale University Press, 1995.

———. *Human Rights Country Reports, Russia.* Washington, DC, 1997.

———. "Kosovo Rape as a Weapon of " 'Ethnic Cleansing.' " *Human Rights Watch Report* (March 2000).

Hunt, D. M. *Screening the Los Angeles "Riots": Race, Seeing, and Resistance.* New York: Columbia University Press, 1997.

Hurtado, Albert. "When Strangers Met: Sex and Gender on Three Frontiers." In *Writing the Range: Race, Class, and Culture in the Women's West*, ed. Elizabeth Jameson and Susan Armitage, 122–42. Norman: University of Oklahoma Press, 1997.

———. *Intimate Frontiers: Sex, Gender, and Culture in Old California*. Albuquerque: University of New Mexico Press, 1999.

Hutchinson, Earl Ofari. *The Assassination of the Black Male Image*. New York: Touchstone, [1994] 1997.

Hutchinson, John, and Anthony D. Smith, eds. *Nationalism*. New York: Oxford University Press, 1994.

Inglis, Tom. "Sexual Transgression and Scapegoats: A Case Study from Modern Ireland." *Sexualities* 5 (2002): 5–24.

Ireland, Kevin. *Wish You Weren't Here: The Sexual Exploitation of Children and the Connection with Tourism and International Travel*. London: Save the Children Working Paper, No. 7, 1993.

Jacobs, Sue-Ellen, Wesley Thomas, and Sabine Lang, eds. *Two-Spirit People: Native American Gender Identity, Sexuality, and Spirituality*. Urbana: University of Illinois Press, 1997.

Jagose, Annamarie. *Queer Theory: An Introduction*. New York: New York University Press, 1996.

Jalata, Asafa. *Fighting against the Injustice of State and Globalization: Comparing the Black and Oromo Movements*. New York: Palgrave, 2001.

Jayawardena, Kumari. *Feminism and Nationalism in the Third World*. London: Zed Books, 1986.

Jefferson, Thomas. *Notes on the State of Virginia*. Edited by William Peden. Chapel Hill: University of North Carolina Press, [1787] 1995.

Jeyasingh, Shobana. "Imaginary Homelands: Creating a New Dance Language." In *Border Tensions: Proceedings of the Fifth Study of Dance Conference*, 191–97. Guildford: University of Surrey, 1995.

Johnson, Chalmers. *Blowback: The Costs and Consequences of American Empire*. New York: Metropolitan Books, 2000.

Carolina Press, [1787] 1995.

Johnson, Lyman L., and Sonya Lipsett-Rivera. *The Faces of Honor: Sex, Shame, and Violence in Colonial Latin America*. Albuquerque: University of New Mexico Press, 1998.

Johnson, Walter. *Soul by Soul: Life inside the Antebellum Slave Market*. Cambridge, MA: Harvard University Press, 1999.

Jolly, Margaret. "From Point Venus to Bali Ha'i: Eroticism and Exoticism in Representations of the Pacific." In *Sites of Desire, Economies of Pleasure: Sexualities in Asia and the Pacific*, ed. Lenore Manderson and Margaret Jolly, 99–122. Chicago: University of Chicago Press, 1997.

Jones, Eldred D. *The Elizabethan Image of Africa*. Charlottesville: University of Virginia Press, 1971.

Jones, James H. *Bad Blood: The Tuskegee Syphilis Experiment*. New York: Free Press, 1993.

Jordan, Winthrop D. *White over Black: American Attitudes toward the Negro, 1550–1812*. Chapel Hill: University of North Carolina Press, 1968.

Julien, Isaac, and Kobena Mercer. "True Confessions: A Discourse on Images of Black Male Sexuality." *Ten-8* 22 (1986): 6.

Kane, June. *Sold for Sex*. Brookfield, VT: Arena, 1998.

Kang, Jerry. "Cyber-Race." *Harvard Law Review* 113 (2000): 1131–1208.

Kantrowitz, Stephen. "White Supremacist Justice and the Rule of Law: Lynching, Honor, and the State in Ben Tillman's South Carolina." In *Men and Violence: Gender, Honor, and Rituals in Modern Europe and America*, ed. Pieter Spierenburg, 213–39. Columbus: Ohio State University Press, 1998.

Kaplan, Amy. "Romancing the Empire: The Embodiment of American Masculinity in the Popular Historical Novels of the 1890s." *American Literary History* 2 (1990): 659–90.

Karlen, Arno. *Sexuality and Homosexuality: A New View*. New York: W.W. Norton, 1971.

Karner, Tracy X. "Masculinity, Trauma, and Identity: Life Narratives of Vietnam Veterans with Post Traumatic Stress Disorder." Ph.D. diss., University of Kansas, 1994.

Katz, Jonathan Ned. *The Invention of Heterosexuality*. New York: Dutton, 1995.

Kaufman, Donald L. "The Indian as Media Hand-Me-Down." In *The Pretend Indians: Images of Native Americans in the Movies*, ed. Gretchen M. Bataille and Charles L. P. Silet, 22–34. Ames: Iowa State University Press, 1980.

Keck, Margaret, and Katherine Sikkink. *Activists beyond Borders: Advocacy Networks in International Politics*. Ithaca: Cornell University Press, 1998.

———. "Historical Precursors to Modern Transnational Social Movements and Networks." In *Globalization and Social Movements: Culture, Power, and the Transnational Public Sphere*, ed. John A. Guidry, Michael D. Kennedy, and Mayer N. Zald, 35–53. Ann Arbor: University of Michigan Press, 2000.

Keith, Verna M., and Cedric Herring. "Skin Tone and Stratification in the Black Community." *American Journal of Sociology* 97 (1991): 760–78.

Kelley, Jack. "Kuwait Slow to Deal with Rapes." *USA Today* (July 29, 1991): 9.

Kelley, Robin D. G. *Race Rebels: Culture, Politics, and the Black Working Class*. New York: Free Press, 1994.

Kelly, Mary E. "Ethnic Conversions: Family, Community, Women, and Kinwork." *Ethnic Studies Review* 19 (1996): 81–100.

———. "Ethnic Pilgrimages: People of Lithuanian Descent in Lithuania." *Sociological Spectrum* 20 (2000): 65–91.

Kelsky, Karen. *Women on the Verge: Japanese Women, Western Dreams*. Durham: Duke University Press, 2001.

Kemble, Frances Anne. *Journal of a Residence on a Georgian Plantation in 1838–1839*. Chicago: Afro-Am Press, 1969.

Kempadoo, Kamala. "The Migrant Tightrope: Experiences from the Caribbean." In *Global Sex Workers: Rights, Resistance, and Redefinition*, ed. K. Kempadoo and J. Doezema, 124–38. New York: Routledge, 1998.

———. *Sun, Sex, and Gold: Tourism and Sex Work in the Caribbean*. Lanham, MD: Rowman and Littlefield, 1999.

Kempadoo, Kamala, eds. *Global Sex Workers: Rights, Resistance, and Redefinition*. New York: Routledge, 1998.

Kestler, Frances Roe. *The Indian Captivity Narrative: A Woman's View*. New York: Garland Publishing Company, 1990.

al-Khalil, Samir. *Republic of Fear: The Politics of Modern Iraq*. Berkeley: University of California Press. 1989.

Khan, Shivananda. "Through a Window Darkly: Men Who Sell Sex to Men in India and Bangladesh." In *Men Who Sell Sex: International Perspectives on Male Prostitution and HIV/AIDS*, ed. Peter Aggleton, 195–212. Philadelphia: Temple University Press. 1999.

Kimmel, Michael S. *Manhood in America: A Cultural History*. New York: Basic Books, 1995.

———. *The Gendered Society*. New York: Oxford University Press, 2000.

Kimmel, Michael S., and Michael A. Messner, *Men's Lives*. New York: Allyn and Bacon, 1995.

King, C. Richard, and Charles F. Springwood. "Fighting Spirits: The Racial Politics of Sports Mascots." *Journal of Sport and Social Issues* 24 (2000): 282–304.

———. *Team Spirits: The Native American Mascot Controversy*. Lincoln: University of Nebraska Press, 2001.

Kinsey, Alfred C., Wardell B. Pomeroy, Clyde E. Martin, and Paul H. Gebhard. *Sexual Behavior in the Human Male*. Philadelphia: W.B. Saunders, 1948.

———. *Sexual Behavior in the Human Female*. Philadelphia: W.B. Saunders, 1953.

Kivisto, Peter. "Theorizing Transnational Immigration: A Critical Review of Current Efforts." *Ethnic and Racial Studies* 24 (2001): 549–77.

Klein, Cecile. *Sentenced to Live*. New York: Holocaust Library, 1988.

Kole, William J., and Aida Cerkez-Robinson. "U.N. Police Accused of Involvement in Prostitution in Bosnia." Associated Press (July 6, 2001) (http://fpmail.friends-partners.org/mailman/listinfo.cgi/stop-traffic).

Kopinak, Kathryn. *Desert Capitalism: Maquiladoras in North America's Western Industrial Corridor*. Tucson: University of Arizona Press, 1996.

Koven, Seth. "From Rough Lads to Hooligans: Boy Life, National Culture, and Social Reform." In *Nationalisms and Sexualities*, ed. Andrew Parker, Mary Russo, Doris Sommer, and Patricia Yaeger, 365–91. New York: Routledge, 1991.

Kraus, Richard. "Public Monuments and Private Pleasures in the Parks of Nanjing: A Tango in the Ruins of the Ming Emperor's Palace." In *The Consumer Revolution in Urban China*, ed. Deborah S. Davis, 287–311. Berkeley: University of California Press, 2000.

Krishnaswamy, Revathi. *Effeminism: The Economy of Colonial Desire*. Ann Arbor: University of Michigan Press, 1998.

Kruks, G. "Gay and Lesbian Homeless/Street Youth: Special Issues and Concerns." *Journal of Adolescent Health* 12 (1991): 515–18.

Kutschera, Chris. "Algeria's Fighting Women." *The Middle East* (April 1996): 4–41.

Laitin, David D. *Hegemony and Culture: Politics and Religious Change among the Yoruba*. Chicago: University of Chicago Press, 1986.

Lambevski, Sasho A. "Suck My Nation—Masculinity, Ethnicity, and the Politics of (Homo)Sex." *Sexualities* 2 (1999): 397–419.

Lancaster, Roger N. *Life Is Hard: Machismo, Danger, and the Intimacy of Power in Nicaragua*. Berkeley: University of California Press, 1992.

———, and Micaela di Leonardo, eds. *The Gender/Sexuality Reader: Culture, History, Political Economy*. New York: Routledge, 1997.

Lang, Daniel. *Casualties of War*. New York: McGraw-Hill, 1969.

Laqueur, Thomas. *Making Sex: Body and Gender from the Greeks to Freud*. Cambridge, MA: Harvard University Press, 1990.

Larvie, Patrick. "Natural Born Targets: Male Hustlers and AIDS Prevention in Urban Brazil." In *International Perspectives on Male Prostitution and HIV/AIDS*, ed. Peter Aggleton, 159–77. Philadelphia: Temple University Press, 1999.

Laumann, Edward O., John H. Gagnon, Robert T. Michael, and Stuart Michaels. *The*

Social Organization of Sexuality: Sexual Practices in the United States. Chicago: University of Chicago Press, 1994.

Law, Lisa. "A Matter of 'Choice': Discourses on Prostitution in the Philippines." In *Sites of Desire, Economies of Pleasure: Sexualities in Asia and the Pacific,* ed. L. Manderson and M. Jolly, 233–61. Chicago: University of Chicago Press, 1997.

Laws of the State of Missouri, first session, twentieth general assembly, Monday, December 27, 1858. Jefferson City: C.J. Corwin, Public Printer, 1859.

Leckie, Shirley A. *Elizabeth Bacon Custer and the Making of a Myth.* Norman: University of Oklahoma Press, 1993.

Leheny, David. "A Political Economy of Asian Sex Tourism." *Annals of Tourism Research* 22 (1995): 367–84.

di Leonardo, Micaela. *The Varieties of Ethnic Experience.* Ithaca: Cornell University Press, 1984.

———. "White Lies, Black Myths: Rape, Race, and the Black 'Underclass.'" In *The Gender/Sexuality Reader,* ed. Roger N. Lancaster and Micaela di Leonardo, 53–68. New York: Routledge, 1997.

Leong, R, ed. *Asian American Sexualities: Dimensions of the Gay and Lesbian Experience.* New York: Routledge, 1996.

Lesch, Ann Mosely. *The Sudan.* Bloomington: Indiana University Press, 1998.

Liguori, Ana Luisa, and Peter Aggleton. "Aspects of Male Sex Work in Mexico City." In *Men Who Sell Sex: International Perspectives on Male Prostitution and HIV/AIDS,* ed. Peter Aggleton, 103–25. Philadelphia: Temple University Press, 1999.

Lim, Lin Lean. "Child Prostitution." In *The Sex Sector: The Economic and Social Bases of Prostitution in Southeast Asia,* ed. Lin Lean Lim, 170–205. Geneva: International Labor Office, 1998.

Lim, Shirley Geok-Lin, and Wimal Dissanayake. "Introduction." In *Transnational Asia Pacific: Gender, Culture, and the Public Sphere,* ed. Shirley G. Lim, Larry E. Smith, and Wimal Dissanayake, 1–9. Urbana: University of Illinois Press, 1999.

Limerick, Patricia. *The Legacy of Conquest: The Unbroken Past of the American West.* New York: W.W. Norton and Company, 1987.

Linebaugh, Peter, and Marcus Rediker, *The Many-Headed Hydra: Sailors, Slaves, Commoners, and the Hidden History of the Revolutionary Atlantic.* Boston: Beacon Press, 2000.

Lipsitz, George. *The Possessive Investment in Whiteness: How White People Profit from Identity Politics.* Philadelphia: Temple University Press, 1998.

Littlewood, Ian. *Sultry Climates: Travel and Sex since the Grand Tour.* London: John Murray, 2001.

Loftus, Jeni. "America's Liberalization in Attitudes toward Homosexuality." *American Sociological Review* 66 (2001): 762–82.

Long, Edward. *The History of Jamaica,* 3 volumes. London, 1774.

Longman, Phillip J. "The World Turns Gray." *U.S. News and World Report* (March 1, 1999).

Lorber, Judith. *Paradoxes of Gender.* New Haven: Yale University Press, 1994.

Low, Bobbi S. *Why Sex Matters: A Darwinian Look at Human Behavior.* Princeton: Princeton University Press, 2000.

Lowe, Lisa. *Critical Terrains: French and British Orientalisms.* Ithaca: Cornell University Press, 1991.

————. *Immigrant Acts: On Asian American Cultural Politics.* Durham: Duke University Press, 1998.

Luker, Karen. *Dubious Conceptions: The Politics of Teenage Pregnancy.* Cambridge, MA: Harvard University Press, 1996.

Lumley, Robert, and Jonathan Morris. *The New History of the Italian South: The Mezzogiorno Revisited.* Exeter: University of Exeter Press, 1997.

Luszki, Walter A. *A Rape of Justice: MacArthur and the New Guinea Hangings.* Lanham, MD: Madison Books, 1991.

MacDonald, Robert H. *Sons of the Empire: The Frontier and the Boy Scout Movement, 1890–1918.* Toronto: University of Toronto Press, 1993.

MacKenzie, John M. "The Imperial Pioneer and Hunter and the British Masculine Stereotype in Late Victorian and Edwardian Times." In *Manliness and Morality: Middle-Class Masculinity in Britain and America, 1800–1940,* ed. J. A. Mangan and J. Walvin, 176–98. Manchester: Manchester University Press, 1987.

MacKinnon, Catherine. *Toward a Feminist Theory of the State.* Cambridge, MA: Harvard University Press, 1989.

Mailly, Hugh D. "Haole." In *Encyclopedia Mythica.* (http://www.pantheon.org/mythica/articles/h/haole.html).

Mailly, Hugh D. "Haole." In *Encyclopedia Mythica* (http://www.pantheon.org/mythica/articles/h/haole.html).

Malinowski, Bronislaw. *Sex and Repression in Savage Society.* New York: Harcourt, Brace and Company, 1927.

————. *The Sexual Life of Savages in North-Western Melanesia.* New York: Horace Liveright, 1929.

Manderson, Lenore. "Public Sex Performances in Patpong and Explorations of the Edges of Imagination." *The Journal of Sex Research* 29 (1992): 451–75.

Marinetti, Filippo Thommaso. *Democrazia Futurista.* In *The Untameables/F.T. Marinetti,* trans. Jeremy Parzen. Los Angeles: Sun and Moon Press, 1994.

Martin, Emily. *The Woman in the Body: A Cultural Analysis of Reproduction.* Boston: Beacon Press, 1989.

————. *Flexible Bodies.* Boston: Little Brown, 1994.

Marx, Karl. *New York Daily Tribune* (July 22, 1853).

Mason, Michael. *The Making of Victorian Sexuality.* Oxford, 1994.

Massey, Douglas S., and Nancy A. Denton. *American Apartheid: Segregation and the Making of the Underclass.* Cambridge, MA: Harvard University Press, 1993.

Masters, William H., and Virginia E. Johnson. *Human Sexual Response.* Boston: Little, Brown, 1966.

Matsui, Yayori. *Women in the New Asia: From Pain to Power.* New York: Zed Books, 1999.

Mayer, Tamar. "Gender Ironies of Nationalism: Setting the Stage." In *Gender Ironies of Nationalism: Sexing the Nation,* ed. Tamar Mayer, 1–12. New York: Routledge, 2000.

McAdam, Doug. *Political Process and the Development of Black Insurgency, 1930–1970.* Chicago: University of Chicago Press, 1982.

————. *Freedom Summer.* New York: Oxford University Press, 1988.

McAlister, Melani. *Epic Encounters: Culture, Media, and U.S. Interests in the Middle East, 1945–2000.* Berkeley: University of California Press, 2001.

McClain, Ellen Jaffe. *Embracing the Stranger: Intermarriage and the Future of the American Jewish Community.* New York: Basic Books, 1995.

McClintock, Anne. *Imperial Leather: Race, Gender, and Sexuality in the Colonial Contest.* New York: Routledge, 1995.

McCrone, David. *The Sociology of Nationalism.* New York: Routledge, 1998.

McFadden, Robert D., Ralph Blumenthal, M. A. Farber, E. R. Shipp, Charles Strum, and Craig Wolff. *Outrage: The Story Behind the Tawana Brawley Hoax.* New York: Bantam Books, 1990.

McGovern, James R. "David Graham Phillips and the Virility Impulse of the Progressives." *New England Quarterly* 39 (1966): 33–55.

McKittrick, David, Seamus Kelters, Brian Feeney, and Chris Thornton. *Lost Lives: Stories of the Men, Women, and Children Who Died as a Result of the Northern Ireland Troubles.* Edinburgh: Mainstream Publishing, 1999.

McLaurin, Melton. *Celia, A Slave.* Athens: University of Georgia Press, 1991.

Mead, Margaret. *Coming of Age in Samoa.* New York: William Morrow, 1928.

———. *Sex and Temperament in Three Primitive Societies.* New York: William Morrow and Company, 1935.

Mehdid, Malika. "En-Gendering the Nation-State: Woman, Patriarchy and Politics in Algeria." In *Woman and the State: International Perspectives,* ed. S. M. Rai and G. Lievesley, 78–102. London: Taylor and Francis 1996.

Mendleberg, Tali. *The Race Card: Campaign Strategy, Implicit Messages, and the Norm of Equality.* Princeton: Princeton University Press, 2001.

Mercer, Kobena. "Skin Head Sex Thing: Racial Difference and the Homoerotic Imaginary." In *How Do I Look: Queer Film and Video,* ed. Bad Object-Choices, 169–222. Seattle: Bay Press, 1991.

Meyer, John, John Boli, George M. Thomas, and Francisco O. Ramirez. "World Society and the Nation-State." *American Journal of Sociology* 103 (1997): 14–81.

Michael, Robert T., John H. Gagnon, Edward O. Laumann, and Gina Kolata. *Sex in America: A Definitive Survey.* Boston: Little, Brown and Company, 1994.

Midgley, Clare. "Anti-Slavery and the Roots of 'Imperial Feminism.'" In *Gender and Imperialism,* ed. Clare Midgley, 161–79. Manchester: Manchester University Press, 1998.

Miles, Nelson A. *Serving the Republic: Memoirs of the Civil and Military Life of Nelson A. Miles.* New York: Harper and Brothers, 1911.

Miles, William F. S. *Hausaland Divided: Colonialism and Independence in Nigeria and Niger.* Ithaca: Cornell University Press, 1994.

Miller, Joseph C. *Way of Death: Merchant Capitalism and the Angolan Slave Trade, 1730–1830.* Madison: University of Wisconsin Press, 1988.

Miller, Judith. "Atrocities by Iraqis in Kuwait: Numbers Are Hard to Verify." *New York Times* (December 16, 1990):1, 20.

Mills, Charles W. *The Racial Contract.* Ithaca: Cornell University Press, 1997.

Modood, T., and P. Werbner, eds. *The Politics of Multiculturalism in the New Europe: Racism, Identity, and Community.* London: ZED, 1997.

Moeller, Robert G. *Protecting Motherhood: Women and the Family in the Politics of Postwar West Germany.* Berkeley: University of California Press, 1993.

Moghissi, Haideh. *Feminism and Islamic Fundamentalism: The Limits.* London: Zed Books, 1999.

Montgomery, Heather. "Children, Prostitution, and Identity: A Case Study from a Tourist Resort in Thailand." In *Global Sex Workers: Rights, Resistance, and Redefinition,* ed. K. Kempadoo and J. Doezema, 139–50. New York: Routledge, 1998.

Moon, Katharine H. S. *Sex among Allies: Military Prostitution in U. S.-Korea Relations.* New York: Columbia University Press, 1997.

Moraga, Cherrie, and Gloria Anzaldua, eds. *This Bridge Called My Back: Writings by Radical Women of Color*. Watertown, MA: Persephone, 1981.

Moran, L. J. "The Uses of Homosexuality: Homosexuality for National Security." *International Journal of the Sociology of Law* 19 (1991): 149–70.

Morgan, Philip D. "British Encounters with Africans and African-Americans, circa 1600–1780." In *Strangers within the Realm: Cultural Margins of the First British Empire*, ed. Bernard Bailyn and Philip D. Morgan, 157–219. Chapel Hill: University of North Carolina Press, 1991.

———. "Encounters Between British and 'Indigenous' Peoples, 1500–1800." In *Empire and Others: British Encounters with Indigenous Peoples, 1600–1850*, ed. Martin Daunton and Rick Halpern, 42–78. Philadelphia: University of Pennsylvania Press, 1999.

Morris, Douglas. "Internetworked Social Movements: Comparing the Alternative Globalization Movement and Terrorist Networks." Paper presented at the annual meeting of the American Sociological Association, Chicago, 2002.

Morse, Edward V., Patricia M. Simon, and Kendra E. Burchfiel. "Social Environment and Male Sex Work in the United States." In *Men Who Sell Sex: International Perspectives on Male Prostitution and HIV/AIDS*, ed. Peter Aggleton, 83–101. Philadelphia: Temple University Press, 1999.

Moses, L. G. *Wild West Shows and the Images of American Indians, 1883–1933*. Albuquerque: University of New Mexico Press, 1996.

Mosse, George L. *Nationalism and Sexuality: Middle Class Morality and Sexual Norms in Modern Europe*. Madison: University of Wisconsin Press, 1985.

———. *The Image of Man: The Creation of Modern Masculinity*. New York: Oxford University Press, 1996.

Motyl, Alexander J., ed. *Encyclopedia of Nationalism*. San Diego: Academic Press, 2000.

Mowforth, Martin, and Ian Munt, *Tourism and Sustainability: New Tourism in the Third World*. New York: Routledge, 1998.

de Moya, E. Antonio, and Rafael Garcia. "Three Decades of Male Sex Work in Santo Domingo." In *Men Who Sell Sex: International Perspectives on Male Prostitution and HIV/AIDS*, ed. Peter Aggleton, 127–39. Philadelphia: Temple University Press, 1999.

de Moya, E. Antonio, Rafael Garcia, Rosario Fadul, and Edward Herold. *Sosua Sanky-Pankies and Female Sex Workers*. Santo Domingo: Instituto de Sexualidad Humana, Universidad Autonoma de Santo Domingo, 1992.

Mukherjee, Rudrangshu. "'Satan Let Loose Upon Earth' The Kanpur Massacres in India in the Revolt of 1857." *Past and Present* 128 (1990): 92–116.

Mullings, Beverly. "Fantasy Tours: Exploring the Global Consumption of Caribbean Sex Tours." In *New Forms of Consumption: Consumers, Culture, and Commodification*, ed. Mark Gottdiener, 227–50. Lanham, MD: Rowman and Littlefield, 2000.

Mumford, Kevin J. " 'Lost Manhood' Found: Male Sexual Impotence and Victorian Culture in the United States." In *American Sexual Politics: Sex, Gender, and Race since the Civil War*, ed. John C. Fout and Maura S. Tantillo, 75–99. Chicago: University of Chicago Press, 1993.

———. *Interzones: Black/White Sex Districts in Chicago and New York in the Early Twentieth Century*. New York: Columbia University Press, 1997.

Mydans, Seth. "Inside a Wartime Brothel: The Avenger's Story." *New York Times* (November 12, 1996): A3.

Myers, Rex C. "Montana Editors and the Custer Battle." In *The Great Sioux War, 1876–77*, ed. Philip L. Hedren, 177–91. Helena: Montana Historical Society Press, 1991.

Na'Allah, Abdul-Rasheed, ed. *Ogoni's Agonies: Ken Saro-Wiwa and the Crisis in Nigeria*. Trenton, NJ: Africa World Press, 1998.

Nagel, Joane. *American Indian Ethnic Renewal: Red Power and the Resurgence of Identity and Culture*. New York: Oxford University Press, 1996.

Namias, June. *White Captives: Gender and Ethnicity on the American Frontier*. Chapel Hill: University of North Carolina Press, 1993.

Nategh, Homa. "Women: Damned of the Iranian Revolution." In *Women and Political Conflict*, ed. R. Ridd and H. Callaway, 45–60. New York: New York University Press, 1987.

Neal, Mark Anthony. *What the Music Said: Black Popular Music and Black Public Culture*. New York: Routledge, 1998.

Nero, Charles I. "Toward a Black Gay Aesthetic: Signifying in Contemporary Black Gay Literature." In *Brother to Brother: New Writings by Gay Black Men*, ed. Essex Hemphill, 229–52. Boston: Alyson Publications, 1991.

New York Times. "Once-hidden Slave Trade A Growing U.S. Problem"(April 2, 2000): 1.

Nobles, Melissa. *Shades of Citizenship: Race and the Census in Modern Politics*. Stanford: Stanford University Press, 2000.

Noll, Stephen F. "What the Anglican Bishops Said about Sex: The Lambeth Conference's Resolution 1.10, with Introduction and Commentary" (May 28, 2000) (http://www.tesm.edu/writings/nolllamb.htm).

Nomberg-Przytyk, Sarah. *Tales from a Grotesque Land*. Chapel Hill: University of North Carolina Press, 1985.

Northrup, Solomon. *Twelve Years a Slave*. Edited by Sue Eakin and Joseph Logsdon. Baton Rouge: Louisiana State University Press, 1968.

Nugent, Daniel, and Ana Maria Alonso, "Multiple Selective Traditions in Agrarian Reform and Agrarian Struggle: Popular Culture and State Formation in the *Ejido* of Namiquipa, Chihuahua." In *Everyday Forms of State Formation: Revolution and the Negotiation of Rule in Modern Mexico*, ed. Gilbert M. Joseph and Daniel Nugent, 209–46. Durham, NC: Duke University Press, 1994.

Nye, Robert A. *Masculinity and Male Codes of Honor in Modern France*. New York: Oxford University Press, 1993.

Octomo, Dede. "Masculinity in Indonesia: Genders, Sexualities, and Identities in a Changing Society." In *Framing the Sexual Subject: The Politics of Gender, Sexuality, and Power*, ed. Richard Parker, Regina Maria Barbosa, and Peter Aggleton, 46–59. Berkeley: University of California Press, 2000.

Odzer, Cleo. *Patpong Sisters*. New York: Blue Moon-Arcade, 1994.

Olzak, Susan. *The Dynamics of Ethnic Competition and Conflict*. Stanford: Stanford University Press, 1992.

O'Merry, Rory. *My Wife in Bangkok*. Berkeley, CA: Asia Press, 1990.

Omi, Michael, and Howard Winant, *Racial Formation in the United States: From the 1960s to the 1980s*. New York: Routledge and Kegan Paul, 1986, 1994.

Opperman, Martin. *Sex Tourism and Prostitution: Aspects of Leisure, Recreation, and Work*. New York: Cognizant Communications, 1998.

Ortner, Sherry. "Is Female to Male as Nature Is to Culture?" *Feminist Studies* 1 (1972): 5–31.

———. "Borderland Politics and Erotics: Gender and Sexuality in Himalayan Mountaineering." In *Making Gender: The Politics and Erotics of Culture*, ed. Sherry B. Ortner, 181–212. Boston: Beacon Press, 1996.

———. *Making Gender: The Politics and Erotics of Culture*. Boston: Beacon Press, 1996.

Page, Clarence. *Showing My Color: Impolite Essays on Race and Identity*. New York: Harper, 1996.

Pares, John. *A West-India Fortune*. London: Longmans, Green, and Company, 1950.

Parker, Andrew, Mary Russo, Doris Sommer, and Patricia Yaeger, eds. *Nationalisms and Sexualities*. New York: Routledge, 1992.

Parrenas, Rhacel Salazar. "The Global Servants: (Im)Migrant Filipina Domestic Workers in Rome and Los Angeles." Ph.D. diss., University of California, Berkeley, 1998.

———. *The Global Servants: (Im)Migrant Filipina Domestic Workers in Rome and Los Angeles*. Stanford: Stanford University Press, 2001.

Patton, Cindy. "To Die For." In *Novel Gazing: Queer Readings in Fiction*, ed. Eve K. Sedgwick, 330–52. Durham: Duke University Press, 1997.

Paxton, Nancy L. "Mobilizing Chivalry: Rape in British Novels about the Indian Uprising of 1857." *Victorian Studies* 36 (1992): 5–30.

Pearce, Roy Harvey. "The Significance of the Captivity Narrative." *American Literature* 19 (1947): 1–20.

Pedraza, Silvia. "Women and Migration: The Social Consequences of Gender." *Annual Review of Sociology* 17 (1991): 303–25.

———. "Cuba's Refugees: Manifold Migrations." In *Origins and Destinies: Immigration, Race, and Ethnicity in America*, ed. Silvia Pedraza and Ruben G. Rumbaut, 263–79. Belmont, CA: Wadsworth Publishing Company, 1996.

———. "Cuba's Revolution and Exodus." *The Journal of the International Institute*, University of Michigan 5 (1998): 8–9.

Penn, Donna. "Queer: Theorizing Politics and History." *Radical History Review* 62 (1995): 2–42.

Perdue, Theda. *Cherokee Women: Gender and Cultural Change, 1700–1835*. Lincoln: University of Nebraska Press, 1998.

———. "Native Women in the Early Republic: Old World Perceptions, New World Realities." In *Native Americans and the Early Republic*, ed. Frederick E. Hoxie, Ronald Hoffman, and Peter J. Albert, 85–102. Charlottesville: University Press of Virginia, 1999.

Peteet, Julie. "Gender and Sexuality: Belonging to the National and Moral Order." In *Hermeneutics and Honor: Negotiating Female "Public" Space in Islamic/ate Societies*, ed. Asma Afsaruddin, 70–88. Cambridge, MA: Center for Middle Eastern Studies of Harvard University, Harvard University Press, 1999.

Petkov, Kiril. *Infidels, Turks, and Women: The South Slavs in the German Mind, circa 1400–1600*. New York: Peter Lana, 1997.

Pfeil, Fred. *White Guys: Studies in Postmodern Domination and Difference*. London: Verso, 1995.

Phelan, Peggy. *Unmarked: The Politics of Performance*. New York: Routledge, 1993.

Phelan, Peggy, and Jill Lane, *The Ends of Performance*. New York: New York University Press, 1998.

Phongpaichit, Pasuk. *From Peasant Girls to Bangkok Masseuses*. Geneva: International Labour Office, 1982.

———. "Trafficking in People in Thailand." In *Illegal Immigration and Commercial Sex: The New Slave Trade*, ed. Phil Williams, 74–104. London: Frank Cass, 1999.

Phongpaichit, Pasuk, and Chris Baker. *Thailand: Economy and Politics.* New York: Oxford University Press, 1995.

Pierce, Paulette, and Brackette F. Williams, "And Your Prayers Shall Be Answered through the Womb of a Woman." In Brackette F. Williams, *Women out of Place: The Gender of Agency and the Race of Nationality,* 186–215. New York: Routledge, 1996.

Pini, Maria. "Cyborgs, Nomads, and the Raving Feminine." In *Dance in the City,* ed. H. Thomas, 111–29. New York: St. Martin's Press, 1997.

———. "Women and the Early British Rave Scene." In *Back to Reality: Social Experience and Cultural Studies,* ed. A. McRobbie, 152–69. New York: Manchester University Press, 1997.

Plane, Ann Marie. *Colonial Intimacies: Indian Marriage in Early New England.* Ithaca: Cornell University Press, 2000.

Plummer, K. *Telling Sexual Stories: Power, Change, and Social Worlds.* New York: Routledge, 1995.

Porter, Robert B. "The Demise of the *Ongwehoweh* and the Rise of the Native Americans: Redressing the Genocidal Act of Forcing American Citizenship upon Indigenous Peoples." *Harvard BlackLetter Law Journal* 15 (1999): 107–83.

Portes, Alejandro, and Alex Stepick, *City on the Edge: The Transformation of Miami.* Berkeley: University of California Press, 1993.

Prucha, Francis Paul. *The Great Father,* volume 1. Lincoln: University of Nebraska Press, 1984.

Pruit, Deborah, and Suzanne LaFont. "For Love and Money: Romance Tourism in Jamaica." *Annals of Tourism Research* 22 (1995): 421–40.

Queen, Carol, and Lawrence Schimel. "Don't Fence Me In: Bi-/Pan-/Omni-Sexuals." In *PoMoSexuals: Challenging Assumptions about Gender and Sexuality,* ed. C. Queen and L. Schimel, 69. San Francisco, Clies Press, 1997.

Queen, Carol, and Lawrence Schimel, eds. *PoMoSexuals: Challenging Assumptions about Gender and Sexuality.* San Francisco: Clies Press, 1997.

Rabasa, Jose. *Inventing America: Spanish Historiography and the Formation of Eurocentrism.* Norman: University of Oklahoma Press, 1993.

Rable, George C. *Civil Wars: Women and the Crisis of Southern Nationalism.* Urbana: University of Illinois Press, 1989.

Rajamoorthy, T. "Globalization and Citizenship in Malaysia." In *Globalization and Citizenship in the Asia-Pacific,* ed. Alastair Davidson and Kathleen Weekley, 87–93. New York: St. Martin's Press, 1999.

Ramet, Sabrina Petra. *Gender Reversals and Gender Cultures: Anthropological and Historical Perspectives.* New York: Routledge, 1996.

Raphael, Jody. *Saving Bernice: Battered Women, Welfare, and Poverty.* Boston: Northeastern University Press, 2000.

Rashid, Ahmed. *Taliban: Militant Islam, Oil, and Fundamentalism in Central Asia.* New Haven: Yale University Press, 2000.

Ratnapala, Nandasena. "Male Sex Work in Sri Lanka." In *Men Who Sell Sex: International Perspectives on Male Prostitution and HIV/AIDS,* ed. Peter Aggleton, 213–21. Philadelphia: Temple University Press, 1999.

Ratti, Rakesh, ed. *A Lotus of Another Color.* Boston: Alyson, 1993.

Ray, Sangeeta. *En-Gendering India: Woman and Nation in Colonial and Postcolonial Narratives.* Durham: Duke University Press, 2000.

Redhead, Steve, ed. *Rave Off: Politics and Deviance in Contemporary Youth Culture.* Brookfield, VT: Avebury, 1993.

Reid-Pharr, Robert F. *Black Gay Man: Essays.* New York: New York University Press, 2001.

Reiss Jr., Albert J. "The Social Integration of Peers and Queers." *Social Problems* 9 (1961): 102–20.

Ren, X. "China." In *Prostitution: An International Handbook on Trends, Problems, and Policies,* ed. Nanette Davis, 102–3. Westport, CT: Greenwood Press, 1993.

Rhodes, Jane. "Fanning the Flames of Racial Discord: The National Press and the Black Panther Party." *Harvard International Journal of Press Politics* 4 (1999): 95–118.

———. *Framing the Panthers: Media, Race, and Representation in America.* New York: The New Press, 2003.

Rhoodie, Eschel. *Discrimination in the Constitutions of the World.* Atlanta: Orbis, 1983.

Rich, Adrienne. "Compulsory Heterosexuality and Lesbian Existence." *Signs* 5 (1980): 631–60.

Richard, Amy O'Neill. "International Trafficking in Women to the United States: A Contemporary Manifestation of Slavery and Organized Crime." Central Intelligence Agency, Center for the Study of Intelligence. Washington, DC: Government Printing Office, 1999.

Richardson, Diane, ed. *Theorizing Heterosexuality: Telling It Straight.* Philadelphia: Open University Press, 1996.

———. "Sexuality and Citizenship." *Sociology* 32 (1998): 83–100.

Rieff, David. *The Exile: Cuba in the Heart of Miami.* New York: Simon and Schuster, 1993.

Ritter, John. "California Racial Data Shifts." *USA Today* (June 19, 2001) (http://usatoday.com/news/census/ca.htm#more).

Roach, Joseph. *Cities of the Dead: Circum-Atlantic Performance.* New York: Columbia University Press, 1996.

Robinson, Christine. "The Web of Talk: Social Control and the Production of a Lesbian Community." Ph.D. diss., University of Kansas, 2002.

Rochlin, M. "The Heterosexual Questionnaire." In *Men's Lives,* ed. Michael S. Kimmel and Michael A. Messner, 405. Boston: Allyn and Bacon, 1995.

Rodriguez, Clara E. *Changing Race: Latinos, the Census, and the History of Ethnicity in the United States.* New York: New York University Press, 2000.

Roediger, David R. *Colored White: Transcending the Racial Past.* Berkeley: University of California Press, 2002.

Rojek, Chris, and John Urry, *Touring Cultures: Transformations of Travel and Theory.* New York: Routledge, 1997.

Rollins, Peter C., and John E. O'Connor, eds. *Hollywood's Indian: The Portrayal of the Native American in Film.* Lexington: University Press of Kentucky, 1998.

Romero, Mary. *Maid in the U.S.A.* New York: Routledge, 1992.

Ronda, James. *Lewis and Clark among the Indians.* Lincoln: University of Nebraska Press, 1984.

Roosevelt, Theodore. *The Winning of the West: From the Alleghenies to the Mississippi, 1769–1776,* volume 1. Lincoln: University of Nebraska Press, [1894] 1995.

Root, Deborah. *Cannibal Culture: Art, Appropriation, and the Commodification of Difference.* Boulder: Westview Press, 1996.

Roscoe, Will. *The Zuni Man-Woman.* Albuquerque: University of New Mexico Press, 1991.

Rosenblum, Karen E. "Rights at Risk: California's Proposition 187." In *Illegal Immigration in America: A Reference Handbook*, ed. David W. Haines and Karen E. Rosenblum, 367–82. Westport, CT: Greenwood Press, 1999.

Rossetti, Christina Georgina. "In the Round Tower at Jhansi." In *The Harvard Classics: English Poetry: From Tennyson to Whitman*, vol. 3, ed. Charles W. Eliot. New York: P.F. Collier and Son, 1910.

Rothschild, Mary Aickin. *A Case of Black and White: Northern Volunteers and the Southern Freedom Summers, 196–1965*. Westport, CT: Greenwood Press, 1982.

Rotundo, Anthony. *American Manhood: Transformations in Masculinity from the Revolution to the Modern Era*. New York: Basic Books, 1993.

Roughton Jr., Bert. "Incredibly Falling Birth Rate Heralds Changing Face of Italy." Cox Newspapers On-Line (July 25, 2001) (http://www.coxnews.com/washingtonbureau/staff/roughton/11-05-00COXITALYBIRTHSADV051STLD.html).

Roy, Sanjay. "Dirt, Noise, Traffic: Contemporary Indian Dance in the Western City; Modernity, Ethnicity, and Hybridity." In *Dance in the City*, ed. H. Thomas. New York: St. Martin's Press, 1997.

Roy, Tapti. *The Politics of a Popular Uprising: Bundelkhand in 1857*. New Delhi: Oxford University Press, 1994.

Rubin, Gayle. "The Traffic in Women: Notes on the 'Political Economy' of Sex." In *Toward an Anthropology of Women*, ed. Rayna R. Reiter, 157–210. New York: Monthly Review Press, 1975.

Rus, Jan. "The 'Communidad Revoluctionaria Institucional': The Subversion of Native Government in Highland Chiapas, 1936–1968." In *Everyday Forms of State Formation: Revolution and the Negotiation of Rule in Modern Mexico*, ed. Gilbert M. Joseph and Daniel Nugent, 265–300. Durham: Duke University Press, 1994.

Ryan, Cornelius. *The Last Battle*. New York: Simon and Schuster, 1966.

al-Sabah, Saud Nasir. "Kuwait's Position." *USA Today* (March 6, 1992): 8.

Safa, Helen I. *The Myth of the Male Breadwinner: Women and Industrialization in the Caribbean*. Boulder: Westview Press, 1995.

Said, Edward W. *Orientalism*. London: Penguin, 1978.

Saldivar, Jose David. *Border Matters: Remapping American Cultural Studies*. Berkeley: University of California Press, 1997.

Salzinger, Leslie. "From High Heels to Swathed Bodies: Gendered Meanings under Production in Mexico's Export-Processing Industry." *Feminist Studies* 23 (1997): 549–73.

Sandefur, Gary D., and Trudy McKinnell, "American Indian Intermarriage." *Social Science Research* 15 (1986): 347–71.

Santiago-Valles, Kevin. "The Sexual Appeal of Racial Differences: U.S. Travel Writing and Anxious American-ness in Turn-of-the-Century Puerto Rico." In *Race and the Production of Modern American Nationalism*, ed. Reynolds J. Scott-Childress, 127–48. New York: Garland Publishing, 1999.

Santos, Aida F. "Gathering the Dust: The Base Issue in the Philippines." In *Let the Good Times Roll: Prostitution and the U.S. Military in Asia*, ed. Saundra Pollock Sturdevant and Brenda Stoltzfus, 32–44. New York: The New Press, 1992.

Sassen, Saskia. *Globalization and Its Discontents*. New York: The New Press, 1998.

Saunders, Kay. "In a Cloud of Lust: Black GIs and Sex in World War II." In *Gender and War: Australians at War in the Twentieth Century*, ed. Joy Damousi and Marilyn Lake, 178–90. Cambridge: Cambridge University Press, 1995.

Sayigh, Rosemary, and Julie Peteet. "Between Two Fires: Palestinian Women in Lebanon." In *Women and Political Conflict*, ed. R. Ridd and H. Callaway, 106–37. New York: New York University Press, 1987.

Scales-Trent, Judy. *Notes of a White Black Woman*. University Park: Pennsylvania State University Press, 1995.

Schaeffer, Robert K. *Understanding Globalization: The Social Consequences of Political, Economic, and Environmental Change*. Lanham, MD: Rowman and Littlefield, 1997.

Schein, Louisa. "Multiple Alterities: The Contouring of Gender in Miao and Chinese Nationalisms." In *Women Out of Place: The Gender of Agency and the Race of Nationality*, ed. Brackette F. Williams, 70–102. New York: Routledge, 1996.

———. "The Consumption of Color and the Politics of White Skin in Post-Mao China." In *The Gender/Sexuality Reader: Culture, History, Political Economy*, ed. Roger N. Lancaster and Micaela di Leonardo, 473–86. New York: Routledge, 1997.

Schellstede, Sangmie Choi. *Comfort Women Speak: Testimony by Sex Slaves of the Japanese Military*. New York: Holmes and Meier, 2000.

Schifter, Jacobo. *Lila's House: Male Prostitution in Latin America*. New York: Haworth Press, 1998.

Schifter, Jacobo, and Peter Aggleston. "*Cacherismo* in a San Jose Brothel—Aspects of Male Sex Work in Costa Rica." In *Men Who Sell Sex: International Perspectives on Male Prostitution and HIV/AIDS*, ed. Peter Aggleton, 141–58. Philadelphia: Temple University Press, 1999.

Scholberg, Henry. *The Indian Literature of the Great Rebellion*. New Delhi: Promilla and Company, 1993.

Schutte, Gerhard. *What Racists Believe: Race Relations in South Africa and the United States*. Thousand Oaks, CA: Sage Publications, 1995.

Schwalbe, Michael. *Unlocking the Iron Cage: The Men's Movement, Gender, Politics, and American Culture*. New York: Oxford University Press, 1995.

Schwartz, Marie Jenkins. *Born in Bondage: Growing Up Enslaved in the Antebellum South*. Cambridge, MA: Harvard University Press, 2000.

Scott, Joan. *Gender and the Politics of History*. New York: Columbia University Press, 1988.

Scott, Julie. "Sexual and National Boundaries in Tourism." *Annals of Tourism Research* 22 (1995): 385–403.

Seale, Bobby. *Seize the Time: The Story of the Black Panther Party and Huey P. Newton*. Baltimore: Black Classic Press, [1970] 1991.

Sedgwick, Eve Kosofsky. *The Epistemology of the Closet*. Berkeley: University of California Press, 1990.

———. "Queer Performativity: Henry James's *The Art of the Novel*. " *GLQ* 1 (1993): 1–16.

Seidman, Steven, ed. *Queer Theory/Sociology*. New York: Blackwell, 1996.

Seifert, Ruth. "War and Rape: A Preliminary Analysis." In *Mass Rape: The War against Women in Bosnia-Herzegovina*, ed. Alexandra Stiglmayer, 54–72. Lincoln: University of Nebraska Press, 1994.

Sell, Henry Blackman, and Victor Weybright. *Buffalo Bill and the Wild West*. Basin, WY: Big Horn Books, 1979.

Shank, Barry. *Dissonant Identities: The Rock 'n' Roll Scene in Austin, Texas*. Hanover, NH: Wesleyan University Press, 1994.

Sharpe, Jenny. *Allegories of Empire: The Figure of Woman in the Colonial Text.* Minneapolis: University of Minnesota Press, 1993.

Shelley, Lore. *Auschwitz: The Nazi Civilization.* Lanham, MD: University Press of America, 1992.

Shen, Hsiu-hua. "Dangerous Liaisons: Representations of Chinese Women across the Taiwan Strait." Paper presented at the annual meeting of the American Sociological Association, Anaheim, 2001.

———. "Crossing the Taiwan Strait: The Gender and Sexual Politics of Identity Construction in the Global Economy." Ph.D. diss., University of Kansas, 2003.

Shih, Shu-mei. "Gender and a New Geopolitics of Desire: The Seduction of Mainland Women in Taiwan and Hong Kong Media." *Signs* 23 (1998): 287–319.

Shrage, Laurie. "Do Lesbian Prostitutes Have Sex with Their Clients? A Clintonesque Reply." *Sexualities* 2 (1999): 259–61.

Silber, Nina. *The Romance of Reunion: Northerners and the South, 1986–1900.* Chapel Hill: University of North Carolina Press, 1993.

da Silva, Lindinalva Laurindo. "*Travestis* and *Gigolos:* Male Sex Work and HIV Prevention in France." In *Men Who Sell Sex: International Perspectives on Male Prostitution and HIV/AIDS,* ed. Peter Aggleton, 41–60. Philadelphia: Temple University Press, 1999

Simon, William. *Postmodern Sexualities.* New York: Routledge, 1996.

Simons, Marlise. "Bosnian Serb Trial Opens: First on Wartime Sex Crimes." *New York Times* (March 21, 2000): 3.

Simons, Marlise, with Carlotta Gall. "Milosevic Is Given to U.N. for Trial in War-Crime Case." *New York Times* (June 29, 2002): 1.

Sinha, Mrinalini. *Colonial Masculinity: The 'Manly Englishman' and the 'Effeminate Bengali' in the Late Nineteenth Century.* Manchester: Manchester University Press, 1995.

Skrobanek, Siriporn, Nattaya Boonpakdee, and Chutima Jantateero. *The Traffic in Women: Human Realities of the International Sex Trade.* London: Zed Books, 1997.

Skurski, Julie. "The Ambiguities of Authenticity: *Dona Barbara* and the Construction of National Identity." *Poetics Today* 15 (1994): 605–42.

Sleightholme, Carolyn, and Indrani Sinha. *Guilty without Trial: Women in the Sex Trade in Calcutta.* New Brunswick: Rutgers University Press, 1997.

Slotkin, Richard. *Regeneration through Violence: The Mythology of the American Frontier, 1600–1860.* Middletown, CT: Wesleyan University Press, 1973.

Smith, Anthony D. *The Ethnic Origins of Nations.* New York: Blackwell, 1986.

———. "The Origins of Nations." *Ethnic and Racial Studies* 3 (1989): 340–67.

Smith, Bernard. *Imagining the Pacific: In the Wake of the Cook Voyages.* New Haven: Yale University Press, 1992.

Smith, Dinitia, and Nicholas Wade. "DNA Tests Offer Evidence That Jefferson Fathered a Child with His Slave." *New York Times on the Web* (November 1, 1998) (http://www.shamema.com/dnajeff.htm).

Smith, Dorothy. "Introduction." In *Home Girls: A Black Feminist Anthology,* ed. Barbara Smith, xxi–lviii. New York: Kitchen Table Press, 1983.

Smith, Graham. *When Jim Crow Met John Bull: Black American Soldiers in World War II Britain.* New York: St. Martin's Press, 1988.

Smith, Leef. "Jefferson Group Bars Kin of Slave: Hemings Family Remains Unshaken." *Washington Post* (May 6, 2002): B1.

Smith, Lois M., and Alfred Padula. *Sex and Revolution: Women in Socialist Cuba.* New York: Oxford University Press, 1996.

Smith, Sherry L. *The View from Officers' Row: Army Perceptions of Western Indians.* Tucson: University of Arizona Press, 1990.

Smits, David D. " 'Squaw Men,' 'Half-Breeds,' and Amalgamators: Late Nineteenth-Century Anglo-American Attitudes toward Indian-White Race-Mixing." *American Indian Culture and Research Journal* 15 (1991): 29–61.

Snipp, C. Matthew. *American Indians: The First of This Land.* New York: Russell Sage Foundation, 1989.

Snitow, Ann, Christine Stansell, and Sharon Thompson, eds. *Powers of Desire: The Politics of Sexuality.* New York: Monthly Review Press, 1983.

Somerville, Sioban. *Queering the Color Line: Race and the Invention of Homosexuality in American Culture.* Durham: Duke University Press, 2000.

Sommerville, Diane M. "The Rape Myth in the Old South Reconsidered." *Journal of Southern History* 61 (1995): 481–518.

Spackman, Barbara. *Fascist Virilities: Rhetoric, Ideology, and Social Fantasy in Italy.* Minneapolis: University of Minnesota Press, 1996.

Spear, Jennifer M. " 'They Need Wives': Metissage and the Regulation of Sexuality in French Louisiana, 1699–1730." In *Sex, Love, Race: Crossing Boundaries in North American History,* ed. Martha Hodes, 25–59. New York: New York University Press, 1999.

Specter, Michael. "Population Implosion Worries a Graying Europe." *The New York Times* (July 10, 1998): 10.

Spector, Malcolm, and John I. Kitsuse. *Constructing Social Problems.* New York: Aldine de Gruyter, 1977.

Sponsel, Leslie E. *Endangered Peoples of Southeast and East Asia: Struggles to Survive and Thrive.* Westport, CT: Greenwood Press, 2000.

Stannard, Ed. "Lambeth Showcases Conservative Anglican World" *Episcopal Life* (August, 1998) (http://www.episcopalchurch.org/episcopal-life/LambOver.html).

Stedman, John Gabriel. *Narrative, of a five years' expedition, against the Revolted Negroes of Surinam, in Guiana, on the Wild coast of South America; from the year 1772 to 1777.* London, 1796

Stedman, Raymond William. *Shadows of the Indian: Stereotypes in American Culture.* Norman: University of Oklahoma Press, 1982.

Steinberg, Deborah Lynn. "Technologies of Heterosexuality: Eugenic Reproductions Under Glass." In *Border Patrols: Policing the Boundaries of Heterosexuality,* ed. D. L. Steinberg, D. Epstein, R. Johnson, 66–97. London: Cassell, 1997.

Steinfels, Peter. "In Algeria, Women are Caught in the Cross-Fire of Men's Religious and Ideological Wars." *New York Times* (July 1, 1995): 8, 10.

Stiehm, Judith Hicks. "United Nations Peacekeeping: Men's and Women's Work." In *Gender Politics in Global Governance,* ed. M. K. Meyer and E. Prugl, 41–57. Lanham, MD: Rowman and Littlefield Publishers, 1999.

Stiglmayer, Alexandra. "The Rapes in Bosnia-Herzegovina." In *Mass Rape: The War against Women in Bosnia-Herzegovina,* ed. Alexandra Stiglmayer, 82–169. Lincoln: University of Nebraska Press, 1994.

Stoler, Ann. "Making Empire Respectable: The Politics of Race and Sexual Morality in 20th Century Colonial Cultures." In *Imperial Monkey Business: Racial Supremacy in Social Darwinist Theory and Colonial Practice,* ed. Jan Breman, 35–70. Amsterdam: Vu University Press, 1990.

———. "Sexual Affronts and Racial Frontiers: European Identities and the Cultural

Politics of Exclusion in Colonial Southeast Asia." *Comparative Study of Society and History* 24 (1992): 514–51.

———. *Capitalism and Confrontation in Sumatra's Plantation Belt, 1870–1979*, second edition. Ann Arbor: University of Michigan Press, 1995.

Stoller, Robert J., and Gilbert Herdt. "Theories of Origins of Homosexuality." *Archives of General Psychiatry* 42 (1985): 399–404.

Sturdevant, Saundra Pollock, and Brenda Stoltzfus. *Let the Good Times Roll: Prostitution and the U.S. Military in Asia.* New York: The New Press, 1992.

———. "Olongapo: The Bar System." In *Let the Good Times Roll: Prostitution and the U.S. Military in Asia*, ed. Saundra Pollock Sturdevant and Brenda Stoltzfus, 45–47. New York: The New Press, 1992.

Stychin, Carl F. *A Nation by Rights: National Cultures, Sexual Identity, Politics, and the Discourse of Rights.* Philadelphia: Temple University Press, 1998.

Sweet, Timothy. "Masculinity and Self-Performance in the *Life of Black Hawk.*" *American Literature* 65 (1993): 475–99.

Taibbi, Mike, and Anna Sims-Phillips. *Unholy Alliances: Working the Tawana Brawley Story.* New York: Harcourt Brace Jovanovich, Publishers, 1989.

Tan, Michael L. "Walking the Tightrope: Sexual Risk and Male Sex Work in the Philippines." In *Men Who Sell Sex: International Perspectives on Male Prostitution and HIV/AIDS*, ed. Peter Aggleton, 241–61. Philadelphia: Temple University Press, 1999.

Tanaka, Yuki. *Japan's Comfort Women: Sexual Slavery and Prostitution during World War II and the U.S. Occupation.* New York: Routledge, 2002.

Tehran Times. "Kuwait Court Rejects Women's Right to Vote." (July 4, 2000) *Middle East News On-Line* (http://www.middleeastwire.com/kuwait/stories/20000705_meno.shtml).

Terry, Jennifer. *An American Obsession: Science, Medicine, and Homosexuality in Modern Society.* Chicago: University of Chicago Press, 1999.

Testimony of Colonel Jefferson Jones. *State of Missouri v. Celia, a Slave.* Fulton, MO: Callaway County Courthouse, October Term, 1855.

Theweleit, Klaus. *Male Fantasies*, volume 1. Translated by Stephen Conway. Minneapolis: University of Minnesota Press, 1987.

Thiesmeyer, Lynn. "The West's 'Comfort Women' and the Discourses of Seduction." In *Transnational Asia Pacific: Gender, Culture, and the Public Sphere*, ed. Shirley G. Lim, Larry E. Smith, and Wimal Dissanayake, 69–92. Urbana: University of Illinois Press, 1999.

Thomas, Dorothy Q. *Criminal Injustice: Violence Against Women in Brazil—An Americas Watch Report.* New York: Human Rights Watch, 1992.

Thornton, Russell. *American Indian Holocaust and Survival.* Norman: University of Oklahoma Press, 1987.

Thurow, Roger. "A Bosnian Rape Victim Suffers from Scars That Do Not Fade." *Wall Street Journal* (July 17, 2000): 18.

Tilly, Charles. "Globalization Threatens Labor's Rights." *International Labor and Working-Class History* 47 (1995): 1–23.

Ting, Jennifer P. "The Power of Sexuality." *Journal of Asian American Studies* 1 (1998): 65–82.

Tohidi, Neyereh. "Gender and Islamic Fundamentalism: Feminist Politics in Iran." In *Third World Women and the Politics of Feminism*, ed. C. T. Mohanty, A. Russo, and L. Torres, 251–65. Bloomington: Indiana University Press, 1991.

Tolentino, Rolando B. "Bodies, Letters, Catalogs: Filipinas in Transnational Space."

In *Transnational Asia Pacific: Gender, Culture, and the Public Sphere,* ed. Shirley G. Lim, Larry E. Smith, and Wimal Dissanayake, 43–68. Urbana: University of Illinois Press, 1999.

Tolnay, Stewart E., and E. M. Beck. *A Festival of Violence: An Analysis of Southern Lynchings, 1882–1930.* Urbana: University of Illinois Press, 1995.

Torres, Maria de los Angeles. "Encuentros y Encontronazos: Homeland in the Politics and Identity of the Cuban Diaspora." *Diaspora* 4 (1995): 211–38.

Trachtenberg, Alan. *The Incorporation of America: Culture and Society in the Gilded Age.* New York: Hill and Wang, 1982.

Trotter Jr., Joe William, ed. *The Great Migration in Historical Perspective: New Dimensions of Race, Class, and Gender.* Bloomington: Indiana University Press, 1991.

Trumbach, Randolph. "Sex, Gender, and Sexual Identity in Modern Culture: Male Sodomy and Female Prostitution in Enlightenment London." *Journal of the History of Sexuality* 2 (1991): 186–203.

Truong, Thanh-Dam. *Sex, Money, and Morality: Prostitution and Tourism in South-East Asia.* London: Zed Books, 1990.

Truscott, James J. "Statement on the Interim Report issued by the Membership Advisory Committee of the Monticello Association, May 2000, 2 (http://www.monticello-assoc.org/interim.html).

Tsuda, Takeyuki (Gaku). "Japanese Emigration to Brazil." *Ethnic and Racial Studies* 24 (2001): 412–32.

Turner, Frederick Jackson. "The Significance of the Frontier in American History." *Annual Report of the American Historical Association for the Year 1893.* Washington, DC: U.S. Government Printing Office, 1894.

Twinam, Ann. *Public Lives, Private Secrets: Gender, Honor, Sexuality, and Illegitimacy in Colonial Spanish America.* Stanford: Stanford University Press, 1999.

Udry, J. Richard. "Biological Limits of Gender Construction." *American Sociological Review* 65 (2000): 443–57.

United Nations. "Assembly Adopts Convention against Transnational Organized Crime and Two Protocols." Press Release GA/9822 (November 15, 2000) (http://srch1.un.org:80/plweb-cgi/).

Unrau, William E. *Mixed-Bloods and Tribal Dissolution: Charles Curtis and the Quest for Indian Identity.* Lawrence: University Press of Kansas, 1989.

Urdang, Stephanie. *And Still They Dance: Women, War, and the Struggle for Change in Mozambique.* New York: Monthly Review Press, 1989.

Urry, John. *Consuming Places.* New York: Routledge, 1995.

U.S. Census Bureau. "Race of Wife by Race of Husband: 1960, 1970, 1980, 1991, and 1992" (http://www.census. gov/population/socdemo/race/interractab1/txt).

———. Table FG3: "Married Couple Family Groups, by Presence of Own Children Under 18, and Age, Earnings, Education, and Race and Hispanic Origin of Both Spouses: March 2000" (http://www.census.gov/population/socdemo/hh-fam/p20-537/2000/tabFG3.txt).

———. Population Division, Fertility and Family Statistics Branch. "America's Families and Living Arrangements, March 2000" (June 29, 2001).

U.S. Department of State, *Trafficking in Persons Report.* Washington, DC: Government Printing Office, 2001.

———. "Release of the 2001 Trafficking in Person's Report." Press release (July 12, 2001).

U.S. Office of Technology Assessment. *Indian Health Care.* Washington, DC: Government Printing Office, 1986.

Utley, Robert. *The Last Days of the Sioux Nation.* New Haven: Yale University Press, 1963.

Vaba, Lembit, Juri Viikberg, and Andres Heinapau. *The Endangered Uralic Peoples* (http://www.suri.ee/eup/samis.html).

Van Kirk, Sylvia. "The Role of Native Women in the Creation of Fur Trade Society in Western Canada, 1670–1830." In *The Women's West,* ed. Susan Armitage and Elizabeth Jameson, 53–62. Norman: University of Oklahoma Press, 1987.

Van Ness, G. "Parades and Prejudice: The Incredible True Story of Boston's St. Patrick's Day Parade and the United States Supreme Court." *New England Law Review* 30 (1996): 625–94.

Vargas, Zaragosa. "Rank and File: Historical Perspectives on Latino/a Workers in the U.S." In *The Latino Studies Reader: Culture, Economy, and Society,* 243–56. Blackwell, Malden, MA: 1998.

Vespucci, Amerigo. *Mundus Novus, Letter to Lorenzo Pietro di Medici.* Translated by George T. Northrup. Princeton: Princeton University Press, 1916.

Vickerman, Milton. *Crosscurrents: West Indian Immigrants and Race.* New York: Oxford University Press, 1999.

Vizenor, Gerald. *Fugitive Poses: Native American Indian Scenes of Absence and Presence.* Lincoln: University of Nebraska Press, 1998.

Walby, Sylvia. "Woman and Nation." In *Ethnicity and Nationalism,* ed. Anthony D. Smith, 81–99. New York: E.J. Brill, 1992.

Wallace, Michele. *Black Macho and the Myth of the Superwoman.* London: Verso, [1979] 1990.

Wallerstein, Immanuel M. *The Modern World System: Capitalist Agriculture and the Origins of the European World-Economy in the Sixteenth Century.* New York: Academic Press, 1974.

Walvin, James. "Symbols of Moral Superiority: Slavery, Sport, and the Changing World Order, 1900–1940." In *Manliness and Morality: Middle-Class Masculinity in Britain and America, 1800–1940,* ed. J. A. Mangan and J. Walvin, 242–60. Manchester: Manchester University Press, 1987.

Ward, Andrew. *Our Bones Are Scattered: The Cawnpore Massacre and the Indian Mutiny of 1857.* New York: H. Holt and Company, 1996.

Ware, Vron. *Beyond the Pale: White Women, Racism, and History.* London: Verso, 1991.

———. "Island Racism." *Feminist Review* 54 (1996): 65–86.

———. "Purity and Danger: Race, Gender and Tales of Sex Tourism." In *Back to Reality? Social Experience and Cultural Studies,* ed. Angela McRobbie, 133–51. Manchester: Manchester University Press, 1997.

Warner, Michael. "Introduction." In *Fear of a Queer Planet: Queer Politics and Social Theory,* ed. Michael Warner, vii–xxx. Minneapolis: University of Minnesota Press, 1993.

———. *The Trouble with Normal: Sex, Politics, and the Ethics of Queer Life.* New York: The Free Press, 1999.

Warren Jonathan W., and France Winddance Twine. "White Americans, the New Minority?: Non-Blacks and the Ever-Expanding Boundaries of Whiteness." *Journal of Black Studies* 28 (1997): 200–18.

Watanabe, Kazuko. "Trafficking in Women's Bodies, Then and Now: The Issue of Military Comfort Women." *Peace and Change* 20 (1995): 501–14.

Waters, Mary. *Ethnic Options: Choosing Identities in America*. Berkeley: University of California Press, 1990.

———. *Black Identities; West Indian Immigrant Dreams and American Realities*. Cambridge, MA: Harvard University Press, 2000.

Weber, Max. *Economy and Society: An Outline of Interpretative Sociology*, volume 1. Edited by Gunther Roth and Claus Wittich. Berkeley: University of California Press, 1978.

Weiner, Marli F. *Mistresses and Slaves: Plantation Women in South Carolina, 1830–80*. Urbana: University of Illinois Press, 1997.

Weitz, Margaret Collins. *Sisters in the Resistance: How Women Fought to Free France, 1940–45*. New York: John Wiley and Sons, 1995.

Weld, Theodore Dwight. *American Slavery as It Is: Testimony of a Thousand Voices*. New York: Arno Press, [1839] 1968.

Wells-Barnett, Ida B. *Crusade for Justice: The Autobiography of Ida B. Wells*. Edited by Alfreda M. Duster, Chicago: University of Chicago Press, 1970.

West, Cornel. *Race Matters*. Boston: Beacon Press, 1993.

Wheelwright, Julie. *The Fatal Lover: Mata Hari and the Myth of Women in Espionage*. London : Collins and Brown, 1992.

White, Edmund. *Jean Genet: A Biography*. New York: Vintage Books, 1993.

White, Kevin. *The First Sexual Revolution: The Emergence of Male Heterosexuality in Modern America*. New York: New York University Press, 1993.

White, LeeAnn. "The Civil War as a Crisis in Gender." In *Divided Houses: Gender and the Civil War*, ed. Catherine Clinton and Nina Silber, 3–21. New York: Oxford University Press, 1992.

White, Turnbull. *Our New Possessions: Four Books in One (The Philippine Islands, Puerto Rico, Cuba, The Hawaiian Islands)*. Chicago: Monarch Book Company, 1898.

Wiegman, Robin. "The Anatomy of Lynching." In *American Sexual Politics: Sex, Gender, and Race since the Civil War*, ed. John C. Fout and Maura S. Tantillo, 223–45. Chicago: University of Chicago Press, 1993.

Wilde, Oscar. *A Woman of No Importance*. Edited by Ian Small. New York: W.W. Norton, [1893] 1993.

Williams, Daryl. "The 'Soul Patrol': Gatekeepers of THE BLACK Identity." Paper presented at the annual meeting of the Midwest Sociological Society, Kansas City,1998.

Williams, Linda. *Playing the Race Card: Melodramas of Black and White from Uncle Tom to O.J. Simpson*. Princeton: Princeton University Press, 2001.

Williams, Phil. "Trafficking in Women and Children: A Market Perspective." In *Illegal Immigration and Commercial Sex: The New Slave Trade*, ed. Phil Williams, 145–70. London: Frank Cass, 1999.

Williams, Simon J., and Gillian Bendelow. *The Lived Body: Sociological Themes, Embodied Issues*. New York: Routledge, 1998.

Williams, Walter L. *The Spirit and the Flesh: Sexual Diversity in American Indian Culture*. Boston: Beacon Press, 1986.

Williamson, Joel. *The Crucible of Race: Black-White Relations in the American South since Emancipation*. New York: Oxford University Press, 1984.

———. *New People: Miscegenation and Mulattoes in the United States*. Baton Rouge: Louisiana State University Press, 1995.

Wilson, Ara. "American Catalogues of Asian Brides." In *Anthropology for the*

Nineties: Introductory Readings, ed. Johnetta B. Cole, 114–25. New York: The Free Press, 1988.

Winant, Howard. *Racial Conditions: Politics, Theory, and Comparisons.* Minneapolis: University of Minnesota Press, 1994.

Wing, Adrien Katherine. *Global Critical Race Feminism: An International Reader.* New York: New York University Press, 2000.

Wolfe, Thomas. *Radical Chic and Mau-Mauing the Flak Catchers.* New York: Farrar, Straus and Giroux, 1970.

Wood, Marcus. *Blind Memory: Visual Representations of Slavery in England and America, 1780–1865.* New York: Routledge, 2000.

Yegenoglu, Meyda. *Colonial Fantasies: Towards a Feminist Reading of Orientalism.* Cambridge: Cambridge University Press, 1998.

Yetman, Norman R. "The 'New Immigrant Wave': Migration Pressures and the American Presence." Paper presented at the annual meeting of the American Studies Association, Philadelphia, 1983.

———. *Majority and Minority: The Dynamics of Race and Ethnicity in American Life.* Boston: Allyn and Bacon, 1999.

Yin, James, and Shi Young. *The Rape of Nanking: An Undeniable History in Photographs.* Chicago: Innovative Publishing Group, 1997.

Ying Ho, Petula Sik, and Adolf Kat Tat Tsang. "Negotiating Anal Intercourse in Inter-Racial Gay Relationships in Hong Kong." *Sexualities* 3 (2000): 299–324.

Yoneda, Sayoko. "Sexual and Racial Discrimination: A Historical Inquiry into the Japanese Military's 'Comfort' Women System of Enforced Prostitution." In *Nation, Empire, Colony: Historicizing Gender and Race,* ed. Ruth Roach Pierson and Nupur Chaudhuri, 237–50. Bloomington: Indiana University Press, 1989.

Young, Crawford. *The Politics of Cultural Pluralism.* Madison: University of Wisconsin Press, 1976.

———. *The Rising Tide of Cultural Pluralism.* Madison: University of Wisconsin Press, 1993.

Youssef, Ibrahim M. "Bareheaded Women Slain in Algiers: Killings Following Islamic Threats." *New York Times* (March 31, 1994): A3.

Yuval-Davis, Nira, and Floya Anthias, eds. *Woman-Nation-State.* New York: St. Martin's Press, 1989.

Zangrando, Robert L. *The NAACP Crusade against Lynching, 1909–1950.* Philadelphia: Temple University Press, 1980.

Zeeland, Steven. *The Masculine Marine: Homoeroticism in the U.S. Marine Corps.* New York: Harrington Park Press, 1996.

Zuilhof, Wim. 'Sex for Money between Men and Boys in the Netherlands: Implications for HIV Prevention." In *Men Who Sell Sex: International Perspectives on Male Prostitution and HIV/AIDS,* ed. Peter Aggleton, 23–39. Philadelphia: Temple University Press, 1999.

Zulaika, Joseba. *Basque Violence: Metaphor and Sacrament.* Reno: University of Nevada Press, 1988.

INDEX

SOAS LIBRARY